Imprints of Revolution

DISRUPTIONS

Disruptions is a series that interrogates and analyses disruptions within and across such fields and disciplines as culture and society, media and technology, literature and philosophy, aesthetics and politics.

Titles in Series

Bearing Society in Mind: Theories and Politics of the Social Formation, Samuel A. Chambers
Open Education: A Study in Disruption, Pauline van Mourik Broekman, Gary Hall, Ted Byfield, Shaun Hides and Simon Worthington
What Lies Between: Void Aesthetics and Postwar Politics, Matt Tierney
Martial Arts Studies, Paul Bowman
Living Screens: Melodrama and Plasticity in Contemporary Film and Television, Monique Rooney
Word: Divine, Dissonant and Digital, Mariam Motamedi Fraser
Culture and Eurocentrism, Qadri M. Ismail
Against Value in the Arts and Education, edited by Sam Ladkin, Robert McKay and Emile Bojesen
Imprints of Revolution: Visual Representations of Resistance, Lisa B. Y. Calvente and Guadalupe García
Disrupting Maize: Food, Biotechnology and Nationalism in Contemporary Mexico, Gabriela Méndez Cota

Imprints of Revolution

Visual Representations of Resistance

Edited by Lisa B. Y. Calvente and Guadalupe García

ROWMAN &
LITTLEFIELD
INTERNATIONAL
London • New York

Published by Rowman & Littlefield International Ltd
Unit A, Whitacre Mews, 26-34 Stannary Street, London SE11 4AB
www.rowmaninternational.com

Rowman & Littlefield International Ltd. is an affiliate of Rowman & Littlefield
4501 Forbes Boulevard, Suite 200, Lanham, Maryland 20706, USA
With additional offices in Boulder, New York, Toronto (Canada),
and Plymouth (UK)
www.rowman.com

British Library Cataloguing in Publication Data
A catalogue record for this book is available from the British Library

ISBN: HB 978-1-78348-505-5
PB 978-1-78348-506-2

Library of Congress Cataloging-in-Publication Data
Names: Calvente, Lisa B. Y., author. | García, Guadalupe, 1975– author.
Title: Imprints of revolution : visual representations of resistance / Lisa B. Y. Calvente and Guadalupe García.
Description: Lanham : Rowman & Littlefield International Ltd, 2016. | Series: Disruptions | Includes bibliographical references and index.
Identifiers: LCCN 2015050985 (print) | LCCN 2016011072 (ebook) | ISBN 9781783485055 (cloth : alk. paper) | ISBN 9781783485062 (pbk. : alk. paper) | ISBN 9781783485079 (Electronic)
Subjects: LCSH: Revolutions. | Art and revolutions. | Social change.
Classification: LCC HM876 .C35 2016 (print) | LCC HM876 (ebook) | DDC 303.4—dc23
LC record available at http://lccn.loc.gov/2015050985

∞™ The paper used in this publication meets the minimum requirements of American National Standard for Information Sciences—Permanence of Paper for Printed Library Materials, ANSI/NISO Z39.48-1992.

Printed in the United States of America

Contents

Introduction

Decolonizing Revolution through Visual Articulations

Lisa B. Y. Calvente

> In historical agitation, only the word Revolution dominates the customary confusion and carries with it the promise that answers the unlimited demands of the masses.
>
> —Georges Bataille, "The Notion of Expenditure" (1933)

> Haiti is the country where Negro people stood up for the first time, affirming their determination to shape a new world, a free world.
>
> —Aimé Césaire, "An Interview with Aimé Césaire" (1967)

With the words "Liberty or Death" inscribed onto the newly imaged blue and red flag, Jean-Jacques Dessalines led the colonized and enslaved people's army to defeat the French troops on the island of Saint-Domingue.[1] The removal of the white from the tricoloured red, white, and blue French flag and the replacement of the initials R. F. that stood for the République Francaise with the affirmation "Liberty or Death" became the visual representation of a new becoming for the former island of Saint-Domingue and its inhabitants.[2] The flag, once a symbol of European enlightenment, modernity, and humanity, became emblematic of an ongoing formation of liberated modernity and black subjectivity. By 1805, less than two years after Toussaint L'Ouverture's death, Jean-Jacques Dessalines established the independent nation of Hayti, an Arawak name for "high land."[3] In addition, regardless of ancestry or phenotype, Dessalines constituted all of Hayti's citizens both free and black.[4]

The materialization of the Haitian Revolution (1791–1804) demonstrated that European enlightenment was not in fact universal, and, if it was, universality was not intended for those who existed under slavery and colonial rule.[5] As Robin Blackburn states, "Haiti was not the first independent American state but it was the first to guarantee civic liberty to all its inhabitants."[6] Through Haiti's constitution, the discourse of revolution was articulated to colonialism, slavery, and blackness, which was reserved solely to the universal politics of European enlightenment prior to the revolt on the island. According to Stuart Hall, the process of articulation illustrates the ways in which discourses are connected, formed, and transformed under particular material conditions that enable social change.[7] The significance of articulation is the disruption of history with the voices and actions of those who are silenced and defined as silent. It is within this disruption and articulation of history that new cultural formations, systems of belonging, and subjectivities arise.[8]

Revolution as a discursive formation marks how Western modernity as a project both created and maintained disciplinary and regulatory practices that were necessarily tied to its colonization endeavors.[9] Discourses of revolution also underscore the slippages and excesses, embodied resistances, to these hegemonic formations that aimed to maintain and strengthen colonial power relations. Haiti and its revolution symbolize these excesses of resistance. The Haitian Revolution marked a conjunctural moment where decolonization was successfully practiced.[10] As the impetus of a decolonization project, the Haitian Revolution actively called into question the colonial relationship of which the modern world is derived.

The emergence of the early modern state coincides with the expansion of overseas exploration that began in the fifteenth century, which reconfigured existing power relations between empires. New technologies made possible the initial contact and exchange between people who have never encountered each other throughout the globe. This early form of globalization, inspired by the tropes of capitalism—privatization and capital—established violence and terror as foundational components of territorialization.[11] Thus, first contact and colonialism emerge and encompass every*thing* "founded" through these encounters—land, resources, and people—as territorial gain. Modernity as a European project necessarily relied upon the colonial relationship to constitute itself in each and every aspect of political, economic, and social life.

Wealth extracted from newly colonial spaces became the quintessential symbol of how Western empires understood themselves to be modern vis-à-vis their colonial territories.[12] The political and social relationship between the colonizer and colonized was regulated by policies and practices of violence, terror, and discipline in order to ensure the continuance of capital gain and in turn the European modernity project. The modern Western citizen came to be defined as white and enlightened only by way of defining its *darkened* colonial subjects.[13] Through philosophical and scientific discourses, the colonized subjects and spaces as objects of knowledge and production established the modern Western citizen as its opposition.[14] Revolution as a discourse also articulated the modern state and the human subject—that is, one who was capable of rational thought, political action, and, most important, freedom. As Jean-Paul Sartre has argued, "For with us there is nothing more consistent than a racist humanism since the European has only been able to become a man through creating slaves and monsters."[15] Revolution as a symbol of freedom became a natural, political act that possessed its own history and was of biological essence to the whitened modern subject, the Western human. Revolution added to the body of racial knowledge by marking what the racialized, primitivized, and colonized other(ed) was not, albeit through the racial *in*visibility of the universal human.[16]

By the sixteenth century, almost one century after first contact, the term *revolution* passed from its original use in scientific references into the lexicon of political philosophy. It was first used to describe the regular movement of celestial bodies in philosophy and science. Copernicus, for example, in his treatise *On the Revolutions of Heavenly Spheres*, cited the regular movement of the planets in his discussion of the term.[17] From this scientific description of regularity and repetitiveness, Richard Pipes notes, the term then went on to describe the "abrupt and unforeseen events" that sixteenth-century astrologers, looking to the heavens to explain political occurrences, designated the term to mean.[18] Similar to processes of conquest, the discursive (trans)formation of revolution relied heavily on the combined support of metaphysics and science. Political and ontological foundings pushed the concept of revolution toward a teleology that helped to naturalize revolution as a collective act that was taken on by rational beings with freedom as the qualifying factor. Revolution was made to unfold in history much like European modernity, both naturally and inevitably.

By the late seventeenth century, freedom became the spirit of universal political and ontological value through philosophers such as Thomas Hobbes, John Locke, and Jean-Jacques Rousseau.[19] The "Glorious Revolution" in England in 1688–1689 helped to begin to solidify these philosophical discourses as natural and historical. Liberty as a natural state of human existence within philosophical thought developed alongside revolutionary action, as the American Revolution of 1776 and the French Revolution of 1789 demonstrated. Philosophers such as Adam Smith and Georg Wilhelm Friedrich Hegel furthered liberty as human nature.[20] By the eighteenth century, revolution became an essential extension of liberation while the violence and profit of colonialism and slavery continued and heightened.[21] The "Glorious Revolution," the American Revolution, and the French Revolution all mark the rise of modern nations that have enacted in multiple versions of liberatory change and state transformations.

These transformations hinged upon the categorization and regulation of the national population in ways that actively denied this enlightened human spirit in colonized peoples and territories.[22] With racism as its foundational core, the categorization of the population was embedded within discourse and relations of production that rested on colonialism. These racial hierarchies were disseminated and justified throughout all forms of knowledge and everyday life.[23] These three-pronged processes of hierarchical categorization and disciplinary regulation were applied to the local, national, and transnational spheres simultaneously. The globality of the colonial relationship ensured that the modern national consciousness with its patterns of categorization was transmuted throughout the globe. The unforeseen excesses of this transmutation became the ways in which colonized and enslaved parts of the global population transformed these revolutionary discourses into performative collectives of decolonization—revolution as applied to the indigenous, colonized, and enslaved. It was through these processes of power and resistance that the transformation of Saint-Domingue by its people became the collective living force of excess that history could not deny.

Prior to the Age of Revolution marked by the constitution of Haiti, rebellions were recurring but localized in scope. Even with the resistances as a mounting problem for colonial and national administrations, these were contained within the framework of colonial and national rule; these resistances were often perceived as manageable rebellions with, for instance, changes in overseers, reductions in taxes, or civil employment. The disciplinary and regulatory practices that maintained subgrouped divisions throughout the colonized and enslaved population continued to ensure social order and secured power relations within the colonial and enslaved territories as well as the nation state.[24] Opportunities to assimilate with colonial and national power alongside brutal and terrifying force exacerbated the colonial and slave relationships.[25] With Haiti as its revolutionary emblem, by 1810, the peoples of the Spanish American colonies (with the Spanish Caribbean as the exception) launched armed revolts against Spain and garnered transnational global solidarity against colonization and slavery.

The very tenet of the modern, enlightened world—humanity = free = rational = history—was ruptured and transformed by its negation: the indigenous, the colonized, and the enslaved.[26] It constituted what Frantz Fanon describes as a program of dis/order that disrupts the world order and creates man anew.[27] For Haiti, national belonging began with an integration of the indigenous, colonized, and enslaved and transformed this integration into black citizenry. The new nation's indigenous name articulated with citizens, who were both free and black, and visually communicated a newly formed national consciousness. This radical articulation of black and citizenship redefined human existence and nullified the objectification of the enslaved, indigenous, and colonized as property and extensions of property that was established through the colonial relationship. As C. L. R. James and the epigraphs remind us, it was "neither Dessalines' army nor his ferocity that won the victory. It was the people. . . . And far from being intimidated, the civic population met the terror with such courage and firmness it frightened the terrorists."[28] The enslaved, the colonized, and other residents of the island *became* a cohesive collective that depended on drawing upon each of their singular experiences, positions, and skills that were derived from the same context: the everyday, terrorizing oppression of European colonization. Through the ritual of naming, the new nation of Hayti and its people symbolized the synthesis of a new black consciousness that was both liberated and modern.

Dessalines's *play* of the modern nation-state and national consciousness continued what the imagery of the new flag set to establish. Blackness was redefined as a liberated, active becoming that could not be reduced to normative discursive modes of categorization such as biology, culture, or phenotype. Blackness became *both* indigenous *and* diasporic, and the people themselves embodied the new black nation and consciousness. As the citizens of Haiti *became* black, they also became the living signs that revealed the great fabrication fostered through European modernity, enlightenment, and humanity. Biologized and naturalized discourses that sustained European, colonial, and white supremacy were disrupted as blackened Polish and German citizens of Haiti went about their days as legally and equally black.[29] This designation of black citizenry also extended to white European women who were married to Haitian citizens.[30] These visual representations materialized as the impetus for the ongoing processes of decolonization, global revolution, and justice. As such, visual representation and articulation became foundational for the ongoing process of revolution as decolonization. With the Haitian Revolution as the quintessential symbol of decolonization, resistances throughout the globe took revolutionary form.

In 1810, the regions that would become part of Mexico, Venezuela, and the United States led the first revolts and were subsequently followed by Gran Colombia (Colombia, Venezuela, Panamá, Ecuador, Peru, Guyana, and northwest Brazil).[31] The resistance spread further against Portugal by the 1820s. However, national consolidations that occurred as a result of these revolts continued to suffer from regional conflicts and violence that were rooted in the colonial division of cultural and ethnic subgroups. These international and interregional processes continued for decades until well into the nineteenth century when revolutionary decolonization reignited throughout the remaining colonial territories.[32] Territories throughout Africa, Asia, and the Americas moved toward decolonization through particular acts of a universal sentiment that mirrored that of the Haitian Revolution: liberation and decolonization toward a newly formulated modernity.[33] These collectivities of universal particulars enabled (neo) colonized peoples to organize their resistances against the exploitative brutalities of (neo)colonization beyond their locales toward the possibility of global alliance for a truly liberated, decolonized modernity. Visual representation would materialize as the way in which revolutionary decolonization was articulated as a modern global force.

Revolutionary decolonization against neocolonial processes would last well into the twentieth and twenty-first centuries and continue on to the time of this writing.[34] Revolutionary decolonization included but was not limited to China, Puerto Rico, Cuba, Vietnam, Congo, Ruanda-Urundi, Algeria, Sudan, Libya, South Africa, Angola, Ghana, Bolivia, and Venezuela.[35] The sentiment of decolonization was not confined to colonial territories as it also became the impetus for civil and human rights struggles within Western modern nations. Revolutionary decolonization came to symbolize performative acts of resistance against racist processes altogether as these processes were understood to stem from colonialism and slavery. These radical acts of resistance incorporated violence even when the strategies were nonviolent in nature as violence continues to be the primary strategy to maintain neocolonial(ity) power relations.[36] Many of the people within these spaces partook in multiple decolonization movements during different times with different strategies yet visual representation was often positioned at the center of these struggles.[37]

In the struggle against Spanish colonialism, for example, the flag for Puerto Rican independence was designed in 1892 to reflect the transnational ties with the revolution in Cuba that was unfolding during the same period. The flags are identical in color and design to signify unity; however, the colors are inverted to symbolize the different experiences and struggles of the islands and their peoples. The flags visually communicated a moment of possibilities as they symbolized the transnational solidarity that was formed by the Puerto Rican Revolutionary Committee and the Cuban Revolutionary Committee at the time, both of which were stationed in New York City.[38] This multilayered temporal and spatial matrix was the site at which differing peoples coalesced in a transnational struggle over hegemony and the flag was the visual mode of communicating and archiving this conjunctural moment. In the next century, the flag remained a primary mode to symbolically communicate liberty and solidarity in the decolonization struggle. As a visual sign, it inspired momentum for the ongoing revolutions while also representing the struggles as both within the nation and beyond it. These flags mirrored the temporal and spatial play that their revolutions engendered, as illustrated by the flags of Pan-Africanism.[39]

Similar to those of Cuba and Puerto Rico, the flags for these nations resembled each other through the adaptation of green, red, yellow, and/or black but utilized different designs to express national identity in these overlapping struggles. The adaptation of the colors and design called on past struggles to galvanize national consciousness that extended beyond national and continental borders.[40] Ghana's use of all four colors, for instance, illustrated its interlocking Pan-Africanist identity with the new nations as well as past struggles that occurred in multiple spaces across the globe. With its horizontal stripes of red, yellow, and green, the Ghanaian flag articulated itself alongside Ethiopia, the oldest independent nation in Africa; the flag also linked itself to earlier struggles of Pan-Africanism with its use of black and, finally, its black star was derivative of Marcus Garvey's *Black Star Line*. The flag articulated possibilities of a new modernity that existed beyond spatial borders and the various temporalities with decolonization as its center. The flags symbolized a new mode of connectedness that opened possibilities of new temporalities, modernities, and histories to occur through revolution and liberation. They symbolized how the visual communicates ongoing struggles over hegemony and the materialized possibility of new histories and modernities. In so doing, the visual also reveals multiple temporalities within varying spaces that disrupt the teleological trajectory of archived history.

The chapters in this volume demonstrate how both visual communication and the discourse of revolution continue to play primary roles in the ongoing struggle over hegemony.[41] They each demonstrate how nations, national consciousness, and dissent have been, and continue to be, haunted by the (neo)colonial(ity) relationship. This collection illustrates the significance of visual representation as a primary communicative practice that archives the discursive formations of revolution in multiple temporalities and spaces.[42] The use of the visual in these chapters examines the complexities of everyday life, revolution, and (trans)national consciousness through theorizing on the visual and through the visual itself. The contributors utilize images as part of a critical methodology that includes images as history and not as *evidence* of history.[43] As a collection, the visual is pushed forth as an intricate part of popular culture. By taking on the visual and how it is used to both sustain and produce a collective mass, the visual image allows us to further investigate the popular as a terrain where the struggle over hegemony occurs.[44] Within the context of revolution, the visual as a site of study opens new perspectives on how struggles against the modernity-coloniality relationship have been and in turn can be formed. It is the intersections of the visual and of revolution that underscore processes of reimagining and reconstituting decolonization for solidarity, social change, and justice. These chapters begin the critical analyses of these intersections of possibility and imagery.

In this collection, the visual serves as a means to interrogate the material culture of revolutionary movements in ways that highlight the aforementioned colonial relationship. The contributors each focus on the affective and experiential interactions between historical actors and the revolutionary movements they engage.[45] Their approach to the public image of revolution draws upon the ways in which new relations of globalization have occurred and can potentially occur. The chapters illustrate the ways in which archived and unarchived histories shape contemporary global issues such as mass tourism, urbanization, war, and migration. The contributors have collectively marked and transformed the legacies of historic movements through the analysis of documents that are outside of what is written and said. The focus on visual representation highlights how historic movements are reconstituted through the visual to reveal histories not otherwise apparent. The visual for this collection encompasses print media, public art, civic and government performances, architectural forms, rituals of naming, social media, material culture, and people as embodied signs and portraits. The chapters span more than a century and take as their points of departure the countries of Mexico, China, Cuba, Vietnam, Ethiopia, Venezuela, Argentina, and Peru.

We begin in the twentieth century with the Mexican Revolution of 1910 against neocolonialism, just one century after the region's war for liberation against Spain, to illustrate these ongoing processes of struggle and how images can reconstitute a movement. Chapter 1, "Icons of Revolution: Constructions of Emiliano Zapata in *Prints of the Mexican Revolution*," analyzes the Taller de Gráfica Popular in Mexico City. Theresa Avila retraces the graphic art collective that was founded in Mexico City in 1937. She locates the collective and its visual production as an alternative site for the narrative of revolutionary change. Through the visual prints of the Taller de Gráfica Popular, Avila critically questions the state's narrative of revolution after 1910. The visual prints retell the Mexican Revolution vis-à-vis imagery of democratic reform and agricultural restructuring. Avila highlights how these images reveal polyvalent meanings *beyond* the conflicting narratives presented by splintering factions of the 1910 war. She concludes with how these images reconstruct the subsequent institutionalization of the movement by the Mexican government and argues that these images can be rearticulated with occurring national and transnational resistances.

The next three chapters continue the theme of the importance of images within ongoing struggle and expand upon visual representation through the use of multiple mediums—namely, poster art, billboards, and magazine prints. Chapter 2, "Imprinting Industriousness in the Quest for the Good Life: Lineages of the Chinese Revolutionary Image from 1949 to the Present," turns toward the significance of print media in shaping national consciousness and belonging. Alison Hulme centers on poster art as imagery of everyday life in the People's Republic of China. Through a comparative analysis, Hulme critically discusses China's poster campaigns of the 1950s that urged people to be productive, selfless national citizens. She illustrates how these images engage with Deng Xiaoping's post-1978 campaigns that center on the accumulation of wealth as a positive and successful lifestyle. Hulme also examines how the themes of "industriousness" and "the good life" are articulated together in the print media of China's Communist Party. She argues that the image of a "good life" remains a unifying theme between the changing landscapes of China.

Chapter 3, "Image in Revolution: Articulating the Visual Arts and Becoming Cuban," theorizes on how articulation and interdependency played a primary role in the national image of the Cuban nation post-1959. Lisa B. Y. Calvente and Guadalupe García analyze how the visual produced a revolutionary ethos after the Revolution of 1959. Calvente and García analyze visual representations of architectural form, photographs, billboards, and graffiti, primarily in urban spaces throughout the island. The authors examine the appropriation of space, style, posters, and billboards to focus on the ways in which these visual mediums serve to narrate, articulate, and negotiate revolutionary meaning. As part of a repertoire of visual cultural production, they illustrate how these objects also form part of a new, revolutionary methodology that is at once national and global.

In chapter 4, "The Image of Difference: Racial Coalition and Social Collapse by Way of Vietnam," Brynn Hatton continues with the theme of global revolutionary representations and solidarity introduced in the previous chapter. Hatton examines poster images, short films, and print publications about Vietnam during the antiwar movement that were produced worldwide. She demonstrates how the imagery of Vietnamese revolutionary subjectivity constituted a medium through which multiple political movements articulated their own political claims. Brynn Hatton illustrates how global protest art functioned as a way for local struggles to be part of a larger revolutionary geopolitical landscape. Her intervention highlights a global, pan-revolutionary sensibility that centers on decolonization. The focus on a decolonizing global revolution segues into a contextual analysis of how nations can simultaneously produce national and global Pan-Africanist consciousness that is explored in chapter 5.

Chapter 5, "Ethiopia Tiqdem? The Influence of the Mythic, Protest, and Red Terror Periods on Ethiopian Pan-Africanism," explores the significance of Ethiopia to the African Diaspora's experience of liberation. Meron Wondwosen examines the evolution of Ethiopia within the African Diaspora's visual representations of the nation, such as paintings, sculptures, and photographs. Wondwosen critically discusses how the image of Ethiopia during the Italian invasion of 1935 galvanized hundreds of black men and women across the globe to volunteer for the armed struggle. She also details how the imagery of Ethiopia garnered a far less enthusiastic response within the African Diaspora during the Marxist struggle of the 1970s and 1980s. In her articulation of these struggles, Wondwosen highlights the difference in public support through the visual representation of Ethiopia. Meron Wondwosen shifts revolution away from the discourse of nation and into a collective mass through a sense of belonging that she locates as the African Diaspora. This articulation of an African Diaspora collective was inspired in part by Ethiopia's historic image.

Similar to the previous chapter, chapter 6 moves away from the nation and instead explores the effects of capitalism on national discourse through tourism. "Incas for Sale: Commodified Images of Historical Sites" addresses heritage sites as a locus of commodification and depoliticization. Coauthors Silvia Nagy-Zekmi and Kevin J. Ryan Jr. focus on the site of Machu Picchu, Peru, as a space of possibility that has been limited by tourism. The authors theorize upon this space as a heritage site that corresponds to the historic processes where indigenous identities are enacted and reconstituted. They utilize photographs of Machu Picchu to explore the built environment and architectural forms that inspire Western sensibility through tourism. Nagy-Zekmi and Ryan conclude that heritage sites as tourist sites transform possibilities of engagement with authenticity to spaces limited by hegemonic conformity. Nagy-Zekmi and Ryan's introduction of authenticity provides a starting point for the discussion of how Hugo Chávez, the former leader of Venezuela, (re)appropriates seemingly authentic national memory as political inspiration in chapter 7.

Chapter 7, "Hugo Chávez, Iconic Associationism, and the Bolívarian Revolution," introduces and defines iconic associationism as a rhetorical strategy of visual representation. Joshua Frye theorizes on iconic associationism through an analysis of Hugo Chávez's appropriation of the image of the nineteenth-century revolutionary Simón Bolívar. He argues that Chávez's use of Bolívar's image during his numerous public and televised addresses and press conferences was a unique form of visual rhetoric that helped Chávez gain political support throughout the nation. Frye highlights how the visual, material culture, and framing intersected in Chávez's appropriation of the national memory of Bolívar. He examines this rhetorical strategy through the exploration of a decade of manufactured associations between Chávez and Bolívar. Frye argues that the iconic associationism of Simón Bolívar helped Chávez reconstitute Venezuelan national identity and extended the Bolívarian Revolution through the reconstitution of the region's history.

The next two chapters highlight the ongoing processes of neoliberalism that inspire reconstitutions of revolution and social change. Chapter 8, "Crisis and Revolution: Activist Art in Neoliberal Buenos Aires," discusses the symbolic occupation of downtown Buenos Aires that was carried out by the Grupo de Arte Callejero (GAC) in 2001. Leonora Souza Paula showcases how the street performance in which hundreds of toy soldiers were dropped over the Buenos Aires urban space constitutes a radical act of resistance. She illustrates how this revolutionary performance of dissent critically articulated Argentina's authoritarian past with the contemporary neoliberal moment. By examining GAC's action as visual radical performance, the author demonstrates how the movement disrupted the flow of Argentina's financial center. Paula argues that these radical performances were not simply attuned to the anti-neoliberal sentiment of twenty-first-century social movements but also provide a link to contemporary movements that utilize similar strategies of disruption across the globe.

The final chapter of the collection returns to Mexico to conclude with an examination of the continuance of revolution through social media. Nasheli Jiménez del Val analyzes how the #YoSoy132 movement functions as a critique of an authoritarian Mexican government. Through her analysis, Jiménez del Val illustrates how the political platform of media as political democratization enables the #YoSoy132 movement to link Mexican student youth to one another and fight for greater transparency and political democracy within Mexican national politics. The chapter analyzes how the movement focuses on media as part of its political agenda and also as its strategy for political gain. Jiménez del Val examines how the uses of visual mediums such as online videos, digital posters, and street performances illustrate a repertoire of resistance strategies and connect to global movements that range from the Chilean student movement, the Arab Spring, and Occupy Wall Street to the Spanish 15M. As in the preceding chapter, Jiménez del Val demonstrates the confluence of the local and the global through the visual strategies of the twenty-first century.

The collection's return to Mexico a century after the country's first revolution underscores the ongoing and global nature of the decolonization struggle and the transformative power of the visual. Across the globe, from the Americas to Africa to Asia and Europe, movements continue to coalesce around a visual iconography that appeals to a global sense of struggle and belonging. These movements are not limited to physical spaces, as the migration of peoples enables the creation and re-creation of new meanings for revolutionary iconographies. The contemporary mobilization of the visual in public spaces and the use of technology and new media both facilitate this understanding of belonging at the same time that they rearticulate the meaning of revolution. Take again, for example, the flags of Puerto Rico and Cuba that were created from the experience of the nineteenth-century independence struggles against Spain. These flags represented a political solidarity under colonial rule that is materially visible in their design. When juxtaposed against the contemporary backdrop of street parades in Miami, New York City, and Chicago, their ability to mobilize revolutionary discourses and practices is dependent on far more than their archived histories. Instead, their meaning is mediated through the deployment of the visual within the local contemporary context.

The presence of expatriates, new and old migrants and immigrants, enmeshed in overlapping communities and the conditions of the urban space are key factors in the flags' ability to be rearticulated into another symbolic formation. The flag not only can resonate with a shared sense of history but also can form part of collective solidarity within a geopolitical landscape that also gives new meaning to the term *revolution*. The chapters in this volume are part of this attempt to rearticulate the twenty-first-century meaning of the term through multiple spaces and mediums. The process is one that requires thinking across fields and disciplines as well as across spatial temporalities to reexamine how discursive formations can be rearticulated to set movements in motion. To aid in this ongoing process, we have included a section on further readings in lieu of a conclusion to reconstitute a contemporary, everyday significance of *revolution*. And the struggle continues.

NOTES

1. C. L. R. James, *The Black Jacobins: Toussaint L'Ouverture and the San Domingo Revolution* (New York: Vintage Books, 1989), 365–70.

2. Ibid, 365.

3. Susan Buck-Morss, *Hegel, Haiti, and Universal History* (Pittsburgh, PA: University of Pittsburgh Press, 2009).

4. Ibid.

5. Ibid.

6. Robin Blackburn, *The Overthrow of Colonial Slavery, 1776–1848* (London: Verso, 1988), 260.

7. Stuart Hall, "On Postmodernism and Articulation: An Interview with Stuart Hall," in *Stuart Hall: Critical Dialogues in Cultural Studies*, eds. David Morley and Kuan-Hsing Chen, 131–50 (New York: Routledge, 1996).

8. Ibid.

9. For more on Western modernity as a project that was dependent on colonialism and its colonized counterpart for the validation of its own existence, see Jean-Paul Sartre's "Preface" in Frantz Fanon's *The Wretched of the Earth* (New York: Grove Press, 1963), 7–31. See also Cedric Robinson's *Black Marxism: The Making of the Black Radical Tradition* (Chapel Hill: University of North Carolina Press, 1983).

10. Drawing upon the work of cultural studies and Stuart Hall, Lawrence Grossberg defines a conjunctural moment as "constituted by, at, and as the articulation of multiple, overlapping, competing, reinforcing, etc., lines of force and transformation, destabilization and (re-)stabilization, with differing temporalities and spatialities, producing a potentially but never actually chaotic assemblage or articulations of contradiction and contestations." Lawrence Grossberg, *Cultural Studies in the Future Tense* (Durham, NC: Durham University Press, 2010).

11. For more on the difference between global exchange and colonialism, as well as the relationship between capitalism and colonialism, see Aimé Césaire's *Discourse on Colonialism* (New York: Monthly Review Press, 2000).

12. Sartre, "Preface."

13. See Tamar Herzog on early modern notions of citizenship, *Defining Nations: Immigrants and Citizens in Early Modern Spain and Spanish America* (New Haven, CT: Yale University Press, 2011), and François Soyer, "Faith, Culture and Fear: Comparing Islamophobia in Early Modern Spain and Twenty-First-Century Europe," *Ethnic and Racial Studies* 36, no. 3 (2013): 399–416.

14. See Karl W. Butzer, "From Columbus to Acosta: Science, Geography, and the New World," *Annals of the Association of American Geographers* 82, no. 3 (September 1992): 543–65.

15. Sartre, "Preface," 26.

16. For more on racial knowledge, see David Theo Goldberg, *Racist Culture: Philosophy and the Politics of Meaning* (Hoboken, NJ: Wiley-Blackwell, 1993).

17. See Nicolas Copernicus, *On the Revolution of Heavenly Spheres* (Amherst, NY: Prometheus Books Great Minds Series, 1995).

18. Richard Pipes, *A Concise History of the Russian Revolution* (Vancouver, WA: Vintage, 1996).

19. Buck-Morss, *Hegel, Haiti, and Universal History*.

20. Ibid.

21. Ibid. See also David Brion Davis, *The Problem of Slavery in the Age of Revolution, 1770–1823* (Ithaca, NY: Cornell University Press, 1975).

22. For more on the categorization and regulation of the population, see Michel Foucault, *Security, Territory, Population: Lectures at the Collège de France, 1977–1978* (London: Picador, 2009), and *Society Must Be Defended* (London: Picador, 2003). See also Herzog, *Defining Nations*.

23. For more on racism and the biological division of the population, see Foucault, *Society Must Be Defended*.

24. See, for example, Achilles Mbembe, "Necropolitics," *Public Culture* 15, no. 1 (Winter 2003): 11–40.

25. See, for example, Homi K. Bhabha's discussion on colonial mimicry in *The Location of Culture* (New York: Routledge, 2004).

26. Here I refer to the colonized as the antithesis of modern Europe. I draw on the body of work from critical race scholars, such as Frantz Fanon and Audre Lorde, who theorize on the relationship between dialectical materialism, race, and social justice. See Frantz Fanon, *Black Skin, White Masks* (New York: Grove Press, 1990), and *The Wretched of the Earth* (New York: Grove Press, 1963), and Audre Lorde, *Sister Outsider: Essays and Speeches* (Berkeley, CA: Crossing Press, 2007).

27. Fanon, *The Wretched of the Earth*.

28. James, *The Black Jacobins*, 361.

29. See James, *The Black Jacobins*, and Buck-Morss, *Hegel, Haiti, and Universal History*.

30. Ibid.

31. See Henry Eugene Sterkx and Brooks Thompson, "Philemon Thomas and the West Florida Revolution," *Florida Historical Quarterly* 39, no. 2 (April 1961): 378–86; John Charles Chasteen, *Born in Blood and Fire: A Concise History of Latin America*, 3rd ed. (New York: W. W. Norton, 2011).

32. See Peter Zinoman, "Colonial Prisons and Anti-colonial Resistance in French Indochina: The Thai Nguyen Rebellion, 1917," *Modern Asian Studies* 34, no. 1 (2000): 57–98; Niels Kastfelt, "African Resistance to Colonialism in Adamawa," *Journal of Religion in Africa* 8, no. 1 (1976): 1–12.

33. Ho Chi Minh, *The Prison Diary of Ho Chi Minh* (New York: Bantam Books, 1971); Aimé Césaire, "Letter to Maurice Thorez," *Social Text* 28, no. 2 (2010): 145–52.

34. *Neocolonialism* refers to the continuance of economic, political, and social dominance for capital gain that was established during Western colonialism. In its late nineteenth- and twentieth-century form, neocolonialism was not limited to the direct exercise of one country over another but a distanced economic, cultural, and political dominance; it also referred to global effects and hierarchies that colonialism engendered. See Kwame Nkrumah, *Neo-colonialism: The Last Stage of*

Imperialism (New York: International Publishers, 1966). See also Jean-Paul Sartre, *Colonialism and Neocolonialism* (New York: Routledge, 2006).

35. *Neocolonialism* is used to encompass stages of colonialism and imperialism in varying temporal spaces.

36. Adding to neocolonialism, *coloniality* refers to the varied continuation of colonial processes, their domination, and their effects throughout the world (see the aforementioned definition for *neocolonialism*). *Coloniality* highlights the contemporary moment and how race and racial hierarchy play a primary role at both the micro and macro level within the global capitalist system of modernity/coloniality. See Anibel Quijano, "Coloniality of Power and Eurocentrism in Latin America," *International Sociology* 15, no. 2 (2000): 215–32; Walter Mignolo, *The Darker Side of the Renaissance: Literacy, Territoriality, and Colonization*, 2nd ed. (Ann Arbor: University of Michigan Press, 2003); Sylvia Wynter, "Unsettling the Coloniality of Being/Truth/Power/Freedom: Towards the Human, After Man, Its Overrepresentation—an Argument," *CR: The New Centennial Review* 3, no. 3 (Fall 2003): 257–337; Nelson Maldonado-Torres, "On the Coloniality of Being: Contributions to the Development of a Concept," *Cultural Studies* 21, no. 2 (2007): 240–70. See also Richard Iton, *In Search of the Black Fantastic: Politics and Popular Culture in the Post–Civil Rights Era* (London: Oxford University Press, 2010).

37. Through the work of Antonio Gramsci, Stuart Hall accounts for the struggle over hegemony as an ongoing process that is not won or lost in an instant. See Stuart Hall, "Gramsci's Relevance for the Study of Race and Ethnicity," in *Stuart Hall: Critical Dialogues in Cultural Studies*, eds. David Morley and Kuan-Hsing Chen, 411–40 (New York: Routledge, 1996); see also Stuart Hall, "What Is This 'Black' in Black Popular Culture?" in *Stuart Hall: Critical Dialogues in Cultural Studies*, eds. David Morley and Kuan-Hsing Chen, 465–75 (New York: Routledge, 1996).

38. Celiany Rivera-Velázquez, "The Importance of Being Rita Indiana-Hernández: Women-Centered Video, Sound, and Performance Interventions within Spanish Caribbean Culture Studies," in *Globalizing Cultural Studies: Ethnographic Interventions in Theory, Method, and Policy*, eds. Cameron McCarthy, Aisha S. Durham, Laura C. Engel, and Alice A. Filmer, 205–28 (New York: Peter Lang, 2007).

39. See C. L. R. James, *A History of Pan-African Revolt* (Oakland, CA: PM Press, 2012); Ronald W. Walters, *Pan Africanism in the African Diaspora: An Analysis of Modern Afrocentric Political Movements* (Detroit, MI: Wayne State University Press, 1997). See also Getachew Metaferia, "The Ethiopian Connection to the Pan-African Movement," *Journal of Third World Studies* 12, no. 2 (Fall 1995): 300–325.

40. The use of red, black, and green linked these midcentury struggles with the earlier Pan-Africanist revolts that peaked just after the turn of the century; the colors and design were appropriations of the Universal Negro Improvement Association's flag, propelled by Marcus Garvey. The use of green, red, and yellow were similarly appropriated and linked the struggles with Ethiopia, the oldest independent nation in the African continent. See Tony Martin, *Race First: The Ideological and Or-*

ganizational Struggles of Marcus Garvey and the Universal Negro Improvement Association (Westport, CT: Greenwood Press, 1976); Metaferia, "The Ethiopian Connection to the Pan-African Movement."

41. For more on visual culture, including its impact on area studies and social movements, see Stuart Hall and Jessica Evans, eds., *Visual Culture: The Reader* (Thousand Oaks, CA: Sage, 1999); Marita Sturken and Lisa Cartwright, *Practices of Looking: An Introduction to Visual Culture*, 2nd ed. (Oxford: Oxford University Press, 2009); Richard Howells and Joaquim Negreiros, eds., *Visual Culture*, 2nd ed. (Cambridge: Polity, 2012); Nicholas Mirzoeff, *The Visual Culture Reader* (London: Routledge, 1998), and *An Introduction to Visual Culture* (London: Routledge, 1999).

42. The use of the visual is not a new concept as apparent in visual studies, visual culture, communication studies, and traditional disciplines such as history and anthropology. However this edited collection utilizes the visual as part of a larger cultural studies project and draws heavily on its body of literature. This collection also takes into account how the development of visual culture stems largely from cultural studies as method, theory, and politics. See, for example, James Elkins, *Visual Studies: A Skeptical Introduction* (London: Routledge, 2003), and *Theorizing Visual Studies: Writing through the Disciplines* (London: Routledge, 2012). See also W. J. T. Mitchell, "Showing Seeing: A Critique of Visual Culture," *Journal of Visual Culture* 1, no. 2 (2002): 165–81.

43. In 2006, the American Historical Association (AHA) issued a statement encouraging the use of moving and still images as documents of history and illustrations of historical processes. See Anna Pegler-Gordon, "Seeing Images in History," *Perspectives on History: The Newsmagazine of the American Historical Association* (February 2006); Adrienne D. Hood, "Material Culture: The Object," in *History Beyond a Text: A Student's Guide to Approaching Alternative Sources*, eds. Sarah Barber and Corinna M. Peniston-Bird, 176–98 (New York: Routledge, 2008).

44. Stuart Hall, "Notes on Deconstructing 'the Popular,'" in *People's History and Socialist Theory*, ed. Raphael Samuel, 227–40 (Boston: Routledge & Kegan Paul, 1981).

45. For the potential of the visual culture as historical method, see Sandria B. Freitag, "The Visual Turn: Approaching South Asia across the Disciplines," *South Asia: Journal of South Asian Studies* 37, no. 3 (2014): 398–409, and Andrea Noble, "Visual Culture and Latin American Studies," *CR: The New Centennial Review* 4, no. 2 (2004): 219–38.

BIBLIOGRAPHY

Bhabha, Homi K. *The Location of Culture.* New York: Routledge, 2004.

Blackburn, Robin. *The Overthrow of Colonial Slavery, 1776–1848.* London: Verso, 1988.

Buck-Morss, Susan. *Hegel, Haiti, and Universal History.* Pittsburgh, PA: University of Pittsburgh Press, 2009.

Butzer, Karl W. "From Columbus to Acosta: Science, Geography, and the New World." *Annals of the Association of American Geographers* 82, no. 3 (September 1992): 543–65.

Césaire, Aimé. *Discourse on Colonialism*. New York: Monthly Review Press, 2000.

———. "Letter to Maurice Thorez." *Social Text* 28, no. 2 (2010): 145–52.

Chasteen, John Charles. *Born in Blood and Fire: A Concise History of Latin America*, 3rd edition. New York: W. W. Norton, 2011.

Copernicus, Nicolas. *On the Revolution of Heavenly Spheres*. Amherst, NY: Prometheus Books Great Minds Series, 1995.

Davis, David Brion. *The Problem of Slavery in the Age of Revolution, 1770–1823*. Ithaca, NY: Cornell University Press, 1975.

Elkins, James. *Theorizing Visual Studies: Writing through the Disciplines*. London: Routledge, 2012.

———. *Visual Studies: A Skeptical Introduction*. London: Routledge, 2003.

Fanon, Frantz. *Black Skin, White Masks*. New York: Grove Press, 1990.

———. *The Wretched of the Earth*. New York: Grove Press, 1963.

Foucault, Michel. *Security, Territory, Population: Lectures at the Collège de France, 1977–1978*. London: Picador, 2009.

———. *Society Must Be Defended.* London: Picador, 2003.

Freitag, Sandria B. "The Visual Turn: Approaching South Asia across the Disciplines." *South Asia: Journal of South Asian Studies* 37, no. 3 (2014): 398–409.

Goldberg, David Theo. *Racist Culture: Philosophy and the Politics of Meaning.* Hoboken, NJ: Wiley-Blackwell, 1993.

Grossberg, Lawrence. *Cultural Studies in the Future Tense*. Durham, NC: Durham University Press, 2010.

Hall, Stuart. "Gramsci's Relevance for the Study of Race and Ethnicity." In *Stuart Hall: Critical Dialogues in Cultural Studies*, edited by David Morley and Kuan-Hsing Chen, 411–40. New York: Routledge, 1996.

———. "Notes on Deconstructing 'the Popular.'" In *People's History and Socialist Theory*, edited by Raphael Samuel, 227–40. Boston: Routledge & Kegan Paul, 1981.

———. "On Postmodernism and Articulation: An Interview with Stuart Hall." Edited by Lawrence Grossberg. In *Stuart Hall: Critical Dialogues in Cultural Studies*, edited by David Morley and Kuan-Hsing Chen, 131–50. New York: Routledge, 1996.

———. "What Is This 'Black' in Black Popular Culture?" In *Stuart Hall: Critical Dialogues in Cultural Studies*, edited by David Morley and Kuan-Hsing Chen, 465–75. New York: Routledge, 1996.

Hall, Stuart, and Jessica Evans, eds. *Visual Culture: The Reader.* Thousand Oaks, CA: Sage, 1999.

Herzog, Tamar. *Defining Nations: Immigrants and Citizens in Early Modern Spain and Spanish America*. New Haven, CT: Yale University Press, 2011.

Howells, Richard, and Joaquim Negreiros, eds. *Visual Culture*, 2nd edition. Cambridge: Polity, 2012.

Hood, Adrienne D. "Material Culture: The Object." In *History Beyond a Text: A Student's Guide to Approaching Alternative Sources*, edited by Sarah Barber and Corinna M. Peniston-Bird, 176–98. New York: Routledge, 2008.

Iton, Richard. *In Search of the Black Fantastic: Politics and Popular Culture in the Post–Civil Rights Era.* London: Oxford University Press, 2010.

James, C. L. R. *The Black Jacobins: Toussaint L'Ouverture and the San Domingo Revolution.* New York: Vintage Books, 1989.

———. *A History of Pan-African Revolt.* Oakland, CA: PM Press, 2012.

Kastfelt, Niels. "African Resistance to Colonialism in Adamawa." *Journal of Religion in Africa* 8, no. 1 (1976): 1–12.

Lorde, Audre. *Sister Outsider: Essays and Speeches.* Berkeley: Crossing Press, 2007.

Maldonado-Torres, Nelson. "On the Coloniality of Being: Contributions to the Development of a Concept." *Cultural Studies* 21, no. 2 (2007): 240–70.

Martin, Tony. *Race First: The Ideological and Organizational Struggles of Marcus Garvey and the Universal Negro Improvement Association.* Westport, CT: Greenwood Press, 1976.

Mbembe, Achilles. "Necropolitics." *Public Culture* 15, no. 1 (Winter 2003): 11–40.

Metaferia, Getachew. "The Ethiopian Connection to the Pan-African Movement." *Journal of Third World Studies* 12, no. 2 (Fall 1995): 300–325.

Mignolo, Walter. *The Darker Side of the Renaissance: Literacy, Territoriality, and Colonization*, 2nd edition. Ann Arbor: University of Michigan Press, 2003.

Minh, Ho Chi. *The Prison Diary of Ho Chi Minh.* New York: Bantam Books, 1971.

Mirzoeff, Nicholas. *An Introduction to Visual Culture*. London: Routledge, 1999.

———. *The Visual Culture Reader*. London: Routledge, 1998.

Mitchell, W. J. T. "Showing Seeing: A Critique of Visual Culture." *Journal of Visual Culture* 1, no. 2 (2002): 165–81.

Nkrumah, Kwame. *Neo-colonialism: The Last Stage of Imperialism.* New York: International Publishers, 1966.

Noble, Andrea. "Visual Culture and Latin American Studies." *CR: The New Centennial Review* 4, no. 2 (2004): 219–38.

Pegler-Gordon, Anna. "Seeing Images in History." *Perspectives on History: The Newsmagazine of the American Historical Association* (February 2006).

Pipes, Richard. *A Concise History of the Russian Revolution.* Vancouver, WA: Vintage, 1996.

Quijano, Anibal. "Coloniality of Power and Eurocentrism in Latin America." *International Sociology* 15, no. 2 (2000): 215–32.

Rivera-Velázquez, Celiany. "The Importance of Being Rita Indiana-Hernández: Women-Centered Video, Sound, and Performance Interventions within Spanish Caribbean Culture Studies." In *Globalizing Cultural Studies: Ethnographic Interventions in Theory, Method, and Policy*, edited by Cameron McCarthy, Aisha S. Durham, Laura C. Engel, Alice A. Filmer, Michael D. Giardina, and Miguel A. Malagreca, 205–28. New York: Peter Lang, 2007.

Robinson, Cedric. *Black Marxism: The Making of the Black Radical Tradition.* Chapel Hill: University of North Carolina Press, 1983.

Sartre, Jean-Paul. *Colonialism and Neocolonialism*. New York: Routledge, 2006.

———. "Preface." In Frantz Fanon, *The Wretched of the Earth*. New York: Grove Press, 1963.

Soyer, François. "Faith, Culture and Fear: Comparing Islamophobia in Early Modern Spain and Twenty-First-Century Europe." *Ethnic and Racial Studies* 36, no. 3 (2013): 399–416.

Sterkx, Henry Eugene, and Brooks Thompson. "Philemon Thomas and the West Florida Revolution." *Florida Historical Quarterly* 39, no. 2 (April 1961): 378–86.

Sturken, Marita, and Lisa Cartwright. *Practices of Looking: An Introduction to Visual Culture*, 2nd edition. Oxford: Oxford University Press, 2009.

Walters, Ronald W. *Pan Africanism in the African Diaspora: An Analysis of Modern Afrocentric Political Movements*. Detroit, MI: Wayne State University Press, 1997.

Wynter, Sylvia. "Unsettling the Coloniality of Being/Truth/Power/Freedom: Towards the Human, After Man, Its Overrepresentation—an Argument." *CR: The New Centennial Review* 3, no. 3 (Fall 2003): 257–337.

Zinoman, Peter. "Colonial Prisons and Anti-colonial Resistance in French Indochina: The Thai Nguyen Rebellion, 1917." *Modern Asian Studies* 34, no. 1 (2000): 57–98.

1

❖ ❖

Icons of Revolution

Constructions of Emiliano Zapata in Prints of the Mexican Revolution

Theresa Avila

The Mexican Revolution erupted in 1910 in response to an oppressive thirty-year dictatorship under José de la Cruz Porfirio Díaz (1876–1910). Aggressive development during the *Porfiriato* resulted in modernization and economic growth in Mexico, but progress came at a high cost. The Porfirian regime's methods for stabilizing Mexico and making resources available for foreign investment and development included coercion and violence, as well as land seizures from small property owners and forced displacement of indigenous groups and villages. Once in place, domestic and foreign agricultural and industrial complexes benefited from preferential treatment from the Porfirian regime in the form of legislation, biased arbitration, and (in some instances) military support.

In response to the injustices and oppression suffered under Porfirio Díaz, outbreaks of rebellion occurred across Mexico throughout the Porfiriato.[1] There was no single issue that motivated individuals to revolt, but reasons included various grievances related to land rights, labor disputes, lack of civil liberties, and an unjust and violent political system. However, Francisco Madero's revolt against Porfirio Díaz, launched on November 20, 1910, has been designated as *the* official beginning of the Mexican Revolution.[2] The war lasted a decade between 1910 and 1920. Following the devastation of ten years of war, the nation rebuilt. The ideologies and issues that motivated the insurrection were made seminal to the reconstruction of the nation through narratives and invented traditions.[3]

The Taller de Gráfica Popular (Workshop for Popular Graphic Art), or TGP, is a graphic art collective founded in Mexico City in 1937 that was motivated by the goals and legacy of the Mexican Revolution.[4] The TGP's 1947 portfolio *Estampas de la Revolución Mexicana* (*Prints of the Mexican Revolution*) consists of eighty-five linocut prints created by sixteen member artists.[5] The album remarks on three distinct periods of Mexican history: one through nineteen address the dictatorship of Porfirio Díaz (1876–1910); twenty through fifty-seven present the violent phase of the Mexican Revolution (1910–1920); and fifty-eight through eighty-five deal with the postwar era in Mexico (1920s–1940s). A "prologue" introduces the project and brief textual captions provide some context for each image.

The figures represented within the portfolio are significant to and symbolic of the historical events, issues, and ideologies associated with the Mexican Revolution. Key figures within the graphic series, based on the number of times represented or referenced, are Porfirio Díaz, Francisco Madero, Venustiano Carranza, Álvaro Obregón, Lázaro Cárdenas, and Emiliano Zapata. National recognition was a tribute paid to these men as part of the process of invention and institutionalization of the war, which promoted most of them as national heroes of the Mexican Revolution. In the graphic series, the TGP heroicized some of these individuals and the collective demonized others.

Emiliano Zapata (1879–1919), the general of the Southern Army of the Mexican Revolution, is the most emphasized figure in the TGP's portfolio on the war.[6] The image of Zapata has a rich and complex history that spans nearly a century. During the rebellion, and more so after his death, Zapata is seen as an agent and symbol of social justice and land reform. Zapata's involvement began as a fight for the reclamation of land and resources on behalf of the disenfranchised villagers of his hometown, Anenecuilco, in the state of Morelos.[7] In this effort, Zapata fought for and promoted agrarian reform and regional autonomy in the form of grassroots self-government.[8] Therefore, fundamentally, the image of Zapata correlates with the concepts of the egalitarian distribution of land, the decentralization of government, and rebellion in the name of justice. Symbolically, Zapata has become the personification of the Mexican Revolution, Mexican national identity, Mexican cultural heritage, and social justice. However, it is important to realize that diverse applications frame Zapata within a variety of contexts and represent him in multiple forms, thus indicating the importance he holds as a symbol, but also making clear the multiplicity of meanings attached to Zapata.

Examination of a select number of prints of Zapata from the TGP's *Prints of the Mexican Revolution* explains how and for what purposes the revolutionary has been remembered, constructed, and transformed into an icon of revolution.[9] Analysis of the visual, textual, historical, and narratological elements in the series of prints reveals the interplay of distinct narratives of the war in the TGP's portfolio, which alludes to the evolving and multiplicitous nature of the legacy of the war. Tracing the narrative(s) of Zapata that the TGP wove into the series of prints, this chapter makes evident the objectives of the TGP for the portfolio.[10] However, although Zapata is represented in nine distinct prints, I will only discuss a select number and focus my discussion on elements that clearly express the focus and intent of the portfolio.

The TGP took the traditional concept of the artisanal workshop and transformed it into a site for artistic production and training motivated by a sense of social justice and political action. The graphic images of the TGP worked to inform and educate the people of Mexico, as well as an international audience.[11] As activists, the artist members of the TGP promoted and lobbied for progressive labor laws, access to education, and control of natural resources. Topics at the core of the workshop's prints include Mexico's heritage and history, the poverty and oppression of the Native American population, human rights, and civil liberties. In alignment with international efforts, the artists in the TGP confronted violence as a state-sanctioned means of social control, encouraged socialism, and remained conscious of global issues in their work. The TGP circulated their prints worldwide and connected with and incorporated numerous international artists.[12]

In *Prints of the Mexican Revolution*, the TGP embraced the origins of the war while it grappled and interacted with the rebellion's history and legacy. The TGP's portfolio is actually a sort of pastiche or collage of narratives of the war. In the the portfolio's "prologue," the TGP describes the motivations behind the portfolio as a response to then president Miguel Alemán's call to "honor and aggrandize Mexico" and a changing political climate. The workshop declared the intended purpose of the album was to "battle against enemies of the insurgency of 1910" and to "revive in an illustrative form the heroic struggle of our country for 'Land and Liberty.'" This statement makes clear the TGP's understanding of the goals of the Mexican Revolution and the ideological focus of the portfolio. In this opening statement, the TGP also indicates their intent to teach the public about the revolutionary struggle of 1910–1920 through the portfolio, which clearly indicates the purposeful nature of what is included, represented, omitted, and expressed.

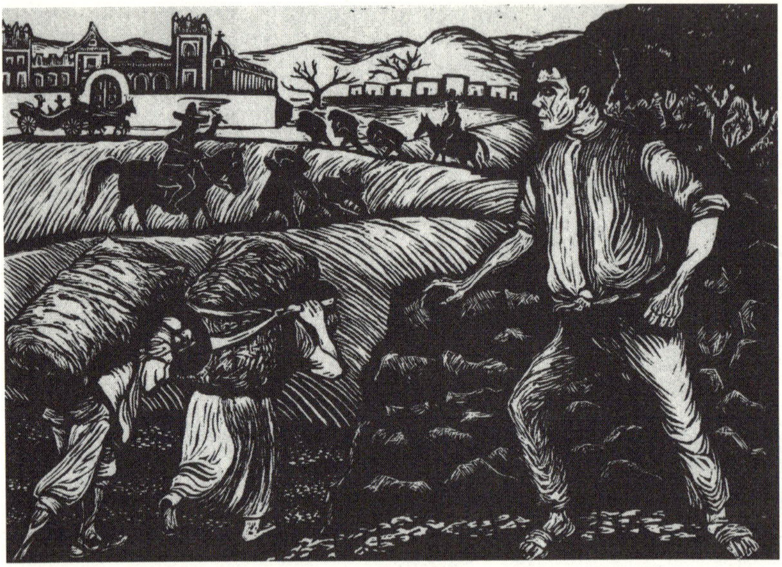

Figure 1.1. Mariana Yampolsky, "La juventud de Emiliano Zapata: Lección objectiva," *Estampas de la Revolución Mexicana*, No. 8, 1947, Linocut. (Courtesy of the University of New Mexico Art Museum, Albuquerque.)

The first nineteen prints of the TGP's graphic series chronicle the tyranny of Porfirio Díaz's dictatorship and focus on the most egregious systems and tactics of the regime to pacify, control, and develop Mexico. Among this set, the artist Mariana Yampolsky introduces Emiliano Zapata as he confronts the tyranny of the Porfirian-era hacienda system. In the eighth print of the portfolio, "*La Juventud de Emiliano Zapata: Lección Objetiva*" ("The Youth of Emiliano Zapata: An Important Lesson"), a young Zapata stands looking out across a sprawling agricultural estate (figure 1.1).[13] During the Porfirian regime, the expansion and domination of large agricultural estates swelled, which disrupted organization of local labor, agricultural production, and economic systems that resulted in the informal colonization of rural Mexico by the domestic elite and by foreign investors and companies. In print 8, Yampolsky describes multiple scenes of abuse suffered by agrarian laborers on these haciendas and indicates how the hacienda system and landscape are instruments of power that encouraged and reinforced uneven development in Mexico.

The text caption connected to this image narrates a key moment of a mythic tale about Zapata as a young man, reading:

> "And why don't the people of the villages come together and take back the land that has been taken away?" Emiliano Zapata asked his father back in the days of his youth. "No son," replied the future leader's father—"nothing can be done against the hacendado's agricultural estates and businessess." In response, Emiliano questioned, "It cannot be done? Let me grow up and they will see that I can recover the lands taken from us." His father's words stayed with him.

The reference to an often-repeated tale about Zapata, who as a youth promised to take back the land stolen from his fellow villagers, harkens to a common myth and the revolutionary's commitment to the issue of agrarian and political reform. The image can be read as a precursor to the conversation between father and son, where Zapata is troubled after seeing the extent of suffering on the hacienda before him and seeks out his father. Although this moment between father and son would have likely taken place near their own village of Anenecuilco, the text and image are nonspecific about location. Instead, the ambiguity of location in the image expands the significance and problems related to land rights, the hacienda system, and labor rights to all of Mexico.

Yampolsky locates Zapata as witness to the working and living conditions on the hacienda and by doing so indicates that the agrarian issue was of personal concern to him. Furthermore, by isolating and making him the sole witness, the artist alludes to Zapata as the only one willing or able to take the land back. Yampolsky further denotes Zapata's intimate association with the agrarian community by dressing him in the traditional attire of rural laborers, white cotton *calzones*. As Samuel Brunk has documented, Zapata's parents were farmers who worked their own plot of village land; therefore, we can assume that Zapata donned the typical attire while performing this type of labor on his own land.[14] As the uniform of the Zapatistas, the calzone also operates as a symbol for Zapata's rebellion and participation in the Mexican Revolution, and, more important, it signifies his demands for agrarian reform.

This image and its narrative attest to Zapata's personal experience with and concern over the agrarian issue, as well as marking him as a key symbol for the ideological platform of agrarian reform. As the first image that introduces Zapata, print 8 establishes how the TGP define him in the portfolio. As the first image of a leader of the Mexican Revolution to be addressed in the portfolio, Zapata is identified as *the* principal revolutionary for the TGP. This also makes it clear that his ideology most closely aligns with that of the TGP and that the organization promoted land rights as a primary issue for them, as well as the Mexican Revolution and its legacy.

Thus, in the portfolio, as in the master narratives of the war, Zapata is *the* historical and symbolic figure, above all others, who constitutes and represents the rural community of Mexico and the agrarian issue.

Zapata plays a significant role within the portfolio and is a principal figure in the group of prints that mark the start of the violent phase of the Mexican Revolution. Zapata's insurgency was part of a larger movement in response to the tyrannical oppression of the Porfirian regime across Mexico. The revolutionary was elected village council president in September 1909, and from that point forward he assumed leadership of the local land struggle in his village of Anenecuilco.[15] Zapata took decisive action in the spring of 1910 when he gathered eighty armed men to protect local villagers who farmed land that was in dispute.[16] Initially, Zapata acted in relation to his local situation, but over time he became aware of Francisco Madero's movement, the Plan of San Luis Potosi, and the wave of rebellion that was occurring across the nation. Article 3 in Madero's declaration addresses the restitution of land unjustly taken by the Porfirian regime from small land owners primarily from the lower classes and motivated the southern rural faction of the war, led by Zapata, to join his effort. When Zapata joined Madero's rebellion on March 10, 1911, it was in alliance with other local leaders, as well as in unison with a national movement. After a shaky start and sporadic bursts of rebellion across the country, a major battle was fought and won at Ciudad Juarez. The outcome was the signing of the Peace Treaty of Ciudad Juarez in May 1911. On May 25, 1911, Porfirio Díaz submitted his resignation to the Mexican congress per the treaty, and the first phase of violence came to an end.[17] Madero was democratically elected president of Mexico in October 1911.

In print 24, "*Emiliano Zapata, Lider de la Revolución Agraria*" ("Emiliano Zapata, Leader of the Agrarian Revolution"), TGP artist member Francisco Mora heralds Zapata's significance in the war and, more important, to the TGP (figure 1.2). Locating Zapata at the beginning of the section of the portfolio that addesses the violent stage of the Mexican Revolution marks him as a crucial actor. Mora depicts Zapata on horseback, armed, and at the forefront of a dense group of armed men also on horseback. The print's caption states:

> General Emiliano Zapata was the Agrarian Leader par excellence. His life is an example of ongoing militancy in favor of the dispossessed of his time. His thinking is embodied in the Plan of Ayala, and over many years, without compromising in any way, he fought for the realization of his noble social ideas. His name and his efforts are revered by all in the rural community of the Republic and in numerous foreign countries.

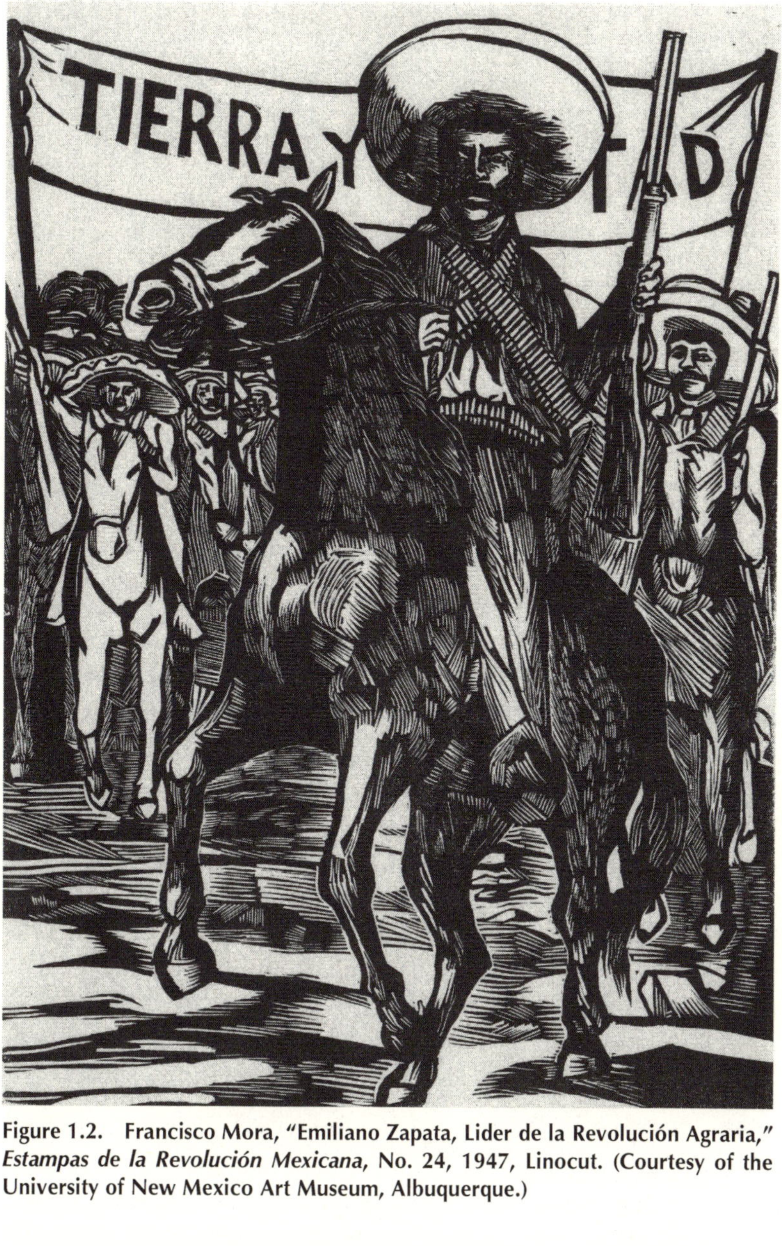

Figure 1.2. Francisco Mora, "Emiliano Zapata, Lider de la Revolución Agraria," *Estampas de la Revolución Mexicana*, No. 24, 1947, Linocut. (Courtesy of the University of New Mexico Art Museum, Albuquerque.)

This text offers an abbreviated summation of Zapata's effort and character. The print alludes to the revolutionary general's rise to power in a manner that resonates with both the personal story and the national dominant narrative, as well as capturing the symbolic meanings attached to Zapata.

In print 24, Mora incorporates the Zapatistas' trademark slogan "*Tierra y Libertad*" ("Land and Liberty"), which is emblazoned on the banner over the army behind Zapata.[18] This text evokes the Zapatista manifesto, the Plan of Ayala. The slogan "Liberty, Justice, and Law" is the last declarative statement attached to this plan, which was circulated in December 1911. The plan was written to explain the goals of *Zapatismo*.[19] It expressed Zapatismo's agenda as primarily land reform on a national scale, but it recognized the significance of political power in this endeavor and promoted decentralized government by self-appointed leaders. Agrarian reform was defined in the Plan of Ayala as the nationalization of estate monopolies and the property owned by enemies of the Mexican Revolution through confiscation and redistribution of land to those who held titles and from whom the land had been unjustly taken.[20] "Emiliano Zapata, Leader of the Agrarian Revolution," as the title of the print, not only describes Zapata's role within the Mexican Revolution but also emphasizes a particular agenda and ideology within the war and the portfolio.

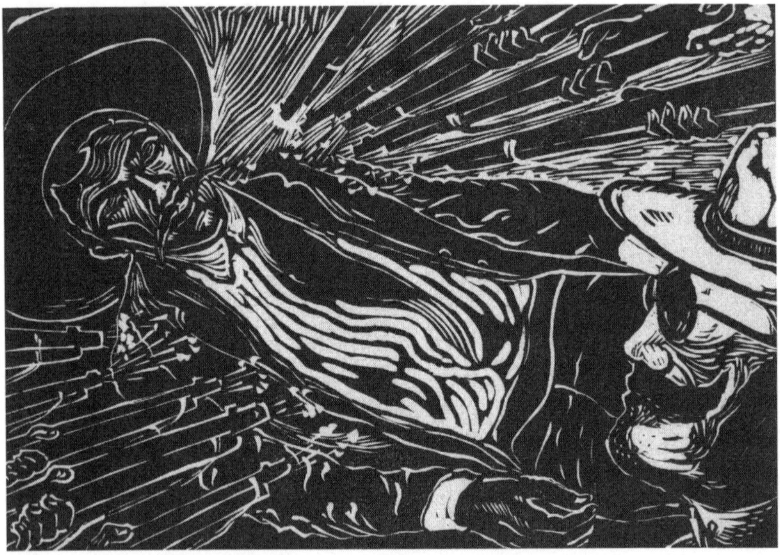

Figure 1.3. Isidoro Ocampo, "La muerte de Emiliano Zapata, 10 de Abril de 1919," *Estampas de la Revolución Mexicana*, No. 57, 1947, Linocut. (Courtesy of the University of New Mexico Art Museum, Albuquerque.)

The ambush assassination of Zapata is the subject of the fifty-seventh print of the portfolio, "*La Muerte de Emiliano Zapata*" ("The Death of Emiliano Zapata"), by Isidoro Ocampo (figure 1.3). The caption for the print declares:

> April 10, 1919 is a day of mourning for the Mexican Revolution. In Chinameca, Morelos, the great revolutionary general Emiliano Zapata was shot dead as a victim of an ambush. After death, his significance grew over time and he is an example for all men who yearn to resolve the problems that plague the rural population of the Republic of Mexico.

The scene is devoid of any reference to place, compelling the viewer to focus on the attack on Zapata. Ocampo confronts the viewer with Zapata's figure by pushing it to the surface of the print. The lifeless body evokes numerous documentary photographs of Zapata in death where he wears this exact outfit.[21] Jutting out from the bottom-left edge and top-right edge of the print are numerous shotguns or rifles directed at Zapata's body. Puffs of smoke emitting from the barrels suggest the weapons have just been fired and create an immediacy that locates the viewer as witness, if not participant, in the attack. Visible are a few hands that hold the weapons, but nothing more of the shooters' identity is depicted. This adds to the reality that there were numerous individuals involved in the murder of Zapata. In history, they are rarely acknowledged, but within the image they are remembered. Captain Guarjardo is seen in profile view lurking in the bottom-right corner of print 57. Guarjardo, under orders from Venustiano Carranza, conned Zapata into thinking he wished to join forces with him and then ambushed him. The captain's presence, as well as the proximity of Carranza in the preceeding print, implicates both men in the murderous act. Reading prints 56 and 57 in chronological sequence alludes to the acrimonious relationship between the two men, as well as to the multiplicity of narratives incorporated within the portfolio.[22]

Print 56, "*Venustiano Carranza, Prometor de la Constitución de 1917*" ("Venustiano Carranza, Promoter of the Constitution of 1917"), by Alberto Beltran, is seemingly focused on celebrating Carranza as the father of Mexico's Constitution. Carranza was the leader of the Constitutionalist Army who became the president of Mexico (1917–1920). He played a significant role in the developments during the Mexican Revolution, particularly after Victoriano Huerta's coup d'etat in 1913 when he led an anti-Huertista offensive. Although Zapatista forces also rebelled against Huerta, they did not align themselves with Carranza. In fact, after Huerta's defeat in 1914, Zapata, as part of the Conventionist forces, went head to head against Carranza's Constitutionalist Army. Carranza's persecution of the Zapatista

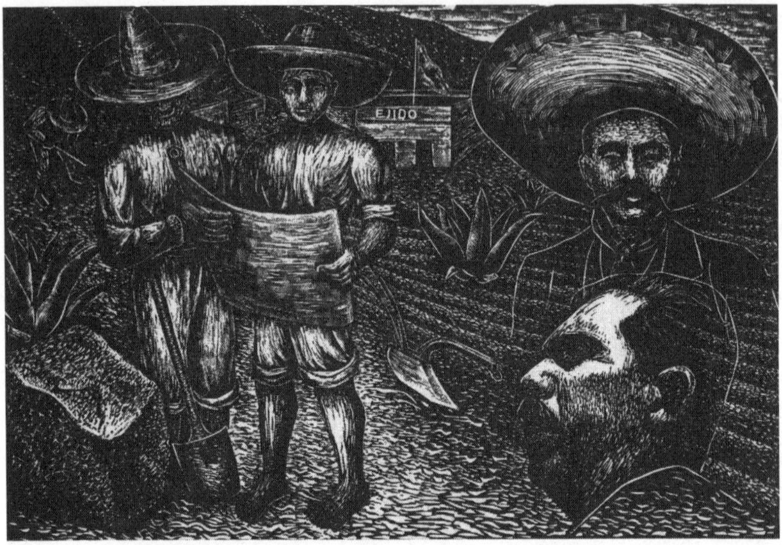

Figure 1.4. Luis Arenal, "Lázaro Cárdenas y La Reforman Agraria, 1934–1940," *Estampas de la Revolución Mexicana*, No. 67, 1947, Linocut. (Courtesy of the University of New Mexico Art Museum, Albuquerque.)

army culminated in Zapata's assassination in 1919. However, the revision of this narrative after the war eventually downplayed Carranza's role in Zapata's assassination. Carranza, like Zapata, became an icon of the Mexican Revolution and a member of the postwar revolutionary family.[23] The juxtaposition of Zapata and Carranza in the portfolio betrays the complex nature of the notion of unification among revolutionaries. The pairing of the prints highlights the TGP's critique of Carranza and their alignment with the Zapatista movement.

The last section of the portfolio presents postwar Mexico between the 1920s and the mid-1940s. In this set of prints, the TGP address each president, some in more depth than others, which often reflects the TGP's assessment of their association to the legacy of the Mexican Revolution and their fulfillment of revolutionary promises. The TGP dedicated a section of prints to the period of Cárdenas's presidency (1934–1940) and his programs. Print 67, "*Lázaro Cárdenas y La Reforman Agraria, 1934–1940*" ("Lázaro Cárdenas and Agrarian Reform, 1934–1940"), by Luis Arenal, pairs Mexican president Cárdenas with Zapata (figure 1.4). The artist also included two rural villagers who stand side by side as both look toward a large sheet of paper, possibly blueprints that likely indicate where their plot of land lies. Behind them in the background, another similarly dressed figure stoops over to hoe the land. A structure in the background with "*EJIDO*" on it refers to an area of communal land used for agriculture, on which community members individually possess and farm a specific parcel. A plow can also be seen at the bottom center of the image. All of these elements come together to evoke not only the promise of land reform but also actual revolutionary change in terms of land reform under Cárdenas.

At the top of the right side of the composition is a bust portrait of Zapata hovering above a profile head shot of Cárdenas. The two national leaders are outlined with a fine and hard white line that suggests a translucency that allows the fields in the background to fill and form the figures, so that each reads as if they are part of the landscape. It is evident that neither Zapata nor Cárdenas actually occupy the space of the rural figures, but in their close proximity to them, and to one another, they are presented as spirits of revolutionary agrarian reform. The pairing of both leaders implies that they are concerned about the same issues and share the same ideals.

The caption for print 67 states:

> President Lázaro Cárdenas relies on the faith of the people to rule the country. He was severely attacked by Mexican conservatives, particularly on the issues that offered justice to the countryside. His regime was characterized by an unheard of distribution of land to farmers throughout the Republic. In the Laguna cotton counties were divided and now, more than ten years later, no one dares to say that agrarian reform there has been a failure.

Cárdenas moved away from the elite- and foreign-driven policies, instead implementing many of the social reforms promised in the Constitution of 1917. The Cárdenas era is typically identified as the most revolutionary period of government after the Mexican Revolution, citing his land-distribution programs, the expansion of labor unions, and the nationalization of natural resources as some of his greatest acts as leader of Mexico. In particular, agrarian reform during the Cárdenas regime meant redistribution of land, development of ejidos, and education for the agricultural class.[24] As such, Cárdenas can be read in the portfolio as (and for many he was) Zapata's successor and the embodiment of revolutionary reform. The TGP's ultimate goal for its portfolio was to address how the postwar regimes constructed and participated in the ongoing revolution.

The TGP produced *Prints of the Mexican Revolution* in the 1940s, an era marked by the departure of President Cárdenas, which punctuated a political shift regarding "revolutionary" ideology. The graphic series was a reaction to the 1940s political regimes' concentrated efforts by postwar leaders to counter the Mexican Revolution. One such effort is legislation passed in 1944 under President Manuel Avila Camacho that allowed foreign participation in the industrialization of Mexico, which was counter to revolutionary ideals and the efforts by President Cárdenas to nationalize the holdings of seventeen foreign oil companies. In December 1946, Miguel Alemán's administration passed thirty-nine new laws that reversed land reform, privatized education, limited free expression, and undermined existing labor organizations.[25] Article 27 of the Mexican Constitution, which originally called for land reform and nationalized Mexican soil, was changed to protect private landholders from further land reform, thus allowing them to increase holdings and to revoke uncultivated lands from *ejidatrios* or collective farm owners/workers.

At the beginning of the portfolio, the TGP remind their viewers/readers of the unjust policies, horrendous practices, and dire conditions that were part of national development during the Porfiriato. In doing this, it establishes a foil against which postwar political regimes and their policies are measured. Hence, as the end of the portfolio parallels and attaches to the beginning, time folds back on itself. In this manner, the TGP relate the historical patterns of oppression and social injustice in Mexico and the nature of the ongoing revolution.

Alfredo Zalce's image "*La Prensa y La Revolución Mexicana*" ("The Press and the Mexican Revolution") is print 82 in the portfolio series and depicts *the* revolutionary family at the top right, which includes, reading from left to right, Alvaro Obregón, Venustiano Carranza, Emiliano Zapata, and Francisco Madero (figure 1.5).[26] Portraits of these figures hover above a field of either sugar cane or corn.[27] Suggestive of the centrality of the agrarian issue to the Mexican Revolution, revolutionary figures wear the agrarian laborer uniform as they march out from the vegetation at the bottom of the image. However, in line with the title, two figures on the left side of the image, both depicted with exaggerated facial features, are surrounded by loose newspaper pages floating around them. The disfigurement of the figures associated with the press portrays newsmen and journalists in a negative light. But the issue of freedom of the press is made more complex when one considers the contradictory support and oppression of the press by the revolutionary leaders, a theme that is emphasized in the title and in the text that accompanies the print, which reads:

> The Mexican Revolution has been extremely generous with the press of the entire nation. It offered absolute freedom of expression, and has followed through on allowing it. Unfortunately, the majority of the national newspapers have taken advantage of the liberties provided thanks to the Constitution of 1917, and have become the most outrageous agents of debauchery. It is necessary to put an end to this outrageous abuse of freedom of expression, which is, as stated, an authentic liberty.

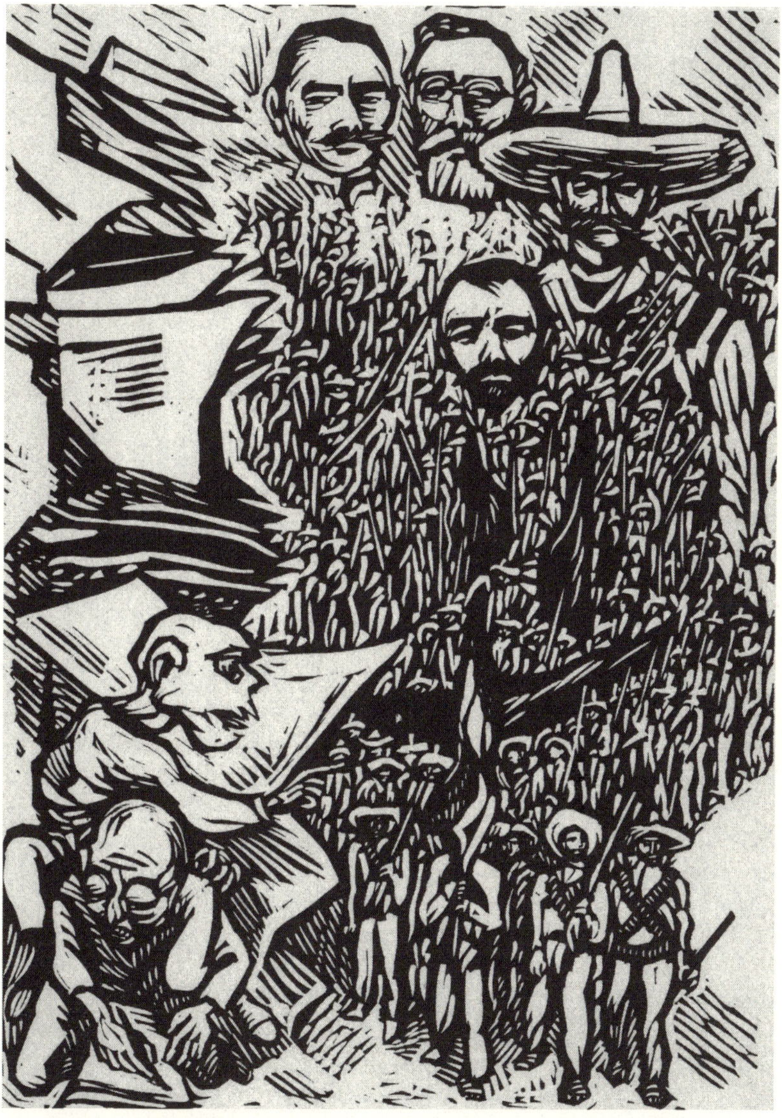

Figure 1.5. Alfredo Zalce, "La prensa y la Revolución Mexicana," *Estampas de la Revolución Mexicana,* No. 82, 1947, Linocut. (Courtesy of the University of New Mexico Art Museum, Albuquerque.)

The image seems to follow the text; however, it diverges in its inclusion of the agrarian theme and in the obvious reference to the revolutionary family, each raising its own set of issues.

In terms of the revolutionary leaders included in the print and their relationship with the press, each had his own distinct points of contention. Madero supported freedom of the press, even at his own expense. Throughout his time as a politician, Madero was regularly and vehemently critiqued, which is documented in the news journals and publications of his day.[28] Zapata's relationship with the press was equally problematic. The press, specifically in Mexico City, was engaged by the elite to criticize and defame Zapata. They blamed him and his followers for most, if not all, wrongdoing that occurred in relation to activities in the south of Mexico during the Mexican Revolution, labeling the revolutionary leader the "Attila of the South."[29] After Huerta's defeat by Constitutional forces in July 1914, Carranza controlled the Mexican press and directed its focus to a pro-Constitutionalism (more specifically, pro-Carrancismo) and anti-Zapatista reports. Thus, each of the figures portrayed in Zalce's print had distinct experiences with the press, and the topic does not necessarily serve to unite the men except to say they all had individual concerns about and relationships with the press, which is also true for all four figures and the issue of land rights.

The agrarian issue affected multiple aspects of political and social life in Mexico as it was connected to land theft, forced removal, and use and ownership of domestic resources, as well as development and modernization of the nation, economic imperialism, and disenfranchisement of agrarian communities. Some revolutionary leaders recognized the question of land distribution as an important issue, but sometimes only as a tool in managing the agrarian masses. Each of the revolutionary leaders portrayed in Zalce's print had a distinct position on agrarian reform, which can be related to their social class: Madero and Carranza were from elite families and, as owners of large agricultural estates themselves, were not interested in dismantling the hacienda system; Obregón was from the middle class and an urban laborer and somewhat disconnected from these concerns; and Zapata, being from a poor rural community, promoted agrarian reform. For Zapata, land reform motivated regional rebellion and demanded immediate attention. A clause in Madero's Plan of San Luis Potosí regarding land rights motivated Zapata to join forces with Madero, until it became apparent to Zapata that land reform was not a priority for Madero.[30]

The close assemblage of these revolutionary leaders within the context of the portfolio and print could be read to imply that these very different men shared common ideological values and were, thus, fighting together to achieve common goals in relation to land rights, campesino rights, and freedom of the press. In fact, the contrary is true, and Zalce would surely have known this, as would have many of the TGP member artists. Actually, each figure in the print represents a divergent group that was in opposition to the others during the Mexican Revolution and whose objectives remained in conflict not only during the violent phase of the civil war (1910–1920) but also long afterward.

That Carranza authorized the assassination of Zapata strikes a major discord in the problematic narrative of unification of revolutionary forces and makes evident the oppositional relationship between these two men. Another example of conflict between the figures of the revolutionary family lies between Obregón and Carranza. Although Obregón fought under Carranza beginning in 1912 during the anti-Huertista offensive, their relationship was one of mutual benefit and mistrust, and eventually Obregón became Carranza's greatest opponent. Obregón's affiliation with Carranza prevented any association with Zapata during the latter's lifetime. It was only after Zapata's death in 1920 that Gildardo Magaña, Zapata's successor, coordinated with Obregón.[31] Zalce's image integrates the revisionist narrative in portraying the revolutionary family while simultaneously revealing the contradictions in this approach. The construction and evocation of a nonexistent alliance through a fabricated revolutionary family was meant to promote the merger of disparate groups. The collapse of divergent groups produced a common history that implies that Mexico imagined itself as a unified nation, particularly after the civil war, which indeed was and is not the case.

Distribution of the TGP's graphic work was accomplished through a variety of venues, which included plastering images on walls throughout Mexico City, publishing in journals, circulating public posters and illustrated leaflets, and producing cinematic illustrations, calendars, books, and portfolios. The price of the portfolio was set at fifty Mexican pesos, or fifteen U.S. dollars, which would have been prohibitive for the working and rural classes. To reach the masses, the TGP regularly published prints from the portfolio in *El Nacional*, a widely distributed publication, during the early months of 1949. Hannes Meyer reported that two-thirds of the portfolios were sold within a year of its release.[32] The price of the portfolio seemingly distinguishes it for a group with expendable cash and was most likely only affordable to the middle and upper classes. Additionally, 50 percent of the portfolios were produced with English text. The price, combined with English text, implies that the intended audience, for at least half of the total production, was an international one. As Meyer recounts, 10 percent (or fifty-five) of the portfolios produced "were presented to progressive cultural organizations all over the world—Cape Town, Buenos Aires, Jerusalem, Montreal, Moscow, New York, Lisbon, Berlin, Geneva."[33] Meyer also took it upon himself to disseminate the work of the TGP in general and the *Prints of the Mexican Revolution* in particular after his departure from the group and Mexico due to illness in 1949.[34] Meyer organized an exhibition of work by the TGP in Zurich, Switzerland, in 1951 that ran between February and May, which likely included work from the 1947 portfolio, since he considered it one of the best examples of the TGP's efforts as a collective. The adept circulation and distribution of the portfolio and its images greatly expanded its popularity, making it a familiar and significant narrative of the Mexican Revolution.

Commonly, leadership that came after the war represented and continues to represent itself as sympathetic to Zapata's ideology—even when their actions demonstrate that they were/are not—in an attempt to validate their distinctive agendas and in order to garner support for themselves politically. Through an association with Zapata, these politicians attempt(ed) to maintain a connection with the Mexican Revolution. Thus, Zapata has frequently been built up as a symbol of the Mexican nation and its government and within this context is portrayed as a national hero across class lines. The tendency has been to reduce Zapata's image to that of an official icon for the nation-state in Mexico. Yet competing narratives of the war in Mexico disallow such a one-dimensional reading. Zapata certainly represents some of the ideals associated with the Mexican Revolution and postwar regimes, but his image is erroneously utilized to suggest alliances that did not exist and his support of ideological values he did not agree with. This propagandistic association with national leaders and government policies has contributed to the elevation of Zapata as a national symbol and his function as a national icon. As a symbol, Zapata's image is evoked to promote distinct ideological messages by various competing groups. Each narrative seeks to claim Zapata's iconic status as a symbol for what they respectively represent. These compelling narratives and illustrations commemorate Zapata, and with each reference, he is deployed to re-signify, encoding his image with new sets of meanings, constructing a multifaceted symbol communicating numerous ideologies and representing various social groups, sometimes simultaneously. This has resulted in a complex sign that denotes Zapata, the man, the legend, the revolutionary spirit, and the symbol, as the chain of signifiers that join, every use, story, and illustration multiplying his significance.

Based on the prologue and the subject of numerous prints, it is clear that the TGP promoted agrarian reform and democratic process in the *Prints of the Mexican Revolution*. The TGP member artists were cautious to not evoke the symbols that had been emptied by postwar regimes of any "true" meaning of revolution and reform. Instead, the TGP reclaimed Zapata by invoking his ideological platform for self-government and agrarian reform with illustrations charged with the revolutionary's demands for justice, land, and civil liberties.

NOTES

1. During the last decade of the Porfiriato, there were a series of events that eventually led to the eruption of outright and nationwide rebellion, such as the 1906 strike by the Mexican copper miners in Cananea, Sonora, and the strikes at the Textile Mills in Rio Blanco, Vera Cruz, in 1907, as well as the establishment of organizations like the Mexican Liberal Party (PLM), founded in 1906.

2. Although the rebellion led by Madero is typically the focus of discussion about the Mexican Revolution, there were actually at least three revolutions that raged on at roughly the same time and included a middle-class revolt, initially led by Francisco Madero, then by Venustiano Carranza and Álvaro Obregón; an agrarian insurrection led by Emiliano Zapata; and a revolution by proletarian or industrial workers. Each of these movements was informed by distinct ideologies. See Carlos Fuentes, chapter 4, in *Nuevo tiempo Mexicano* (Mexico: Aguilar, 1994), for his categorization of the multiple revolutions that sprouted during 1910 and 1920. See also David Craven, *Diego Rivera as Epic Modernist* (New York: G. K. Hall, 1997), 59–61, and David Craven, *Art and Revolution in Latin America, 1910–1990* (New Haven, CT: Yale University Press, 2002), 69.

3. For how invented traditions operate to govern our values and norms of behavior, see Eric Hobsbawm and Terrence Ranger, *The Invention of Tradition* (Cambridge: Cambridge University Press, 2010), 1. Scholars that address the process of nation building in postwar Mexico through civic activities, education, and artistic and cultural productions include Mary Kay Vaughan, *Cultural Politics in Revolution* (Tucson: University of Arizona Press, 1997), and Ilene V. O'Malley, *The Myth of the Revolution: Hero Cults and the Institutionalization of the Mexican State, 1920–1940* (New York: Greenwood Press, 1986).

4. All translations of Spanish into English are by the author, unless otherwise indicated. Additionally, I will only italicize a word in Spanish the first time I include the word, at which point I will either translate or define the term.

5. The TGP member artists who contributed to the 1947 portfolio include, in alphabetical order, Ignacio Aguirre (9 prints), Luis Arenal (1 print), Alberto Beltrán (10 prints), Angel Bracho (1 print), Fernando Castro Pacheco (11 prints), Jesus Escobedo (2 prints), Antonio Franco (1 print), Arturo García Bustos (6 prints), Julio Heller (1 print), Leopoldo Méndez (6 prints), Francisco Mora (7 prints), Isidro Ocampo (5 prints), Pablo O'Higgins (3 prints), Everardo Ramírez (2 prints), Mariana Yampolsky (3 prints), and Alfredo Zalce (18 prints).

6. They include print 8 by Mariana Yampolsky, print 16 by Ignacio Aguirre, print 24 by Francisco Mora, print 25 by Angel Bracho, prints 27 and 33 by Leop-

oldo Méndez, print 57 by Isidoro Ocampo, print 67 by Luis Arenal, and print 82 by Alfredo Zalce. Prints 8, 16, and 57 visually depict scenes from Zapata's life in a consecutive order.

7. For an in-depth history of land issues and oppression in Morelos, see Jesús Sotelo Inclan, *Raíz y razón de Zapata*, 2nd ed. (Mexico: Editorial CFE, 1970), 97–439.

8. Agrarian reform encompasses a variety of issues, including corrupt land seizure and the redistribution of land, as well as foreign imperialism over Mexican natural resources and the nationalization of resources.

9. I refer to Franciso Madero, Emiliano Zapata, and Venustiano Carranza as icons of the Mexican Revolution. Traditionally, the term *icon* refers to the representation of a holy person that was governed by strict theological rules and conventions developed between the fourth and twelfth centuries. These images were deemed sacred and some were even believed to possess and exercise miraculous powers. However, in contemporary use *icon* is applied to prominent and recognizable figures of history and culture. I engage the term with every intention of evoking both sets of meanings, which speaks to the significance and fame of these figures, as well as to the religious connotations ascribed to the Mexican Revolution and its leadership.

10. I am indebted to David Craven for introducing me to the work of the Taller de Gráfica Popular. I am especially grateful to Corey Dzenko and Gay Falk for their support and editorial comments throughout the development of my work on the Taller de Gráfica. I would also like to acknowledge Kirsten Buick, Holly Barnet-Sanchez, Linda Hall, and the anonymous reviewers for this publication project who provided advice and comments that were important to the writing of this chapter.

11. In terms of identifying who the TGP envisioned its international audience to be, one can turn to their declaration of principles, which states, "The T.G.P. lends its professional cooperation to similar workshops and cultural institutions, to popular or labor organization and to all progressive movements and institutions. . . . The T.G.P. protects the professional interests of all artists." Hannes Meyer, *Taller de Gráfica Popular: Doce años de obra artística colectiva* (Mexico: La Estampa Mexicana, 1949), i.

12. For names of specific international artists who worked directly and interacted with the TGP, see ibid.

13. I have previously published parts of my discussion on print 8 from the TGP's *Estampas de la Revolución Mexicana*; see Theresa Avila, "Laborious Arts: El Taller de Gráfica Popular & the Meaning of Labor in *Las Estampas de la Revolución Mexicana*," *Hemisphere: Visual Cultures of the Americas* 1 (Spring 2008): 62–82.

14. Samuel Brunk, *¡Emiliano Zapata! Revolution and Betrayal in Mexico* (Albuquerque: University of New Mexico Press, 1995), 6.

15. See John Womack, *Zapata and the Mexican Revolution* (New York: Vintage Books, 1970), 75–79.

16. Ibid., 64.

17. Michael C. Meyer, William L. Sherman, and Susan M. Deeds, *The Course of Mexican History* (New York: Oxford University Press, 2003), 373.

18. It is important to acknowledge that Zapata was not the only person concerned about and fighting for land rights, nor was he the originator of the concept of and demands for agrarian reform in Mexico. A significant predecessor is the Mexican Liberal Party (PLM), founded in 1906 and led by the Flores Magón brothers. Another precedent for the slogan is the Leyvistas slogan "*Tierra y Agua*" ("Land and Water") from the 1909 governmental race in Morelos. Sotelo Inclan, *Raíz y razón de Zapata*, 474.

19. The plan was directed, partially, toward critics who considered the southern forces barbarians aimlessly bent on wreaking havoc on Mexican society. A constant vilification of Zapata in the press during the Mexican Revolution heightened public interest in this leader while also fueling fears and swaying popular opinion against "the bandit" he was portrayed to be. Techniques to denigrate Zapata included false reports, unfounded accusations, and labels such as "bandit," "rebel," "insurgent," "thief," "arsonist," "scoundrel," and, eventually, "Attila of the South."

20. For discussion of the agenda of the Plan de Ayala, see Womack, *Zapata and the Mexican Revolution*, 393–404, and Brunk, *¡Emiliano Zapata!* 63–70.

21. For a discussion of photographs of Zapata in death, see Theresa Avila, "Zapata: Figure, Image, Symbol" (master's thesis, University of New Mexico, 2005), chapter 1.

22. See Brunk, *¡Emiliano Zapata!* 190–92 and 205, for descriptions of the ferocity and brutality Carrancistas engaged in to derail Zapatismo.

23. Womack (*Zapata and the Mexican Revolution*, 323) asserts that Zapata's death was planned by Pablo González, who was authorized, if not directed, by Carranza. Brunk (*¡Emiliano Zapata!* 227) indicates that González immediately telegraphed Carranza after Zapata had fallen to inform him of their success.

24. See Adolfo Gilly for an explanation of Cárdenas's contributions in terms of agrarian reform in "Rural Economy and Society: 1920–1940," in *Encyclopedia of Mexico*, vol. 2, ed. Michael S. Werner, 1309–13 (Chicago: Fitzroy Dearborn, 1997), 1313. See also Héctor Aguilar Camín and Lorenzo Meyer, *In the Shadow of the Mexican Revolution: Contemporary Mexican History, 1910–1989* (Austin: University of Texas Press, 1993), 132, and Meyer, Sherman, and Deeds, *The Course of Mexican History*, 576.

25. See Stephen R. Niblo, *Mexico in the 1940s: Modernity, Politics, and Corruption* (Wilmington, DE: Scholarly Resources, 1999), 83–237.

26. Parts of this discussion about print 82 have been previously published in Avila, "Zapata," and Theresa Avila, "El Taller de Gráfica Popular and the Chronicles of Mexican History and Nationalism," *Third Text* 28, no. 3, Special Issue: Art and Revolution in Mexico (2014): 311–21.

27. Sugar cane was a common crop grown in the state of Morelos, Zapata's home state and an important site of rebellion. Corn is a crop that has legendary significance to the Mexican people extending back to pre-Columbian times. Both crops also signify sustenance and labor, particularly in relation to the lower classes of the agrarian regions of Mexico.

28. Ross identifies a long list of journals that attacked Madero, including *El Imparcial*, *El Diario*, *El Heraldo*, *El País*, *La Nación*, *El Mañana*, *El Debate*, *El*

Noticioso Mexicano, *Frivolidades*, and *Multicolor*. See Stanley R. Ross, *Francisco I. Madero, Apostle of Mexican Democracy* (New York: Columbia University Press, 1955), 231–32. Zapata's plan, which denounced Madero as a traitor to the revolution, was made public and circulated, with Madero's permission, in Mexico City on December 15, 1911, in *El Diario del Hogar* in "Revolutionary Mexico in Newspapers, 1900–1929" (microfilm set), edited by Adán Benavides and Agnes L. McAlester, Nettie Lee Benson Latin American Collection, General Libraries, University of Texas at Austin, 2002. Madero's allowance of Zapata's public critique of him speaks to his stance on a free press.

29. See the headline on the front page and the accompanying article "Zapata es el Moderno Attila," *El Imparcial*, June 20, 1911.

30. Article 3 of the Plan of San Luis Potosí addressed the restitution of land to Indian communities. A published copy of the Plan of San Luis Potosí is available as Francisco I. Madero, "October 1910," in *Plan de San Luis: Documentos Facsimilares* (Mexico: PRI, Comisión Nacional Editorial, 1976). For a useful interpretation of the plan, see Ross, *Francisco I. Madero, Apostle of Mexican Democracy*, 116–17.

31. See Linda Hall, *Álvaro Obregón: Power and Revolution in Mexico, 1911–1920* (College Station: Texas A&M University Press, 1981), 241. Association with the Zapatistas aided the establishment of a new revolutionary coalition and guaranteed support from the campesinos.

32. Meyer, *Taller de Gráfica* Popular, xv. A 20 percent commission was given to each person who personally sold a portfolio. Additionally, it appears as if the portfolios were sold in nonsequential order and that individual prints from the portfolio were sold. For sales records, see *Taller de Gráfica Popular Records*, reel 6, box 1, folder 51.

33. Meyer, *Taller de Gráfica Popular*, xiii.

34. Helga Prignitz-Poda, *El Taller de Gráfica Popular en México, 1937–1977*, trans. Elizabeth Siefer (Mexico City: Instituto Nacional de Bellas Artes, 1992), 133 and 444. See also Hannes Meyer and Johannes Itten, *"Mexikanische Druckgraphik," Die Werkstatt fur graphische Volkskunst in Mexico* (Zurich, Switzerland: Kunstgewerbemuseum de la ciudad de Zurich, 1951).

BIBLIOGRAPHY

Avila, Theresa. "El Taller de Gráfica Popular and the Chronicles of Mexican History and Nationalism." *Third Text* 28, no. 3, Special Issue: Art and Revolution in Mexico (2014): 311–21.

———. "Laborious Arts: El Taller de Gráfica Popular & the Meaning of Labor in *Las Estampas de la Revolución Mexicana.*" *Hemisphere: Visual Cultures of the Americas* 1 (Spring 2008): 62–82.

———. "Zapata: Figure, Image, Symbol." Master's thesis, University of New Mexico, 2005.

Brunk, Samuel. *¡Emiliano Zapata! Revolution and Betrayal in Mexico.* Albuquerque: University of New Mexico Press, 1995.

Camín, Héctor Aguilar, and Lorenzo Meyer. *In the Shadow of the Mexican Revolution: Contemporary Mexican History, 1910–1989.* Austin: University of Texas Press, 1993.

Craven, David. *Art and Revolution in Latin America, 1910–1990.* New Haven, CT: Yale University Press, 2002.

———. *Diego Rivera as Epic Modernist.* New York: G. K. Hall, 1997.

El Diario del Hogar. In "Revolutionary Mexico in Newspapers, 1900–1929" (microfilm set), edited by Adán Benavides and Agnes L. McAlester. Nettie Lee Benson Latin American Collection, General Libraries, University of Texas at Austin, 2002.

Fuentes, Carlos. *Nuevo tiempo Mexicano.* Mexico: Aguilar, 1994.

Gilly, Adolfo. "Rural Economy and Society: 1920–1940." In *Encyclopedia of Mexico,* volume 2, edited by Michael S. Werner, 1309–13. Chicago: Fitzroy Dearborn, 1997.

Hall, Linda. *Álvaro Obregón: Power and Revolution in Mexico, 1911–1920.* College Station: Texas A&M University Press, 1981.

Hobsbawm, Eric, and Terence Ranger. *The Invention of Tradition.* Cambridge: Cambridge University Press, 2010.

Madero, Francisco I. "October 1910." In *Plan de San Luis: Documentos Facsimilares.* Mexico: PRI, Comisión Nacional Editorial, 1976.

Meyer, Hannes. *Taller de Gráfica Popular: Doce años de obra artística colectiva.* Mexico: La Estampa Mexicana, 1949.

Meyer, Hannes, and Johannes Itten. *"Mexikanische Druckgraphik," Die Werkstatt fur graphische Volkskunst in Mexico.* Zurich, Switzerland: Kunstgewerbemuseum de la ciudad de Zurich, 1951.

Meyer, Michael C., William L. Sherman, and Susan M. Deeds. *The Course of Mexican History.* New York: Oxford University Press, 2011.

Niblo, Stephen R. *Mexico in the 1940s: Modernity, Politics, and Corruption.* Wilmington, DE: Scholarly Resources, 1999.

O'Malley, Ilene V. *The Myth of the Revolution: Hero Cults and the Institutionalization of the Mexican State, 1920–1940.* New York: Greenwood Press, 1986.

Prignitz-Poda, Helga. *El Taller de Gráfica Popular en México, 1937–1977.* Translated by Elizabeth Siefer. Mexico City: Instituto Nacional de Bellas Artes, 1992.

Ross, Stanley R. *Francisco I. Madero, Apostle of Mexican Democracy.* New York: Columbia University Press, 1955.

Sotelo Inclan, Jesús. *Raíz y razón de Zapata,* 2nd edition. Mexico: Editorial CFE, 1970.

Vaughan, Mary Kay. *Cultural Politics in Revolution.* Tucson: University of Arizona Press, 1997.

Womack, John. *Zapata and the Mexican Revolution.* New York: Vintage Books, 1970.

2

❖ ❖

Imprinting Industriousness in the Quest for the Good Life

Lineages of the Chinese Revolutionary Image from 1949 to the Present

Alison Hulme

THE NOTION OF THE GOOD LIFE IN HISTORICAL PERSPECTIVE

The China that Mao Tse-tung officially took control of on the first day of October 1949 was a China ravaged by both internal and external wars, paranoid about its own failure to embrace the scientific developments witnessed elsewhere in the world, and with an inferiority complex bred from over a century of foreign exploitation in trade matters. The opium wars (1839–1842 and 1856–1860) had seen Hong Kong leased to Britain in an attempt to contain the illegal trade to some extent, and they also left a huge percentage of the population addicts[1] for decades afterward. The first Sino-Japanese war (1894–1895) had seen China forced to relinquish Korea, Formosa (now Taiwan), and Port Arthur to Japanese forces. The combination of these two events left an overwhelming sense of humiliation at the hands of foreign powers in its wake, and an increasing discontentment with the ruling Qing dynasty.

This dissatisfaction and sense of frustration at the weakness of the country's leaders created a rising tide of nationalistic sentiment and eventually led to the victory of the Nationalists lead by Sun Yat Sen (1866–1925) in 1911. This was the birth of republican China; yet warlords from the dynastic era continued to plague the stability of the country and Chiang Kai-shek's new leadership from 1926 did little to improve this. Chiang was struggling with the threat of another Japanese invasion as well as the rising popularity of Li Dazhao[2] and Chen Duxiu's Chinese Communist Party (CCP). With Chiang's attention split between fighting the Communists internally[3] and the Japanese externally, the warlords settled comfortably into the remaining void. The Second World War saw the Communists and Nationalists manage a brief accord (although suggesting they were united against the external threats would be an overstatement), but, not surprisingly, this broke down as soon as the war was over. The years 1945–1949 were effectively a period of domestic anarchy in China as Chiang and Mao both attempted to gain control of the country.

It was due to the toll created by all of these events over the course of the preceding century that when Mao took official control of China on October 1, 1949, it was in many ways a broken country he inherited. There was a fervent energy to repair and develop, alongside a sense of righteousness concerning how downtrodden the nation had been as a result of foreign powers. In fact, despite the victory of the Communists over the Nationalists, the sentiments of communist supporters were, at this stage, avowedly nationalist*ic*, if not nationalist, on the whole. These nationalistic sentiments did not of course strictly concur with orthodox Marxist-Leninist internationalist thinking on the spread of Communism across the globe, but at this stage the nation-state was seen as a necessary evil in China's path to Communism.

Alongside this desire to repair the war-ravaged country was an acknowledgment, popular among left-wing thinkers of the time, of the way in which dynastic rule and Confucian thought had held back the nation and created gaping inequalities. Through writers such as Lu Xun,[4] Confucianism came to be associated with privilege and laziness. The literary stereotypes created at the time remain part of popular imagination and common parlance today. A classic example is Lu Xun's character Kong Yi Ji—a Confucian failed scholar who typifies laziness by drinking and being largely unemployed, and who possesses arcane knowledge that is irrelevant to a modernizing China. In the eponymously titled short story, Kong Yi Ji regularly drinks at a specific bar, where he often owes money on his tab, and spends his time quoting erudite texts to anyone who will listen. His pomposity and use of archaic phrases are portrayed as only serving to maintain a rigid class system and therefore being truly oppressive. Lu Xun's creation of this character was a reaction against the norms of Confucian scholarship and the traditions and privileges that came along with it. In the story, Kong has his legs broken and is forced to beg for a living, eventually fading away, presumed dead. If we accept Frederic

Jameson's[5] view that Lu Xun writes characters as allegories for China (or parts of Chinese culture), we can see what happens to the character of Kong as representing the breaking of Confucian norms and the disintegration of the privileges associated with dynastic rule.

Mao built on the thinking of left-wing writers such as Lu Xun and was to ban Confucianism as a result. Not only did its insistence on the legitimacy and positive impact of hierarchy sit in direct opposition to his stance on social equality, but he also blamed its traditionalism for China's "backwardness" in terms of science and development. This backdrop of righteous frustration with the state China was in, its "humiliation," and the desire to quash any tradition that maintained social inequalities added force to Mao's rhetoric of industriousness in order to gain a "happy life for all." "Catching up" with the West was of the utmost importance according to him, and was to be gained through the physical exertions and incredible labor capacity of the population—which was proudly celebrated. The industriousness of the masses was China's great blessing and would be its salvation, enabling the creation of a world of plentiful provision for all, in which comradely relations and the lack of concerns about life's necessities would provide the basis for a new utopia—the communist "happy life." It was via this powerful rhetoric and the positing of this utopian vision that Mao was able to galvanize the population despite their exhaustion following extended periods of global and domestic war and unrest. And so, the twin paradigms of industriousness and its reward—the good life—were born and they would continue with greater or lesser influence throughout Mao's reign.

Following the interim two years of Hua Guofeng's leadership, Deng Xiaoping would then once again call upon the energy of the masses. He too would utilize the idea that China was downtrodden and could now take its rightful place, but under very different auspices and with a very different vision of the good life than that put forward by Mao. Both used very specific visual devices to promote these visions of industriousness and the good life—posters depicting happy workers and family life became commonplace and various designers were employed to create such images throughout both Mao's and Deng's reign. They became an important and established part of party messaging and many have since become iconic pieces of visual history displayed in museums[6] and online archives. What follows will explore how the continuity of rhetoric of the good life was built, among other things, through imprinting visions of industriousness and galvanized action that could be seen to have originated in the context of 1949 onward.

THE COMRADELY INDUSTRIOUS MASSES AND THE GOOD LIFE UNDER MAO

It is perhaps not surprising that Mao capitalized on the frustrations of those who felt the Nationalists had once again allowed the nation to be trampled on by foreign powers. Whether intentionally or not, the "century of humiliation" became a long century of humiliation due to the way in which the mythologizing of Mao's rise elongated the subjugation of the Chinese to the point of liberation in 1949. While for the Nationalists this subjugation had been blamed on the foreign and dynastic powers, for Mao this was of course blamed specifically on Chiang Kai-shek's Nationalist Party (as it was this group that had expelled Communists from its ranks), with Sun Yat Sen continuing to be hailed as the founder of modern China. Maintaining a continuity between Sun and himself was desirable for Mao not only in creating a historical trajectory for his own part in China's history but also in terms of enabling (arguably by exaggerating) a continuity of political philosophy. Continuity has always been an important concept in Chinese culture, as witnessed by the continued respect given to the *I Ching*,[7] which promotes "continuity through change." In the case of Mao and Sun, this continuity was, however, not pure construct and had some credence, as both had entertained the work of Li Dazhao. Indeed, Li's thinking can be seen as a clear thread running through what was to become "Mao Tse-tung Thought." More crucially, it was Li's specific brand of Narodnik populism that introduced the idea of the potency and capacity of the masses (i.e., their ability to be industrious) to the young Mao. In fact, industriousness in the post-1945 context was a direct consequence of the Narodnik belief in the importance of unified and abrupt action.

To explain this further it is necessary to briefly explore the development of Narodnik thought from its Russian origins. The Narodnik worldview was developed by Alexander Herzen and Pyotr Lavrov. Herzen's firm belief was that the most desirable model of social structure was that of agrarian collectivity and he placed great emphasis on the potential of the peasantry. Coupled with this, the Narodniks founded their philosophy on Bakunin more than Marx, emphasizing the latter's belief that revolution could and should be started directly from the people, regardless of the existing state of material conditions. This was, of course, in direct contrast to Marx's belief that only capitalist societies had the "correct" material conditions for a socialist revolution. Bakunin's insistence that people were revolutionary by instinct, and his calls for direct action, proved irresistible for a Russian youth contingent impatient for change and unprepared to sit out the long wait for Marx's revolution.[8] It is this idea of using the power of the peasant masses to start a revolution from scratch with hard work and commitment that Mao translated into the notion of industriousness.

It is worth noting alongside this, however, that this denial of orthodox Marxist logic as to how the revolution should come about was not only a desire to make revolution happen on the part of the Narodniks but also a firm belief that Russia had specific unique conditions that meant it was on a "special" path of historical development. This is, of course, also precisely the rationale used by Mao to explain the use of Marxism in the Chinese context and the legitimacy therefore of "Chinese Marxism" (or, indeed, Maoism). This idea of having specific conditions is in many ways a truism of any country—in that all countries have a unique set of conditions—and can be seen in contemporary China in the idea of "Chinese characteristics."

It was these key differences between Bakunin and Marx concerning which class should instigate revolution, and under what conditions, that influenced the Narodniks and therefore Li Dazhao. This difference in viewpoint has also caused "Chinese Marxism" to be seen as an oxymoron to orthodox Marxist-Leninists, for whom the "Chinese" element (i.e., the Narodnik element) is simply un-Marxist.[9] In fact, the idea of industriousness can be seen as one constantly fought over by communist and capitalist forces. Mao interprets it to the people as the binary opposite of Confucian privilege and arrogance; yet he is concerned about the point at which it becomes entrepreneurial on an individual level, as this, he believes, is capitalistic. In doing so, he unwittingly creates a strange schism in which Confucianism sits at one extreme, with entrepreneurialism/capitalism at the end of one axis and Communism at the end of another. Yet, in doing this, Communism is also pitted against entrepreneurialism—especially if we see entrepreneurialism as necessarily an individual urge used for individualistic ends. Indeed, Seldon argues that the entire history of the PRC can be seen as "the persistent . . . effort from below to restore the role of markets."[10] However, this assumes that entrepreneurialism can only exist in capitalistic domains, when in actual fact it can fit within the realms of communist thought and organization just as well. It also does not account for the notion of creative entrepreneurialism as requisite for survival and implicitly suggests that entrepreneurialism is a "natural" urge in rather the same way that Schumpeter posits his "wild spirits."[11]

Regardless, in the Chinese context, it is with the move from land socialization to land nationalization (collectivity) that the notion of industriousness was sealed. Suddenly, mass labor units and huge development projects abound and people are expected to work at the pace dictated by the unit leaders. The Great Leap Forward (GLF) was Mao's determined push to harness the industriousness of the masses in order to prove that China could have an output as high as those of Western developed countries. Although the great productive power of the masses had been harnessed shortly after Mao came to power, this was nothing compared to the exertions demanded during the GLF. Effectively, it brought industriousness to the peasantry under the rubric of power redistribution and cooperative ownership.

It was in this context that the propaganda posters of the 1950s (figures 2.1 and 2.2) urged people to "produce more, contribute more" based on a classic Marxist ideology of "from each according to ability." Figure 2.1 urges "Work more! Produce more!" and depicts a muscled and focused worker looking happy to be part of an impressive industrial development,

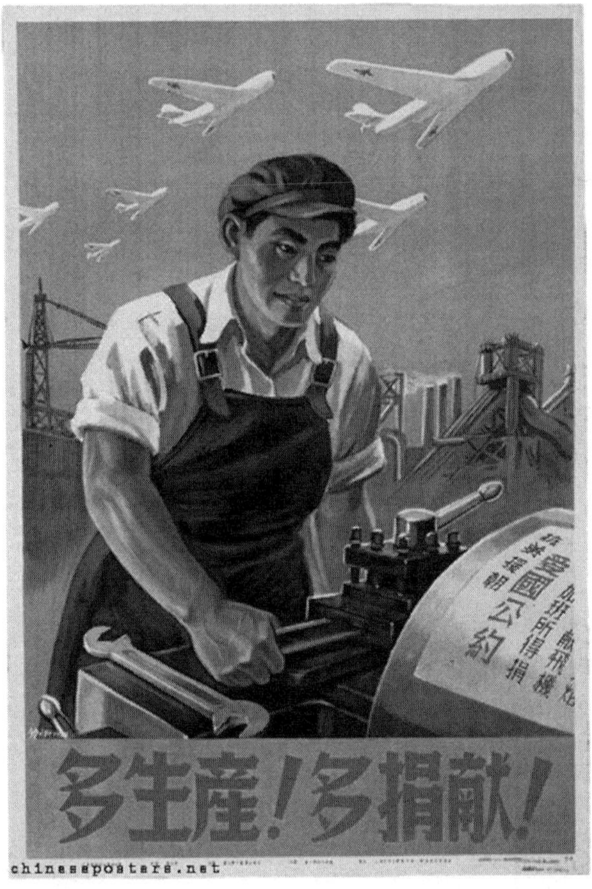

Figure 2.1. "Work more! Produce more!" 1951. (Designer: Qian Daxin)

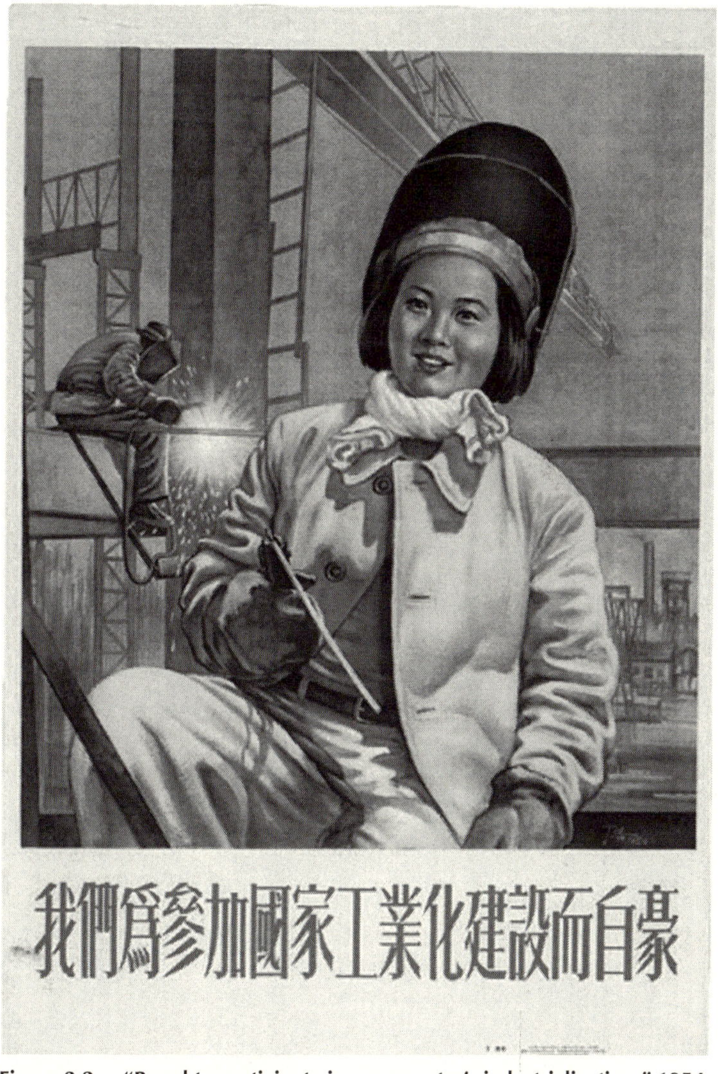

Figure 2.2. "Proud to participate in our country's industrialization." 1954. (Designer: Ning Hao)

shown by the factories in the background and the planes flying overhead. (It is worth noting that the planes in China at this point would have been those provided by the Soviets.) The worker wears a traditional "Mao cap," a symbol of the peasantry, again tapping into the idea of the potency and energy of the peasant masses. The colors are those of industry (grey) and the military (muted greens), with a flash of red/orange to evoke the color of Communism at the bottom. Figure 2.2 specifically speaks to a female audience, playing on the stated importance of women's role in China's industrial, as well as industrious, revolution. Mao had famously stated that "women hold up half the sky" and, as part of providing them with equal rights to men in many ways, had made it clear that they were 50 percent of the revolution and could do everything that men could do. Hence the caption plays on the pride that many women felt in being able to work alongside men as equals, saying, "Proud to participate in our country's industrialization." Again, the background is of a highly industrial scene, with what looks to be a male coworker in the background. The woman is in traditionally masculine mode, with one leg raised and a confident look. This would have been a long way removed from the depictions of women and expected demure behavior that were the norm in previous eras. The woman wears one of the three versions of uniform of the time—the beige military suit (the others being khaki and blue—the traditional Mao suit). Her hair is cut short, again a sign of the times, as Mao felt that buns and long hair pinned up were a way of curtailing women's freedom of movement just as foot-binding had been. Like the male in figure 2.1, she looks slightly off camera, into the distance, signifying a positive look to the future, her expression hopeful, happy, and determined. In emphasizing the pride to be gained in being part of industrialization, both images are typical of the way industriousness was harnessed during these years.

And what was the promise of reward for the industriousness of the Mao-era masses? How did Mao manage to motivate such a bedraggled nation, tired from external and internal wars, into such energies of production? The answer, of course, lies in the second half of Marx's maxim "from each according to ability" (or, in Mao's case, ability to work)—"to each according to need." The good life under Mao was specifically based on the idea of provision, and it was this "guarantee" of having enough that motivated industriousness. The promise of the "iron rice bowl"[12] was extremely attractive to a populace who had suffered extreme poverty at the hands of past leaders who enabled a hierarchical distribution of resources. Mao's revolution promised the provision of resources and services for all according to their personal circumstances and needs—it was about provision in a fair system. This was part of being comradely—the sharing of effort, and the sharing of the results of effort. And, as Vladislav Todorov argues, it was precisely this sharing of production processes (as depicted in the posters) in condensed spaces (such as factories) that created "technological togetherness" and led to a "fellowship of collaboration" that would come

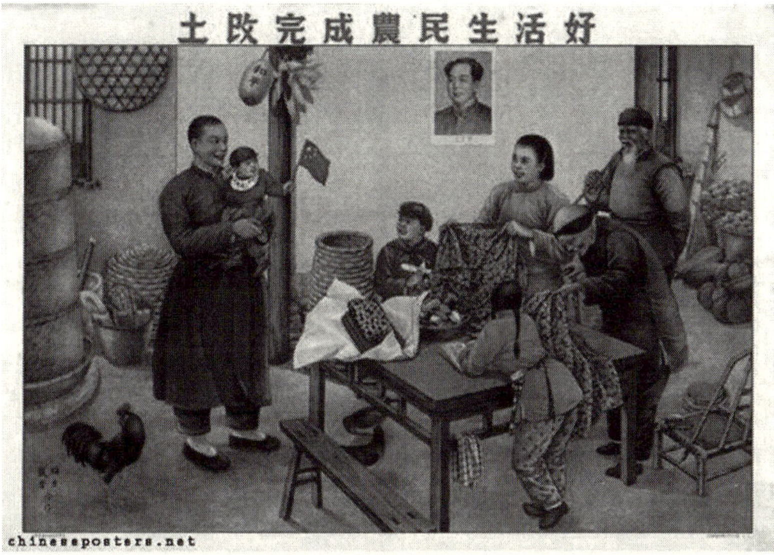

Figure 2.3. "The life of the peasants is good after land reform." 1951. (Designer: Jin Meisheng)

to be known as comradeship.[13] Industriousness then created the way of the comrade, and its reward was a mutual enjoyment of the gains.

This enjoyment is well illustrated in posters of the time depicting the Maoist vision of the good life. They tended to show domestic scenes of families with food on the table—a simple but happy life with no worries about money, shelter, or food (see figure 2.3). Such images were typically home based—an intimate portrayal of Chinese everyday life that was almost fly on the wall in the spectator view it gave. Figure 2.3 is from 1951 and reads, "The life of the peasants is good after land reform." It shows three generations of a family eagerly examining the delivery of fabric and surrounded by fresh produce. It specifically posits itself as a depiction of everyday life under Mao, with food on the table, Mao looking upon the scene benevolently from a picture on the wall, and the solidarity of the family to the communist cause shown by the wearing of Mao caps and, in the case of the young son, military uniform.[14] These intimate family scenes of happiness are typical of the time—showing the Chinese subject looking at him- or herself in an extremely localized way, representative of the insular nature of China as a country at this time. The good life under Mao was, much like the man himself, a rather telluric vision, rooted in a largely inward-looking culture that was, in this sense, strangely conservative despite its revolutionary nature.

THE ENTREPRENEURIAL INDUSTRIOUS MASSES AND THE GOOD LIFE FROM DENG TO THE PRESENT DAY

In the latter years of Mao's reign, the notion of industriousness was overshadowed by Cultural Revolution concerns with being sufficiently "revolutionary" in one's political outlook and behavior—although hard physical labor was of course part of "correct" revolutionary fervor. However, years of ill-conceived economic policies and emphasis on political cleansing saw the country stripped of much of the progress it had made in the early Maoist period. So it was that in 1978, when Deng Xiaoping came to power, he once again called upon the great capacity of the masses to put extreme energies into their work.

We may ask how, following the suffering of the GLF and the Cultural Revolution, it is possible that a leader could once again ask the people to make such immense effort. In many ways it was precisely the rhetoric surrounding the GLF and the acknowledgment, even in official circles, that it was a leap *back*ward that allowed Deng Xiaoping to talk about industriousness in much the same way Mao had, without this appearing unconvincing to the general populace. The acknowledged economic failure of much of the Mao era allowed Deng to insist on the necessity for fast economic development and convincingly assert, once again, that this was absolutely reliant on the efforts and abilities of the masses. Having been through the disastrous famines of the GLF, followed by the insecurities of the Cultural Revolution, when called on to be industrious once again, the nation heaved itself into fervent action—an incredible feat psychosocially, not to mention materially. But what was, once again, behind this call to arms was effectively a nationalism that played on the same rhetoric of "humiliation" that Mao had done, and Sun Yat Sen before him. Communism, of course, was not to blame, but in a famous interview with the Italian journalist Oriana Fallaci, Deng acknowledged that Mao had made certain mistakes, rating his life as "70% good, 30% bad."[15] This was later written into official doctrine in the document titled "Resolution on Certain Questions in the History of Our Party," which admitted the harm caused by the GLF and the Cultural Revolution while insisting on the continued legitimacy of the party (and indeed of Mao Tse-tung Thought more generally).[16]

The main thrust of Deng's rhetoric, however, was to insist that, aside from the parts of Mao's reign that were to blame, the long century of China's humiliation had been elongated and it was time for the nation to rise up and take its rightful place in the world. For Deng, of course, this meant implementing the open-door policy beginning with Special Economic Zones (SEZs) and urging the nation that it was "glorious" to get rich. The idea being promulgated here was that of getting rich *as a nation*, but Deng had no qualms about this happening on an individual level, believing firmly (or at least purporting to) in the trickle-down factor. Mao's concerns about triggering "capitalistic tendencies" were the very motivating factors of Deng's call. This time, the great energy of the people was being called on, with the dramatic new caveat that economic progress created as a result was allowed to be enjoyed by individuals, not just the masses as a whole. This was a new revolution of sorts; yet it was never acknowledged as such because of the necessity of continuity in the CCP's political line, and the fact that anything that went against the original Marxist-Leninist revolution was referred to as "anti-revolutionary," making any new revolution effectively invisible.

Figure 2.4 shows the far less industrial depiction of industriousness under Deng, effectively combining a new vision of enjoyment and *leisure*—that

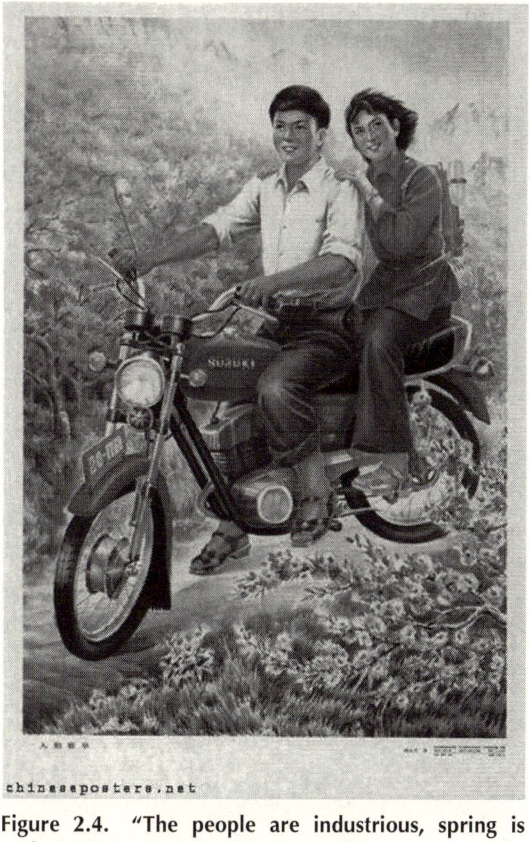

Figure 2.4. "The people are industrious, spring is early." 1987. (Designer: Liu Yuanxing)

newest of inventions. It reads, "The people are industrious, spring is early," positing the abundance of spring as the direct result of industriousness in a way not dissimilar to Maoist depictions, but showing a scene that under Mao would have been interpreted as a rather unrevolutionary image of romantic (bourgeois) love. It is also rather unusual that the motorbike is a Japanese make, perhaps showing a period of tolerance for foreign goods.

It is also worth noting here that the industriousness of the Mao era, despite emphasizing China's ability to independently provide for its own people, to some extent had involved making comparisons between itself and other countries. However, with the industriousness of the Deng era came direct comparisons of China to the developed world along with the beginnings of the normative assumptions of classic economics when it came to ways of measuring growth and wealth—faith in the reliability of the trickle-down factor being indicative of this. This fundamentally changed the nature of China's industriousness—it was no longer about self-sufficiency and proving the workability of a specific political regime; it was all about "catching up" with the rest of the world and taking their rightful place in that world. The nationalism of Deng's revolution had in many ways a tinge of righteous anger that was less perceptible in that of Mao's. Catch-up tactics were sometimes fueled by a kind of resentment, as opposed to the idealism of the early Mao era, by comparison rather than creation, and this was in part because the object of blame (Mao himself) had been partially exonerated by Deng, thus creating a void into which "the rest of the world" could, in time, be placed, as dealing with it steadily increased.

It is perhaps not surprising that the current *fenqing* (angry youth) promote an extreme nationalist rhetoric, the roots of which could quite easily be argued to have begun with Deng's determination to "catch up" with the rest of the world. The fenqing of Deng's own era were fighting for freedom of speech and/or a certain form of democracy—a legacy of the Mao era—which many of them saw as going hand in hand with the economic changes taking place. Their Mao-era counterparts had fought not to be sent to the countryside to farm when they had skills and qualifications they wanted to use outside that realm. Whereas previously the Chinese populace had been told it was downtrodden by foreigners, under Deng it was also told that it had a rightful place that was as yet unoccupied. It is precisely this righteousness that changes the mood of the nationalism at play from Mao to Deng and that, arguably, has set the scene for the major concern of today's angry youths—the right to the kind of jobs and wealth witnessed in the West.

This strain of nationalism was at play anyway, but following the events of Tiananmen Square, Deng began a huge national campaign to divert attention away from the party and outward, once again toward the ills forced on China by foreign imperialists. From 1989 onward, the party began a campaign of "patriotic education," reinventing itself as the defender of national interests in a global society that was scared and jealous of China's rise. The campaign was carried out via school textbooks, newspapers, films, and public monuments and drew constant attention to the "humiliation" of China beginning with the opium wars.

So, with humiliation firmly in focus and the encouraging of individual desire for wealth, what was to be the reward for the nation's industriousness this time around? What was the good life under Deng? Deng, of course, attempts to maintain continuity with the Maoist past by evoking ever more virulent images of the century of humiliation and insisting on wealth creation being a national project. But these are simply strands of thought designed to reassure the party conservatives (i.e., nonreformists). In actuality, Deng is determined to transform the notion of the good life, making sure it is no longer about universal provision and having "enough," but rather that it is about individual wealth in the name of national wealth and creating *abundance.* The words "to get rich is glorious" relied on Western economists' concept of the trickle-down effect. So while Deng was calling for individuals to gain wealth, he was able to promote this as a way of enabling all people to gain wealth—he turned classic liberal trickle-down economics into a pseudo-Maoist logic.

While "the family" was still present in words, it was far less present in images, with "the good life" now being entirely about wealth generation. To allay concerns that this message was simply capitalistic, poster designers in the Deng era often returned to far older and/or "spiritual" traditions such as Daoism and Confucianism, using cartoon depictions of Confucius and traditional Daoist artistic style and colors. The harking back to Confucianism also enabled a reappropriation of its values to suit the new economic aims, but with the benefit of a moral tone to set it apart from the perceived debauchery of Western capitalism. Deng encouraged neo-Confucianism in the new context of business entrepreneurship, for example, by emphasizing the importance of family ties and encouraging would-be business people to borrow money from relatives in order to cover their start-up costs and provide them with initial capital. The family was therefore present as economic backdrop, rather than intimate domestic group and/or unit of production. In reality, of course, this was positing the family as the basis of profit-oriented entrepreneurialism in exactly the way that Mao, Lenin, and Stalin had been concerned about in regards to the potential for spontaneous capitalistic urges. Deng, in fact, wanted nothing more than to utilize these capitalistic urges in the name of a communism that was almost unrecognizable to that of Mao. In the process, he managed to attach Confucianism to industriousness once again, via the notion of family responsibility, whereas Mao (and the preceding generation of authors and thinkers) had attached it firmly to laziness, unearned privilege, and lack of efficiency.

Post-Deng, Mao's "happy life" has found its voice in a series of policy lines that exert a very different image of how life could be. This is best evidenced through Hu Jintao's "scientific development" theory, which emphasized sustainable development and social welfare in pursuit of a "socialist harmonious society." The thrust of the theory is that sustainable development can be created via proven methodologies of social and economic governance that minimize the potential for conflict among different groups in society while contemporaneously improving economic and cultural wealth. It is logical that Hu would emphasize such a theory, as he had inherited a China with growing wealth disparity and less welfare guarantee than ever before. Worse, the bulk of the population were still not at all well off, despite the new emergence of a middle class in China (with upper strata too), and an increasing number of social disturbances and protests were being recorded.

Creating a "harmonious society" was therefore a genuine concern, although Hu chose to return to the Confucian language of balance and modesty in order to convey it, also starting to use the term *Xiaokang*, meaning "basically" or "functionally" well off or middle class but without huge wealth, living comfortably but ordinarily. The suggestion was that the enabling of all to reach this state would create the desired "balance" and "harmony" within Chinese society. Like *harmonious society*, this term was also originally Confucian and used to describe a society of modest means that sees the need for economic growth to provide prosperity, while making sure that prosperity is broadly distributed. However, Deng had also used it in 1979, positing it as the ultimate goal of Chinese modernization—so Hu was following a safe lineage of thought here.

The combination of tireless economic development with societal compassion and equality is not the only anomaly in Hu's thought, though. The current usage of the term *Xiaokang* also attempts to make ancient Chinese thought support Chinese Marxism when in actual fact it may not. In ancient Chinese thought, a Xiaokang society progressed to become the "great unity," this being roughly equivalent to world communism. However, in the ancient tradition Xiaokang society sees the middle classes subsume elements of both the poor and the well off. This can hardly be likened to orthodox Marxism, in which what is required is the bottom-up creation of an urban proletariat whose existence is certainly not a melting pot that includes the extremes of wealth and poverty from other sections of society.

At some point, it has to be asked whether the desire to create a Xiaokang society is really about building the urban proletariat, or rather simply a manifestation of the bourgeoisie spreading across the surface of China.

Certain cities were promoted on state television channels as having the required facets to be called "harmonious"—such as "harmonious Hangzhou"—and shown as clean, "modern," and developed, yet as having history in the form of architectural features such as pagodas, bridges, half-moon gates, and so on. The word *harmonious* was thereby linked to physical aspects of the built environment whose origins lie in the Confucian era. These elements are combined in the "Better City, Better Life" campaign of 2010 (see figure 2.5), which tended to feature classical pagodas in the

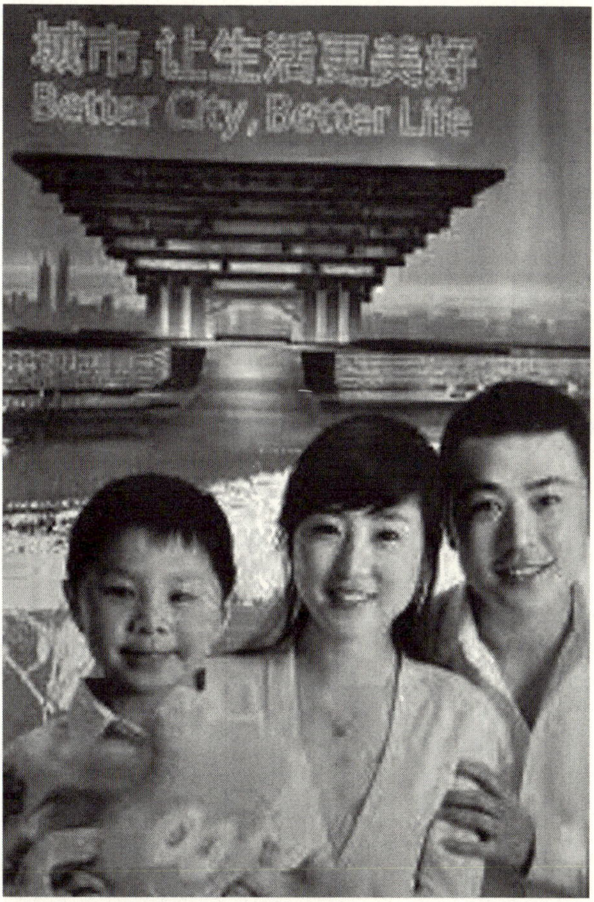

Figure 2.5. "Better city, better life."

foreground juxtaposed with the skyscraper offices behind. This campaign, used in the run-up to the Shanghai Expo, in many ways encapsulates Hu's combination of development and harmony and the ways in which it relates to earlier depictions of "the good life." Most telling is the use of the cartoon mascot "*Haibao*" (as seen in figure 2.5) to teach *wenming*, or "manners," to those present in Shanghai. These "manners" were the manners of Westerners, and were designed to ensure that the visits of Westerners resulted in business, as well as a favorable impression left of China in the minds of the Western visitors. They therefore revolved around teaching U.S. and European culture, such as forming queues, not spitting, and understanding where certain food types and music come from.

Note, too, how the family in figure 2.5 has changed from that pictured in the post-1949 depictions. They are no longer a rural, intimate domestic unit but decidedly urban dwelling, with one child, and probably (therefore) Han. They are also looking out of the poster into the world—the Chinese subject is no longer looking in on his or her own intimate reality, as in the Mao era posters; rather, he or she sees him- or herself as a global citizen gazing proudly out at a globalized future in which China is a rising star.

Hu Jintao's somewhat strangely opposing twin policies of scientific management and "harmonious society" are arguably a combination of the "industrious" rhetoric and the "good life" rhetoric—in fact, it is a tempering of the first with the second. This can be seen as quite typical of a leadership that was purportedly (and, to a large extent, genuinely, although more due to concerns about unrest than poverty in and of itself) concerned with the livelihoods of China's less well off while simultaneously relentlessly pushing for greater and greater economic growth. The Hu/Wen legacy is therefore one of a rather awkward combination of the manufacturing dragon versus the rural idyll—yet quality of life and lifestyle carry little weight in the daily reality of the average worker. However, it is a rhetoric that enables China to reimagine and promote itself both domestically and globally. Internal tourism campaigns promote scenes of half-moon gates and pagodas on the banks of misted lakes, drawing on connotations of a peaceful, "old" China steeped in gentle tradition but coupled with a modernist rationality and forward-looking mentality. Thus, drawing on its lineages and reappropriating the various imprints of revolution, China presents itself to the world as both a manufacturing superpower and a beautiful backwater.

This unlikely mix of ideas is precisely what Xiaobing Tang attempts to analyze by dividing them into features that belong to either revolutionary or postrevolutionary culture. For Tang, revolutionary features include a dedication to communality, the work unit, politics, unilateralism, homogeneity, content over form, production oriented, romantic/utopian, collective concerns, rural. In contrast, postrevolutionary features are those of domestic commodification, the market (as opposed to the work unit), economics (as opposed to politics), pluralism (as opposed to the mass line), heterogeneity, form over content, an emphasis on consumption (as opposed to production), a pragmatic/utopian vision, consumer desires, and the urban (as opposed to the rural). However, Tang argues that certain revolutionary features can offer themselves as alternatives in the postrevolutionary era: "When everyday life is affirmed and accepted as the new hegemony, when commodification arrives to put a price tag on human relations and even private sentiments, participatory communal action may offer itself as an oppositional discourse and expose a vacuity underlying the myriad of commodity forms."[17]

This "schizophrenia" is, of course, not specific to China—far from it. However, it can certainly be seen in the determination to continue certain rates of economic growth while attempting to build a more solid welfare state and provide a compassionate society. It can also be seen in the determination to depict China as at once modern and deeply historical. And it can be seen in the outright rejection and then easy acceptance of historical philosophies such as Confucianism. It can be seen in the desire for the Western as a sign of wealth, contemporaneous to the accusations of foreign imperialism levied by the angry youth. And it can be seen in the uneasy line between modernism and "functional" wealth and its fall into all things bourgeois. This line is often blurred by fuzzy concepts such as "Chinese characteristics," which allow bourgeois products and services to be legitimized and made part of an allegedly specifically Chinese (and therefore revolutionary) path. Adverts are often doctored to provide a more "appropriate" angle for the party's purposes.

It is perhaps precisely because of these mixed messages that the image of the good life has had to adapt to changing party ideals if it is still to inspire the industriousness required for the continuation of the capitalist-communist revolution China is currently engaged in. Therefore, while the good life is still the motivating factor for industriousness, the vision of what constitutes it has changed significantly in the period of 1949 to the present. It has become more determinedly modernist and outward looking—a China acknowledging itself as part of a globalizing world and indeed using the vision of the good life as a form of soft power to the world looking in, as well as the Chinese populace.

CONCLUSION

The industrious revolution of the post-1978 years seeks to promote a happy lifestyle just as the Communist revolution post-1949 did. Similarly, it attempts to emphasize sheer capacity in a way that has strong resonances with those earlier images of abundant food production and gleaming construction machinery. However, the image of the "good life" has changed drastically in the years from 1949 to the present day, becoming more globally oriented and more urban, reflecting China's desire to continue the burgeoning creation of a professional, comfortable, middle class, or Xiaokang.

However, these lineages are largely for domestic consumption; they enable the Communist Party to create a continuity that legitimates its existence and consolidates the party idea of "socialism with Chinese characteristics." The imprints of the Chinese revolutions appear as a continuous and simplistic rhetoric about the power of the masses to put China in its rightful place in order that its citizens may experience a lifestyle of great quality. Ironically, this "quality" is frequently modeled on that of the West, despite the extreme nationalist sentiments often witnessed toward foreign powers and systems. Regardless, the twenty-first-century version of the life that will be the reward for the industriousness of the people has just as little truth in reality as the post-1949 promise did.

Despite the many more complicated movements and sentiments that underlie this ongoing trajectory linking industriousness to the good life throughout China's recent history, the need for continuity (now largely due to the need to legitimize the CCP) can also be seen as a simplifying of the political rhetoric offered to the populace. It therefore also constitutes a simplification of the revolutionary journey and its imprints—the national rhetoric has been presented in such a way as to deny the complicated changes that lie beneath the surface. And this is likely to continue; as the CCP is increasingly legitimized by its ability to maintain economic growth and facilitate the continued expansion of the new middle class in China, the continuity with the rhetoric of past eras remains just as important as it has been to date. Thus, despite the many ways in which China is far from monolithic in reality, the continuity of political rhetoric surrounding industriousness in the quest for "a good life" has maintained a sense that China is indeed "one" and that its history is a single unified strand.

NOTES

1. The opium wars occurred as British desire for Chinese products—namely, tea—grew. Since British traders lacked the silver to pay for the goods they wanted, they began to illegally sell opium to the Chinese in order to obtain the silver that could then be used to purchase tea. The most common statistic given is 1 percent of the population in rural regions, but up to 90 percent of all males under forty years of age in coastal regions were addicted. The anti-opium commissioner at the time—Lin Ze Xu (1785–1850)—modestly estimated the number of addicts to be four million, but trade records show that in 1836 enough opium was imported to cater to twelve million addicts (see Travis Hanes and Frank Samello, *The Opium Wars: The Addiction of One Empire and the Corruption of Another* [London: Sourcebooks, 2004]).

2. Li Dazhao is credited with bringing Marxism to China via Russian Narodnik thought. Li worked as a librarian at the Beijing University, where Mao was an assistant. Along with Chen Duxiu, he founded the Chinese Communist Party (CCP) in 1921. He supported the Bolshevik government in the USSR and built close relations with the Comintern. Indeed, it was the Comintern who recommended they join Sun Yat Sen's Nationalists and Li was elected to the Central Executive Committee in 1924. However, the relationship between the CCP and the Guomindang (Nationalists) deteriorated quickly, and by 1927, following Sun's death, Chiang Kai-shek had taken over the leadership and was attempting to purge the Communists. Li was captured in one of these purges and executed in 1927.

3. Following Sun Yat Sen's death, Chiang Kai-shek had expelled the Communists from the Nationalist Party. Previously, they had joined up with the Nationalists as part of an agreement between China and the Communist USSR. In fact, Sun himself was very sympathetic to Marxism; Chiang, however, was far more conservative and created an enemy of the Communists, massacring many of them (including Li Dazhao) in his purges.

4. Lu Xun (1881–1936) was a famous Chinese author best known for "Diary of a Madman" and "The Real Story of Ah Q." His work has been seen as presenting many allegorical characters that represent China as a nation (see Frederic Jameson's "Third World Literature in the Era of Multinational Capitalism," *Social Text* 15 [1986]: 65–88, on this point). Lu Xun was part of a left-wing writer's scene in Shanghai and has been entirely appropriated by the CCP in the contemporary era despite certain anomalies in his own thought that meant he never joined the Communist Party.

5. Jameson, "Third-World Literature in the Era of Multinational Capitalism."

6. For example, the Propaganda Poster Art Centre in Shanghai—a museum located in the basement of a private apartment block that exhibits posters from the Maoist period. The owner is Mr. Yang Pei Ming, who started collecting the posters as a hobby but is keen to preserve them as an art form.

7. The *Ching*—otherwise known as the Book of Changes—is a Chinese book of hexagrams thought to date back to the second or third millennium BC.

8. Alan Woods, *Bolshevism: The Road to Revolution* (London: WellRead Books, 1999), 26.

9. Maurice Meisner explores this in his seminal work on Li Dazhao (*Li Ta-chao and the Origins of Chinese Marxism* [Cambridge, MA: Harvard University Press, 1967]).

10. Mark Seldon, *China in Revolution: The Yenan Way Revisited* (New York: M. E. Sharpe, 1995), 150.

11. Joseph Schumpeter, *Capitalism, Socialism, and Democracy*, 3rd ed. (New York: Harper Perennial Modern Thought, 2008).

12. *Iron rice bowl* (鐵飯碗; *tiě fàn wǎn*) is used to refer to the benefits gained if one is employed in an occupation that guarantees job security and provision of housing and so on, such as party positions. The term is often compared to "cradle to grave socialism." As during much of Mao's era, people were attached to "work units" run by the party/system, and their membership of such units meant they were given accommodation, food, education, and health care; it was felt that everyone under Communism had an "iron rice bowl." Famine and societal disorder, of course, proved this not to be the case. From 1978 onward, the iron rice bowl began to be diminished as Deng Xiaoping began to decrease the number of government jobs and state-owned enterprises as part of his wide-reaching labor reforms.

13. Vladislav Todorov, *Red Square, Black Square* (New York: SUNY Press, 1995), 48.

14. Chris Hughes (*Chinese Nationalism in a Global Era* [London: Routledge, 2006]) argues that militarization was (and is) the overriding factor in China's history from the Mao period onward. There is, of course, a great deal of truth in this, although the layers of meaning in the wearing of military uniforms may extend to elements beyond the purely military. For example, uniforms connoted a distinctly unglamorous and therefore antibourgeois mentality, making them safe symbols of Communist allegiance—this was perhaps especially true for women. Mao's own wife, Jiang Ching, often chose to wear a military uniform and no makeup in order to be above ridicule (and out of a determination that her past life as an actress should not be brought up against her). She had left behind her acting career in Shanghai after the Japanese invasion of the city and joined a Red Army faction in Yan'an, where she met Mao. She transformed herself from glamorous wannabe starlet of the stage and screen to plain and devoted comrade, although her sincerity was always doubted by many party members and the public. She was instrumental in the Cultural Revolution, ordering the destruction of hundreds of works of culture and art that were deemed too bourgeois, including (strangely but perhaps wisely) many of those she herself had had a hand in.

15. Orville Schell and David Shambaugh, *The China Reader* (New York: Random House, 1999), 29.

16. Ibid.

17. Xiaobing Tang, "The Anxiety of Everyday Life in Post-revolutionary China," in *The Everyday Life Reader*, ed. Ben Highmore (London: Routledge, 2002), 125.

BIBLIOGRAPHY

Arrighi, Giovanni. *Adam Smith in Beijing: Lineages of the 21st Century*. London: Verso, 2009.

Bakunin, Mikhail. *Statism and Anarchy*. Cambridge: Cambridge University Press, 1990.

Hanes, Travis, and Frank Samello. *The Opium Wars: The Addiction of One Empire and the Corruption of Another*. London: Sourcebooks, 2004.

Hughes, Chris. *Chinese Nationalism in a Global Era*. London: Routledge, 2006.

Jameson, Frederic. "Third-World Literature in the Era of Multinational Capitalism." *Social Text* 15 (1986): 65–88.

Lenin, V. "Left-Wing Communism: An Infantile Disorder." In *Collected Works*, volume 31. Moscow: Progress Publishers, 1964.

Lu, Xiufen. "Li Dazhao's Materialist Conception of History." *East-West Connections* 9, no. 1 (2009).

Marx, Karl, and Frederich Engels. *The Communist Manifesto*. London: Penguin, 1967.

Meisner, Maurice. *Li Ta-chao and the Origins of Chinese Marxism*. Cambridge, MA: Harvard University Press, 1967.

Schell, Orville, and David Shambaugh. *The China Reader*. New York: Random House, 1999.

Schumpeter, Joseph. *Capitalism, Socialism, and Democracy*, 3rd edition. New York: Harper Perennial Modern Thought, 2008.

Seldon, Mark. *China in Revolution: The Yenan Way Revisited*. New York: M. E. Sharpe, 1995.

Tang, Xiaobing. "The Anxiety of Everyday Life in Post-revolutionary China." In *The Everyday Life Reader*, edited by Ben Highmore. London: Routledge, 2002.

Todorov, Vladislav. *Red Square, Black Square*. New York: SUNY Press, 1995.

Woods, Alan. *Bolshevism: The Road to Revolution*. London: WellRead Books, 1999.

3

❖ ❖

Image in Revolution

Articulating the Visual Arts and Becoming Cuban

Lisa B. Y. Calvente and Guadalupe García

> This . . . will be translated concretely into the reconquering of man's true nature through liberated labor, *and the expression of his own human condition through culture and art.*
>
> —Ernesto Che Guevara, "Man and Socialism" (1965)

In 1961, directors Alberto Cabrera Infante and Orlando Jiménez Leal documented black urban spaces as a complement to the political ideology of the Cuban revolution. The experimental documentary (approximately fifteen minutes), titled *P.M.*,[1] highlighted nightlife in Havana clubs and bars that were heavily populated with the city's working-class and black urban population. The realist short underscores the communicative interactions in these urban spaces through visual imagery of dancing, drinking, and revelry. Upon the film's completion, Cabrera Infante and Jiménez Leal sought out the Instituto Cubano del Arte e Industria Cinematográfica (Cuban Institute of Cinematographic Arts—ICAIC)[2] for permission to publicly showcase *P.M.* Instead, the ICAIC condemned the film. The condemnation was premised on the idea that *P.M.* depicted sexual promiscuity, prostitution, and drug use—all vices associated with the Cuban republic.[3] The ICAIC promptly censored the film and argued that *P.M.* was in fact in opposition to the goals of the revolution.

P.M.'s censorship immediately ignited a public debate within the intellectual community over the nature of cultural production and visual production in particular. The growing contentiousness of this debate was the catalyst for the speech "Words to the Intellectuals," which Fidel Castro delivered on the steps of the National Library later that year.[4] In the speech, Castro identified artistic creators and cultural producers as the vanguard of the emerging nation-state. Castro further stressed the role of the vanguard and the importance of cultural production within the emerging revolutionary government. The most (in)famous lines of that speech—"within the Revolution, everything; against the Revolution, nothing" ("*dentro de la Revolución, todo; contra la Revolución, nada*")—articulated the revolution into anything that could be created by and for the people.

That the speech was delivered at the National Library, which stands adjacent to the "Revolutionary Square" (*Plaza de la Revolución*), a space dedicated to political gatherings, is evidence of the importance of urban space within the production, image(ing), and regulation of the visual arts in Cuba. The often-quoted slogan from "Words to the Intellectuals" has since been interpreted as evidence of an increasing authoritarianism within the Cuban state as well as a continued commitment to the arts. As a whole, however, the speech signifies how cultural and visual production is central to revolutionary change and practice.[5] "Words to the Intellectuals" served to catapult artistic realism and the visual arts into a medium of and for revolution.

As cultural production in Cuba achieved global recognition, the ICAIC continued to serve as a medium for mass mobilization through its visual production and promotion of artistic materials. The institute and its collaborators, as one of the first cultural organizations created by the new Cuban government, became one of the pioneers in flagging the importance of visual arts in the articulation of revolution. It is through the process of articulation that the particular discourses of visual arts, revolution, and the Cuban masses were connected and, in turn, new alliances and revolutionary, transnational, Cuban subjectivities were created.[6] Through a dialectical process, the theme of revolution became a unifying ideology that created a united social force with a collective subjectivity. This theme also reinvented the urban landscape from capitalist strategies of imperialism to the visual and visionary political embodiment of revolution.

This chapter examines the Revolution of 1959 as the primary communicative mode of a shared collective experience and what the practice of visual arts and imagery in relation to the revolution has meant for Cuba.[7] Instead of conflating the period after 1959 into a single political era, the chapter takes into consideration the changes that have taken place. This chapter analyzes the public, revolutionary, and political appropriation of these images to discuss how the visual plays a predominant role in Havana's socioeconomic infrastructure since tourism became a major component of Cuba's economic recovery. It explores how urban space in Havana functions as a medium of expression through an analysis of the imagery and articulation within the political transitions between the 1960s and the collapse of the Soviet Union. It also accounts for the economic catastrophe of the 1990s, which forced a recalibration of political goals among the revolutionary leadership and opened up new channels of visual expression within civil society in Cuba. Lastly, the chapter concludes with questions of how the struggle over hegemony continues within popular visual culture in contemporary Havana, Cuba.

A BRIEF HISTORY OF THE VISUAL ARTS IN CUBA

The history of visual arts in Cuba is necessarily filled with the irony that is endemic to the revolution. This irony arises from the contemporary use of billboards, posters, cinema, and magazines as visual representations of revolution on the island, which was the communication medium most subservient to consumerism during the years of the republic (1902–1959). Since 1910, when the medium of silkscreening was introduced in Cuba, billboards and posters evolved as an art form to serve capitalist needs. Companies such as Coca-Cola, Colgate-Palmolive, Exxon, and Goodyear, to name but a few, claimed areas of the Havana skyline to promote North American products to a Cuban audience. Havana has historically had one of the highest standards of living among Latin American capitals, making it a city with an urban population with access to disposable income and a prime destination for U.S. companies looking for consumer markets abroad. Its long history of reciprocal exchanges with the United States, too, meant that travel, commerce, and proximity gave U.S. companies an economic advantage when doing business on the island. Consumer messages were concentrated in the capital city, where most of these exchanges—cultural, economic, and political—took place.

Since 1959, however, the same visual medium that U.S. companies used to promote goods and services was transformed to serve the political agenda of the new revolutionary government. The island's urban areas became the arena where the struggle over hegemony materialized through strategic articulations of the visual arts and the anti-imperial regime. When the guerrillas entered the cities of Cuba, they became the living image of revolutionary Cuba and the embodiment of the significance of 1959. The image of the rebel army in the city of Santa Clara en route to Havana

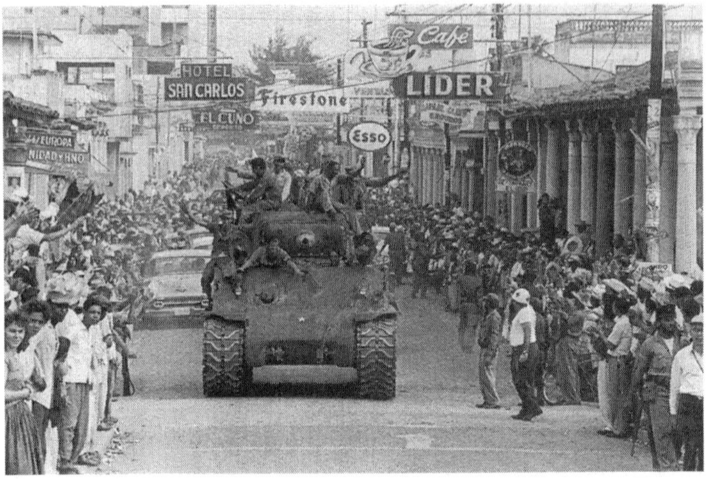

Figure 3.1. "The March to La Habana," 1959 (photo by Burt Glinn; courtesy of Magnum Photos)

transformed into one of the quintessential images of a triumph over capitalism and imperialism. The juxtaposition of the guerillas atop of the military tank against the backdrop of the urban space, saturated with remnants of the former regime and overcrowded with welcoming urban residents, visually illustrates the dialectical process of a new alternative modernity to the one previously offered by neocolonial relations.[8]

The Castro government appropriated the roles that the visual arts held during the Cuban republic. The mediated form remained the same, but the *function* of the visual arts was radically transformed. This dialectical process occurred from the historical, material conditions of the cultural politics of the early revolution against capitalist imperialist regimes. The image that remains the most emblematic of this change is the reappropriation of the Havana Hilton hotel. The hotel was owned and operated by the American Hilton Hotels group and built under the presidency of Fulgencio Batista in March 1958, less than one full year before the July 26 Movement overthrew Batista. When it was built, it was among the most luxurious and largest in Latin America and the Caribbean and advertised Havana as a prime tourist destination.

The rebel army used one of the Hilton's hotel suites as their government headquarters immediately upon entering the city. The military occupation of the hotel suite became the conscious enactment of redefining and politicizing neocolonial space and embodied the contradictions evident within the juxtapositions of the rebel army and the city. The Havana Hilton was allowed to remain in operation until October 1960. This marked the year when relations with the United States began to deteriorate rapidly after the Cuban government continued to radicalize its political agenda. Shortly thereafter, the Castro administration embarked on mass nationalization campaigns of foreign-owned property that would culminate in 1968 with the "Great Revolutionary Offensive," or the final step in the complete nationalization of all private property. The nationalization campaign illustrated a realignment of space with the new nation's agenda. After nationalizing the Havana Hilton, the Cuban government renamed it the Hotel Habana Libre (the Free Havana Hotel), a name that communicated symbolically and publicly the orientation of the new Cuban government.

From their previous use during the Cuban republic, advertisements, posters, and billboards evolved into a medium in which the Cuban government could combat the effects of neocolonialism. Eventually, these mediated objects would also become sites where the Cuban state waged its struggle against globalization and where civic participation also took place. Similar to its imperialist interlocutor, revolutionary Cuba developed posters, billboards, and signage to facilitate mass communication of various types. Communication continued to play a significant role within

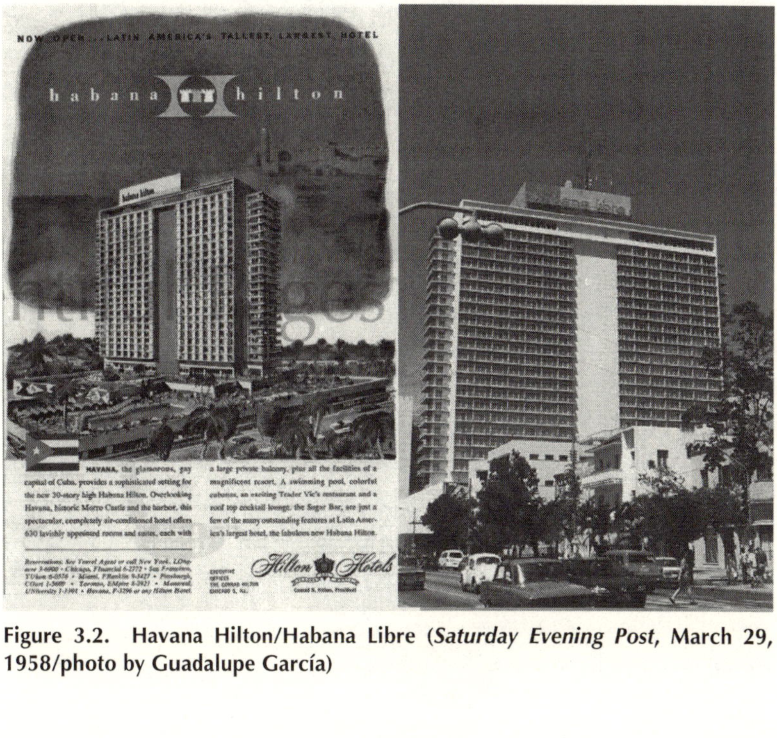

Figure 3.2. Havana Hilton/Habana Libre (*Saturday Evening Post,* March 29, 1958/photo by Guadalupe García)

confidence building for the newly independent nation in the process of freeing itself from imperial control. Internally, posters and billboards were used in literacy campaigns to reach mass audiences and publicize revolutionary programs. The campaigns employed mostly young, Cuban men and women from the urban areas to teach *campesinos* (peasants) literacy by way of Cuban history, global politics, and fine arts.

The literacy campaigns exposed the rural population to the newly formed Cuban education system that was made readily available in the city. In turn, the urban youth would also be exposed to the "backbone" of the Cuban economy and revolution: the campesino, the sugar crop, and the land. The campaign was meant to incorporate all Cuban youth into an already well-established educational system that eradicated the disparities of the old vanguard: urban/rural, rich/poor, and white/black. The campaign would additionally achieve a goal of a newly formed citizen, one that was culturally formulated to become both urban and rural simultaneously; the citizen was completely Cuban, a representative of the entire island, and the island would be completed with its new citizens.[9] These strategies advertised the revolution and extended a political platform to the masses; this platform was twofold, aimed purposefully to the people of the nation-state and strategically toward a global, anti-imperialist decolonization politics.

The campaigns relied on an iconography of revolutionary figures whose purpose was to remind the population that revolution is ongoing and interdependent. Interdependency as revolutionary is best described by Audre Lorde's process of interconnectedness that is necessarily reliant on "mutual (nondominant) differences" of becoming that can produce new forms of knowledge and new futures.[10] Lorde's depiction of interdependency and becoming rests on dialectical processes and agency. Similarly, with the new Cuban agenda, interdependency rested on the idea that every citizen was an embodied actor of change.[11] Imagery that depicted the administration working alongside various sectors of the Cuban population, such as men, women, students, urban laborers, campesinos, and children, reinforced the notion that every citizen was a necessary subject for the national collective.

Images of Ernesto "Che" Guevara and Fidel Castro working in unison with the people signified the guerilla worker, and this embodiment was often made apparent through style of dress, a meshing of the campesino and militant styles. Fatigues, for example, were matched with traditional straw hats, used to block one's face from the sun and debris from the cutting of cane. The imagery also correlated with the idea that 1959 marked the beginning of a revolution—not its end. This starting point of *becoming* created spaces of revolutionary agency that were also underscored by style portrayed in many images: the now-iconic fatigue, footed with combat boots and topped with a military cap. The iconography of the administration working as part of an interdependent Cuban collective articulated these spaces of agency and becoming. The images helped to articulate the masses and the nation as one body of guerilla workers who gain revolutionary agency from the people.

The Cuban government also introduced mass sugar harvests in which the entire population rallied to cut cane. Like the literacy campaigns, the mass sugar harvest, *La zafra de los diez millones* (The Ten Million Ton Sugar Harvest), employed voluntary Cuban labor and connected the newly formed citizens to each other and to the national body politic. The sugar campaign bridged the interdependent subjects and possessed an economic value that would ensure the island's viability in the global market. After the Revolution of 1959, the government attempted to diversify its market production; however, hundreds of years of colonialism and imperialism stunted industrialization, leaving the island a core producer of raw materials. The emphasis on raw materials meant that the island was dependent on imported products and subject to the fluctuation of market prices. As a means to extricate itself from its colonial and imperialist position within the global economy, Cuba, like decolonized territories before it, had no choice but to turn to its most reliable resource—sugar.

The decision to maintain significance with the continued economic production of its highest-priced natural resource provided the potential surplus that would allow the newly independent nation to build its industrial infrastructure. This became ever more urgent as dividends from the previous administration of Fulgencio Batista dissipated.[12] The government was in dire need of liquid capital, especially after 1963, when the embargo restricted its ability to accrue credit from, and engage in trade with, the United States—its primary trade partner from the 1850s until 1959. The goal of the sugar harvest was to accrue the capital needed to maintain the nation despite the U.S. embargo. Although la zafra did not reach its goal of ten million tons, it far surpassed the crop of previous years, even in the wake of the mass emigration of the island's residents. The success of la zafra was its articulation of a Cuban agency and mass as well as economic sustainability. This campaign would not have been successful without the dissemination of the guerilla worker imagery.

Through the people's interdependency, the campaign strategies lauded the virtues of volunteerism through visual mediums reinforced by Castro's speeches.[13] "*Estudio, trabajo, y fusil*" ("Education, Work, and Arms") likened recruits to military soldiers and became the rallying cries through which the government mobilized the population into crafting the new Cuban nation. The revolution's emphasis on cultural and visual arts led to its continued use in strengthening the Cuban citizen as well as the country. Politics and art were inextricably intertwined, and the ICAIC took center stage in the interlocking of the residential art constituencies.[14] Its members consisted of Cuba's foremost leading intellectuals, who exercised creative license to create, interpret, and visually deploy multiple meanings of revolutionary Cuba. The ICAIC purposely carried out the same strategy of articulation used to rebrand the Hotel Habana Libre throughout the island. Through the visual arts, popular stylistic features utilized during the Cuban republic were rearticulated with the imagination of the revolution and its future possibilities.

Just five years after the creation of the ICAIC, the *Organización de Solidaridad de los Pueblos de África, Asia, y América Latina* (Organization in Solidarity with the People of Asia, Africa, and Latin America—OSPAAAL) was founded in January 1966 by the Primera Conferencia Tricontenental de La Habana (First Tricontinental Conference of Havana). OSPAAAL became the international arm of the ICAIC tasked with global outreach that actively promoted political solidarity and revolutionary change. OSPAAAL's primary role in the nation's global imagery was to articulate that "the art of the Revolution will be internationalist."[15] The distribution of the magazine *Tricontinental* reached populations who otherwise may not

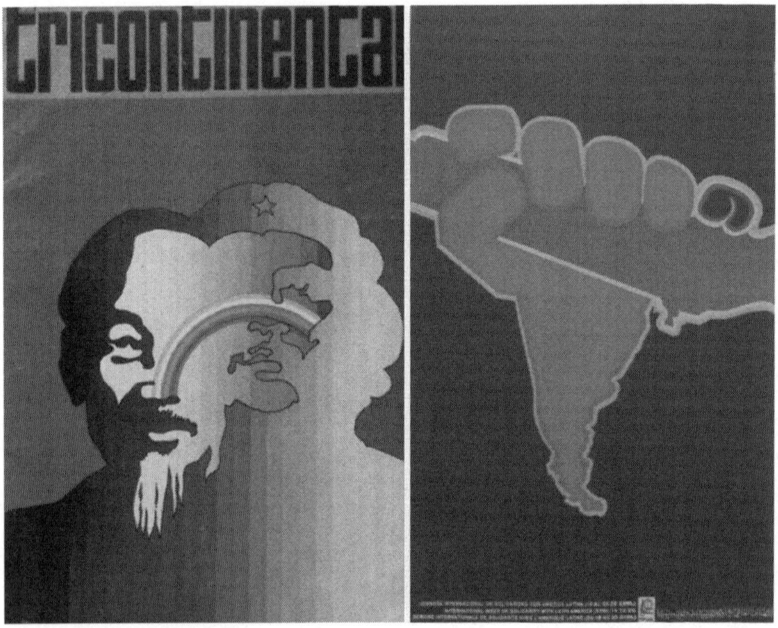

Figure 3.3. OSPAAAL

have had access to the revolution's transnational message of decolonization and liberation as a result of either economic or linguistic barriers. Its visual messages aimed to communicate the struggle against neocolonial oppression through its audience's own affective understandings of their localized struggle and marginalization. Toward this end, it published the magazine *Tricontinental* in eighty-seven countries, in four languages, with a circulation of thirty thousand copies.

Influenced by the possibilities of cinema and contextualized by the historical, material conditions of colonialism and imperialism, the ICAIC was a multifunctional institute whose members not only created film and drew in audiences but also interpreted film, both Cuban and foreign, to Cuban audiences visually. These interpretations did not deviate from its radical ideology. The seminal piece "Toward a Third Cinema," by Octavio Getino and Fernando Solanas, was published in the fourteenth volume of *Tricontinental* in 1969. The manifesto argued that the arts were key to decolonization and the anti-imperialist struggle and would continue to create revolutionary art, subjectivities, and spaces; it located the cinematic arts of both the Soviet Union and the United States as part of the same racist system.[16] Getino and Solanas proclaim, "Isn't it true that a kind of new International is arising through the Third World struggles; through OSPAAAL and through the revolutionary vanguards of the consumer societies? A guerilla cinema . . . is, nevertheless, the only cinema of the masses possible today, since it is the only one involved with the interests, aspirations, and the prospects of the vast majority of the people."[17] The manifesto as a critique highlights colonialism and racializes visual art through cinema as a political medium no longer solely about class struggle.

The messages of Third Cinema were also reinforced through the ICAIC's film production and distribution. The historical film *La última cena* (*The Last Supper*), directed by Tomás Gutiérrez Alea and produced by the ICAIC in 1976, for example, reinstated the significance of unarchived histories through the film's narrative of slave revolt and resistance against the brutality of Western colonialism and Spanish rule.[18] It also redefined Cuban subjectivity through its connection to Africanness, the island's mountainous terrain, the revolutionary spirit, and spirituality. Antiracism, anti-imperialism, and anticolonialism played a primary role in the imagery of the new nation and helped to underscore Cuban cinema as an innovator of Third Cinema across the globe. The acclamation of Cuba's political and artistic approach to film gave way to a global reception for multiple visual representations of revolution.

The ICAIC's posters and billboards publicized political campaigns and cultural production that also spoke to global political events and processes.

The state fostered a shift in how poster art was perceived and transformed it into a primary mode of visual art that was separate from the moving image—cinema. Furthermore, though the function of the medium remained the same as its political predecessor, the message articulated was one that gave it new form. Ideogrammatic style emerged as an extension of republican utility; however, the poster and billboard as art became the graphic symbol of the revolutionary power that the people possess. The articulation of the poster and billboard as art catapulted accessible art and made art in its entirety publicly accessible. Thus, art in itself became a revolutionary act that symbolized each subject as an actor, creator, producer, artist, and, finally, revolutionary. For instance, *salones nacionales de carteles* (national poster workshops) enabled anyone to participate in the creation and reception of art. This process launched popular expression as accepted art forms with the sentiment that "our enemies are capitalism and imperialism, not abstract painting."[19]

The emphasis on posters as an art form underscored the administration's use of the visual arts in its political agenda and also ensured for the medium a respected and independent place in the world of art. For example, the poster for the 1963 highly acclaimed film *Hari Karu* won an honorable mention at the International Film Poster Competition. The honor represented Cuba's effort to highlight the poster as an art form with as much credence as its acclaimed films. The move allowed the island to separate itself from the USSR and assert its independence from Soviet influence through its artistic agenda. Even as the administration faced increasing internal and external criticism as a result of the "sovietization" of its social policy and economy, Cuba's cultural arts continued as the vanguard of the administration's anti-imperialist and anticolonial revolution.

Separate from posters, *vallas*, or billboards, emerged to showcase Cuba's key political positions. The Editora Política del Comité Central del Partido Comunista de Cuba (the publishing house for the Cuban Communist Party), originally the Commission of Revolutionary Orientation (COR) and later the Department of Revolutionary Orientation, was the only government institution with a silkscreen press capable of producing billboard sheets. Though most often noted for his poster art contributions of similar style, especially those of Vietnam independence, René Mederos, a member of the Department of Revolutionary Orientation, was the person responsible for the various billboards distributed and produced annually throughout the island.[20] These were composed of twelve silkscreened sections and offered a way to efficiently produce a means of mass communication.[21] The silkscreen process was affordable and quick; hence the production of billboards proved effective both in time and in cost. Unlike its Latin American predecessors, who often utilized murals as the cultural and political medium of the nation, revolutionary Cuba chose posters and billboards as its cultural and political platform to encompass the flexibility of the guerilla revolution.[22]

As David Kunzle argues, murals "lack the flexibility required by a Revolution full of abrupt changes and constant radicalization."[23] Cuban author Edmundo Desnoes argues against the costly strategy of murals and also critiques their revolutionary utility. Desnoes encompasses the sentiment that through the alternative use of revolutionary billboards, Cuba possessed the ability to manage the radical changes that revolution required. Through vallas, the medium of the message and the message itself are superimposed onto one another. The interplay between medium, message, and reception coalesce and produced a new, unstable revolutionary form that possesses in itself a message that is continuously in flux. The vallas remind the audience that art is organically and constantly produced within the revolution instead of as a mere strategy of and for the revolution. The billboards highlight Cuba as an innovative political strategist among Latin American nations and embody how revolution ideally functioned.

Similar to its billboard complement, *Tricontinental* was also produced through silkscreen. The simplistic and symbolic style both enforced the revolutionary representation and sustained economic feasibility. The magazine used no photographs. Instead, the editors relied on color, humor, and visual wit to advocate for armed struggle. The symbolism of flat color combined with simple visual imagery and text encourages multiple interpretations of the same message, redefining difference as a component of the transnational revolutionary collective. These articulations do not inform but rather leave to interpretation the channeled hopes of imagined futures that revolutions might call into fruition for each subject. Many of the images illustrate liberation struggles such as those in Angola and Vietnam. These illustrations feature "David and Goliath" narratives of armed opposition against colonial and neocolonial empires. They feature images of guerilla soldiers in opposition to imperial soldiers and underscore the heroism and endurance of the guerilla. The significant use of weapons within the images in *Tricontinental* represents the continuity of the revolutionary struggle.

The repetition of the war themes was an extension of the ideological stance in Cuba's foreign policy in particular, and the guerrilla soldier was used as a signifier in opposition to depictions of large weapons associated with empire. "Empire" included not just the countries that had historically colonized and occupied areas of Asia, Africa, and Latin America but also the collective West. These images mobilized affective memory of marginalization, inequality, terror, slavery, and murder within these spaces of reception. *Tricontinental* continued its run from 1966 to 1990 despite objections from both the United States and the Soviet Union. It ended only after the fall of the Soviet Union and at the start of the country's economic crisis; however, *Tricontinental* influences remain through the continued circulation of its images and content.[24]

The economic and political condition in which the Cuban administration found itself after 1989 radically affected the role of the ICAIC. After the dissolution of the USSR, almost overnight 80 percent of all trade with the Soviet Union disappeared. Cuba's gross domestic product (GDP) plummeted by one-third once the USSR, which had subsidized much of Cuba's export economy, exited from the global market. At the same time, the U.S. administration tightened the embargo that had been in effect since 1963 in order to encourage civil unrest on the island. All social programs were reevaluated as the Cuban government attempted to manage the economic crisis and prioritize its social spending. The ICAIC was not exempt from this reevaluation. In an effort to lower costs and reserve resources, cultural institutions in charge of visual representation, such as the Editora Política, reinvented the ways in which the revolution was expressed and imaged prior to the island's Special Period.

Vallas suddenly favored the use of white space juxtaposed with brightly colored imagery. The white background spotlighted the colored slogans and *rostros* (facial images) of revolutionary icons throughout the highways, skylines, and public spaces of urban and rural areas. White paint also served an economic purpose, as it was easier and cheaper to procure and the white background was reusable, allowing for the Editora Política to maintain both its revolutionary content and its form. The vallas' recyclable white space rearticulated revolution to include the economic context of the Special Period and reinforced the notion that the Cuban collective was resilient with revolutionary fervor. "Going green" was now an intricate component of the revolution.

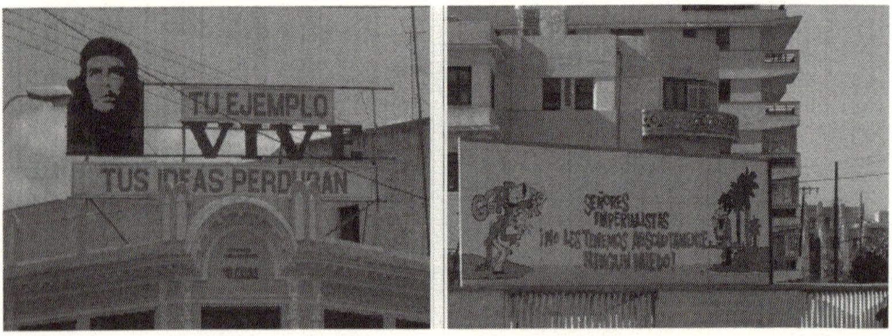

Figure 3.4. Santa Clara and Havana skylines (photos by Guadalupe García)

Austerity measures continued throughout the 1990s as the economic condition of the country worsened. By the fall of 1995, Cuba passed the Foreign Investment Act, which allowed its partial reinstatement in the global market and legalized the informal economy. The scarcity of food and consumer goods as well as the rise of the black market, tourism, and *jineterismo* (forms of hustling that became associated with prostitution) forced the economy to shift toward "dollarization"—the transition into a dual economy. U.S. dollars now functioned as legal tender alongside Cuban pesos, though at significantly different values. Dollarization decriminalized the black market and simultaneously allowed the Cuban government to profit from the sale of previously prohibited goods—imported nonessentials.[25] It also, however, made consumer goods such as paint, ink, film, paper, and chemicals almost impossible to obtain on the Cuban peso salary. This greatly limited the production of Cuban art throughout the island and stunted the growth of potential artists. Dollarization also limited the ability of the Cuban administration to purchase those same goods on the global market as it, too, struggled to gain globally recognized currency.

Through the decade-long period of crisis, the administration reduced various programs in the fields of health, education, and the arts in order to preserve its achievements that were carefully built over the course of thirty years. *Tricontinental* was one of the programs cut as a part of these preservation efforts. The Cuban government additionally explored alternative strategies that would sustain the nation but allow it to continue its tenants of revolution. Havana became the canvas on which the government's revolution was illustrated, and tourism was its primary strategy for economic viability. The use of UNESCO's designation of the city's architecture as a historical landmark aided the administration in securing its place in the global market through tourism, which would eventually displace sugar as the number-one market of the Cuban economy.[26] This was not without consequence as global representations of Havana, and by default Cuba, were ossified to the Revolution of 1959 and the legacy of colonialism. For the island's exiles, Havana became the city on the eve of their departure, and for residents, Havana mirrored its 1959 image. Cuba became "frozen" in time as its representations were regulated to its past.

Revolution as an ongoing act became obsolete as discourses of Western modernity and Third World coloniality were applied to the socialist administration and the island.[27] Iconography that poster art, vallas, and *Tricontinental* inaugurated, in addition to the end of *Tricontinental*'s production, enabled the transformation of the city into a living museum of the antiquated revolution. As of the 1990s, Havana, Cuba, offered political and cultural exoticism for mass consumption with the billboards and posters as exemplars of the unique Cuban experience. Images of Havana, as well as images produced by the ICAIC, became the number-one commodity in the photographic world and reinforced the portrayal of the nation as static. The Cuban administration played a primary role in exporting an image of the nation that expressed the political fantasies, desires, and memories of its visitors. These "expressed a symbolic zone of suspension onto which the gaze of globalization may project its fantasies."[28] The affective appeals were then concretized through *Habana vieja* (Old Havana), 1950s American cars, and the revolutionary posters, billboards, and buildings. The Hotel Havana Libre, for instance, once again helped to reinforce tourist Cuba as a primary symbol of tourist attraction. The Cuban administration utilized these foreign interpretations and perceptions of these artifacts to coincide with Western frameworks of development in order to gain the economic footing that dissipated during the Special Period.[29]

Through its visual narration of the nation, camouflaged as depoliticized, nostalgic images of the past, the administration talked back to the global gaze. By responding safely and strategically, the administration allowed it to exploit itself—Cuban exceptionalism. Cuba as an exception transforms the island into a heterotopia, a layered space in which multiple ideas of the island are projected onto its terrain; these projections come from multiple directions: the tourists, the exiles, allied and hostile nations as well as "neutral" global organizations, and, of course, from within the island itself.[30] However, as a heterotopian space, the island's performed projection of itself materialized through the visual and the city's topography became a space of illusion—a funhouse mirror of the modern Western world.[31] It is through this performative play of the visual and layered space that the administration countered and distorted the imagined projections.

CONCLUSIONS

Political participation remained at the core of crafting the new Cuban nation after 1959. As a medium, the visual arts were a vehicle toward popular mobilization that drew from various stratas of the Cuban population. *Talleres de transformación integral* (neighborhood transformation workshops) and *consejos populares* (neighborhood councils), for example, encouraged political participation and urban engagement that relied on revolution as a dialectical process instead of democratic participation. The images that local governing bodies approved through various community negotiations and interactions gave new life to the city through the transformation of individual neighborhoods. The city as revolutionary is not a contested space but a space of fusion. This additionally allows for the state to utilize the city as a space to work out solutions creatively, in ways that rigid structures won't allow. The emphasis of local participation was most clearly evident during Cuba's Special Period (1989–2000), which contributed to the deterioration of its infrastructure and additionally encouraged the heterotopic visions discussed above. *Tricontinental* and its images continued to circulate in Cuba and abroad despite the end of its production. As the island became a prime tourist destination, the ICAIC produced new serial runs of OSPAAAL posters that were available for purchase in state-run stores. The increase in tourists in addition to Internet and digital media made these readily available for popular consumption and showcased the importance of the visual in the articulation of the revolutionary process.

The visual prints of revolution and the images imposed onto the Cuban landscape underscore the continuity of Cuban collectivity and revolution. In and through these spaces, the mediums of revolution are no longer distinguishable; boundaries between the administration and its people are blurred through the actions and interactions of the Cuban masses, who redefine formal structures without challenging revolution in itself. Graffiti emerges from within the tenets of revolution and functions alongside and in dialogue with the revolutionary iconography implemented by the administration. For example, the economic crisis urged the administration to implement infrastructural changes to generate profit from tourism. One of those implementations was to privatize the same beaches it had opened to the public after ousting Batista. The ironic move provoked an outcry from the island's citizens, and, in response, the administration reopened the privatized Varadero beach to its citizens. Around this same time, an image of Fidel was painted on a pillar on the Varadero beach in a dramatically different form than most of those in Havana. The artistic style of the portrait rests more along the lines of graffiti and other forms of popular art and was left on the pillar unerased. Because we do not know how or by whom the image was produced, the graffiti image of Castro reminds us of the dialectical process of interdependency that arises from the Cuban masses.

Visual art in Cuba continues to be the terrain in which the struggle over hegemony is performed and where revolution is located.[32] When the revolution was first imagined, Ernesto Che Guevara highlighted the process of becoming liberated as part of an intricate web of cultural and artistic expression and production. As the epigraph for this chapter states, "This . . . will be translated concretely into the reconquering of man's true nature through liberated labor, *and the expression of his own human condition through culture and art*." The 1959 arrival of guerilla soldiers in Cuba's urban spaces that inaugurated the beginning of the new revolutionary

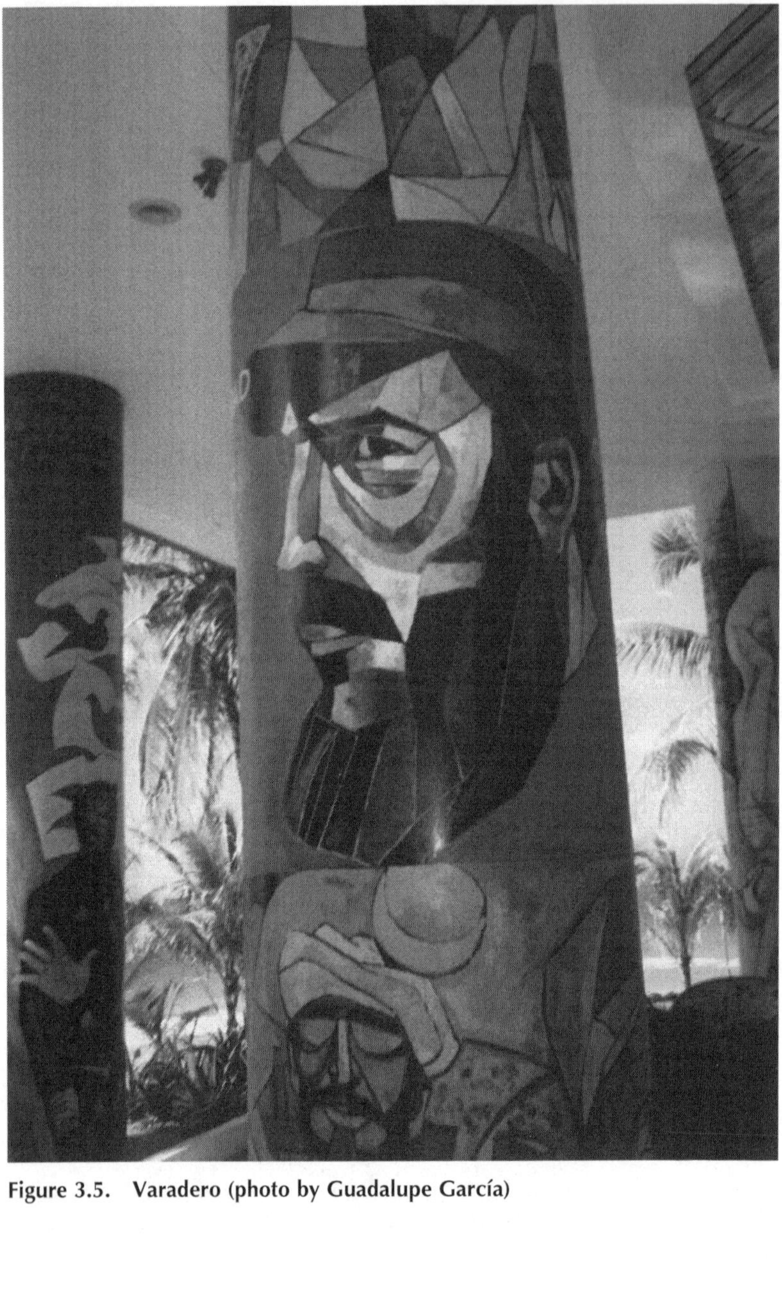

Figure 3.5. Varadero (photo by Guadalupe García)

government occurred against a backdrop of posters and billboards that collectively announced the values of the old Cuban republic. Over the course of the more than five decades that the Cuban revolution has spanned, the collective actions of the administration and the masses reimagined revolution anew. As the island continues to reinvent itself politically and economically, the question remains as to whether the visual will function as the medium through which new revolutions will come into being.

NOTES

1. Alberto Cabrera Infante and Orlando Jiménez Leal, *P.M.* (Havana, Cuba, 1961).

2. The Instituto Cubano del Arte e Industria Cinematográfica (Cuban Institute of Cinematographic Arts—ICAIC) is the primary, state-run production house for Cuban film and cinema. Created in 1961, the institute's purpose was to produce, promote, and disseminate Cuban artistic production. It showcased the revolutionary government's commitment to the cinematic arts and continues to operate into the present day.

3. The first Cuban republic (1902–1958) followed the end of Spanish colonial rule (1898) and the U.S. military occupation (1899–1902) of the country. The period was marked by the continued and growing economic and political presence of the United States.

4. Fidel Castro, "Palabras a los intelectuales," in *Palabras a los intelectuales* (Havana, Cuba: National Cultural Council, 1961), 32.

5. Par Kumaraswami, "Cultural Policy and Cultural Politics in Revolutionary Cuba: Re-reading the Palabras a los intelectuales (Words to the Intellectuals)," *Bulletin of Latin American Research* 28, no. 4 (2009): 527–41.

6. Here we use Stuart Hall's theory of articulation as a process in which history is transformed under specific material conditions through new discursive connections of seemingly unconnected elements. The importance of the process of articulations rests within its ability to create alliances and, in turn, new subjectivities, as well as its potential for social change. For more on the process of articulation, see Stuart Hall's "Ideology and Communication Theory," *Rethinking Communication*, vol. 1, ed. Brenda Dervin, Larry Grossberg, Barbara J. O'Keefe, and Ellen A. Wartella, 40–52 (Newbury Park, CA: Sage, 1989). See also Lawrence Grossberg, "On Postmodernism and Articulation: An Interview with Stuart Hall," in *Stuart Hall: Critical Dialogues in Cultural Studies*, ed. David Morley and Kuan-Hsing Chen, 131–50 (New York: Routledge, 1996).

7. We see communication as the ritualistic practices by which social processes are symbolically formed. For more on communication as representations of real-life experience and of reality, see James W. Carey's "A Cultural Approach to Communication," in *Communication as Culture: Essays on Media and Society*, 13–36 (Boston: Unwin Hyman, 1989).

8. The new and alternative modernity we discuss through articulations of the visual, becoming Cuba(n), and interdependency highlights how, like Western modernity, multiple and alternative modernities are projects. They are actively created and maintained under specific material conditions with particular significant symbols and social processes that cannot be reduced to essentialist, spatial, or cultural notions of colonized natives and difference.

9. The complementarity of the urban and rural can be seen in the ideological underpinning of the Cuban revolution. The armed struggle against Fulgencio Batista included rural (*sierra*) and urban (*llano*) components that worked in tandem to oust the dictator. This was an acknowledgment that a successful movement would require incorporating both sectors of the Cuban population. In the work of Ernesto Che Guevara, written as the armed struggle unfolded and during the early years of consolidating the government, the urban and the rural are positioned as necessary components of the revolutionary Cuban citizen. The guerilla soldier, for example, exploited his or her strengths within specific urban and rural contexts that required that the body and mind were conditioned to the local environment. The literacy and sugar campaigns also linked the population to both urban and rural environments. See Ernesto Che Guevara, *Guerrilla Warfare* (Minneapolis, MN: Ocean Press, 2006), and Julia Sweig, *Inside the Cuban Revolution: Fidel Castro and the Urban Underground* (Cambridge, MA: Harvard University Press, 2004).

10. Audre Lorde, "The Master's Tools Will Never Dismantle the Master's House," in *Sister Outsider: Essays and Speeches*, 110–13 (Berkeley, CA: Crossing Press, 2007).

11. For more on Lorde's concepts of interdependency and difference, see "The Master's Tools Will Never Dismantle the Master's House" and "Age, Race, Class, and Sex: Women Redefining Difference," in *Sister Outsider: Essays and Speeches by Audre Lorde* (Berkeley, CA: Crossing Press, 2007).

12. Fulgencio Batista fostered the growth of the Cuban economy through a series of capital investments in the global market that matured under the leadership of Fidel Castro. Once in power, the new revolutionary government benefited from the dividends. They used the proceeds, along with discounts they received in foreign loans, to offset capital flight from foreign (mainly U.S.) investments on the island, increase workers' wages, and implement new social and economic programs. See Marifeli Pérez-Stable, *The Cuban Revolution: Origins, Course, and Legacy*, 3rd ed. (Oxford: Oxford University Press, 2011).

13. The University of Texas at Austin has compiled a searchable, digital database of speeches by and interviews of Fidel Castro from 1959 to 1996. See http://lanic.utexas.edu/la/cb/cuba/castro.html.

14. The composition of the ICAIC changed soon after the *P.M.* debacle, with political appointees also making up its membership alongside Cuban artists and intellectuals.

15. 1971 Congress on Education, Havana, Cuba.

16. Octavio Getino and Fernando Solanas, "Towards a Third Cinema," *Tricontinental* 14 (October 1969): 107–32.

17. Ibid., 129.

18. Drawing from Michel Foucault and Jacques Derrida, Gyanendra Pandey defines the archive as the "sayable," that which can be understood and located as rational; in contrast, unarchived histories are those histories that are actively obscured and disenfranchised. Colonized and enslaved peoples are a prime example of those marked by unarchivable histories. For a more in-depth discussion on the discursive formations of the "mad" and the "trifling," categories of people who are exiled within the state and who in turn do not possess a history, see Gyanendra Pandey's *Unarchived Histories: The "Mad" and the "Trifling" in the Colonial and Postcolonial World* (New York: Routledge, 2014).

19. In a 1963 interview with the Paris newspaper *Le Monde*, Fidel Castro criticized Cuban party members who asked for a ban on abstract art in Cuba after Nikita Krushchev, attending a Moscow exhibit, criticized the art form. Castro responded and condemned what he called "slavish" supporters of Moscow. He pointed out that support from most socialist countries had been nonexistent during the earlier October blockade of Cuba by the United States. In response, he stated, "Our enemies are capitalism and imperialism, not abstract painting." See Tonya L. Saunders, "The Cuban Remix: Rethinking Culture and Political Participation in Contemporary Cuba," PhD dissertation, University of Michigan, 2008.

20. Lincoln Cushing, *Revolución! Cuban Poster Art* (San Francisco: Chronicle Books, 2003). René Mederos illustrates the articulation of art as politics in Cuba. Originally the art director of a local television channel, he was also an artist. In 1964, his exhibition chronicled the history of the Cuban revolution. His artistic background led him to be appointed director of Intercomunicaciones (1964–1967), where he was in charge of public-health and disease-prevention campaigns and in which he used *carteles* to disseminate information. After Intercomunicaciones was dissolved, he went to work for the Comisión de Orientación Revolucionaria (COR), or the Commission of Revolutionary Orientation, as a graphic artist. He began most of his collaborative art projects with solidarity organizations while at COR.

21. Though revolutionary Cuba was not credited for its innovative influence on the process of silkscreening as an artistic genre, silkscreening became a symbol of artistic style that rested with alternative, urban, and "underground" spaces throughout the globe. Just after Cuba's implementation of silkscreening as an artistic, revolutionary medium, Andy Warhol's iconic image of Marilyn Monroe was made famous through the same medium in the United States, in 1962, in line with the European appropriation of such style. For more on Warhol's adaptation of silkscreening, see Ingrid Schaffner's *The Essential Andy Warhol* (New York: Wonderland Press, 1999).

22. Since the Mexican Revolution of 1910, murals have been used by the state to publicly showcase emerging values and contemporaneous political messages. Mexico incorporated these as part of its political repertoire to incite a cohesive vision of the nation. For more on Mexico, the muralist movements, and art in Latin America, see Leonard Folgarait, *Mural Painting and Social Revolution in Mexico, 1920–1940* (Cambridge: Cambridge University Press, 1998), and Cushing, *Revolución.*

23. See David Kunzle, "Public Graphics in Cuba: A Very Cuban Form of Internationalist Art," *Latin American Perspectives* 2, no. 4 (1975): 89–110.

24. Piero Gleijeses, *Visions of Freedom: Havana, Washington, Pretoria, and the Struggle for Southern Africa, 1976–1991* (Chapel Hill: University of North Carolina Press, 2013).

25. Even during the Special Period, the Cuban administration managed to maintain its ration of necessities, which prevented poverty and famine throughout the island. The *libreta*, or ration card, was still used to dole out rice, beans, dairy, and other essentials.

26. UNESCO's World Heritage Commission added Havana, Cuba, to its list in 1982 and represented the city and the island's 1959 revolution as merely part of its colonial legacy; the revolution was no longer articulated as an independent decolonizing global force but as yet another stage in the process of modern development. For an in-depth discussion on the antiquation and depoliticization of revolution and revolutionary Cuba, as well as how Cubans resist these processes, see Lisa B. Y. Calvente and Guadalupe García, "The City Speaks: Dis/articulating Revolutionary Cuba and Global Belonging," *Cultural Studies* 28, no. 3 (2014): 438–62.

27. See ibid.

28. Ana Maria Dopico, "Picturing Havana: History, Vision, and the Scramble for Cuba," *Nepantla: Views from the South* 3, no. 3 (2002): 451–93.

29. Arturo Escobar critiques the history of development and its connections to Western ideology and modernity; Escobar argues that these frameworks of development reclassify nations and their subjects into hierarchies and reinforce neoliberal logic and neocolonial paternalism. For more, see Arturo Escobar, *Encountering Development: The Making and Unmaking of the Third World*, 2nd ed. (Princeton, NJ: Princeton University Press, 2012).

30. Dopico, "Picturing Havana." Dopico describes the picturing of Cuba through the lens of heterotopia, which she defines as a blank slate that foreigners fill with their ideological projections. She discusses photographs specifically to illustrate her argument and how heterotopia is formed.

31. Juxtaposed with utopias, Michel Foucault describes heterotopias as real spaces where counterhegemony arises through the reversed imagery of these spaces. For more on heterotopia, see Michel Foucault, "Of Other Spaces," *Diacritics* 16 (Spring 1986): 22–27.

32. For an extended analysis on popular culture as a space where the struggle over hegemony occurs, see Stuart Hall's "Notes on Deconstructing 'the Popular,'" in *People's History and Socialist Theory*, ed. Raphael Samuel, 227–40 (Boston: Routledge & Kegan Paul, 1981).

BIBLIOGRAPHY

Cabrera Infante, Alberto, and Orlando Jiménez Leal. *P.M.* Havana, Cuba, 1961. DVD.

Calvente, Lisa B. Y., and Guadalupe García. "The City Speaks: Dis/articulating Revolutionary Cuba and Global Belonging." *Cultural Studies* 28, no. 3 (2014): 438–62.

Castro, Fidel. *Palabras a los intelectuales*. Havana, Cuba: National Cultural Council, 1961.

———. Speech by Cuban prime minister Fidel Castro Ruz. Presented at the closing of the National Congress on Education and Culture, Havana, Cuba, May 3, 1971.

Chanan, Michael. *Cuban Cinema*. Minneapolis: University of Minnesota Press, 2004.

Cushing, Lincoln. *Revolución: Cuban Poster Art*. New York: Chronicle Books, 2003.

Dopico, Ana Maria. "Picturing Havana: History, Vision, and the Scramble for Cuba." *Nepantla: Views from the South* 3, no. 3 (2002): 451–93.

Escobar, Arturo. *Encountering Development: The Making and Unmaking of the Third World*, 2nd edition. Princeton, NJ: Princeton University Press, 2012.

Folgarait, Leonard. *Mural Painting and Social Revolution in Mexico, 1920–1940*. Cambridge: Cambridge University Press, 1998.

Foucault, Michel. "Of Other Spaces." *Diacritics* 16 (Spring 1986): 22–27.

García Espinosa, Julio. "For an Imperfect Cinema." *Jump Cut*. Accessed September 1, 2015. www.ejumpcut.org/archive/onlinessays/JC20folder/ImperfectCinema.html.

Getino, Octavio, and Fernando Solanas. "Towards a Third Cinema." *Tricontinental* 14 (October 1969): 107–32.

Gleijeses, Piero. *Visions of Freedom: Havana, Washington, Pretoria, and the Struggle for Southern Africa, 1976–1991*. Chapel Hill: University of North Carolina Press, 2013.

Guevara, Ernesto Che. *Guerrilla Warfare*. Minneapolis, MN: Ocean Press, 2006.

———. *Man and Socialism*. Atlanta, GA: Pathfinder Press, 1965.

Grossberg, Lawrence, ed. "On Postmodernism and Articulation: An Interview with Stuart Hall." In *Stuart Hall: Critical Dialogues in Cultural Studies*, edited by David Morley and Kuan-Hsing Chen, 131–50. New York: Routledge, 1996.

Hall, Stuart. "Ideology and Communication Theory." In *Rethinking Communication*, volume 1, edited by Brenda Dervin, Larry Grossberg, Barbara J. O'Keefe, and Ellen A. Wartella, 40–52. Newbury Park, CA: Sage, 1989.

———. "Notes on Deconstructing 'the Popular.'" In *People's History and Socialist Theory*, edited by Raphael Samuel, 227–40. Boston: Routledge & Kegan Paul, 1981.

Kumaraswami, Par. "Cultural Policy and Cultural Politics in Revolutionary Cuba: Re-reading the Palabras a los intelectuales (Words to the Intellectuals)." *Bulletin of Latin American Research* 28, no. 4 (2009): 527–41.

Kunzle, David. "Public Graphics in Cuba: A Very Cuban Form of Internationalist Art." *Latin American Perspectives* (1975): 89–110.

Lorde, Audre. "Age, Race, Class, and Sex: Women Redefining Difference." In *Sister Outsider: Essays and Speeches by Audre Lorde*, 114–23. Berkeley, CA: Crossing Press, 2007.

———. "The Master's Tools Will Never Dismantle the Master's House." In *Sister Outsider: Essays and Speeches by Audre Lorde*, 110–13. Berkeley, CA: Crossing Press, 2007.

Organization in Solidarity with the People of Africa, Asia, and Latin America (OSPAAAL). "Digital Archive." Accessed August 30, 2015. www.docspopuli.org/CubaWebCat/gallery-01.html.

Pandey, Gyanendra. *Unarchived Histories: The "Mad" and the "Trifling" in the Colonial and Postcolonial World*. New York: Routledge, 2014.
Pérez-Stable, Marifeli. *The Cuban Revolution: Origins, Course, and Legacy*, 3rd edition. Oxford: Oxford University Press, 2011.
Saunders, Tonya L. "The Cuban Remix: Rethinking Culture and Political Participation in Contemporary Cuba." PhD dissertation, the University of Michigan, 2008.
Schaffner, Ingrid. *The Essential Andy Warhol*. New York: Wonderland Press, 1999.
Sweig, Julia. *Inside the Cuban Revolution: Fidel Castro and the Urban Underground*. Cambridge, MA: Harvard University Press, 2004.
Tricontinental. Accessed August 30, 2015. www.tricontinental.cu.

4

❖ ❖

The Image of Difference

Racial Coalition and Social Collapse by Way of Vietnam

Brynn Hatton

An unattributed propaganda poster produced in Hanoi in 1966 features text in English, French, and Vietnamese, organized around two blockish, loosely stylized male figures conspicuously raced as white. One of the figures extends his right arm outward in a recognizable "halt" gesture. His left arm reaches around the front of his companion's chest, bracing his upper body in a posture that first reads as defensive but also conjures an embrace. Both men look in profile toward formidable blocks of text that seem to encroach on the shallow space already occupied by their bodies; this text reads like a series of directives spoken by a Vietnamese subject to an American military aggressor: "Don't Join the Army and Come to Vietnam," "Stop Bombing North Vietnam," and minimally, but just as poignantly, "Stop." The interplay of body language and text suggests that the men pictured are the ones being invaded, though the historical context and provenance of the poster's production confirms it to be about just the opposite: the Vietnamese resistance to the American occupation. By switching the presumed racial and national identity markers of the implied speakers and their corresponding gestures of protection and resistance, this artist initiates a plurality of other possible subject positions and modes of address.

This plurality is further instantiated in the poster's top-most block of text, which, though written in Vietnamese, makes an appeal to the "world intellectual antiwar youth movement" ("tinh than phan chien cua thanh nien") and, more specifically, American university students ("sinh vien

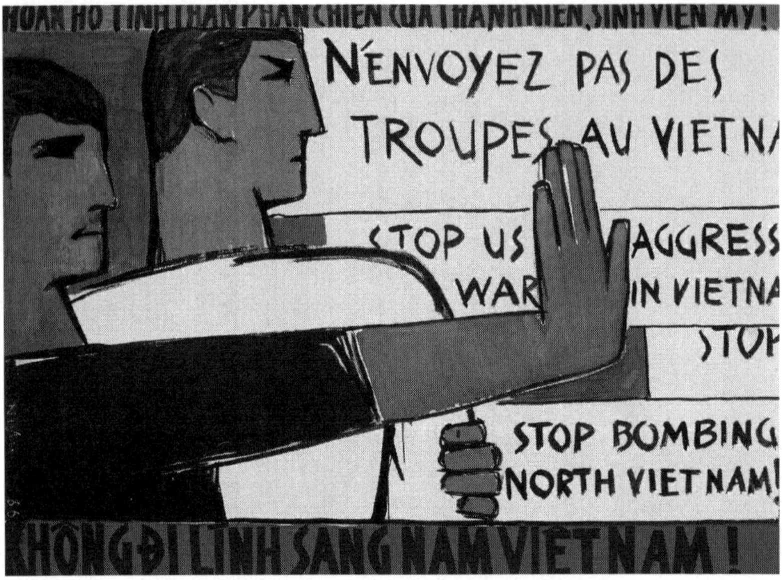

Figure 4.1. "Don't Join the Army and Come to Vietnam" (artist unknown), 1966, Hand-painted poster. (Courtesy of the Dogma Collection.)

My"). Why would this phrase be written in Vietnamese and not English, especially since English already appears in other parts of the composition? Furthermore, how should one account for the lack of tone marks in this particular sentence, whereas the corresponding sentence in the bottom register ("Không đi lính sang nam Việt Nam"/"Don't go to the south, Vietnamese soldiers") includes all the proper tone marks and is apparently directed at a North Vietnamese reader? Tone marks in the Vietnamese language are as essential to understanding the written language as the characters themselves, though Anglified transcriptions often confusingly leave them out. In pared-down graphic form, and in a genre of imagery usually characterized by more straightforwardness and clarity of message, this poster communicates via a series of oblique, inverted semantic and linguistic markers. It addresses several foreign audiences in transliterations left intentionally opaque, suggesting a complex political subjectivity that is generated by way of external reference to, and in comparison with, the image of difference.

During the height of the American-led wars in Southeast Asia (roughly 1965–1975), a global antiwar movement became responsible for the production of hundreds of posters, short films, illustrated print publications, and other quickly reproducible and widely distributable objects of protest art. While eclectic in format and diverse in national provenance, these works composed a genre of transnational protest art formed around the shared strategy of linking local politics with the issue of Vietnamese liberation. The most widely deployed tactic in this genre was the construction of visual comparison with, or proximity to, the idea and signifier of Vietnam. With the decision to picture "oneself," or the constituency to which one belongs, alongside and in comparison with the image of "Vietnameseness," works such as these constructed a version of Vietnam able to service a wide range of political claims. In this way, which is to say by way of Vietnam, locally specific struggles were joined to larger geopolitical contexts to forge a pan-revolutionary sensibility that was as tenuous and circumstantial to the war itself as it was potentially paradigm shattering to greater social realities exceeding it.

This chapter takes as its subject examples of antiwar art produced in the United States, Vietnam, Palestine, Italy, and Cuba between 1962 and 1972. I assemble these geographically disparate works in order to think telegraphically through them as a coherent political aesthetic, highlighting shared aspects of their visual and critical economies of representation, while attending to local specificities of production, circulation, and reception. What unites these works beyond the general topic of demonstrating solidarity is a compositional tendency to distinguish physically between compared subjects, while attempting to merge or conflate them politically. Social categories such as race, nationality, political party, and economic class were all variously recalibrated to appear as institutions of potential cohesion rather than division in protest art of this type. This gesture exhibits both progressive and problematic political ethics, as it depends on utilizing the ingrained social categories under scrutiny in order to bungle, question, and ultimately invalidate them. This sending up and recalibrating of power relations through didactic visuals also rehearsed a familiar Orientalist taxonomy in which the general category "Vietnam" became substitutable by a series of pheno-/stereotypical attributes: brown skin, conical hat, the dark jungle, the guerilla fighter. At the same time, subtle experiments with language, positionality, and co-identity introduce the possibility of multiple and flexible subject positions within these tropes, as the example of "Don't Join the Army" begins to illuminate. Retracing and analyzing these visual experiments opens up new avenues for the historical interpretation of protest art, calling into question the canonical status of certain artistic innovations usually reserved to discussions of Western conceptualism and poststructuralism of the late twentieth century. The model of deploying familiar language to couch a differently coded message, or to examine the fungibility of the language or the message itself, is a well-known feature of the Euro-American avant-garde that I locate in multiple examples of vernacular antiwar art produced in Asia, Latin America, and the Middle East, as well as Europe and North America. By engaging with these works in this way, I question whether this transnational genre of protest art might be viewed as an instance of conceptual art dressed in vernacular art's clothing—as a series of unprecedented pilot propositions, delivered in the form of visual statements, and engaged in an actual and timely politics as opposed to aesthetic "politics" in the abstract.

I identify two major trajectories by which to analyze the pervasive "self-to-(Vietnamese)-other" analogy in the so-called image of difference. The first trajectory recognizes its radicality as a potent visual politics that gives representational form (and thus tangible credence) to total social transformation by way of subjective self-reidentification. This, the more optimistic view, would tend to support the idea that visual artists experimenting in hyperlocal capacities with foreign, alternative political subjectivities amounts to a viable, substantial retort to the binary world order devised by architects of the Cold War. This would also seem to be supported by the fact that a core set of representational modes populates so much of this art, regardless of the country of origin or the specific material conditions of its production. Handmade pop propaganda tinged with socialist realism formed the large part of the graphic program of the global counterculture between 1965 and 1975, a choice that has been recognized by critics of the period as a conscious rebuttal to the polished-machine aesthetic of the ruling technocracy.[1]

The other trajectory of interpretation would look again at this optimistic view in order to critique its primary vehicle of expression—the overdetermination of the visible differences between people—as a visual tactic that resembled too closely the scopic binarism and essentialism of the imperial power it was designed to dismantle. Art historian Hal Foster's investigations of the "ethnographic turn" in art since the 1960s locates a similar problem in the tendency of artists in the avant-garde to look always and ever elsewhere—to the repressed, the subaltern, the postcolonial, any constructed site of the "other"—for the raw material of artistic and political transformation. Foster writes, "The ethnographer paradigm, like the producer model, fails to reflect on its own realist assumption: that the other, here postcolonial, there proletarian, is somehow in reality, in truth, not in ideology, because he or she is socially oppressed, politically transformative, and/or materially productive."[2] Foster's scope of analysis pertains to institutions and practices of high (Western) art as they negotiated the politics of alterity in the 1970s and 1980s, and so the material under consideration in this chapter is not similarly confined to the same art historical canon. Yet the core theoretical problems at stake resonate with Foster's question of what it means when artists politically self-style by way of a manufactured concept of the other.

Both the avant-garde and vernacular protest art leave open the problem of whether the aggrandizement of the other tends more toward transformation or reinscription of status quo power relations. At the intersection of the two contradictory tendencies is a visual politics that, in the realpolitik context of the Vietnam-American war, addresses a core theoretical concern bridging modern critical histories of art and race: namely, the power of the visual to calcify social construction as social fact by reifying sameness or difference.

Particular to the Vietnam-American War period and its vast catalog of experimentation with political identities is a visual and political culture that never fully came to terms with the deeply racialized dimensions of its own transnationally imagined connections and disconnections. Race undergirded the justification of the war and its escalation as much as it constituted the agenda of its various counterpublics. In 1965, the U.S. House on Foreign Affairs Committee was warned in a testimony by the economist and foreign policy analyst Thomas Schelling that if Vietnam "goes Communist," that would exclude "the US and what we call Western Civilization from a large part of the world that is poor and colored and potentially hostile," conflating in unambiguous language, and in an official government document, the direct political relationship between brown skin and potential enemy status.[3]

This same fusion of racial branding and identity formation was mobilized, albeit to the opposite political conclusion, in the numerous manifestos of antiwar groups ranging from the Weathermen Underground to the Havana Tricontinental, Chicago's Yippie Party, the Black Panther Party, and other organizations loosely anchored to the concept of the global radical left. In the official statements of these antiwar groups, the tendency was to assert an essential likeness with the world's racially (and thus politically and economically) disenfranchised populations. These manifestos call attention to the shared oppression felt by Vietnamese, black Americans, Tuparamaros, Aboriginees, Chicanos, Kent State students, Fort Bragg GI's, Tibetans, and so on.[4] According to literary scholar Sylvia Shin Huey Chong, "Activists already embroiled in the epistemic conflict over race and sovereignty made elaborate analogies between these movements and the Vietnam War, showing the political flexibility of this cross-racial identification."[5] This flexibility manifested in a visual language that constructed the idea of "Vietnameseness" in a series of shorthand visuals, able to translate specific political ends via a limited menu of representational means.

The evidence is in the number of images that spontaneously employed similar visual vocabularies in order to demonstrate local solidarity with Vietnam, but tended to signify and iconize Vietnam generically and malleably in accordance with the chief interests of other political claims. A 1972 poster by Ismail Shammout, a narrative painter and officer of the Palestinian Liberation Organization widely known in the Middle East for his patriotic tableaux chronicling the history of Palestinian dispossession, stands out not only for the directness of the equivalence it proposes between the Palestinian and Vietnamese occupations but also for the way in which Vietnamese and Palestinian soldiers are rendered physically identical in nearly all aspects. Physiognomy, skin tone, bodily gesture, and uniform are interchangeable; only certain iconic accessories signifying national and political affiliation (*keffiyeh*, rifle, and *nón lá*, the conical, woven leaf hat prevalent throughout Southeast Asia) serve to distinguish the two figures (figures 4.2a and 4.2b).

The political importance for Palestine of demonstrating cross-national racelessness is useful to consider within the context of Middle Eastern and international affairs at this moment, particularly between the poles of the 1967 Six-Day War with Israel and the 1975 UN General Assembly Resolution. The latter of these marked a substantial, if temporary, shift in tone for Israeli-Palestinian relations in the United Nations (UN), and the resolution

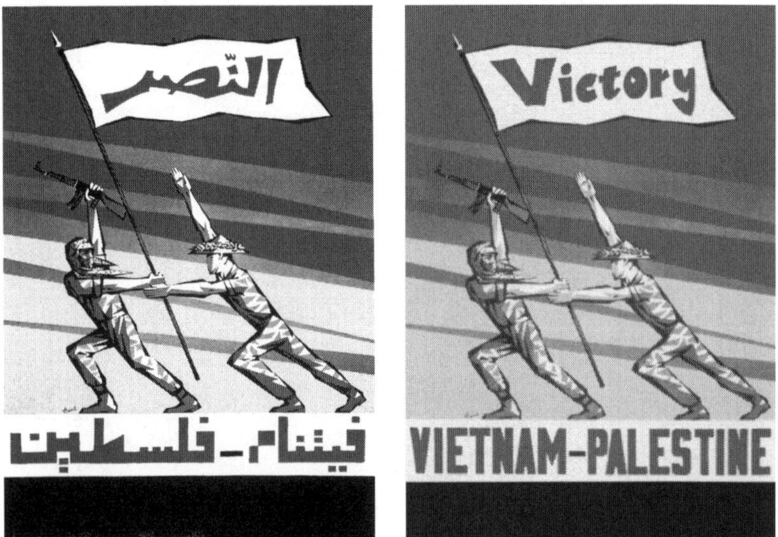

Figure 4.2. Ismail Shammout, "Victory, Vietnam-Palestine," 1972, Poster, Arabic and English versions. (Courtesy of the Palestine Poster Project Archives.)

document declared Zionism to be a structurally instituted form of racism.[6] By the early 1970s, UN delegations were made up of a new majority in the global south, which altered the dominant tenor in the organization from nonrecognition of grievances in these regions toward a new effort at their collective, diplomatic redress. Israeli international policy was put under particular scrutiny, which also presented a political opportunity for Palestinian nationhood to be galvanized vis-à-vis other global conflicts, Vietnam being the most visible and widely represented at the time. Between the Six-Day War and the General Assembly's thirtieth session, Palestine was routinely characterized by political figureheads and in the popular press of the Arab Middle East as a "second Vietnam," and the comparisons most often invoked were that of Deir Yassin to My Lai, and the Karama Operation as the "Arab Tet Offensive."[7] In Shammout's poster, which conveys this synchronicity, nationality is as distinctly and sovereignly Palestinian as it is categorically third world. Here, Palestine and Vietnam are equivalent concepts in the larger framework of Western imperialism.

Palestinian-Vietnamese solidarity as its own cause célèbre and unit of symbolic potency was also transposed onto other leftist and nationalist causes. In Italy, Shammout's imagery informed the poster program of mass worker and student strikes riding the end of the May 1968 wave. Artists from an Italian–Southeast Asian–Middle Eastern branch of the youth solidarity movement repurposed the figure group from "Victory, Vietnam-Palestine" and adapted it for a number of local posters. This instance of social movement triangulation had been operating in Italy at least three years prior to Shammout's image's appearance in the protest lexicon. Like "Victory, Vietnam-Palestine," Italian solidarity posters attempted to convene and collectivize a plurality of political subjectivities by the sheer representational act of placing them close together in a shared space. Though the intent was clearly to dissolve circumstantial distinctions between local conditions of racial and socioeconomic oppression and to emphasize the overarching similarities, the result in this case is that Vietnam becomes the more malleable and flexible image, able to contain and reinforce the whole of the Palestinian nationalist and Italian socialist causes by its sheer appearance in the compositional field. The sameness and coherence that is implied between all three causes is imposed, rather than explained, and this is only possible to do because Vietnam is by this point reducible to a general symbol of oppression. Shammout's image, repurposed and recontextualized across other multinational movements, gets at the core of the racial logic that inflects the image of difference as construed via Vietnam. By leveling and then reasserting physical difference on such resolutely shorthand terms, "Victory, Vietnam-Palestine" embodies racial schematization at its most literal level: as an overdetermined set of visual constructs that actively produces rather than realistically represents human difference and sameness, using a vocabulary that both transforms and reinscribes social hierarchy in the same move. To show this construction so directly, on one hand, destabilizes and disrupts race as a reliable category, confirming its arbitrariness as a structure. The repurposed Italian versions of Shammout's original image also tended to monochromatize or further schematize the figures, which made the already fairly indistinguishable phenotypic markers between the Palestinian and Vietnamese soldiers even harder to parse. Yet the shorthand visual cues that Shammout and his European appropriators used to achieve this destabilization *surpass* and *survive* their semantic deconstruction, because the viewer's comprehension of the image relies on prior knowledge of a racially inflected, if not entirely racially suffused, typology based in visual tropes: *keffiyeh* = Palestinian, *nón lá* = Vietnamese.

As critical studies of race have argued, and as this and other images of cross-national racial solidarity confirm, the visual management of racialization is both self-reflexive and double edged. The concept of race and its social application across groups of people is theorized as having been formulated and arrived at by a number of different motives and forces: economic, religious, juridico-political, technological, performative. Yet race as a category has been argued by scholars of race to be most flexible, transmutable, and resilient when it is exercised and maintained chiefly as a visual mode.[8] A visual system based on the differentiation and the derogation of differently raced subjects was developed in tandem with colonialism in order to sustain its ratiocination as a power structure. Once it became clear that colonial order depended on setting non-Euro-Americans apart as a distinct order of beings other than human, derogatory representations of colonized peoples established a heuristic of distance and difference between colonizer and colonial subject. The genesis of an entire classificatory system, and its attendant religious, scientific, political, and ideological enactments, arose out of these early representations that were invested in creating and confirming the empirical, visual "fact" of racial difference.[9] This visual system has been developed, refined, and leveraged continuously and flexibly for changing political purposes ever since.

The ease and flexibility with which Vietnam tended to be conjured and then emptied of its own content, grafted on to sundry revolutionary platforms, rehearsed some embedded Western-colonial systems of classifying and picturing difference.[10] On another level, the fact that Vietnamese artists also appropriated these same modes in representing themselves in war-era art shows that a more complex ideation was being established that included, but also exceeded, colonial taxonomy and the Orient-Occident binary and indicated Vietnam's keen awareness of its own currency within a global field of politicized aesthetics. Different historical and material realities shaped the forging of local and international politics in Vietnam. Invasion and colonization of Vietnam back to the second century BCE, when the Han Chinese first invaded and changed the territory's name to Nanyue, the Vietnamese pronunciation of which, Nam Viet, became the first name of the consolidated territory later known as independent Viet Nam.[11] Importantly, the successive centuries of foreign rule are popularly interpreted in modern accounts as evidence of the unassailability and uniformity of an essential, Vietnamese core, a pro-nationalist and racially implicated reworking of a fragmented claim to territorial sovereignty.

During the Vietnam-American War, the most recent in the line of imperialist incursions, access to paper and printing technology was sharply limited. Two-sided posters were frequently hand-painted on the backside of imported and recycled Russian, Polish, and North Korean propaganda.[12] This "B-side" poster phenomenon was the practical result of a paper shortage that accompanied the intensification of violence and the stalemate of import-export traffic in the mid-1960s, necessitating the creative repurposing of a number of everyday goods. Yet this specific material limitation also enabled a concrete, physical connection to be materialized between the visual economies of Vietnamese nationality and other political struggles. Practical necessity drove this form of synthesis, and the resulting aesthetic made no direct claims about an inherent fusion or synchronicity between sides A and B. Each side simply had to, and did, exist together, irrespective of the political nuance it implied. On occasion, however, formal and metaphorical relationships serendipitously cohere, as in the example of a Vietnamese poster about protecting the nation, painted on the back of a Polish state poster promoting safety in the workplace (figure 4.3). Both sides share the general theme of care and safekeeping, as well as a top-left-to-bottom-right diagonal organization. Right-aligned text floats above a duo of dominant figures in both compositions. Two connected, slightly anthropomorphized machine parts form the center of the Polish side; two connected male and female soldiers mirror it on the Vietnamese side. The single star of the Vietnamese flag on the B side (the flag of the Socialist Republic of Vietnam already being a modification of the flags of the USSR and the People's Republic of China) corresponds neatly to the star-shaped crank on the A side, and it is again mirrored in the smaller star on the helmet of the male soldier. With minimal cognitive leaps, it is possible to then visually substitute the bandaged lever (A side) for an outstretched arm or backpack strap (B side). Soldier and soldier-like machines fuse with subtle but effective symbolism in this front-to-back comparison. Without necessarily spelling it out, as in "Victory, Vietnam-Palestine," posters such as this Vietnamese-Polish

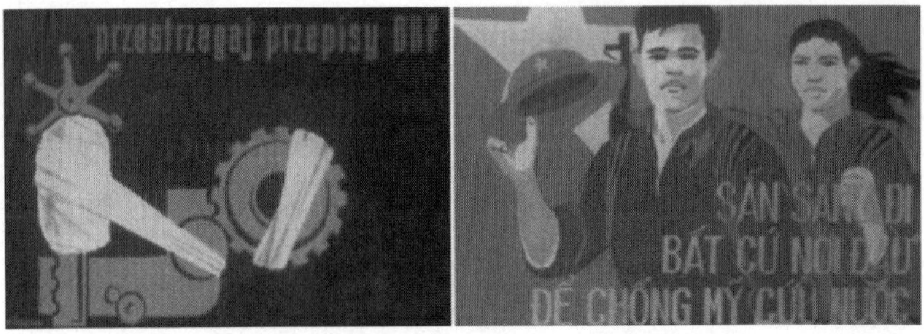

Figure 4.3. A side: Artist Unknown (Poland), "Przestrzegaj Przepisy BHP," Poster, circa 1960–1969 / B side: Artist Unknown (Vietnam), "Ready to Go Anywhere to Protect Our Nation from the Americans," Hand-painted poster, 1969. (Courtesy of the Dogma Collection.)

one conjure a reciprocity between political expressions that is receptive to, and reflective of, the many patterns and possibilities of shared meaning.

This reciprocity, and its related global iterations in antiwar art, relied time and again on the transitive property of an essential element and its ability to be grafted on to a wide range of other revolutionary and nationalist identities, while still standing alone as a specific and nameable unit. The operations in which this image type flourished are partly contextualized by the concurrent and preceding intellectual environment of global decolonization, in which the deepest political investments by the brightest thinkers were committed to exposing the connective tissue between third-world subordination and all forms of racism. The liberatory possibility of radical, subaltern plurality was among the chief cultural products of the midcentury anticolonial elite. By the early 1960s, the vocabulary of transracial resistance was standardized across the antiwar political spectrum. In China, Mao Tse-tung arranged an official meeting with American black nationalist leaders in lieu of the president in 1963, during which he publicly corroborated the Black Panther Party's view that "the evil system of colonialism and imperialism grew on along with the enslavement of the Negroes and the trade in Negroes; it will surely come to its end with the thorough emancipation of the black people."[13] Activist groups in the United States, ranging from the more centrist Martin Luther King camp of black liberation theology to far-left black nationalist movements, to radicalized whites denouncing their structural privilege, all galvanized at some point in the 1960s around the recognition that the situation of black Americans and the situation of the Vietnamese were related and equivalent.[14] King first articulated his public antiwar stance on April 4, 1967, in a speech that collated the two social ills of domestic racism and U.S. Indochina policy on the level of basic immorality, the same year that Che Guevara made his infamous appeal to "create two, three, many Vietnams" at the Havana Tricontinental Conference. Che's vision of a transnational solidarity of the oppressed as the engine of social collapse was landed in the realpolitik of the late 1960s by the black nationalist critic Clyde Taylor, who wrote, "From unheard of places came the news: the big white bubble of the last few centuries has got to burst. Castro, Lumumba, Che, Ho Chi Minh, Nkrumah, Mao and, yes, Malcolm revealed wrinkles in its previously seamless mass that foretold its eventual collapse."[15]

Inside the operational center of the big white bubble, the U.S. government, Georgia state congressman and activist Julian Bond tuned his political brand to communicating connections between Vietnamese liberation and other episodes not necessarily or intrinsically understood as belonging together. A 1973 anthology of essays on Vietnam and black resistance edited by Taylor included an essay by Bond, a founding member of the Student Nonviolent Coordinating Committee (SNCC) who had been elected to his state office largely on the premise of his well-publicized antiwar stance. A *longue durée* theorist more than an on-the-ground agitator, Bond deemphasized the militant action championed and anticipated by the Panthers and other radical groups of the time. Still, his public statements against the war caused the Georgia House to bar him from taking his congressional seat in 1965. A Supreme Court ruling determined this action by the state House to be unconstitutional one year later, but in the interim year, Bond wrote and published a special issue comic book in collaboration with illustrator T. G. Lewis titled *Vietnam*. From its opening pages, *Vietnam* presents slavery as the conceptual-historical link, and racism the present-day iteration, of the domestic and international policies that have long shaped the interconnected social and political histories of Southeast Asia, Africa, Europe, and the United States (figure 4.4).

"Who is against the war in Vietnam?" reads the comic's opening panel, accompanied by a sparse contour drawing of a human face caught in an open-mouthed facial gesture, possibly anticipating speech. The following five frames in succession repeat the schematic image in the background, gradually filling the foreground with a multiplying crowd that grows in front of and eventually obscures the face entirely, first by blocking the area directly in front of the mouth. In response to the book's opening question, as the crowd grows, the text lists a preliminary but powerful roll call of what would become the war's most active and iconic dissenters from within the black activist community: Martin Luther King Jr., the Southern Christian Leadership Conference, Southern Conference Educational Fund, Interracial Civil Rights Group, John Lewis, Stokely Carmichael, SNCC, Cassius Clay, Elijah Muhammad, the Black Muslims, Malcolm X, Adam Clayton

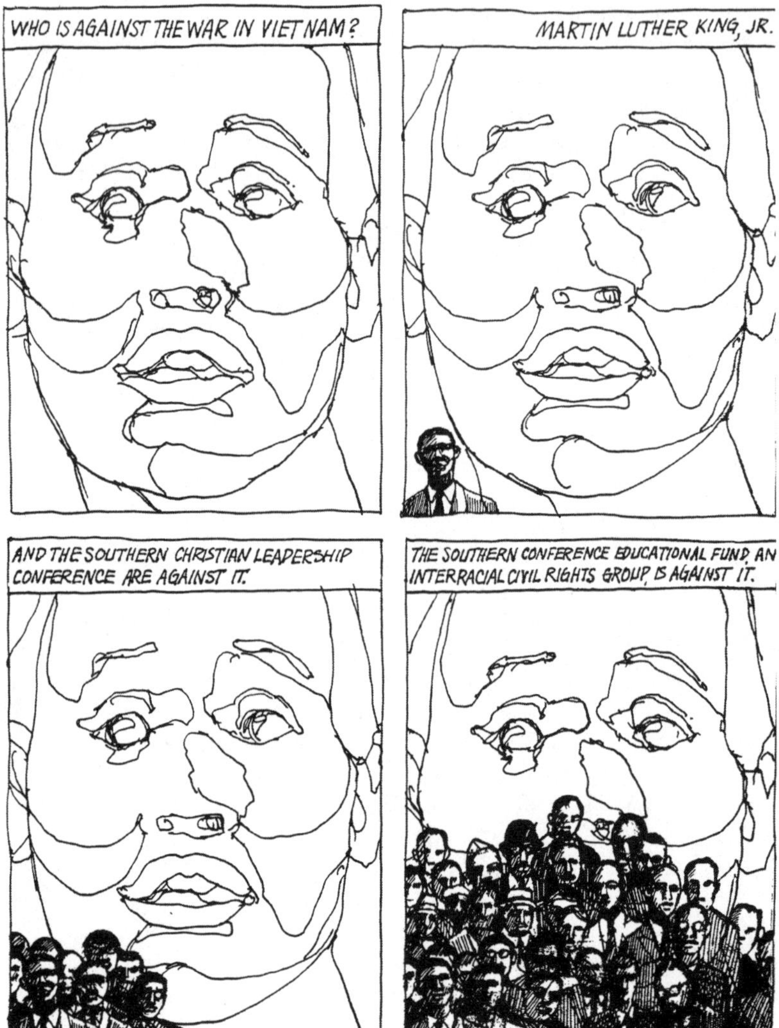

Figure 4.4. Julian Bond (writer) and T. G. Lewis (artist), *Vietnam*, 1967. (Courtesy of the Sixties Project and Viet Nam Generation, Inc., Charlottesville, VA.)

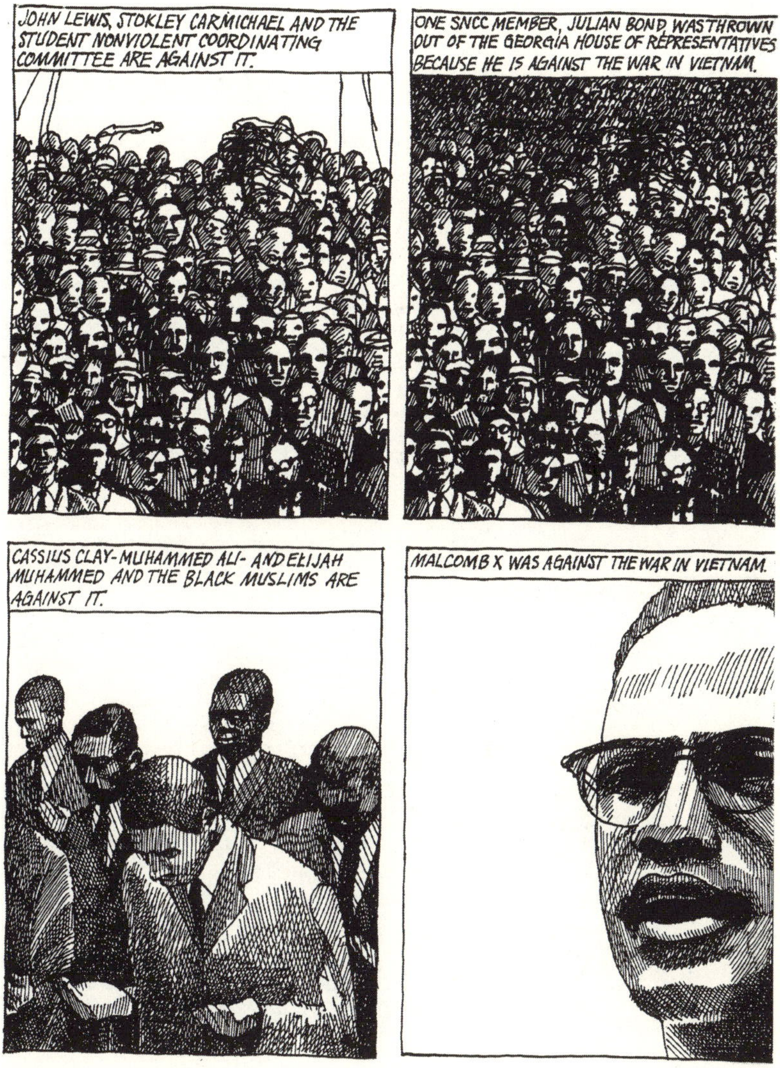

Figure 4.4. (*continued*)

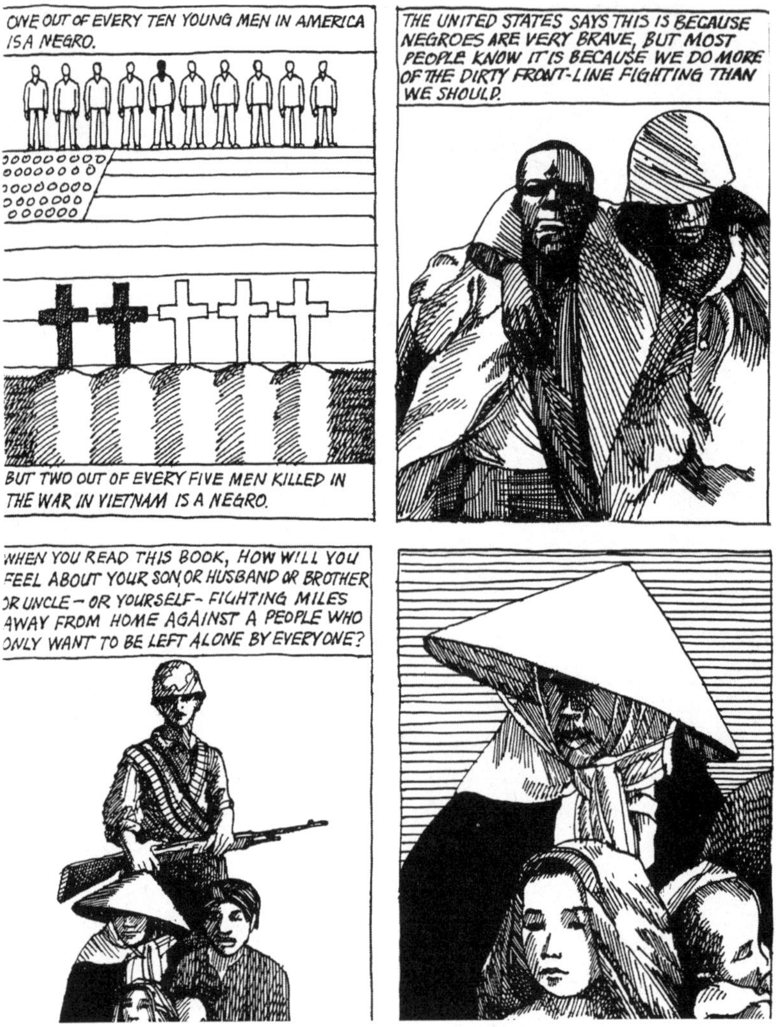

Figure 4.4. (*continued*)

Powell, James Farmer, Floyd McKissick, the Congress of Racial Equality, and most of the Africans at the United Nations. Beginning with a single question and then answering it seemingly ad infinitum, the successive and continuous list of names and organizations, paired visually with the image of a virally multiplying mass, implies that opposition to the war was then growing exponentially among the world's nonwhite population and would continue apace. The text then shifts to a past-tense narrative that links Europe and America's histories of chattel slavery to the current policies of military aggression in Southeast Asia. Bond presents these summations in a plainly stated, cause-and-effect tone reminiscent of an elementary school textbook. One-to-one analogies serve as compound explanations of broad and complex histories: "In 1860, when the United States was fighting a war to free the slaves, the French were fighting a war to make slaves of the people who live in Vietnam. . . . In December 1960, the National Liberation Front was formed. Some people here called it the 'Viet Cong' like people who don't like negroes call us 'Niggers.'" A series of purposeful, diametrically opposed expressions of "fact"—the official line of the American government, juxtaposed against the experience of the Vietnamese people and/or of African Americans—moves the narrative chronologically through two hundred years to the present moment.

Vietnam's writing style resembles the war-themed storylines of the era's major comic book publishers, whose formulae generally supported the Johnson administration and also tackled wide swaths of history in terms of good versus evil and the plight of righteous, patriotic superheroes pitted against enemy Vietcong (and occasionally, countercultural hippie) supervillains. Marvel's Hulk, Thor, Iron Man, and Captain America characters all diversified and adapted during the Vietnam era to incorporate current events, and the pitch of the heroes' adventures adjusted to the rising level of reader sophistication and the war's fluctuating domestic popularity.[16] Though similar in writing style to the offerings of the larger comics industry, Bond and Lewis's independent venture also differed in subtle ways. While it still reduced the explanation of complex realities into simple bifurcations like good and evil, enemy and ally, Bond's treatment positioned those bifurcations as equally weighted counterpoints. The resultant effect tends to encourage discussion and reflection rather than deliver a neatly packaged ideology through storyline. *Vietnam* also enlists the agency of the reader throughout, beginning and concluding with sets of open-ended questions meant to encourage political self-examination. The end of the book mirrors the opening pages with another series of close-up, single-panel portraits: a helmeted soldier, a rural Vietnamese couple, a father and child, a young black man posed in front of an American flag, a single eye looking askance. The panel text is once again interrogative: "What do you think? Should we be fighting in Vietnam, or should we let the Vietnamese people—Catholics, Buddhists, Communists and Democrats—settle their own problems in their own way? You are part of America. You are supposed to be a part of the government. Men you vote for help make this war possible. Will you vote for them again? Or will the war in Vietnam—the war that is fought in your name—keep on killing? What do you think?"

Bond and Lewis chose the graphic legibility and accessibility of the comic book format in order to signal reader familiarity and innocuousness, and to posit through the conventions of that medium a challenging model of political reflection and personal choice. The leveling and conflating of the listed groups and visual archetypes, both written and illustrated, implies that the unanimity of the oppressed as emblematized by Vietnam is itself an open-ended question posed to the reader (and hence to society at large). Art historian Ernst Gombrich famously argued in 1963 for the political efficacy of the cartoon format in a comparative analysis of different forms of didacticism in visual representation. Gombrich compared the cartoon's shorthand distillation of larger ideas into abbreviated archetypes to a similar function found in secular and religious myths. One of the unique strengths of the cartoon, Gombrich writes, is the "flash of pleasant insight" it can offer at having made the unfamiliar clear in an instant, though this is more often than not "the illusion of an explanation while really the analogy is rather incomplete."[17] Beginning and ending the comic with a series of difficult rhetorical questions makes transparent this "illusion of an explanation" and puts pressure on the self-evidence of what are presented structurally throughout as facts. Conscious representational slippages and openings such as this cut through the apparent didacticism of *Vietnam* and resemble the visual vernacular of poster artists working in the same period and context of antiwar popular imagery. Transnational propaganda artists working in multiple mediums recognized the political utility of the didactic analogy and of the "flash of pleasant insight" left purposely incomplete, irresolute, or ambiguous. Upon more prolonged investment with these diverse images, one can start to notice the seams pulling around the established visual conceits of the colonial order.

A different series of panels in the *Vietnam* comic, however, shows these seams from an angle that reveals the doubled edge of anticolonial visuality, as it was produced and received around the subject of Vietnamese liberation. Bond and Lewis devote several pages in the middle of the book to illustrating statistics on black versus white enlisted soldiers and the numbers of corresponding war deaths. Simplified grids and icons do the informational work of conveying the bare statistics, while the depiction of racial difference (used to illustrate the human impact) is again reduced and compounded to typology, the frequent tool and consequence of solidarity clothed in the shorthand of agitprop. Though it is a stylistic staple of the comics format, the illustrated grid itself also carries the cultural imprint of what Mary Louise Pratt has called the "totalizing classificatory schema"[18] of imperial worldmaking. The connection of knowledge production, pedagogy, racial differentiation, and biopower in this schema is exemplified in the format of the *info-graphic*, an explicative mode of communication neutralized in its implication of scientific distance and mathematical facticity. Bond's accompanying text on race versus life expectancy emphasizes "the bravery of Negroes" disproportionately engaged on the front lines in Vietnamese battlefields. His adulatory prose is set against illustrative info-graphics as well as images of supplicant Vietnamese, who are pictured cowering beneath the protective gun of a stalwart American. The heroic Negro soldier is here extracted and liberated from the classificatory schema through the text, whereas the Asian victim is resorbed into Orientalist stereotype in the same set of demonstrative (visual) moves. The combined result does not so much raise a rhetorical question about the nature of the social order and racial subordination as it unintentionally *confirms* and *rehearses* the logic of racism, a larger symptom of a colonially inflected vision that extends even to representations of black heroism under white power.

In cases where nonfigurative graphics substituted for the human form in protest imagery, shorthand visual cues still forged connections between two, three, four, or more political platforms and were woven together and assembled under the umbrella of Vietnamese liberation. Many works produced outside Vietnam, as we have seen with Shammout and Lewis's examples, used the *nón lá* as an indicator of both Vietnamese people and Vietnamese solidarity. A type of actual woven umbrella itself, the *nón lá* in Vietnamese culture is an object imbued with layers of poetic symbolism and affect such that its usage by foreign artists could not help but be partial misappropriations of its full significance. Yet it is precisely this type of disjuncture and partiality in the transfer between cultural codes that allows for symbolic appropriation to become its own type of hybrid language. Cultural appropriation can be an effective, if charged, method by which to establish sameness and difference simultaneously; some antiwar art, as we have seen, accomplished a toggling and collapsing of political identity in this regard by parsing the visual language of racialization in representations of the human figure. Graphic abstraction was also deployed as a leveler of distinction and a visual aid of identity politics, though its application was no less volatile in terms of the capacity to be double edged. The artistic program and internationalist reach of Cuba's Organization in Solidarity with the People of Asia, Africa and Latin America (OSPAAAL), a transnational entity born out of the 1965 Tricontinental conference in Havana, was emblematized in hundreds of mass-produced posters that traveled the Pan-Socialist network between the organization's founding and its near-dissolution at the fall of the Soviet Union.[19] A highly visible and developed system of noncommercial poster art flourished in Cuba as early as 1959, though the vast majority of OSPAAAL's posters were not meant to be pasted up on public spaces per the traditional application of the medium.[20] Rather, the posters were printed, folded up, and stapled inside issues of the organization's self-published journal *Tricontinental* and distributed via mail to a worldwide subscriber base of tens of thousands. Unlike Vietnamese posters, which were almost all individually hand painted, distributed hyperlocally by individual artists, and made with the express functionality of communicating to a largely illiterate population, OSPAAAL posters were mass-produced in large quantity for a literate and mostly affluent international audience. At its peak, *Tricontinental* had a circulation of thirty thousand subscribers in eighty-seven countries, making it the most effective international poster-distribution system in the world.[21]

OSPAAAL's significant international reach and its bold, impactful aesthetic made for perhaps the most effective and iconic oeuvre of transnational protest imagery produced during the Vietnam-American War. According to the organization's manifesto, all Afro-Asiatic states able to transmit their experiences of generalized Western domination and collective oppression could be, and were, cohered and co-represented in a visual and political lexicon termed the "ideo-aesthetic," an expansion and rebranding of the info-graphic format. OSPAAAL's organizational representation of the "new international situation, characterized by the predominance of a unipolar world where the Northamerican imperialism [*sic*] exercises its supremacy,"[22] inspired an abundance of creative visual communications on that theme. The reach and style of the successful poster program also had the effect of narrowing and contracting the intricacies of the global antiwar discourse. The ideo-aesthetic menu was limited and succinct in most of OSPAAAL's Vietnam-themed posters. Abbreviated, graphically reduced versions of the *nón lá* were the most common graphic element, the one that provided the Gombrichian "flash of pleasant insight" to the widest possible audience. Two usages of the *nón lá* from *Tricontinental* in the early 1970s offer a useful comparison of the ways in which visual sameness and difference were managed within this shared visual system. A 1972 poster by Cuban artist Olivio Martínez features a *nón lá* woven from straws labeled "solidarity" in four different languages (English, Spanish, French, and Arabic), upturned in order to catch a guided missile within its conical bowl. A literal catch-all symbol, the intertwinement of the four representative languages of OSPAAAL's international propaganda campaigns here disrupts the weapon's trajectory, which is aimed at the flags of anti-Communist South Vietnam and pro-Communist National Liberation Front (NLF). Ernesto Padrón's 1971 *Together with Viet Nam* is composed of a minimalistic pattern of identical concentric circles, shadowed just enough to suggest a slight three-dimensionality and read visually as a group of *nón lá* seen from above.

Neither composition indicates a particularly refined sensitivity to local political diversities in Vietnam, but both proffer a broad brand of togetherness, oneness, and uniformity across the span of anticolonial Afro-Asia. Martínez's conflation of the flags of two politically opposed Vietnamese factions may read as a statement on how the North and the South mutually suffer at the hand of American forces. It may alternatively read as a failure to differentiate between the NLF, the Viet Minh, the Lao Dong (Vietnamese Communist Party), and the Republic of South Viet Nam (RVN), and the positions each organization occupied in the national and international political milieu.[23] Padrón's repetition of identical *nón lá* in a regularized grid also dispenses with its local meaning, appropriating its form as an object of maximum graphic utility. No Vietnamese persons are represented directly; yet both posters suffuse the subject of Vietnam with a range of projected revolutionary identities having little to do with Vietnam itself. The adaptable, associative properties of Vietnameseness, here exemplified by the *nón lá*, endow it with the highest potential for symbolic co-optation and, ultimately, commoditization.

This aesthetic reduction of Vietnam to the *nón lá* was clearly effective on the level of mass readability and common sense to a wide international reader and viewership. The choice was prescient also, given the lasting commercial potency of this particular object, which persists as one of the most popularly photographed and mass reproduced in the tourism economy of Vietnam. Where it once was coded as part of the language of transnational revolutionary kinship, it now serves as a more blatant apparatus of commodity fetishism grafted onto Orientalist tropes. Contemporary travel literature often highlights the *nón lá* and its long-held associations with a number of vaguely "authentic" and mostly feminized virtues of Vietnamese culture, such as harmony, gentility, romance, and charm.[24] The ways in which race, gender, fantasy, and commodity culture are all mutually implicated in the circulation of object codes, especially as it curtails with historical episodes of atrocity and violence, comprises its own developed area of discourse that is beyond the bounds of this chapter. What bears reinforcing here is the fact that the image economy of a single object was able to move facilely from the lexicon of anticoloniality to the fantasy proffered by tourism and its particular breed of economic neocoloniality.

In Igor Kopytoff's seminal 1986 essay "The Cultural Biography of Things," the adaptive aspect of objects is likened to the construction of identities and the management of human social life. Applied to an analysis of visual tropes in protest art, Kopytoff's social economics is instructive. The template economy he establishes of "things" as they move in and out of commodity status resembles the visual economy of subjects moving in and out of political salience in the transnational protest art of the Vietnam era. Kopytoff's theory of economy and identity reads as a kind of backward operation of solidarity politics. "Things" in "complex society" gain social traction as they gain biography and singularity, whereas humanity in protest art gains greater social traction via the *reduction* of biography and singularity, which is manifested in graphic and taxonomic reduction. Kopytoff is worth quoting at some length to secure the analogy:

> In complex societies . . . a person's social identities are not only numerous but often conflicting, and there is no clear hierarchy of loyalties that makes one identity dominant over the others. Here, the drama of personal biographies has become more and more the drama of identities—of their clashes, of the impossibility of choosing between them, of the absence of signals from the culture and the society at large to help in the choice. The drama, in brief, lies in the uncertainty of identity.
>
> The biography of things in complex societies reveals a similar pattern. In the homogenized world of commoditization, *an eventful biography of a thing becomes the story of the various singularities of it, of classifications and reclassifications in an uncertain world of categories whose importance shifts with every minor change in context.* As with persons, the drama here lies in the uncertainties of valuation and identity.[25]

Between these spheres of commoditization and singularization, culture acts as a policing agent that assesses the status of a person or object's circumstantial entry and exit in and out of either sphere. Culture imposes a collectively shared order on an impossible diversity of objects/people. It carves the path between too much homogeneity ("lumping") and too much heterogeneity ("splitting") in dealing with singular things, by assigning various levels of value as context demands.[26] This Kopytoff regards to be true in every complex society, though modern Western ones do the most work to deny the equivalence of things and people so as to hypocritically reinforce their sameness, waging wars in defense of systems (transatlantic slavery, unfettered neoliberal capitalism, institutional racism) that unselfconsciously fail to distinguish between people and commodities. People and things do not occupy polarized and opposing positions in a projected moral order that would claim to distinguish them. Rather, people and things both become equal-opportunity vehicles for social ordering. Kopytoff again: "What is significant about the adoption of alien objects—as of alien ideas—is not the fact that they are adopted, but the way they are culturally redefined and put to use."[27] To appropriate and resituate this insight to the material at hand: The singular truth of the Vietnamese experience and its biographical synchronicity with the world's oppressed is *not* the major significance or contribution of the transnational antiwar movement, nor should it be its visual legacy. What is significant is the fact that Vietnam, for a time, served as a convenient, effective, translatable visual commodity of oppression for various political economies that had vested, local interests in different versions of social reordering.

In order to substantiate the relevance and proliferation of any culture, it becomes necessary to impose a "collectively shared cognitive order upon the world which, objectively, is totally heterogeneous and presents an endless array of singular things."[28] Without this imposition of order, how would the untenable heterogeneity of all the world's nonwhite cultures be grouped together and understood as ideologically equivalent? "Vietnam" as a cognitive object was constructed and reduced by the capitalist architects of the Cold War as an emerging stronghold and a hapless victim of globalizing Communism. To the antiwar movement, "Vietnam" was used to impose coherence on an equally vast heterogeneity within a cognitive system that organized the world according to sameness and difference. Pro-war and antiwar alike, essentialism cohered the cognitive orders that defined Vietnam and Vietnameseness. Visual culture organized and managed the social systems that these orders imagined and purveyed. As strategies of coalition and leveling, both "Vietnams"—that of the countercultural left and that of the pro-war right—required the collapse, reduction, and repetition of essentially irreducible fields of local meaning. Popular images that traveled, both in the physical sense and in the stylistic emergence and reproduction of a coherent visual vocabulary, helped produce and impose this "collectively shared cognitive order upon the world." How closely, though unintentionally, the antiwar movement's methods resembled those of the very aggressors they designed to dislodge.

POSTCRIPT

The widespread networks of cross-racial identification that defined the voice of the global left during the war years waned significantly in the immediate postwar era, after 1975. Politically, the internationalist dimension of the war ceased to galvanize counterpublics in the same way once the urgency to end the war dissipated as the prevailing grievance. A parlance once defined and emboldened by pluralism and difference was disaggregated into narrower identity politics and isolationist nationalisms, while the language and policies of the late Cold War shifted from more broad-stroke ideologies to the management of scattered counterrevolutionary regimes and volatile economic blocs. Cohesive visual styles that had populated global antiwar art likewise retreated from public view, as did the many seemingly self-evident connections between decolonization struggles and the continuing violence across Southeast Asia well into the 1980s. Whatever political work it temporarily served, the tactic of visualizing racial equivalence in transnational art was abandoned in order to sustain the profitability, both political and economic, of other social needs after 1975. With the end of the Vietnam-American War, new wars broke out between the Communist states of Vietnam, Cambodia, and China, and millions of war refugees repatriated between 1975 and 1992. The brutality of the subsequent wars and a global Indochinese diaspora challenged and complicated the once-rampant translatability of Vietnam as an internationally cohesive symbol, though the tremendous scale of the Indochinese diaspora might have provided fodder for a continued and continually evolving demonstration of transnational solidarity (albeit on the premise of actual as opposed to imagined proximity). In a volume of essays titled *Vietnam and Black America: An Anthology of Protest and Resistance*, R. S. Browne observed that the temporary sense of equivalence between disparate groups was palpable, if not necessarily abiding, driven by "a vague sense of community which [found] special nourishment in the problems of underdevelopment which they all share[d]."[29] It was rather this problem of underdevelopment—a sustained crisis of economics, not a projected ethics of kinship with the Vietnamese—that drove the postwar conversation about capitalism's larger relationship to race and power.

As a tool of social communication, protest art largely tends toward the assumption that the visual sphere—the realm of racial grouping, among other aspects of subject formation—is both stable and representable in relation to the space and articulation of political claims. It is usually compelled and materialized by the stability of its claims, asserting that to name a problem amounts to representing it directly and transparently. "This," according to an incisive catalog essay on a recent exhibition of Vietnamese propaganda art in the Czech Republic, "is the real infamy of war propaganda, whether Italian or Vietnamese, sophisticated or vulgar, from the artistic or conceptual point of view, in favor of fair or unfair matter: it erases any possibility to differentiate the real from the false; it only asks you to join one party against the other one."[30] The apparent positivism in much of the protest imagery against the Vietnam-American War contained encoded symbolic and semiotic disruptions that questioned the basic coherence between the essential structure of subject identification, racial typing, and the assumed function of propaganda. To assert sameness, kinship, and likeness in a visual and political sphere usually produced by conflict and difference leaves open radical fissures in the system of subject identification itself. The image of difference claims therefore claimed likeness with that which was categorically other by representing "self" and "other" equally, and side by side. The effect was a leveling of "an endless array of singular things" into a visual vocabulary that was, for a time, cognitively manageable, if often misappropriated or misconstrued; it bore unintended social consequences as well as radical social potential.

Critics since have questioned the potency and intensity of contemporary art's engagement in dissentionist politics after Vietnam. Recent scholarship in the social sciences on contemporary leftist and antiwar movements, from the Iraq War protests of 2003 to the Occupy Wall Street movement, tend to view the conflation of multiple grievances and topical platforms as evidence of a movement's disorganization, irrationality, ineffectiveness, or outright failure.[31] This problem of perception is perpetuated in art historical circles, notably by the *October* questionnaire of 2008 in which the journal's editors bemoan the lack of any visible, active, counterpublic sphere with regard to the wars in Iraq and Afghanistan "conducted with an intensity comparable to the protests organized during the era of the Vietnam War."[32] In a moment such as this, when the visual products of organized dissent are sometimes harder to see, revisiting and recuperating an art historical moment in which broad and multiple political concerns were mutually reinforcing rather than individually disintegrating provides a productive path by which to understand the lineage of protest art beyond the prevailing grievances of any one local crisis. That is, after all, what these artworks in global solidarity with Vietnam had always intended for us to see. Ongoing, shared struggles over the irregular dynamics of world power—struggles that, for a time, consolidated a global resistance under the sign of Vietnam—have been narrated out of proximity in the years since due to a failure of perception, not a lack of solidarity.

NOTES

1. See Gwen Allen, "Design as a Social Movement," in *Power to the People: The Graphic Design of the Radical Press and the Rise of the Counter-Culture, 1964–1974*, ed. Geoff Kaplan (Chicago: University of Chicago Press, 2012).

2. Hal Foster, "The Artist as Ethnographer," in *Return of the Real: Critical Models in Art and Theory since 1960* (Cambridge, MA: MIT Press, 1996), 174.

3. "Supplemental Foreign Assistance, Fiscal Year, 1966—Vietnam: Hearings before the Committee on Foreign Relations, United States Senate, Eighty-Ninth Congress, Second Session, on S. 2793, to Amend Further the Foreign Assistance Act of 1961, as Amended: January 28, February 4, 8, 10, 17 and 18, 1966" (Washington, DC: U.S. Government Publishing Office, 1966).

4. For a discussion of leftist manifestos and their assertions of equivalence with the Vietnamese, see Noam Chomsky, "The Responsibility of Intellectuals," in *Against the Vietnam War: Writings by Activists*, ed. Mary Susannah Robbins (Syracuse, NY: Syracuse University Press, 1999). In a 1970 statement titled "To My Black Brothers in Viet Nam," Black Panther Party minister of information Eldridge Cleaver made perhaps the most direct appeal toward specific action in this regard. Asking enlisted black soldiers to recognize their moral affinity with Vietnamese as stronger than their American citizenship, Cleaver requests that black GIs defect. See Eldridge Cleaver and Black Panther Party, *To My Black Brothers in Viet Nam* (1970).

5. Sylvia Shin Huey Chong, *The Oriental Obscene: Violence and Racial Fantasies in the Vietnam Era* (Durham, NC: Duke University Press, 2012), 25.

6. "The racist regime in occupied Palestine and the racist regime in Zimbabwe and South Africa have a common imperialist origin, forming a whole and having the same racist structure and being organically linked in their policy aimed at repression of the dignity and integrity of the human being." From "Resolution Adopted by the General Assembly of the United Nations 3379 (XXX): Elimination of All Forms of Racial Discrimination," November 10, 1975.

7. Paul Thomas Chamberlin, *The Global Offensive: The United States, the Palestine Liberation Organization, and the Making of the Post–Cold War Order*, Oxford Studies in International History (Oxford; New York: Oxford University Press, 2012), 26, 46.

8. Tracing the history of the signification of race through visual modes, Michael D. Harris has argued that it was the transatlantic slave economy, driven by its own profit motive, that essentially invented race. A social order based on differentiating black Africans from white Europeans was developed in order to sustain the profitability of the slave trade once it became clear that the industry depended on setting blacks apart as a distinct order of beings other than human. Derogatory representations of blacks arose out of a need to create distance between slavers and slaves for the purpose of sustaining an economic world order, and the genesis of an entire classificatory system—racism—with its corresponding and secondary religious, scientific, ideological principles arose out of these representations. See Michael D. Harris, *Colored Pictures: Race and Visual Representation* (Chapel Hill: University of North Carolina Press, 2003).

9. As a result, my investment in these works engages more meaningfully and closely with critical theories of race that have understood race to be a historical product of the political imagination, produced in order to create, sustain, or supersede other classificatory social systems and sovereign structures. Falguni A. Sheth, *Toward a Political Philosophy of Race* (Albany, NY: SUNY Press, 2009); Amy

Abugo Ongiri, *Spectacular Blackness: The Cultural Politics of the Black Power Movement and the Search for a Black Aesthetic* (Charlottesville: University of Virginia Press, 2009); Harris, *Colored Pictures*; David Theo Goldberg, *The Threat of Race: Reflections on Racial Neoliberalism* (Malden, MA: Blackwell, 2009).

10. Charles W. Mills, *The Racial Contract* (Ithaca, NY: Cornell University Press, 1997), 126.

11. See Marilyn Young, *The Vietnam Wars: 1945–1990*, 1st ed. (New York: HarperCollins, 1991); Huu Ngoc, *Wandering through Vietnamese Culture*, 4th ed. (Hanoi, Vietnam: Thế Giới, 2004); Robert Friend, "Review: *Anthologie de la littérature vietnamienne* by Nguyen Khac Vien, Nguyen Van Hoan, Huu Ngoc, Vu Dinh Lien, Tao Trang," *East and West* 24, nos. 3/4 (September 1974).

12. *A Revolutionary Spirit: Vietnamese Propaganda Art from the Dogma Collection*, exhibition catalog, January 8–18, 2015 (Hanoi: Vietnam Fine Arts Museum, 2015).

13. Mao Tse-tung, "Statement Supporting the American Negroes in Their Just Struggle against Racial Discrimination by U.S. Imperialism of Aug 8, 1963," reprinted in *Peking Review* 9, no. 33 (August 12, 1966): 12–13.

14. See Clyde Taylor, "Black Consciousness and the Vietnam War," *Black Scholar* 5, no. 2 (October 1973): 4.

15. Clyde Taylor, ed., *Vietnam and Black America: An Anthology of Protest and Resistance*, 1st ed. (Garden City, NY: Anchor Press, 1973), 73.

16. Bradford Wright, "The Vietnam War and Comic Books," in *The Vietnam War: A Handbook of the Literature and Research*, ed. James S. Olson, 427–54 (Westport; London: Greenwood Press).

17. Ernst H. Gombrich, "The Cartoonist's Armory," in *Meditations on a Hobby Horse and Other Essays on the Theory of Art* (London: Phaidon, 1963), 132.

18. Mary Louise Pratt, *Imperial Eyes: Travel Writing and Transculturation*, 2nd ed. (London; New York: Routledge, 2008), 28.

19. OSPAAAL produced posters through roughly the mid-1980s until financial austerity led to paper and ink shortages and discontinued further production. In the early 2000s, the organization began reprinting archival posters and granting reproduction rights for publication from its vast and well-maintained print library. See "Ospaaal.com," accessed May 6, 2013, www.ospaaal.com.

20. Production of noncommercial mass poster art was already a bustling arm of the national print media infrastructure in Cuba, having been built up during the revolution roughly a decade prior. See Carlos Francisco Jackson, *Chicana and Chicano Art: ProtestArte, the Mexican American Experience* (Tucson: University of Arizona Press, 2009).

21. Richard Frick, *The Tricontinental Solidarity Poster*, 1st ed. (Bern, Switzerland: Comedia-Verlag, 2003).

22. *Il Manifesto Della OSPAAAL: Arte Della Solidarietà (El Cartel de La OSPAAAL: Arte de La Solidaridad/OSPAAAL's Poster: Art of Solidarity)* (Il Papiro, Italy: Tricontiental, 1997), ix.

23. For a discussion of the differences between the major political and militant groups operating in Vietnam, see Robert K. Brigham, *Guerrilla Diplomacy: The*

NLF's Foreign Relations and the Viet Nam War (Ithaca, NY: Cornell University Press, 1998).

24. From a Vietnam tourism website: "The hat elegantly enhances the sentimental attractiveness of Vietnamese girls because they are mysteriously hidden, showing only their shy blush cheeks and long hair beneath the broad rims of the nón lá. The leaf hat is not only a symbol of Vietnamese girls, but has also become part of the spirit of Vietnam, the nation." See "Vietnam, Vietnam Culture: Leaf Hat," accessed May 7, 2013, www.vietnampeace.com/vietnam/Leaf-hat.html.

25. Igor Kopytoff, "The Cultural Biography of Things: Commoditization as Process," in *The Social Life of Things: Commodities in Cultural Perspective*, ed. Arjun Appadurai (Cambridge: Cambridge University Press, 1986), 89–90.

26. Ibid., 70.

27. Ibid., 67.

28. Ibid., 70.

29. Robert S. Browne, "Is Racism Involved in the Vietnam War?" in *Vietnam and Black America: An Anthology of Protest and Resistance*, 1st ed., ed. Clyde Taylor (Garden City, NY: Anchor Press, 1973), 73.

30. "No War Has a Winner," in Francesco Augusto Razetto, *Vietnam, Plakáty Propagandy [Vietnam, Propaganda posters/Vietnam, Manifesti Di Propaganda]*, exhibition catalog, Národní Galerie Praha (Prague, Czech Republic: Nadacn Fond Eleutheria, 2010), 16.

31. See Mancur Olson, "Logic of Collective Action," in *Social Movements: A Reader*, eds. Vincenzo Ruggiero and Nicola Montagna, 93–94 (London: Routledge, 2008); Sidney Tarrow, "Cycles of Contention," in *Power in Movement: Social Movements, Collective Action, and Politics*, 141–46 (Cambridge: Cambridge University Press, 1994); Donatella della Porta and Mario Diani, "Collective Action and Identity," in *Social Movements: An Introduction*, 83–109 (Oxford: Blackwell, 2006); Sidney Tarrow, "Cycles of Contention," in *Power in Movement: Social Movements, Collective Action, and Politics*, 141–46 (Cambridge: Cambridge University Press, 1994); Mark Irving Lichbach, *The Rebel's Dilemma* (Ann Arbor: University of Michigan Press, 1998); Ashutosh Varshney, "Nationalism, Ethnic Conflict, and Rationality," *Perspectives on Politics* 1, no. 1 (March 2003): 85–99.

32. "Questionnaire," *October* 123 (Winter 2008): 9.

BIBLIOGRAPHY

Allen, Gwen. "Design as a Social Movement." In *Power to the People: The Graphic Design of the Radical Press and the Rise of the Counter-Culture, 1964–1974*, edited by Geoff Kaplan. Chicago: University of Chicago Press, 2012.

Brigham, Robert K. *Guerrilla Diplomacy: The NLF's Foreign Relations and the Viet Nam War*. Ithaca, NY: Cornell University Press, 1998.

Browne, Robert S. "Is Racism Involved in the Vietnam War?" In *Vietnam and Black America: An Anthology of Protest and Resistance*, 1st edition, edited by Clyde Taylor. Garden City, NY: Anchor Press, 1973.

Chamberlin, Paul Thomas. *The Global Offensive: The United States, the Palestine Liberation Organization, and the Making of the Post–Cold War Order*. Oxford Studies in International History. Oxford; New York: Oxford University Press, 2012.

Chomsky, Noam. "The Responsibility of Intellectuals." In *Against the Vietnam War: Writings by Activists*, edited by Mary Susannah Robbins. Syracuse, NY: Syracuse University Press, 1999.

Chong, Sylvia Shin Huey. *The Oriental Obscene: Violence and Racial Fantasies in the Vietnam Era*. Durham, NC: Duke University Press, 2012.

Cleaver, Eldridge, and Black Panther Party. *To My Black Brothers in Viet Nam*. 1970.

Davis, Clyde. "Black Consciousness and the Vietnam War." *Black Scholar* 5, no. 2 (October 1973).

della Porta, Donatella, and Mario Diani. "Collective Action and Identity." In *Social Movements: An Introduction*, 83–109. Oxford: Blackwell, 2006.

Dohrn, Bernadine. "Communiqué #1 from the Weatherman Underground." *Berkeley Tribe*, May 21, 1970. www.freerepublic.com/focus/f-news/2098150/posts.

Foster, Hal. *Return of the Real: Critical Models in Art and Theory since 1960*. Cambridge, MA: MIT Press, 1996.

Frick, Richard. *The Tricontinental Solidarity Poster*, 1st edition. Bern, Switzerland: Comedia-Verlag, 2003.

Friend, Robert. "Review: *Anthologie de la littérature vietnamienne* by Nguyen Khac Vien, Nguyen Van Hoan, Huu Ngoc, Vu Dinh Lien, Tao Trang." *East and West* 24, nos. 3/4 (September 1974).

Goldberg, David Theo. *The Threat of Race: Reflections on Racial Neoliberalism*. Malden, MA: Blackwell, 2009.

Gombrich, Ernst H. *Meditations on a Hobby Horse and Other Essays on the Theory of Art*. London: Phaidon, 1963.

Harris, Michael D. *Colored Pictures: Race and Visual Representation*. Chapel Hill: University of North Carolina Press, 2003.

Huu Ngoc. *Wandering through Vietnamese Culture*, 4th edition. Hanoi, Vietnam: Thế Giới, 2004.

Il Manifesto Della OSPAAAL: Arte Della Solidarietà = El Cartel de La OSPAAAL: Arte de La Solidaridad = OSPAAAL's Poster: Art of Solidarity. Il Paprio, Italy: Tricontinental, 1997.

Jackson, Carlos Francisco. *Chicana and Chicano Art: ProtestArte, the Mexican American Experience*. Tucson: University of Arizona Press, 2009.

Kaplan, Geoff, ed. *Power to the People: The Graphic Design of the Radical Press and the Rise of the Counter-Culture, 1964–1974*. Chicago: University of Chicago Press, 2012.

Kopytoff, Igor. "The Cultural Biography of Things: Commoditization as Process." In *The Social Life of Things: Commodities in Cultural Perspective*, edited by Arjun Appadurai. Cambridge: Cambridge University Press, 1986.

Laclau, Ernesto, and Chantal Mouffe. *Hegemony and Socialist Strategy: Towards a Radical Democratic Politics*. London: Verso, 1985.

Lichbach, Mark Irving. *The Rebel's Dilemma.* Ann Arbor: University of Michigan Press, 1998.

Mao Tse-tung. "Statement Supporting the American Negroes in Their Just Struggle against Racial Discrimination by U.S. Imperialism of Aug 8, 1963." Reprinted in *Peking Review* 9, no. 33 (August 12, 1966): 12–13.

Martin, Susan. "Introduction: The Left Turn." Exhibition catalog. *Track 16 Exhibition: Decade of Protest: Political Posters from the United States, Viet Nam and Cuba, 1965–1975*, March 19, 1996. Accessed May 2013. www2.iath.virginia.edu/sixties/HTML_docs/Exhibits/Track16.html#Viet.

McAdam, Doug, Sidney Tarrow, and Charles Tilly. "Revolutionary Trajectories." In *Dynamics of Contention*, 193–226. New York: Cambridge University Press, 2001.

Mills, Charles. *The Racial Contract.* Ithaca, NY: Cornell University Press, 1999.

Mosquera, Gerardo, and Jean Fisher, eds. *Over Here: International Perspectives on Art and Culture.* Cambridge, MA: MIT Press, 2007.

Mouffe, Chantal. "Strategies of Radical Politics and Aesthetic Resistance." Accessed May 7, 2013. http://truthisconcrete.org/texts/?p=19.

Olson, James S., ed. *The Vietnam War: Handbook of the Literature and Research.* Westport, CT; London: Greenwood Press, 1993.

Olson, Mancur. "Logic of Collective Action." In *Social Movements: A Reader*, edited by Vincenzo Ruggiero and Nicola Montagna, 93–94. London: Routledge, 2008.

Ongiri, Amy Abugo. *Spectacular Blackness: The Cultural Politics of the Black Power Movement and the Search for a Black Aesthetic.* Charlottesville: University of Virginia Press, 2009.

"Ospaaal.com." Accessed May 6, 2013. www.ospaaal.com.

Pratt, Mary Louise. *Imperial Eyes: Travel Writing and Transculturation*, 2nd edition. London; New York: Routledge, 2008.

"Questionnaire." *October* 123 (Winter 2008): 9–10.

Razetto, Francesco Augusto. *Vietnam, Plakty Propagandy [Vietnam, Propaganda posters/Vietnam, Manifesti Di Propaganda].* Exhibition catalog. Prague, Czech Republic: Nadacn Fond Eleutheria, 2010.

"Resolution Adopted by the General Assembly of the United Nations 3379 (XXX): Elimination of All Forms of Racial Discrimination." November 10, 1975. Accessed May 13, 2013. http://unispal.un.org/UNISPAL.NSF/0/761C1063530766A7052566A2005B74D1.

A Revolutionary Spirit: Vietnamese Propaganda Art from the Dogma Collection. January 8–18, 2015. Exhibition catalog. Hanoi: Vietnam Fine Arts Museum, 2015.

Robbins, Mary Susannah, ed. *Against the Vietnam War: Writings by Activists.* Syracuse, NY: Syracuse University Press, 1999.

Said, Edward. *Orientalism.* New York: Vintage Books, 1978.

Sheth, Falguni A. *Toward a Political Philosophy of Race.* Albany, NY: SUNY Press, 2009.

"Supplemental Foreign Assistance, Fiscal Year, 1966—Vietnam: Hearings before the Committee on Foreign Relations, United States Senate, Eighty-Ninth Congress, Second Session, on S. 2793, to Amend Further the Foreign Assistance Act of 1961, as Amended: January 28, February 4, 8, 10, 17 and 18, 1966." Washington, DC: U.S. Government Publishing Office, 1966.

Tarrow, Sidney. "Cycles of Contention." In *Power in Movement: Social Movements, Collective Action, and Politics*, 141–46. Cambridge: Cambridge University Press, 1994.

Taylor, Clyde. "Black Consciousness and the Vietnam War." *Black Scholar* 5, no. 2 (October 1973): 4.

———. *Vietnam and Black America: An Anthology of Protest and Resistance*. Garden City, NY: Anchor Press, 1973.

Varshney, Ashutosh. "Nationalism, Ethnic Conflict, and Rationality." *Perspectives on Politics* 1, no. 1 (March 2003): 85–99.

"Vietnam, Vietnam Culture: Leaf Hat." Accessed May 7, 2013. www.vietnampeace.com/vietnam/Leaf-hat.html.

Wright, Bradford. "The Vietnam War and Comic Books." In *The Vietnam War: A Handbook of the Literature and Research*, edited by James S. Olson, 427–54. Westport, CT; London: Greenwood Press.

Young, Marilyn Blatt. *The Vietnam Wars: 1945–1990*. New York: HarperCollins, 1991.

Young, Marilyn Blatt, and Mark Bradley. *Making Sense of the Vietnam Wars: Local, National, and Transnational Perspectives*. Oxford; New York: Oxford University Press, 2008.

5

❖❖

Ethiopia Tiqdem?

The Influence of the Mythic, Protest, and Red Terror Periods on Ethiopian Pan-Africanism

Meron Wondwosen

The heat was palpable, that July haze seemingly visible and rising from the sidewalk. It was 1935 and while it wasn't the record-setting scorcher that would be the summer of the following year, it was still a sweltering July in New York City. Yet there they were, under the scalding sun, the men wearing their suits and hats, the women in dresses, skirts, and bonnets, fanning themselves. There they were, hundreds of Black[1] men and women, spilling from the wide concrete pavement onto the street. They stood shoulder to shoulder, squeezing together; their rage and their energy, too, were palpable. These African descendants stood for hours in long lines in Harlem, New York, some 6,957 miles away from Addis Ababa, to register to fight on Ethiopian soil against an invading Italian army.

This historic—and unprecedented—galvanization was one of several across the globe, from Europe to the Caribbean to southern Africa, in support of Ethiopia, the only continuously independent African country. People of African descent across the Diaspora organized to arm themselves and defend Ethiopia from a European colonial power. Their actions precisely emphasized the African country's importance to the Diaspora. For centuries, Ethiopia as both a nation and a concept representing freedom has captured the imagination of people of African descent.[2]

For Africans in the Diaspora, brutally stripped of their lands, languages, and cultures, the phenomenon of Ethiopia denoted the majesty of the Black race and the struggle for liberation. Much of Ethiopia's revered status can be traced to three factors: the country's preeminent presence in the Bible, its historical resistance to colonization, and its defeat of Italy at the Battle of Adwa in 1896. When Italy invaded Ethiopia in 1935, the Diaspora relied on Ethiopia's historical significance to rally support against the invasion. The African Diaspora's response was swift and demonstrated the power of Pan-Africanism. Although Italy occupied Ethiopia for five years during World War II, the tremendous response from the Diaspora highlighted Ethiopia's importance. Forty years after the 1935 invasion, an authoritarian Marxist regime would ruthlessly rule Ethiopia from the mid-1970s to 1991. The Diaspora's response to the Marxist revolution contrasted sharply, lacking the intensity and the passion that followed the Italian invasion. In turn, the Marxist revolution almost irrevocably changed the country's perception and its historical iconography and altered its Pan-African trajectory.

Considering this history, public representations of Ethiopia for the better part of the twentieth century were rooted in Pan-African ideology that linked Ethiopia's independence with the liberation of Africans in the Diaspora. Symbols representing Ethiopia, while evolving through various historical periods, remained tied to African liberation. Within the last century, representations of Ethiopia unfolded in three distinct periods, each exhibiting a different depiction of the country and its relationship with the Diaspora. This relationship mainly crystallized Ethiopia as Zion, a utopian home for Africans, and Ethiopia as a symbol of resistance and liberation. Images reflecting these two themes were embedded within the psyche of the African Diaspora for centuries. Yet these depictions of Ethiopia that had survived through different eras were undone within two decades, when a third theme—one of famine and poverty—would emerge within the last thirty years. In this last period, the term *Ethiopia* is removed from its historical definition. Thus, the country since the late 1970s has been synonymous with destitution and underdevelopment—definitions at odds with its rich history, which promoted African pride and independence. This shift in the identification of Ethiopia from a cultural and movement icon to a poverty-stricken nation is explored in the images representing Ethiopia beginning in the late 1800s through 1991.

This chapter will explore public representations, including artistic representations of Ethiopia, during three critical periods: after the Battle of Adwa in 1896, referred to as the "Mythical Period"; during the Italian invasion in 1935, referred to as the "Protest Period"; and during the Marxist revolution in the 1980s, referred to as the "Red Terror Period." Each of these three periods represents a distinct relationship between Ethiopia and Pan-Africanism. The common thread woven between the various periods is the relationship between Ethiopia and the Diaspora through Pan-Africanism.

The Pan-African movement emerged from *Ethiopianism*, a concept that "predict[ed] a 'bright' future for people of African descent and assert[ed] a common heritage shared by Africans and African Americans."[3] With deep biblical roots, Ethiopianism is seen as "a religious-political concept of race revival."[4] It is "a distinctly black nationalist idea. . . . [A] biblically derived myth of black nationality and destiny, it identifies all people of African descent with Ethiopia of the Bible, a respected black land in antiquity, and ordains global black redemption from the sovereignty of all other races."[5] Accordingly, through this movement, Black churches across the Diaspora sought the "establishment of Christian churches according to African ideals, methods and objectives, by and for Africans."[6] In general, themes associated with Ethiopianism were "expressed in three forms: millenarian, migratory and emancipatory."[7] Most relevant to the discussions of this chapter is the "emancipatory" theme and, by extension, how in each of the aforementioned periods Pan-Africanism was either supported or hindered by public representations of Ethiopia.

Pan-Africanism, as a theory and a movement, has many proponents and strains of thoughts. In defining *Pan-Africanism*, this author adopts a description provided by Professor St. Clair Drake, the preeminent scholar and chronicler of social movements. He defines *Pan-Africanism* as "the idea that Africans and people of African descent in the New World should develop racial solidarity for the purpose of dismantling discrimination, enforced segregation and political and economic exploitation of Negroes through the world."[8] This chapter expands the discussion to include a Pan-Africanism that utilizes the cultural and artistic expressions of a global African identity to further liberation movements. Therefore, Pan-Africanism within this chapter necessarily implicates an emancipatory ethos that is explored in three periods in Ethiopian history. In each period, the question is whether Pan-Africanism is present in the public representation of Ethiopia and how, if at all, these representations hindered or supported liberation movements.

"ETHIOPIA SHALL SOON STRETCH FORTH HER HANDS UNTO GOD"

Ethiopia's historical resistance to colonialism established the country's exalted status. Accordingly, the prevailing image of Ethiopia in the 1800s was of a sovereign nation symbolizing resistance to colonialism. The term *Ethiopia* embodied more than the country; in fact, the name was used by many in the Diaspora to generally mean "African" or "Black." Poets, writers, and artists, including Phillis Wheatley, identified as "an Ethiop."[9]

Descriptions of Africans, including in popular publications and in comic strips, referred to Black men and women as Ethiopians. Paul Lawrence Dunbar penned his poem "Ode to Ethiopia"[10] and Black churches adopted names such as "Abyssinia" or "Ethiopia."[11] Several newspapers, including the *Colored Tennessean* and the New Orleans *Black Republican*, used the oft-cited biblical psalm "Ethiopia shall soon stretch forth her hands unto God" on the design of their masthead. In his paper, the *North Star*, Frederick Douglass reminded his readers that "Ethiopia is always mentioned in ancient Mythology with the highest deference, such as could be due to a nation far exceeding the rest in its religion and merit."[12]

Bolstering Ethiopia's historical resistance to colonialism is the country's exalted presence in a biblical psalm interpreted as advocating liberation. For abolitionists, the term *Ethiopia* and the inspirational Psalms 68:31 formed the basis for an aggressive and proactive fight for liberation. The psalm pronouncing that "Ethiopia shall soon stretch forth her hands unto God" explicitly signifies more than a biblical phrase placed on newspapers or alluded to from the church's pulpit. Accordingly "the speeches and sermons of black dignitaries celebrating the abolition of the Atlantic slave trade show an early tendency in Black spiritual circles to apply the Ethiopian passage to the political condition of African Americans."[13] Thus, *Ethiopianism*'s emancipatory theme is evident in how Blacks appropriated the Ethiopia psalm in the fight for their human rights. In a letter to Frederick Douglass, his friend J. M. Glouchester evokes the language of battle and war as he discusses the fight for freedom as "advocating by means, by voice, by moral and intellectual worth and loveliness—using the weapons that God and the Right have placed in our power."[14] He concludes his letter by adding, "Armored for freedom, with the God of freedom, shall battle . . . and we shall be victorious. . . . All of our kindred, shall come out of the house of bondage—Ethiopia shall lift up her unfettered, redeemed hands unto God!"[15] Invoking the Ethiopia psalm, abolitionists interpreted it as a call for Africans to fight for their liberation, rather than one imploring them to wait patiently. Indeed, "by the mid-nineteenth century, Ethiopia was no longer functioning as a nostalgic place of origin for enslaved African Americans, but emerging as a place of Black solidarity, on the one hand, and the foil of American slavery, on the other."[16] Thus Ethiopia's anointing in the Bible combined with its independence amplified the Italian defeat.

THE MYTHICAL PERIOD: ETHIOPIANISM

In the Mythical Period, which extends from the Battle of Adwa in 1896 until 1935, Ethiopia was a state of mind encapsulating the hopes of African people. During this period, "the idea of Ethiopia [was] a source of spiritual and political armor and creativity."[17] This notion was symbolized by Ethiopia's defeat of Italy. Adwa served as a metaphor for the African Diaspora and Ethiopia's victory was tied to the Diaspora's liberation. Consequently, the Ethiopian triumph "heralded the prized view that the colonial enterprise was, after all, not indomitable."[18] Adwa was therefore more than a battle; in fact Adwa "was venerated because it delivered a decisive body blow to the colonial myth of European invincibility."[19] Henceforth, Ethiopia became synonymous with that body blow.

The Italian defeat solidified Ethiopia's mythic image, and public representation of the country in the post-Adwa period included paintings, sculptures, and plays depicting the country romantically and mythically.[20] These symbols of Ethiopia celebrated the country's independence and linked the Adwa victory to the struggles of Africans in the Diaspora. Specifically, the victory at Adwa was seen as a harbinger for the liberation of all Africans[21] and brought to fruition the prophecy in Psalms 68:31. In fact, beyond symbolism, Ethiopia's place in the imagination of the Diaspora supported an emerging Pan-African movement. Adwa was significant "because of its inspirational value as a meaningful prelude and stimulus to a budding African liberation movement of ideas."[22] Hence, the events at Adwa informed the public representations of the country. In turn, the imagery, symbolism, and art galvanized Africans and supported the struggle for liberation. The defeat of a European colonial power "signified an imminent racial resurgence, and the far off country became henceforth an icon for African independence and a source of racial self-assurance."[23]

The Mythical Period coincides with the era of legalized segregation and second-class citizenship for Blacks in the United States. This was exemplified by "separate but equal" laws, the stripping of the few political rights gained during Reconstruction, and violence to maintain white rule. In the midst of this grim reality, the defeat of a colonial European power by Continental Africans was more than symbolic; Adwa was a tangible historical victory exemplifying the African struggle for liberation. The victory led to the resurgence in racial pride and the assertion of fundamental rights.[24] Ethiopia and, in this particular time, Adwa served to connect the plight of Africans across continents—the fight to ward off colonialism in the Horn of Africa and the struggle for human rights following the legal end of slavery in the United States were inextricably linked. In this manner "[the] commemoration of a mythological Ethiopia creates a framework for the performance of [Black] American community that transcends the political borders of the United States."[25] For Africans in the United States, Adwa allowed for a celebration of African independence and for envisioning a defeat of racist policies at home. In the bourgeoning Pan-African movement, the connection between the oppression of Africans on the continent and those of the Diaspora was evident: the same power structure that benefited from the slave trade and the continuation of racist policies sought to rid Africa of its only remaining independent country.

The link between Ethiopia and the Diaspora's struggle for freedom is evident in the paintings, sculptures, and plays of the Mythical Period. In the public artistic representations of this period, the term *Ethiopia* referred generally to Blacks or Africans. In each of the three pieces discussed below—a play, a sculpture, and a painting—a Black woman represents Ethiopia. In addition, each representation alludes to the same themes: (a) Ethiopia represents Africans in general and the invocation of that term is synonymous with racial uplift, (b) a celebration of African history, and (c) a determination to work toward a "brighter future," as envisioned by Ethiopianism. The three pieces discussed below demonstrate a concerted, if not coordinated, effort by artists and scholars of the time period to portray a certain image of Africa and Africans. That image—a romantic and mythic Ethiopia—is used to reenergize and "awaken" Blacks by invoking their history and compelling them to ascend from their current circumstances to freedom.

W. E. B. Du Bois—*The Star of Ethiopia* (1913)

Historian and proponent of the concept of Ethiopianism, W. E. B. Du Bois, along with Carter G. Woodson and other scholars, was engaged in a tactical effort to convey racial solidarity and raise consciousness through education about the accomplishments of Africans.[26] Woodson introduced Black History Month and Du Bois employed many avenues, including the NAACP publication titled *Crisis*, to achieve these goals.

Seizing on the interest in pageants during that period, Du Bois also employed the play *The Star of Ethiopia* as an educational tool on Black history.[27] In his ambitious play, the term *Ethiopia* encompasses the history of Continental and Diaspora Africans. Concretely, Du Bois wrote "the pageant with Pan-Africanism in mind,"[28] and it was seen as "the most patent, expansive use yet made by Du Bois of an ideology of black supremacy in order to confound one of white supremacy."[29] Through the pageant, Du Bois made a determined effort "to claim an historical past and affirm a national culture,"[30] both of which are "important to the psycho-affective equilibrium of a people."[31] Thus *The Star of Ethiopia* was an illustration of Du Bois's claim that all art is propaganda and the purpose of his art was the promotion of the Black race. His Pan-African pageant served as an intellectual and political armor, fulfilling Du Bois's vision of melding art and politics with the goal of uplifting the race.

The Star of Ethiopia was a historical pageant, depicting ancient African civilizations and Black contributions. The pageant "celebrated black uniqueness."[32] Beginning in 1913, Du Bois used hundreds of, and at times one thousand, cast members to produce the play four times in four different cities.[33] The premiere show was in New York City in October 1913.[34] The play used history, music, dance, costumes, and pageantry to impart the story of African descendants in the United States in six parts: "The Gift of Iron," "The Gift of Civilization," "The Gift of Faith," "The Gift of Humiliation" (slavery), "The Gift of Struggle towards Freedom," and "The Gift of Freedom." These six scenes provided reenactments of critical events in Black history, including the Middle Passage, slavery, the struggle for freedom, Reconstruction, and the conditions of Blacks in the United States at the time of the play.

The pageant references both Mythical Ethiopia and the emancipatory themes of Ethiopianism. Throughout the play, Du Bois references emancipation by using themes of the awakening and resurrection. The pageant portrays "the black race writh[ing] back to life and hope . . . on which the Star of Ethiopia gleams forever."[35] Du Bois chose a Black woman to depict Ethiopia and to represent the struggles of Africans throughout history. Portrayed as a veiled woman and as "Ethiopia, Mother of Men," the Black woman begins the march of historic proceedings.[36] She symbolizes Africa as the "Mother of All Men" and represents the history of humanity. Furthermore, the Black woman (Ethiopia) was present through the journey from the African continent, through the horrors of the Middle Passage to the Americas. Du Bois describes the Black woman as having "followed the race from Africa to the New World."[37] The reference to Ethiopia as a Black woman is particularly daunting when viewed in the context of a mother watching her children (Africans), born of a majestic legacy, suffer through a transatlantic slave trade. The Black woman, by following Africans from the continent, continues the link between the continent and the "New World." The Black woman and therefore Ethiopia is the connection between the two worlds, first by representing Africa and second by her presence during all aspects of African history.

Throughout the pageant, Du Bois continually pays homage to Ethiopia. He includes classical references to Ethiopia including two selections from Giuseppe Verdi's *Aida*, an opera written about an Ethiopian princess who is enslaved in Egypt. He also includes two of the most well-known queens of Ethiopia, Sheba and Candance (or Makeda). In addition, in presenting the history of Blacks in this pageant, Du Bois used various titles for the play, including *The People of the Peoples and Their Gifts to the World* as well as *The Jewel of Faith* and *The Jewel of Ethiopia*, before settling on *The Star of Ethiopia* as the final title. Du Bois's choice of Ethiopia to represent Africa and a Black woman to depict Ethiopia is emulated by other artists and other art forms, two of which are discussed below.

Finally, Du Bois's pageant was revolutionary in that it portrays African history from a Black perspective, ensuring that Africans, including Black freedom fighters, are credited for their own liberation.[38] *The Star of Ethiopia* was also Pan-Africanist in its presentation and portrayal of African history—it draws from the inextricable link between the African continent and the Diaspora. In the years surrounding the pageant, Du Bois would organize three Pan-African congresses in 1919, 1921, and 1923.[39] Therefore, while Du Bois's use of Ethiopia in his play is homage to the mythic image of the country, his invocation of Africa's history was a deliberate pedagogical and unifying effort.

Meta Warrick Fuller—*Ethiopia Awakening* (1914)

Similar to *The Star of Ethiopia*, Meta Warrick Fuller's sculpture *Ethiopia Awakening* (figure 5.1) also uses the mythical image of Ethiopia to depict the rise of Africans. As with Du Bois's pageant, Fuller's sculpture depicts a Black woman referred to as "Ethiopia" who also represents all Africans. Again, the country is depicted as a woman, and while some scholars may view this trope as the "hackneyed image of Africa-as-mother"[40] in recounting a tale of Africans stripped from their lands, the use of a woman and by extension a mother is powerful imagery.

Acknowledging ancient Egypt, the other African nation that served as an inspiration to Blacks,[41] the woman in Fuller's sculpture is adorned in a headdress generally associated with ancient Egypt. The Black woman is swathed in bandages; although her lower half appears tightly wrapped and restricted, her upper half is portrayed as unwrapping.[42] The emancipatory theme of Ethiopianism is also evident in this sculpture, where the Black woman is depicted as escaping bondage. Since she represents Ethiopia, which in turn represents all Africans, the sculpture portends a reality in which Africans escape bondage. The figure is *awakening*; therefore, the sculpture "clearly references [the Ethiopian] Psalms 68:31, with her rendering of the figure's hand breaking free from the bindings."[43] The placement of her head (turned) and her hand (raised) "implies the artist's understanding of what Ethiopia denoted within and without the African American community. It seems that Fuller recognized a new sense of Africa in the black imagination: her awakening from a deep slumber, during which she was overtaken by slavery and colonialism."[44] In that sense, *Ethiopia Awakening* also connotes a "resurrection" of Blacks from the darkness of slavery and a call to challenge Jim Crow.

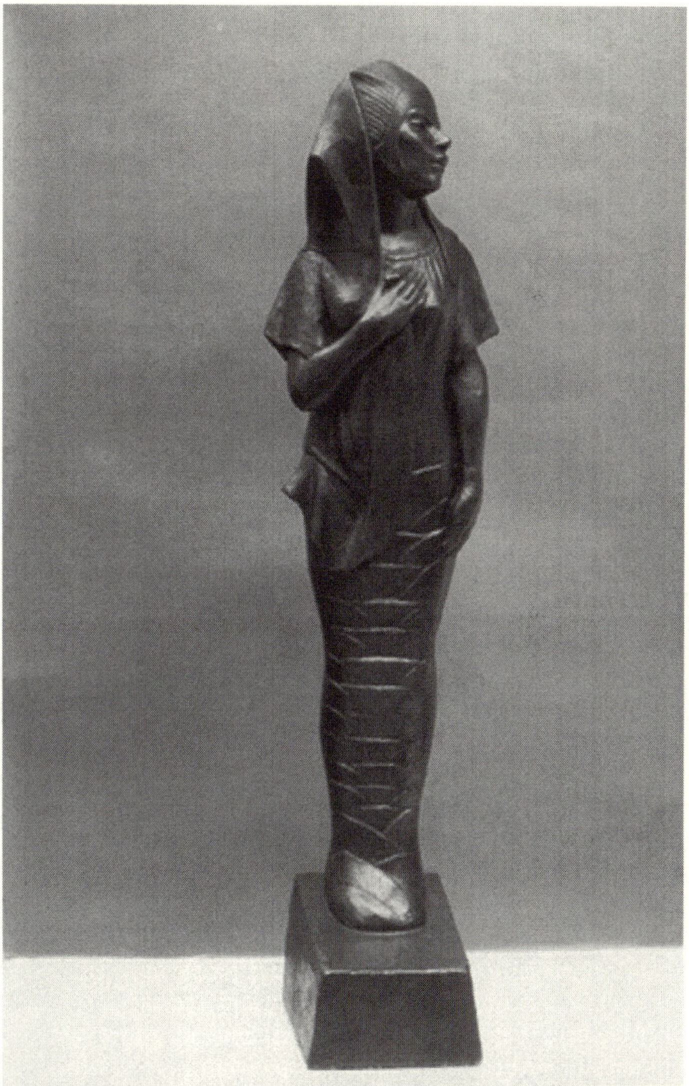

Figure 5.1. Meta Warrick Fuller's sculpture, *Ethiopia Awakening*. (Courtesy of New York Public Library Photographs.)

Fuller's sculpture also fits within the aforementioned efforts by Black historians and scholars to counter racist images and perception of Blacks, instill racial pride, and raise the consciousness of Africans.[45] The sculpture "embodied these new conceptualizations with its references to ancient Egypt and to *Ethiopianism*; Fuller's awakening black woman indicated a nation reclaiming its rightful place in history and asserting racial pride."[46] Although some contend that Fuller's "signature piece, Ethiopia Awakening . . . focuses on racial uplift rather than protest,"[47] the title of the sculpture itself denotes a protest. The sense of awakening conveys uplift, awareness, and consciousness. As such that very sense of racial awareness and awakening is counter to the notion of a people who are beleaguered under a sustained attack of white supremacy. Furthermore, Fuller's reference to Ethiopia—a symbol of defiance—is a protest against the negative perceptions of Blacks. *Ethiopia Awakening* highlights a dignified Black woman and therefore a dignified Black race that is rising out of its slumber.

Lois Mailou Jones—*The Ascent of Ethiopia* (1932)

Lois Mailou Jones's painting *The Ascent of Ethiopia* (figure 5.2) continues the theme of racial progress and of Ethiopia representing Africans. The painting prominently displays a journey by people of African descent. Central to the painting is a large depiction of a Black woman representing Ethiopia. Similar to the Fuller sculpture, this figure is also wearing an Egyptian headdress and resembles the Sphinx. Thus, *The Ascent of Ethiopia* is a description not of the rise of indigenous Ethiopians alone but of the journey of all Africans from the continent, through the Middle Passage, to the Americas, through slavery, freedom from slavery, and ultimately upward to liberation. The painting recalls Du Bois's *The Star of Ethiopia* in its depiction of the journey and the history of Africans from the continent to the "New World." In Jones's painting, this journey is represented by Black figures ascending a series of steps. The piece also prominently displays the iconic North Star. This constellation, followed by enslaved Africans to route their escape to freedom, has long been associated with liberation and has served as its symbol, most notably as the name of Frederick Douglass's newspaper.

Jones's painting also highlights the important role of the arts in the life of Africans and in the history of liberation. Similar to Du Bois, Jones uses art to pay homage to the history of Africans, and in this piece, she portrays art as symbolizing liberation. Jones's painting includes the words *art*, *brushes*, and *paint*, as well as portions of the word *drama*, which is represented by *dra* and masks. The painting also depicts portions of the word *music*, represented by *mu* as well as music notes.

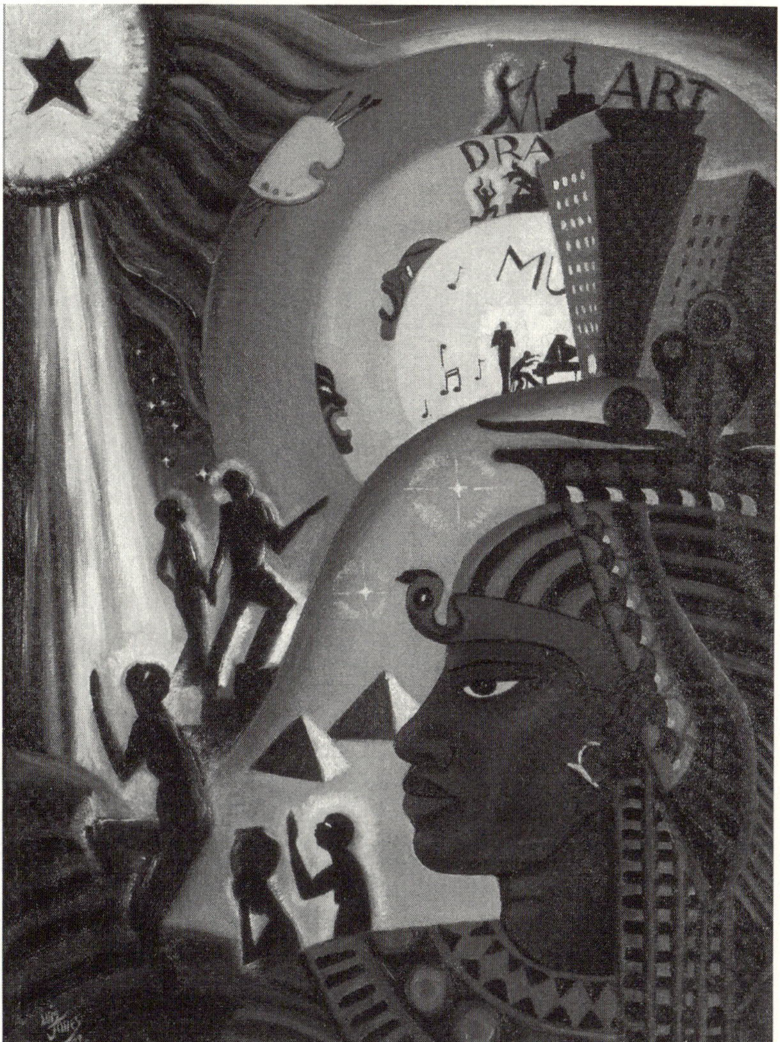

Figure 5.2. Lois Mailou Jones (American, 1905–1998), *The Ascent of Ethiopia*, 1932. Oil on canvas. 23.5 × 17.25 in. (59.69 × 43.82 cm). Milwaukee Art Museum, Purchase, African American Art Acquisition Fund, matching funds from Suzanne and Richard Pieper, with additional support from Arthur and Dorothy Nelle Sanders. M1993.191. (Photo credit: John R. Glembin. Lois Mailou Jones Pierre-Noel Trust. Courtesy of the Milwaukee Art Museum.)

Du Bois's pageant, Fuller's sculpture, and Jones's painting represent three different genres of art that reference Ethiopianism and promote racial pride and Pan-Africanism. These three pieces also inspired one another—Fuller was influenced by Du Bois's play and his interpretation of Africa as a Black woman. Du Bois was a friend and a mentor to Fuller.[48] In turn, Fuller, whose African heritage is reflected in her art, studied under the famed French sculptor Auguste Rodin; she mentored Jones, advising her to follow in her path and study in Paris.[49] Jones's *The Ascent of Ethiopia* was inspired by Fuller's *Ethiopia Awakening*.[50]

It would be remiss to dismiss the Mythical Period as empty symbolism. The importance of symbolism and artistic representations of freedom are well established in the annals of African liberation theory.[51] Black artists and activists were "cognizant of the special significance of symbols to an oppressed people."[52] Indeed, the use of art and symbolism fits within a "longstanding and conscience tactic of African American leaders and activists during the postbellum era to use aural and visual means to reach the black masses."[53]

The public artistic representations of Ethiopia during the Mythical Period ultimately served two objectives. First, they were used to educate, uplift, and raise the consciousness of Blacks in the Diaspora. Second, they also sustained the image of *Ethiopia* as a hallowed space for people of African descent. Thus each of the three pieces precisely capture the mythical era: the representation of Ethiopia "creates a perspective on the present, past and future of black experience, configuring the memory of a black public."[54] It is this very memory that heralded the tremendous response from the Diaspora in defense of the country following the Italian attack on Ethiopia at the onset of the Second World War.

PROTEST PERIOD: THREAT TO "MYTHICAL ETHIOPIA"

The coronation of Haile Selassie as emperor of Ethiopia in the 1930s may be considered the pinnacle of the Mythical Period. He was a prophesized Black king of the only continuously independent African nation, whose rule and name, Ras Tafari, would serve as inspiration for a Jamaican religious movement that proclaimed Ethiopia as Zion. The Mythical Period was interrupted in 1935 with Italy's second attack on Ethiopia, almost forty years after the Battle of Adwa. With this attack, the mythic image of Ethiopia was shattered and the country's historical standing was threatened, thereby ushering in a new era of public representations of Ethiopia in the African Diaspora—the Protest Period. In this era, the bourgeoning

Pan-African movement galvanized and expressed international solidarity with Ethiopia. The public representations of Ethiopia in this period drew on the images of Mythical Ethiopia to inform the Diaspora's response to the Italian attack. These representations included demonstrations and protests, organizing and mobilization drives, protest poetry, and music. This era differs from the Mythical Period in that the public representations were based on activities aimed at destroying or curbing the attack on Ethiopia physically and on the Mythical Period theoretically. Ethiopia is therefore viewed "as a community bound together through shared experiences in political and mythical time. This temporal framework recollects the dispersed elements of the African Diaspora, providing a framework for understanding transnational black community."[55] Such a community, one that extends beyond the boundaries of the United States, allowed Africans in the United States to express their solidarity with Ethiopians through their actions.

While the term *Ethiopia* in the Mythical Period denoted all Africans, in the Protest Period, when the territorial integrity of the country was under attack, *Ethiopia* in the songs, poems, demonstrations, and petition drives referred to the indigenous people and their land. It was the collective "Ethiopians" of the Diaspora who organized to defend the country from the Italian invasion. Newspapers from Black communities in the United States zealously reported on all aspects of the war and many editorials urged Blacks to support the Ethiopian cause. The response from the Diaspora was swift and tremendous and evident in the public representations. From scholars to organizers to ordinary citizens, Blacks were energized. One of the most vocal supporters of the cause of Ethiopia was Langston Hughes, who penned poems including "Broadcast on Ethiopia" and "Call on Ethiopia"—which served as the *cris de coeur* for the movement.

In addition to defending the territorial integrity of Ethiopia, the public representations sought to galvanize Africans in the Diaspora by invoking Mythical Ethiopia. Accordingly, Black experiences with racism and segregation in the United States were linked with the fascist attack on Ethiopia. In connecting the two experiences, the Protest Period also introduced a new art genre in commemoration of Ethiopia. Blues, a musical form that was borne out of the Black experience in the United States and typically conveyed messages of spirituality, love, heartbreak, and struggle, was used to condemn the attack on Ethiopia. A protest song titled "Cockeyed World" by blues artist Minnie Wallace was released ten days after the Italian invasion. The song, which laments the attack on Ethiopia and the possibility of the singer's loved one leaving her to join the war effort, includes the lyrics "it's war on Ethiopia and mama's feeling blue."[56] The singer, who was from Jackson, Mississippi, mourns the Italian attack, which to Africans in the United States was the ultimate expression of white aggression against Blacks.[57] Thus an art form, which is borne out of the quintessential experience of African descendants in the United States, is used to draw the link between the colonial aggression on the African continent and the racist atrocities committed against Blacks at home. These artistic public representations, including protest poems and songs, set the stage for the activities conducted in the Protest Period. Discussed below are two photographs that depict actions undertaken in support of Ethiopia in this period.

"We Protest Murders by Fascist Troops in Addis Ababa"

In addition to public artistic representations, Africans in the United States also engaged in social protests and mobilized to show their solidarity with Ethiopia. In Harlem, "African American rage about the Ethiopian crisis was publicly displayed."[58] For many, this rage was channeled into actions, including forming groups in support of Ethiopia. For instance, at City College in New York City, students formed a "Defense Group for Ethiopia."[59] Blacks in the United States also boycotted Italian-owned shops and held protests against the invasion.[60] In May 1936, a protest picketed the Italian consulate in New York City (figure 5.3). Photographs depict a multiracial

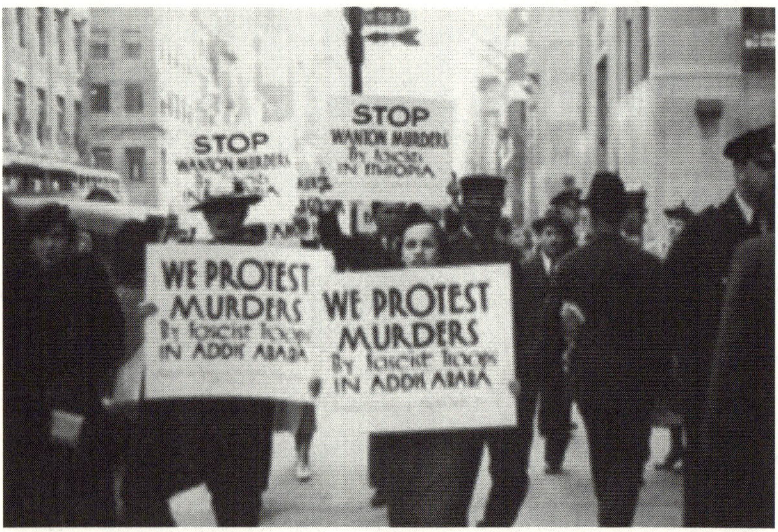

Figure 5.3. Members of the American League Against War and Fascism picket the Italian Consulate on Fifth Avenue, New York, protesting against the brutality of the Italian troops during their invasion of Abyssinia, May 1936. (Photo by FPG/Hulton Archive/Getty Images.)

group holding placards and signs declaring, "We protest murders by fascist troops in Addis Ababa" and "Stop wanton murders by fascists in Ethiopia." The sentiments expressed in the pictures denouncing the attacks were not limited to protests in the United States. In Paris, Diaspora Africans held rallies in support of Ethiopia.[61] Protests also took place in other countries in the Caribbean, including St. Kitts, Barbados, Guyana, and Trinidad.[62]

"Hands off Ethiopia" Campaign

Black communists also organized on behalf of the Ethiopian cause. Two such supporters were Harry Haywood and Oliver Law, who formed a "Hands off Ethiopia" campaign in Chicago. City officials had refused to grant a permit to the duo's Defense of Ethiopia Committee's request to hold a parade denouncing the attack on Ethiopia.[63] In refusing the permit, the mayor of Chicago indicated that the parade would be offensive to Italy, which was considered a powerful ally.[64] In reality, city officials were cognizant of the links that Africans would make between their struggles on the Southside of Chicago and those of the Ethiopians.[65] To discourage the Black masses from organizing, the city banned the anti-fascist parade. Organizers responded by holding demonstrations where they wore T-shirts declaring "Down with Mussolini" and "Hands off Ethiopia."[66]

When the Hands off Ethiopia campaign held its rally, police arrested many participants and in the process attacked and brutalized some of the protestors. One of those arrested was Haywood, who in his biography describes how he was giving a speech on Ethiopia when the police brutally struck his head with batons and dragged him off the stage. In his speech, Haywood was likening the denial of the parade permit by city officials to Mussolini's fascist tactics, continuously linking the plight of Africans in the United States with Ethiopia.[67]

"Register for Ethiopia"

The commitment to support Ethiopia extended beyond boycotts and demonstrations. In Harlem, Blacks organized registration drives (figure 5.4) and solicited volunteers to fight on behalf of Ethiopia. One of the most profound images of this period is that of hundreds of Black men and women in queues waiting to register to join the war effort in Ethiopia. The U.S. State Department declared that the petition drives would result in a fine of $2,000, as well as imprisonment, and pose a threat to one's citizenship.[68] Despite such threats directed at Black citizens, there were no repercussions for Fiorello La Guardia, who would serve as mayor of New York City, despite his "tenure in the Italian army 15 years" prior to the Harlem registration drives.[69] Moreover, while prohibited from fighting in Africa, Blacks from the United States fought against Franco's fascist regime in Spain, thereby prompting one such fighter to allegedly exclaim, "It ain't Ethiopia, but it will do."[70] Yet the U.S. State Department declared that registering to fight on behalf of Ethiopia presented a threat to the citizenship of Blacks—a group whose tenuous rights of citizenship in the United States (including voting rights and the right to be free of discrimination) had yet to be solidified by the highest court of the land. Indeed, the Supreme Court would not overturn the infamous *Plessy v. Ferguson* case until twenty years after the beginning of the Protest Period, in the landmark 1954 *Brown v. Board of Education* case. Thus barred from physically fighting in Africa, Diaspora Africans collected supplies and funds bound for Ethiopia.

The interest in fighting on behalf of Ethiopia was not limited to Blacks in Harlem or in the United States. In Guyana, a group of Africans petitioned the British Crown to volunteer to fight on behalf of Ethiopia.[71] Similarly, South Africans also requested permission to join the fight against the Italians in Ethiopia.[72] None of these requests were granted. Yet, despite the inability of Blacks in the Diaspora to physically assist

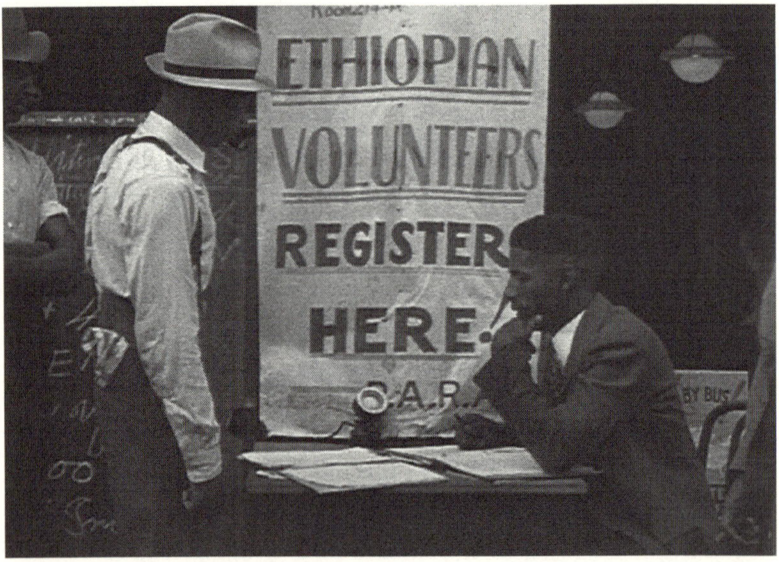

Figure 5.4. People of African descent register themselves as Ethiopian volunteers in New York for the war effort against Italy's invasion of Ethiopia in 1936. (Courtesy of Critical Past LLC.)

Ethiopia, two pilots from the United States arrived on Ethiopian soil for humanitarian purposes—Hurbert Fauntleroy Julian ("Black Eagle") and John C. Robinson ("Brown Condor").[73] In fact, as evidence of the cooperation between Diaspora Africans and Ethiopians, Robinson, originally from the Southside of Chicago, is credited with assisting in the development of the Ethiopian air force.[74]

The mobilization of the Diaspora in support of Ethiopia was a clear expression of Pan-Africanism. Indeed, "no event in recent times stirred the rank and file of Negroes than the Italian-Ethiopian War."[75] This sentiment expressed the enormity of not only the invasion but also the groundswell of support for the movement. Witnessing the lack of U.S. government assistance to Ethiopia, which even barred Blacks from fighting, many Blacks felt compelled to defend Ethiopia since the lack of support was attributed to Ethiopia's race. The overwhelming sentiment was that "[the United States] won't do more for Ethiopia than she will do to stop [white] mob rule in the south."[76] Thus, Ethiopia's fate of defending itself against a colonial attack is tied with the Black struggle against Jim Crow in the Diaspora. Even as the public representations sought to support indigenous Ethiopians, the Diaspora's response placed the Italian aggression within the larger context of the struggle of Africans in the United States. Accordingly, groups that were established for the aid of Ethiopia, such as the Ethiopian World Federation, "lobbied for anti-lynching legislation,"[77] thereby linking the cause of Ethiopian liberation with that of the Diaspora through a concrete effort to combat lynching, a genocidal practice and policy in the United States.

The Diaspora's support of Ethiopia during the Protest Period encouraged and furthered Pan-Africanism. Indeed, "the Italian fascist invasion of Ethiopia became the rallying ground of Pan-African nationalism."[78] These activities formed a cohesive effort, confronting the Italian attack. Although ultimately not successful in thwarting the Italian occupation,[79] the tremendous response from the Diaspora strengthened Pan-Africanism. The public representations of this era demonstrated these efforts and ultimately documented how the image of Ethiopia in the Protest Period supported Pan-Africanism. Yet these iconic representations of Ethiopia—first as mythical and then as defiant in the face of fascist aggression during the Protest Period—would disintegrate and be replaced with one wholly inconsistent with its history. In fact, the public representations of Ethiopia—artistic and otherwise—in the latter part of the twentieth century could be captured in two words: Red Terror—*red* to denote Marxism and bloodshed, and *terror* to denote the human rights crisis of the 1980s.

RED TERROR PERIOD: THE MARXIST REVOLUTION

The imperial period of Ethiopia ended with social unrest stemming from "recurring drought and growing economic disparity between the wealthy elite and subsistence-farming majority."[80] As a result, Emperor Haile Selassie's government was overthrown in 1974 by a Marxist revolution that was supported by a broad coalition. Yet this support for the revolution waned as the military controlled all aspects of Ethiopian life under the guise of reordering society to align with Marxist ideals. The revolution ushered in almost twenty years of brutal reprisals, disappearances, and despotic rule. Perversely, the motto of revolutionary Ethiopia[81] was *yaale menem dem, Ethiopia tiqdem* ("without the shedding of any blood, let Ethiopia advance"). The term *Red Terror* refers to the Ethiopian government's campaign aimed at exposing "reactionaries" and enemies of the revolution.[82] In reality, innocent civilians were imprisoned, disappeared, and murdered without any evidence of subversive or treasonous activity. The disastrous policies of the government resulted in a massive human rights crisis: the severe famines of the 1980s. In this section, the "Red Terror Period" encompasses the reign of the Marxist regime, between 1974 and 1991.

Initially, Ethiopia's revolution appeared to join the explosion of the Marxist and anti-imperialist fervor seizing much of the world during that period.[83] However, the revolution led to Ethiopia's isolation and undermined its historical standing in the Pan-African movement. Much of this can be credited to the isolationist nature of the Marxist revolution. While Ethiopia under Haile Selassie sought interactions with outsiders, including the West and the Diaspora, during the Red Terror Period, engagement was limited to other communist enclaves, mainly the Soviet satellites. Second, Marxist Ethiopia was Eurocentric and its architects presumed that organizing on the basis of class was primary,[84] even to the exclusion of Ethiopia's unique identity and history. The Ethiopian Marxists "did not address how and to what extent the Eurocentric foundations of Marxism 'fit' into a non-Western country like Ethiopia."[85] Instead of providing an analysis of Marxism that conformed to Ethiopia's unique history, the revolutionaries rendered unsacred traditions held for millennia. For instance, "the family of [those] murdered [by the government] had to pay for the bullet, with mourning forbidden under penalty of death."[86] In a country where tradition is primary, the Marxist regime violated age-old cultural norms, refusing to allow families to bury or even acknowledge their dead.[87] It is this attempt at the erasure of and disdain for historical Ethiopia that rendered revolutionary Ethiopia a terror state. As such, not only did the Marxist regime apply a system of government inconsistent with Ethiopia's identity, but it also resulted in two catastrophic events: First, the country became engulfed in a massive human rights crisis. Second, the Marxist regime changed the focus of Ethiopia's external interactions and the country marched out of its Pan-African trajectory.

The human rights crisis, in the form of the severe famines of the 1980s in Ethiopia, was by no means the making of the Marxist regime alone. Indeed, Haile Selassie's government allowed the disaster to fester without addressing it[88] and ultimately passed on the crisis to the Marxist regime. Although initially the regime sought to hide the famines, when discovered, government officials reveled in the ensuing crisis management and the attention of famous entertainers and dignitaries, as though the human rights disaster did not result from the regime's malfeasance. It is estimated that half a million Ethiopians perished during the famines of 1983, 1984, and 1985 and, notably, "over half of this mortality, can be attributed to human rights abuses, causing the famine to come earlier, strike harder and extend further than would otherwise have been the case."[89] That is, the lack of clean water, access to health facilities, violence directed at political dissidents, and economic strangulation, among a myriad of other human rights violations, exacerbated what many thought was a "natural disaster." To the outside world, the haunting images of human suffering would leave an indelible mark. Ultimately, these images of sorrow, helplessness, and wretched poverty, wholly incongruent with historical representations of Ethiopia, would dominate the discussion.

In between the fervent support of Ethiopia during World War II and the advent of the Marxist regime, there was a critical shift in the support for Ethiopia. Some historians contend that the African independence movements of the 1960s, propelled by Pan-Africanism, may have perversely eliminated or diminished Ethiopia's importance to the Diaspora. They surmise that following the second Italian attack, there was a "dissipation of Ethiopian symbolism from African American political thought. With the independence of several African states . . . and the rise of a . . . group of African nationalist leaders, black Americans no longer felt duty bound in their support for Ethiopia."[90] While this analysis may be valid, a more pressing question is how the lack of racial consciousness and the absence of Pan-African public representations of Ethiopia during this period may have not only contributed to the distance between the country and the Diaspora but ultimately hampered any efforts to alleviate the crisis.

The rooting of Ethiopia's Marxist revolution in Eurocentrism is not unique to the country. In fact, some Pan-African communists, including the influential George Padmore, initially dismissed racial awareness as a "bourgeois concept."[91] Consequently, Ethiopia during the Red Terror Period limited its support of Pan-Africanism. Rather than focusing on the entire African Diaspora, the government's contributions to Pan-Africanism came in the form of support for anticolonial movements on the continent. The government of Ethiopia provided training to the South West Africa People's Organization (SWAPO) and the African National Congress (ANC), revolutionary groups that fought to remove white colonial rule from Namibia and South Africa, respectively. According to an International Labor Office report on apartheid:

> The government of Ethiopia has provided ANC and SWAPO representatives in Addis Abeba with free offices and residence facilities. Both organizations also use Ethiopian radio stations to broadcast reports on their activities. Ethiopia also provides free scholarships for South African and Namibian freedom fighters and issues them with work permits to enable them to support themselves on completion of their study if they wish to do so.[92]

Thus, Marxist Ethiopia supported antiapartheid and anticolonial movements in Africa and built alliance with those countries. Indeed, since his ouster in 1991, the head of revolutionary Ethiopia, Mengistu Haile Mariam, has received asylum from Robert Mugabe of Zimbabwe, a one-time anticolonial fighter and current president.

In the disorder that was famine-afflicted Marxist Ethiopia, art and public representations of this period appeared to dispel any Diaspora connections. This decline of Mythical Ethiopia was aided by the emerging dual public representations of the country during this period: the first depicting it as a Marxist haven and the second as a failed state that disappeared hundreds of thousands and made the country synonymous with famines.[93] These two conflicting public representations were a far cry from the turn of the century when the word *Ethiopia* evoked images of an independent nation, a free people, and resonated with the liberation movements of the Diaspora. Indeed, "by the late-twentieth century, images of famine and abject poverty—not obelisks, rock-hewn churches, and grand mosques—would be the most popular points of reference of Ethiopia for the West."[94] The Marxist aesthetic of the Red Terror Period became synonymous with these images of famine and human suffering.

Posters, Slogans, and Gates

Much of the art produced during the Red Terror Period was propaganda intended to indoctrinate the population. Artists were mandated to produce "mural art and monumental sculpture as well as graphic design for innumerable political posters."[95] The overtly Marxist public artistic representations of the period are the statues and the "soviet monuments . . . erected, including massive arches over the roads entering what was then called Abiot (Revolution) Square."[96] Discussed below are three examples of public representations of Ethiopia during the Red Terror Period. The first picture is of a mass rally in front of a poster of Marx, Engels, and Lenin for the thirteenth anniversary of the Marxist revolution. The second picture depicts a march, as well as revolutionary slogans erected atop city buildings. The third example discusses a historical gate in a large Ethiopian city, decorated with pictures of revolutionary leaders. Each of these representations reflects Marxist themes without alluding to the country's rich history of supporting African liberation and Pan-Africanism.

Marx, Engels, and Lenin Poster

Trademark images of Marxist regimes, particularly autocratic ones, include compelled demonstrations of mass support at public gatherings. Revolutionary Ethiopia was no exception. Pictures of rallies and marches invariably portray a large number of Ethiopians attending government-orchestrated rallies. For instance, figure 5.5 is a photograph depicting such an event—a commemoration of the thirteenth anniversary of the Ethiopian Revolution. The rally is held in front of a typical poster of Marx, Engels, and Lenin and flanked by hundreds and possibly thousands of members of

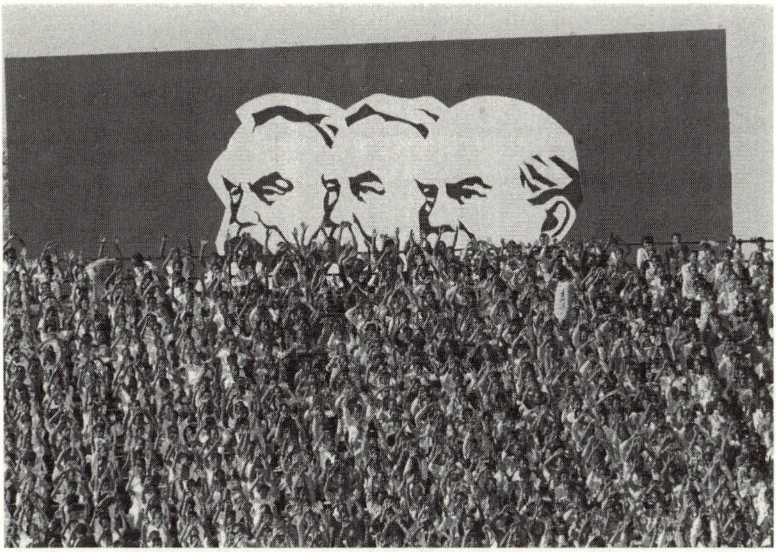

Figure 5.5. Supporters of the pro-communist Ethiopian Workers' Party wave in front of a huge portrait of the founders of the "scientific socialism": (from left) Karl Marx, Friedrich Engels, and Russian Bolshevik revolutionary leader Vladimir Ilyich Lenin. (Photo credit: ALEXANDER JOE/AFP/Getty Images.)

the Workers' Party of Ethiopia. Some posters depicted the leaders of the Ethiopian Revolution or included other prominent revolutionaries, such as Ernesto "Che" Guevara or Mao Tse-tung. However, the majority of the posters depicted the Eurocentric Marxist and communist trinity of Karl Marx, Friedrich Engels, and Vladimir Lenin. Posters of these images were erected at "nearly every important juncture in the city."[97]

Absent in the posters are any African revolutionaries or any Pan-African representation of the revolution. Furthermore, the history of revolutionary Ethiopia aiding emerging African democracies is not readily available in the public artistic representations of the country. Unlike the other periods when the images of Ethiopia portrayed a symbol of liberation for Africans, revolutionary Ethiopia, despite its support of anticolonial movements, was not synonymous with Pan-Africanism.

Slogans: "Long Live Proletarian Internationalism"

In addition to posters of revolutionary leaders, public artistic representations also included Marxist slogans. In September 1987, a march was held in celebration of the thirteenth anniversary of the Marxist revolution. In this photograph (figure 5.6), members of the Workers' Party of Ethiopia,

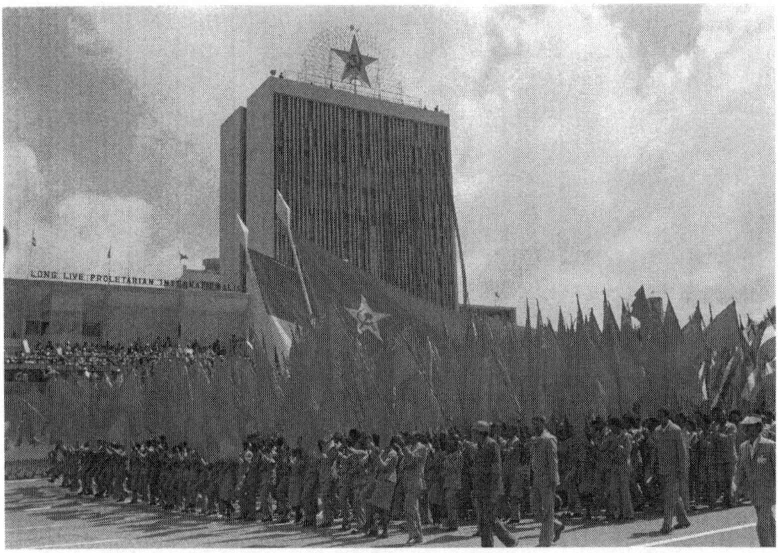

Figure 5.6. Supporters of the pro-communist Ethiopian Workers' Party holding Ethiopian and communist flags parade at Revolution Square in Addis Ababa. (Photo credit: ALEXANDER JOE/AFP/Getty Images.)

the only party permitted under the regime, are marching while wearing mandated blue uniforms. Under the Marxist regime, the government assigned dress codes for all civil servants and officials of the regime. This served as the "uniform of the proletariat"[98] and the regime could then rely on ordinary citizens to maintain order and adherence to its doctrine. Prominent in the photograph is a building decorated with the red communist star as well as the workers' symbol of the sickle and the hammer. An adjacent building is decorated with the phrase "Long Live Proletarian Internationalism," a revolutionary slogan espousing the ideals of a united working or proletarian class. As though emphasizing the Eurocentric nature of Marxism in Ethiopia, the slogan is written in English and not Amharic, the national language of Ethiopia.

As the country's public presentations increasingly became attached to the human rights crisis, the regime continued to cultivate its image as a successful Marxist experiment, holding marches and producing propaganda artwork to promote the revolution. The celebration of the thirteenth anniversary of the Ethiopian Revolution, depicted in the two images discussed thus far in this section, was held on the heels of what is the worst famine crisis in recorded history.[99]

Gates

The Marxist revolution also installed its propaganda on historical buildings. The city of Harar, a UNESCO world historical site, dates back to the mid-1500s. It is renowned for its five gates that surround the city and historically defended it from invaders. During revolutionary Ethiopia, some of the gates were adorned with pictures of communist and Marxist leaders. One particular gate, leading into the center of the city, was decorated with a picture of Leonid Brezhnev, Mengistu Haile Mariam, and Fidel Castro—the head of the USSR, the head of revolutionary Ethiopia, and the head of communist Cuba, respectively. Ethiopia and Cuba received funds and military support from the Soviet Union. Each of the leaders in the posters represented a distinct leadership style. And while Cuba aided Ethiopia in its war with Somalia in the late 1970s, there is no evidence of a distinctly Pan-African approach to the support.

These images support the theory that public artistic representation of Ethiopia during the Red Terror Period lacked a Pan-African perspective. Generally, the images reflected Marxist ideals without any reference to either the rich culture of Ethiopia or its historical role in the Pan-African movement. The primary reason for the absence could be attributed to the Eurocentric nature of Marxism in Ethiopia. As a result, the country was isolated from the Diaspora during the Red Terror Period. When famine and drought engulfed the country, resulting in a devastating human rights crisis, the lack of a Pan-African perspective, including the absence of such artistic representations, undermined the response from the Diaspora.

Unlike the broad support from the Diaspora during the Italian invasion of 1935, the response to the human rights crisis in Ethiopia in the 1980s was not intense and did not elicit the same fervor. There was, however, assistance from some groups and individuals in the Diaspora. In fact, "from Trinidad and Tobago alone, a check for $88,000 was delivered to the [Ethiopian] patriarchate in person by Deacon Tekle-Mariam Greene of Port-of-Spain, accompanied by Qes Miskale Engida of Toronto."[100] In addition, Black newspapers also reported on the human rights crisis and some held events, including a drive organized by the Chicago Black Press to provide aid to Ethiopia.[101] Yet a large-scale response from the Diaspora, akin to the Protest Period, is not represented artistically or historically. In fact, with the exception of writings by Rastafarians, African scholars, and Black nationalists, public representations of Ethiopia in the Diaspora during revolutionary Ethiopia were devoid of its rich historical significance to African liberation. Thus, Ethiopia, hidden behind a Marxist veneer, without the benefit of the artistic representations of its historical importance or Diaspora organizing, distanced from its history of Pan-Africanism, witnessed the death of five hundred thousand of its citizens.

In discussing the Ethiopian human rights crisis of the 1980s, one must distinguish between a Pan-African response and the Western aid/nongovernmental organization industrial complex. The latter was successful in that it seized the crisis and created an industry and a lifestyle that continues unabated today.[102] Concerts held in many countries in the West to raise money for Ethiopia, such as Live Aid, and the general consumer-driven "philanthropy" around the human rights crisis in Ethiopia were capitalist ventures very much removed from Pan-Africanism. In fact, "while ultimately [offering] few new options to those starving in Africa, Live Aid offered many economic and cultural opportunities for the cities in which the concerts were held, for celebrity organizers and participants, for corporate sponsors, and for concert-goers."[103]

Unlike Live Aid and its progeny, a Pan-African response to the famine in Ethiopia would have framed the human rights crisis within the overall context of the struggle of Africans and used the historical significance of Ethiopia to challenge the Marxist regime. Such a response would have relied on an "Ethiopian state of mind [that] transcends state borders and develops within the struggle against bureaucratic power, against authority that retards the development of human potential."[104] Further, a Pan-African response would have criticized the role of the Western aid/nongovernmental organizations in the crisis and squarely positioned the self-determination of Africans as a central piece to any galvanization efforts, rather than as a cash cow for a bourgeoning aid industry.

Yet the crisis was not framed within that Pan-African context. In describing the human rights disaster, one author notes, "The images on the television screen shocked, but they did not clarify."[105] It is this clarification, an explanation of how such a crisis transpired, that a Pan-African perspective could have provided. None was forthcoming and historical expectations of support from the Diaspora did not materialize. The "memory of a black public" that nurtured the notion of Ethiopia in the Mythical Period and came to her rescue in the Protest Period is absent in the Red Terror Period.

In addition to the devastating loss of human life, the famine crisis and the lack of response from the Diaspora irrevocably changed the public representation of Ethiopia. The country, outside of scholarly circles, is no longer synonymous with freedom or the rich history of African liberation movements. Rather, the images of poverty and starvation overwhelmed historical accomplishments, literary influences, and the immutable fact that the country inspired two human rights movements, Ethiopianism and Pan-Africanism, which served to galvanize Africans for well over a century.

ETHIOPIA THROUGH TIME: MYTHICAL, PROTEST, AND RED TERROR

Ethiopia has captured the imagination of Africans in the Diaspora for several reasons. Historically, Ethiopia is referenced in a biblical psalm that Africans associated with liberation from slavery. In addition, the country's status as the only continuously independent African country and the defeat of the invading Italian army in 1896 rendered Ethiopia's independence legendary. As a result, the country and the term *Ethiopia* became synonymous with freedom and the struggle for African human rights. This chapter examined public representations of Ethiopia through three periods: Mythical, Protest, and Red Terror. Through each of these periods, public representations of Ethiopia shifted, as did the country's relationship with Pan-Africanism. Each period described a unique public representation of Ethiopia and reflected how these images encouraged or hindered Pan-Africanism.

A NECESSARY RETURN TO ETHIOPIANISM

After the fall of revolutionary Ethiopia in 1991, the country's hope for a reprieve from autocratic rule was shattered. For the past two decades, the regime in control of Ethiopia, with complicity from the West, has committed grave human rights violations with impunity.[106] The government controls media outlets and interferes with communication methods, including e-mails and Skype,[107] thereby controlling the flow of news and information from and into Ethiopia. Thus the public representations of modern-day Ethiopia, at the behest of the government and the business class, reflect a different reality to the world. This constructed reality posits Ethiopia and particularly its capital as an affluent metropolis with the necessary accoutrements for investors and expats. While such a public image might be a welcome reprieve from the 1980s poverty-stricken Ethiopia, it merely shifts the public's gaze from the atrocities committed by the government. Yet the violations persist, despite the scant attention paid by the world.

Modern-day Ethiopia is very much in need of a return to a combination of the Mythical and Protest Periods. The task would be to engage in that "memory of a black public" that allows for the commemoration of Ethiopia's history with a concrete plan for visioning a different future for the country. Through a return to Ethiopianism, the Diaspora can, as it did during the Italian attack, "crea[te] a now that includes both past and future."[108] Perhaps the Diaspora can, to paraphrase the biblical psalm, "stretch forth [their] hands unto" Ethiopia and support her through public representations that not only are outwardly romantic and welcoming to investors but also address the human rights and dignities of Ethiopia's citizens.

NOTES

1. Throughout this chapter, people of African descent are referred to as Black, African, African descendants, or people of African descent. These terms could be referring to those Africans born on the African continent as well as those who were not. Much of the meaning will depend on context. Other than for the important purpose of preserving historical accuracy when recounting events, the author purposefully conflates discussions of "Continental Africans" and "Diaspora Africans" as a political statement intended to convey the common bond between all Africans. When referring to those Africans who were born on the African continent, when necessary to make such a distinction, the author refers to them as Continental Africans. In turn, when referring exclusively to those Blacks who were born outside of the continent, the author uses the term *Diaspora Africans*. In this chapter, *Black* is capitalized since it is referring to and describing the race and culture of Africans. Other than when using direct quotes, the author does not use the term *African Americans*.

2. *African Diaspora* or *Diaspora* refers to the community of people of African descent born and living outside of the African continent. Specifically in this chapter, *Diaspora* or *African Diaspora* refers to those communities of Africans who reside in the United States, the Caribbean, South America, and Europe.

3. A. Poikāne-Daumke, *African Diasporas: Afro-German Literature in the Context of the African American Experience* (Piscataway, NJ: Transaction, 2006), 22.

4. W. Scott, "The Ethiopian Ethos in African American Thought," *International Journal of Ethiopian Studies* 1, no. 2 (Winter/Spring 2004): 44.

5. Ibid.

6. C. Contee, "The Emergence of Du Bois as an African Nationalist," *Journal of Negro History* 54, no. 1 (January 1969): 48–63.

7. F. N. Gebrekidan, *Bond Without Blood: A History of Ethiopian and New World Black Relations, 1896–1991* (Trenton, NJ: Africa World Press, 2005), 37.

8. R. Walters, *Pan-Africanism in the African Diaspora: An Analysis of Modern Afrocentric Political Movements* (Detroit, MI: Wayne State University Press, 1997), 43.

9. D. Dagmawi Woubshet, S. Tillet, and E. Wolde Giorgis, "The Romance of Ethiopia," *Callaloo* 33, no. 1 (2010): 12.

10. P. L. Dunbar, *The Complete Poems of Paul Laurence Dunbar* (New York: Dodd, Mead, 1926), 15.

11. L. Rollins, "Ethiopia, African Americans, and African-Consciousness: The Effect of Ethiopia and African-Consciousness in Twentieth-Century America," *Journal of Religious Thought* 54/55, nos. 2/1 (2000): 1.

12. F. Douglass, *North Star* 2, no. 12 (March 16, 1849): 1.

13. Scott, "The Ethiopian Ethos in African American Thought," 45.

14. F. Douglass, *Frederick Douglass Papers* 7, no. 25 (1854): 3.

15. Ibid.

16. Dagmawi Woubshet, Tillet, and Wolde Giorgis, "The Romance of Ethiopia," 12.

17. Ibid., 8.

18. K. Abraham, *Adwa: Decolonization, Pan-Africanism, and the Struggle of the Black Diaspora* (Addis Ababa: The Ethiopian International Institute for Peace and Development and the Horn of Africa Democracy and Development International Lobby, 2007), 48.

19. Ibid.

20. Gebrekidan, *Bond Without Blood.*

21. Ibid.

22. Abraham, *Adwa*, 48.

23. Gebrekidan, *Bond Without Blood*, 39.

24. Ibid.

25. A. Putnam, "Ethiopia Is Now: J. A. Rogers and the Rhetoric of Black Anticolonialism during the Great Depression," *Rhetoric and Public Affairs* 10, no. 3 (2007): 434.

26. R. Hewett, "'Looking at One's Self through the Eyes of Others': Representations of the Progressive Era Middle Class in W. E. B. Du Bois's *The Star of Ethiopia*," *Theatre History Studies* 30 (2010): 187–201; R. Ater, "Making History: Meta Warrick Fuller's 'Ethiopia,'" *American Art* 17, no. 3 (2003): 12–31.

27. F. Giles, "Star of Ethiopia 1913," in *Black Theater USA Revised and Expanded Edition: Plays by African Americans*, volume 1, *The Early Period 1847–1938*, edited by James V. Hatch and Ted Shine (New York: Simon & Schuster, 1974).

28. Alessandra Lorini, *Rituals of Race: American Public Culture and the Search for Racial Democracy* (Charlottesville: University of Virginia Press, 1999), 224.

29. Ibid.

30. Nagueyalti Warren, "Pan-African Cultural Movements: From Baraka to Karenga," *Journal of Negro History* 75, nos. 1/2 (Winter/Spring 1990): 19.

31. Ibid.

32. P. D. Krasner, "The Pageant Is the Thing: Black Nationalism and *The Star of Ethiopia*," in *Performing America*, eds. J. Ellen Gainor and Jeffrey Mason, 106–22 (Ann Arbor: University of Michigan Press, 2000), 109.

33. Giles, "Star of Ethiopia."

34. Hewett, "Looking at One's Self through the Eyes of Others."

35. Krasner, "The Pageant Is the Thing," 109.

36. W. E. B. Du Bois, *The Star of Ethiopia* (Alexandria, VA: Alexander Street Press, 2001 [1913]).

37. Ater, "Making History," 26.

38. Krasner, "The Pageant Is the Thing."

39. S. Hay, *African American Theatre: An Historical and Critical Analysis* (Cambridge: Cambridge University Press, 1994).

40. P. Rothwell, "Momple's Melancholia: Mourning for Mozambique," *Portuguese Studies Review* 10, no. 1 (2002): 188.

41. Ater, "Making History."

42. Ibid.

43. Ibid., 22.

44. I. Okafor-Newsum, "A Passage to Afrotopia," *Research in African Literatures* 32, no. 4 (2001): 176.

45. Ater, "Making History."

46. Ibid., 22.

47. J. B. Armstrong, "'The People . . . Took Exception to Her Remarks': Meta Warrick Fuller, Angelina Weld Grimké, and the Lynching of Mary Turner," *Mississippi Quarterly* 61, nos. 1/2 (2008): 122.

48. Ater, "Making History."

49. B. LaDuke, "Lois Mailou Jones: The Grand Dame of African-American Art," *Women's Art Journal* 8, no. 1 (1987).

50. C. Rowell, "An Interview with Lois Mailous Jones," *Callaloo* 39 (1989): 357–78.

51. African liberation theory in this context loosely refers to the common use of certain methods, practices, and mores by people of African descent in various human rights movements. These may include marches, protest writings, civil disobedience, revolutionary violence, and other tactics.

52. W. F. Cheek and A. L. Cheek, *John Mercer Langston and the Fight for Black Freedom (1829–1865)* (Urbana: University of Illinois Press, 1996), 456.

53. W. F. Brundage, "Meta Warrick's 1907 'Negro Tableaux' and (Re)Presenting African American Historical Memory," *Journal of American History* 89, no. 4 (2003): 1369.

54. Putnam, "Ethiopia Is Now," 434.

55. Ibid., 420.

56. P. Oliver, *Blues Fell This Morning: Meaning in Blues* (Cambridge: Cambridge University Press, 1960), 231.

57. Ibid.

58. Rollins, "Ethiopia, African Americans, and African-Consciousness," 13.

59. Ibid., 14.

60. Ibid.

61. R. G. Weisbord, "British West Indian Reaction to the Italian-Ethiopian War: An Episode in Pan-Africanism," *Caribbean Studies* 10, no. 1 (1970): 34–41.

62. R. Lewis, "Marcus Garvey and the Early Rastafarians: Continuity and Discontinuity," in *Chanting Down Babylon,* edited by Nathanial Samuel Murrell, William David Spencer, and Adrian Anthony McFarland (Philadelphia: Temple University Press, 1998), 151.

63. M. G. Hall and H. Haywood, *A Black Communist in the Freedom Struggle: The Life of Harry Haywood* (Minneapolis: University of Minnesota Press, 2012).

64. Ibid.

65. Ibid.

66. Ibid., 218.

67. Hall and Haywood, *A Black Communist in the Freedom Struggle.*

68. R. Kelley, *Race Rebels: Culture, Politics and the Black Working Class* (New York: The Free Press, 1994).

69. Putnam, "Ethiopia Is Now," 439.

70. Kelley, *Race Rebels.*

71. Weisbord, "British West Indian Reaction to the Italian-Ethiopian War."

72. B. G. Plumber, *Rising Wind: Black Americans and U.S. Foreign Affairs, 1935–1960* (Chapel Hill: University of North Carolina Press, 1996).

73. J. Carver, J. A. Ennels, and D. L. Haulman, *The Tuskegee Airmen: An Illustrated History, 1939–1949, with a Comprehensive Chronology of Missions and Events* (Montgomery, AL: NewSouth, 2011).

74. Ibid.

75. J. H. Meriwether, *Proudly We Can Be Africans: Black Americans and Africa, 1935–1961* (Chapel Hill: University of North Carolina Press, 2002), 27.

76. Putnam, "Ethiopia Is Now," 422.

77. Ibid., 436.

78. T. Tibebu, "Ethiopia: The 'Anamoly' and 'Paradox' of Africa," *Journal of Black Studies* 26, no. 4 (1996): 426.

79. Italy used chemical weapons against the Ethiopian population. See Lina Grip and John Hart, "The Use of Chemical Weapons in the 1935–36 Italo-Ethiopian War," in *SIPRI Arms Control and Non-proliferation Programmme*, October 2009. Italy also "bombed Red Cross Ambulances, and when in control, massacred most

of the country's educated elite." See A. De Waal, *Evil Days: Thirty Years of War and Famine in Ethiopia* (New York: Human Rights Watch, 1991).

80. P. Klemm and M. Niederstadt, "Beyond Wide-Eyed Angels: Contemporary Expressive Culture in Ethiopia," *African Arts* 42, no. 1 (2009): 9.

81. "Revolutionary Ethiopia" in this section encompasses the regime in power during the Marxist revolution in Ethiopia between 1974 and 1991. Therefore, references to revolutionary Ethiopia within this section are synonymous with "Ethiopia during the Red Terror Period" as well as "Marxist Ethiopia."

82. T. Tibebu, "Modernity, Eurocentrism, and Radical Politics in Ethiopia, 1961–1991," *African Identities* 6, no. 4 (2008): 345–71.

83. Ibid.

84. Ibid.

85. Ibid., 360.

86. T. Riccio, "Ethiopia and Its Double," *TheatreForum* 41 (2012): 55.

87. Tibebu, "Modernity, Eurocentrism, and Radical Politics in Ethiopia, 1961–1991."

88. De Waal, *Evil Days*.

89. Ibid., 5.

90. Gebrekidan, *Bond Without Blood*, 232.

91. Ibid., 231.

92. International Labor Office, *Special Report of the Director-General on the Application of the Declaration concerning Action against Apartheid in South Africa and Namibia* (International Labor Conference, 77th session, 1990), 94.

93. The Ethiopian famines of the 1980s are discussed within the context of human rights violations. Accordingly, in this section, the term *human rights crisis* refers to the politically motivated famines of the 1980s. In addition, the author has consciously chosen not to include public representations of the famine within this discussion since those images are most readily accessible to most readers. Instead, the chapter will focus on images of Marxist representations in Ethiopia and their relationship with Pan-Africanism.

94. Dagmawi Woubshet, Tillet, and Wolde Giorgis, "The Romance of Ethiopia," 10.

95. Klemm and Niederstadt, "Beyond Wide-Eyed Angels," 9.

96. Ibid.

97. E. C. Zeleke, "Addis Ababa as Modernist Ruin," *Callaloo* 33, no. 1 (2010): 125.

98. Ibid.

99. H. L. Davis, "Feeding the World a Line? Celebrity Activism and Ethical Consumer Practices from Live Aid to Product Red," *Journal for Nordic Studies in English* 9, no. 3 (2010): 89–118.

100. Gebrekidan, *Bond Without Blood*, 220.

101. N. Clay, "Black Press Drive to Aid Ethiopia Gets in Gear," *Chicago Metro News*, January 5, 1985, p. 3.

102. Live Aid and Feed Africa, while garnering worldwide attention to the singers and the organizers, did not alleviate the core of the human rights crisis impacting

millions. Indeed, the most successful result of the response to the crisis has been the proliferation of hundreds of aid agencies.

103. Davis, "Feeding the World a Line?" 96.

104. Putnam, "Ethiopia Is Now," 433.

105. R. D. Kaplan, *Surrender or Starve: Travels in Ethiopia, Sudan, Somalia, Eritrea* (New York: Vintage, 2008), 11.

106. Amnesty International, *Amnesty International Report 2012: The State of the World's Human Rights* (New York: Amnesty International, 2012).

107. K. Moskvitch, "Ethiopia Clamps Down on Skype and Other Internet Use on Tor," *BBC News*, June 15, 2012, www.bbc.co.uk.

108. Putnam, "Ethiopia Is Now," 434.

BIBLIOGRAPHY

Abraham, K. *Adwa: Decolonization, Pan-Africanism, and the Struggle of the Black Diaspora.* Addis Ababa: The Ethiopian International Institute for Peace and Development and the Horn of Africa Democracy and Development International Lobby, 2007.

Amnesty International. *Amnesty International Report 2012: The State of the World's Human Rights*. New York: Amnesty International, 2012.

Armstrong, J. B. "'The People . . . Took Exception to Her Remarks': Meta Warrick Fuller, Angelina Weld Grimké, and the Lynching of Mary Turner." *Mississippi Quarterly* 61, nos. 1/2 (2008): 113–41.

Ater, R. "Making History: Meta Warrick Fuller's 'Ethiopia.'" *American Art* 17, no. 3 (2003): 12–31.

Brundage, W. F. "Meta Warrick's 1907 'Negro Tableaux' and (Re)Presenting African American Historical Memory." *Journal of American History* 89, no. 4 (2003): 1368–1400.

Carver, J., J. A. Ennels, and D. L. Haulman. *The Tuskegee Airmen: An Illustrated History, 1939–1949, with a Comprehensive Chronology of Missions and Events.* Montgomery, AL: NewSouth, 2011.

Cheek, W. F., and A. L. Cheek. *John Mercer Langston and the Fight for Black Freedom (1829–1865)*. Urbana: University of Illinois Press, 1996.

Clay, N. "Black Press Drive to Aid Ethiopia Gets in Gear." *Chicago Metro News*, January 5, 1985, p. 3.

Contee, C. "The Emergence of Du Bois as an African Nationalist." *Journal of Negro History* 54, no. 1 (January 1969): 48–63.

Dagmawi Woubshet, D., S. Tillet, and E. Wolde Giorgis. "The Romance of Ethiopia." *Callaloo* 33, no. 1 (2010): 8–14.

Davis, H. L. "Feeding the World a Line? Celebrity Activism and Ethical Consumer Practices from Live Aid to Product Red." *Journal for Nordic Studies in English* 9, no. 3 (2010): 89–118.

De Waal, A. *Evil Days: Thirty Years of War and Famine in Ethiopia.* New York: Human Rights Watch, 1991.

Douglass, F. *Frederick Douglass Papers* 7, no. 25 (1854): 3.

———. *North Star* 2, no. 12 (March 16, 1849): 1.

Du Bois, W. E. B. *The Star of Ethiopia.* Alexandria, VA: Alexander Street Press, 2001 [1913].

Dunbar, P. L. *The Complete Poems of Paul Laurence Dunbar.* New York: Dodd, Mead, 1926.

Gebrekidan, F. N. *Bond Without Blood: A History of Ethiopian and New World Black Relations, 1896–1991.* Trenton, NJ: Africa World Press, 2005.

Giles, F. "Star of Ethiopia 1913." In *Black Theater USA Revised and Expanded Edition: Plays by African Americans*, volume 1, *The Early Period 1847–1938*, edited by James V. Hatch and Ted Shine. New York: Simon & Schuster, 1974.

Grip, Lina, and John Hart. "The Use of Chemical Weapons in the 1935–36 Italo-Ethiopian War." In *SIPRI Arms Control and Non-proliferation Programmme*, October 2009.

Hall, M. G., and H. Haywood. *A Black Communist in the Freedom Struggle: The Life of Harry Haywood.* Minneapolis: University of Minnesota Press, 2012.

Hay, S. *African American Theatre: An Historical and Critical Analysis.* Cambridge: Cambridge University Press, 1994.

Hewett, R. "'Looking at One's Self through the Eyes of Others': Representations of the Progressive Era Middle Class in W. E. B. Du Bois's *The Star of Ethiopia.*" *Theatre History Studies* 30 (2010): 187–201.

International Labor Office. *Special Report of the Director-General on the Application of the Declaration concerning Action against Apartheid in South Africa and Namibia.* International Labor Conference, 77th session, 1990.

Kaplan, R. D. *Surrender or Starve: Travels in Ethiopia, Sudan, Somalia, Eritrea.* New York: Vintage, 2008.

Kelley, R. *Race Rebels: Culture, Politics and the Black Working Class.* New York: The Free Press, 1994.

Klemm, P., and M. Niederstadt. "Beyond Wide-Eyed Angels: Contemporary Expressive Culture in Ethiopia." *African Arts* 42, no. 1 (2009): 6–13.

Krasner, P. D. "The Pageant Is the Thing: Black Nationalism and *The Star of Ethiopia.*" In *Performing America*, edited by J. Ellen Gainor and Jeffrey Mason, 106–22. Ann Arbor: University of Michigan Press, 2000.

LaDuke, B. "Lois Mailou Jones: The Grand Dame of African-American Art." *Women's Art Journal* 8, no. 1 (1987).

Lewis, R. "Marcus Garvey and the Early Rastafarians: Continuity and Discontinuity." In *Chanting Down Babylon*, edited by Nathanial Samuel Murrell, William David Spencer, and Adrian Anthony McFarland, 145–58. Philadelphia: Temple University Press, 1998.

Lorini, Alessandra. *Rituals of Race: American Public Culture and the Search for Racial Democracy.* Charlottesville: University of Virginia Press, 1999.

Meriwether, J. H. *Proudly We Can Be Africans: Black Americans and Africa, 1935–1961.* Chapel Hill: University of North Carolina Press, 2002.

Moskvitch, K. "Ethiopia Clamps Down on Skype and Other Internet Use on Tor." *BBC News*, June 15, 2012. www.bbc.co.uk.

Okafor-Newsum, I. "A Passage to Afrotopia." *Research in African Literatures* 32, no. 4 (2001): 172–86.

Oliver, P. *Blues Fell This Morning: Meaning in Blues*. Cambridge: Cambridge University Press, 1960.

Plumber, B. G. *Rising Wind: Black Americans and U.S. Foreign Affairs, 1935–1960*. Chapel Hill: University of North Carolina Press, 1996.

Poikāne-Daumke, A. *African Diasporas: Afro-German Literature in the Context of the African American Experience.* Piscataway, NJ: Transaction, 2006.

Putnam, A. "Ethiopia Is Now: J. A. Rogers and the Rhetoric of Black Anticolonialism during the Great Depression." *Rhetoric and Public Affairs* 10, no. 3 (2007): 419–44.

Riccio, T. "Ethiopia and Its Double." *TheatreForum* 41 (2012): 46–55.

Rollins, L. "Ethiopia, African Americans, and African-Consciousness: The Effect of Ethiopia and African-Consciousness in Twentieth-Century America." *Journal of Religious Thought* 54/55, nos. 2/1 (2000): 1–25.

Rothwell, P. "Momple's Melancholia: Mourning for Mozambique." *Portuguese Studies Review* 10, no. 1 (2002): 185–93.

Rowell, C. "An Interview with Lois Mailous Jones." *Callaloo* 39 (1989): 357–78.

Scott, W. "The Ethiopian Ethos in African American Thought." *International Journal of Ethiopian Studies* 1, no. 2 (Winter/Spring 2004): 40–57.

Tibebu, T. "Ethiopia: The 'Anamoly' and 'Paradox' of Africa." *Journal of Black Studies* 26, no. 4 (1996).

———. "Modernity, Eurocentrism, and Radical Politics in Ethiopia, 1961–1991." *African Identities* 6, no. 4 (2008): 345–71.

Walters, R. *Pan-Africanism in the African Diaspora: An Analysis of Modern Afrocentric Political Movements.* Detroit, MI: Wayne State University Press, 1997.

Warren, Nagueyalti. "Pan-African Cultural Movements: From Baraka to Karenga." *Journal of Negro History* 75, nos. 1/2 (Winter/Spring 1990): 16–28.

Weisbord, R. G. "British West Indian Reaction to the Italian-Ethiopian War: An Episode in Pan-Africanism." *Caribbean Studies* 10, no. 1 (1970): 34–41.

Zeleke, E. C. "Addis Ababa as Modernist Ruin." *Callaloo* 33, no. 1 (2010): 117–35.

6

❖ ❖

Incas for Sale

Commodified Images of Historical Sites

Silvia Nagy-Zekmi and Kevin J. Ryan Jr.

The word *revolution* brings up different images depending on the plurality of contexts in which people live. Political, economic, technological, and sociocultural cases of revolution vary from instances of bloody upheaval to peaceful transitions, dystopian nightmares to utopian paradise, and tectonic historical shifts to minor symbolic changes. As such, exploring its polysemy in the semantic field expands the term *revolution* considerably. Change may be subtle at one time, yet influential in the future of a society. Nonviolent resistance may well be associated with revolution as a catalyst for reshaping the future. Scrutinizing cultural practices associated with nonviolent resistance through a revisionist view of history is our aim in this piece.

More specifically, we shall argue that certain cultural spaces are situated at a crossroads: either they may lead to a revolution beneficial to the masses through the cultivation and support of various forms of cultural agency and cultural exchange or they may provide further subjugation of marginalized groups through evolving forms of economic and social hegemony. We thus plan to examine the difficulty of leveraging heritage and tourist sites as possible loci for cultural agency. According to Baram and Rowan, a tradition of "active reconstruction of the past toward a specific purpose"[1] is perceivable throughout history, particularly in the construction of nationalist discourses. As things stand, we suggest that tourist sites, while offering a strong potential for cultural agency, are particularly targeted by such discourses that portrayed them as manifestations of the "essence" of an indigenous past and need rethinking and restructuring to actually become such loci.

Our arguments are built around the contradiction inherent in the commodification of a site of historical significance.[2] In the "business" of tourism, the mark of capital becomes essential in altering the significance of different cultural signs. Venturing into semiotics and elaborating on the Saussurean sign of signification, we suggest that the tourist is the cultural equivalent to Duchamp's *Fountain* or Warhol's *Brillo Boxes* in the art world, for the tourist reorients the meaning of cultural boundaries, just as Warhol and Duchamp reoriented our understanding of the meaning of art.

Starting from a framework in which basic concepts of space and spatiality are called into question, this chapter critically analyzes the commodification of historical spaces, such as monuments or ruins, both in the literal sense of the physical space around specific sites and in the metaphorical sense of the social and historical elements encountered within or mediated through them. A nonexclusive sense of what we mean by "basic concepts of spatiality" includes terms such as *inside*, *outside*, *above*, *below*, *between*, *near*, and *far*. Moreover, space here must be understood in terms of both a physical space *and* a metaphorical site.

Considering the scope of our inquiry, this chapter focuses in particular on one specific case study—Machu Picchu—first by introducing key background information about Machu Picchu as a historical monument and popular tourist site. Second, in order to scrutinize the cultural meaning of the site in both the past and the present, we establish a theoretical framework based on the concepts of *thirdspace* and *deadspace*, along with the broader concerns that originally gave rise to them. Third, we flesh out important concerns and considerations about how the tension inherent in these concepts can be applied to the case of Machu Picchu. Likewise, in what follows we assume that at least a portion of cultural agency should be understood in the context of historical spaces as an avenue for increasing political, social, and economic power for individuals and groups who are and have been historically maligned by dominant modes of economic and political control and stratification.

MACHU PICCHU AND TOURISM

Machu Picchu is a double-peak mountain in Peru that consists of Machu Picchu (Old Mountain) and Huayna Picchu (Young Mountain), known first and foremost for its famous indigenous ruins whose origins date back

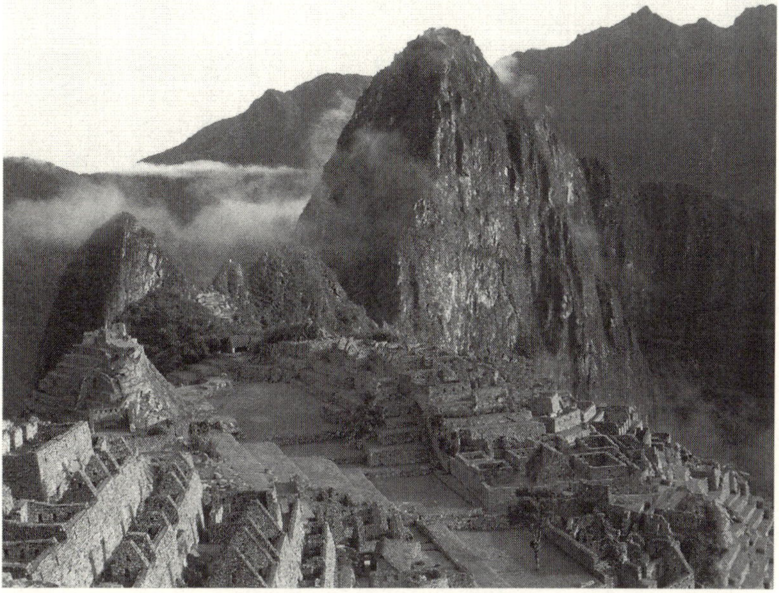

Figure 6.1. Photo by Allard Schmidt (the Netherlands; own work) [Public domain, GFDL (http://www.gnu.org/copyleft/fdl.html) or CC-BY-SA-3.0 (http://creativecommons.org/licenses/by-sa/3.0/)], via Wikimedia Commons: https://upload.wikimedia.org/wikipedia/commons/d/da/Peru_Machu_Picchu_Sunrise_2.jpg; https://commons.wikimedia.org/wiki/File%3APeru_Machu_Picchu_Sunrise_2.jpg.

to the Inca Empire, which rose from the kingdom of Cuzco in the twelfth century and was devastated in the sixteenth century by the Spanish colonizers whose *criollo*[3] descendants are still in power today. The site was built by the emperor Inca Pachacuti Yupanqui (1438–1472) in 1450[4] as a winter retreat, and after his death it became his mausoleum. However, the chronicles of the conquest of Peru do not mention the site at all, not even by the most famous chronicle writer of mestizo origin, Garcilaso de la Vega, El Inca (1539–1616),[5] who was born in the city of Cuzco next to Machu Picchu. Supposedly, Machu Picchu was discovered as an archeological site by the American Hiram Bingham in 1911 as he was led to the ruins by local shepherds.

However, Peruvian intellectuals claim otherwise. Historian Mariana Mould de Pease writes that the site has never been "lost" to Peruvians,[6] the native population. The Peruvian president at the time, Augusto Leguía, residing in the coastal town of Lima[7] with a self-image as the leader of a country populated by people of European (Spanish) descent, allowed Bingham's account of his "discovery" to be transmitted to the world straight from Yale University. Subsequently, in his book, *Lost City of the Incas: The Story of Machu Picchu and Its Builders*, Bingham declares himself the discoverer of Machu Picchu. According to Mould de Pease, the Peruvian government wasted an opportunity "to demonstrate with historical evidence that Machu Picchu was never really lost to Peruvians."[8] Let us remember that Bingham was *led to the site* by native Peruvians—namely, a boy named Pablo.[9]

With these considerations in mind, we suggest that the space today is not a barren physical site but a space of cultural dif/fusion akin to what Mary Louise Pratt referred to as the "contact zone,"[10] which is a space in which a variety of identities come into contact, primarily between groups interlocked in different levels of unequal power relations. These contacts may occur simultaneously, such as the interaction among tourists[11] from other areas of the country and abroad, guides, vendors, local inhabitants, and other individuals and entities working on and around the site. In diachronic (historic) terms of the contact zone, we can think of a palimpsest with the superimposition of different cultural strata where identities can be enacted and reconstituted into a variety of symbolic and concrete meanings with individual, national, and international dimensions. These are embodied in moments such as the recent debate between the government of Peru and Yale University concerning the return of local artifacts from the United States back to Machu Picchu.

In turn, Machu Picchu, a pre-Columbian Inca site near Cusco, Peru, exemplifies a historic space in which nationalist discourses are embodied; it does not exclude commodification, and contemporary interpretations of the site disallow historic uniqueness, creating instead a generic image to appeal to every taste—in other words, an image fashioned for popular consumption. For instance, John Roach quotes Carolyn Bointon, the former manager of the Cusco clubhouse of the South American Explorers club, as saying, "It certainly has appeal to everyone, whether they are interested in the history, or the magic, or just the stupendous beauty." Tourism, particularly in the twenty-first century, can be understood as an industry that sells the experiences of (i.e., commodifies) specific historical and geographical sites. Tourism, after all, has proven to be an important economic catalyst throughout the world. According to the UN World Tourism Organization's (UNWTO) 2013 annual report, there were 1,087,000,000 tourist arrivals around the world, with the industry experiencing a 5 percent growth from the previous year and a projection to hit approximately 1.8 billion tourist arrivals within the next twenty years.[12]

At the same time, tourism cannot be narrowly defined in purely economic terms. According to Dean MacCannell, tourism is "not just an aggregate of merely commercial activities; it is also an ideological framing of history, nature and tradition; a framing that has the power to reshape culture and nature to its own needs."[13] Although the pool of potential tourists is large, the growth has promoted a rise in competition. Those who wish to be players in the growing tourism industry cannot simply set up a sign and expect tourists to flow and business to jump on its own. While there are many different venues for promoting tourism, the practice itself carries certain normative implications. From the simple expectation of having (or lacking) certain amenities to the more intricate attempt at cultivating a lasting image, tourism is concerned not simply with getting visitors but also with selling a product.

Popularizing historical spaces as tourist destinations corresponds to a specific interpretation of history where identities come to be enacted and reconstituted into a variety of cultural spheres, individual, national, and international in character and scope. The process of interpretation, insofar as it occurs simultaneously at these multiple levels and at differing timescales, takes place as a set of conflicting interpretations. There is, therefore, not one entity that controls the process of popularizing major tourist attractions, but rather competing images created by various agencies. Nevertheless, we suggest that a noticeable portion of attempts at attracting tourists to locations like Machu Picchu seems to find a locus within the colonizing dichotomy of Europeanness and alterity. The colonizing dichotomy, here, is primarily rooted in the process of presenting the Incan space as a static photo of what once was, without reference to how it relates to the lives of indigenous people today. For example, the www.machupicchu.info website, specifically created for (potential) tourists by the Cosmic Travel Network, has the following description (under "History of Machu Picchu"):

> The site is made up of single buildings arranged in groups, along streets, adjacent to plazas and terraces. Most of the buildings *are residences*, some of white granite masonry such as that seen in the city of Cusco. Some of the buildings, which *must have been for special purposes*, are partly carved into the bedrock and partly built from finely cut white granite.[14]

In a typical fashion, the description is quite unspecific as to the historical significance and the social structure of the site. However, it is added that "due to its impressive buildings and gorgeous natural surroundings, Machu Picchu is among the seven 'wonders of the world.'" One tends to think of the seven wonders of the ancient world, among which Machu Picchu does not figure; however, it appears in the list of the so-called new

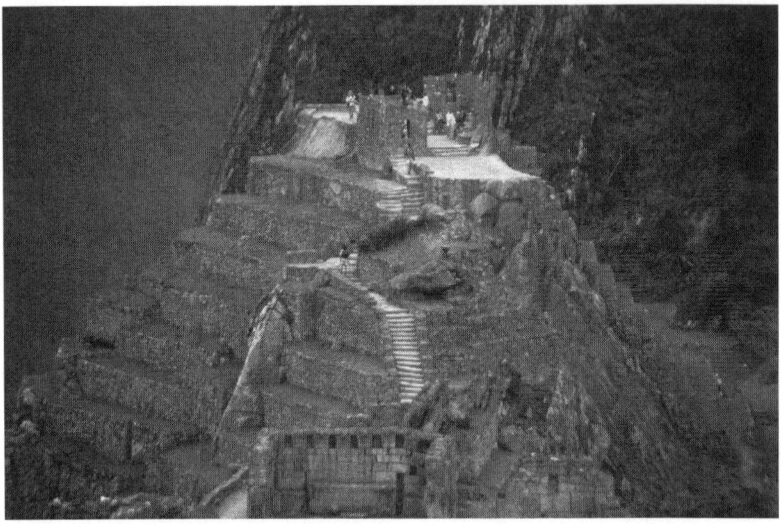

Figure 6.2. Photo by Colegota [CC BY-SA 2.5 es (http://creativecommons.org/licenses/by-sa/2.5/es/deed.en)], via Wikimedia Commons: https://upload.wikimedia.org/wikipedia/commons/d/d5/Machu-picchu-c03.jpg; https://commons.wikimedia.org/wiki/File%3AMachu-picchu-c03.jpg.

seven wonders from an effort initiated in the early 2000s to list the two hundred most remarkable historic or geographic sites in today's world. This ambiguity is advantageously used by the Cosmic Travel Network. The images created by the tourism industry, or by tourists themselves, blatantly disregard the site itself. The tourist presence may become a mere exercise in narcissism, as the following news bit exemplifies. As the CNN site notes, "Watch out for bare butts when traveling in Machu Picchu—incidents of 'naked tourism' at the 15th-century Inca citadel are on the rise, and getting under the skin of Peru officials."[15]

In addition to the description of the structures in the site built by those long gone, the local population is described in exotic terms, such as in an advertisement of a Machu Picchu tour where tourists are invited to visit "Andean people that know magical secrets, such as Andean and Amazonian Mother of Nature."[16] There is an intentional cultural homogenizing of the Andean and Amazonian areas, even though they are not only different from one another but also considerably diverse in themselves. For instance, the Andean deity Pachamama (literally, "Mother Earth") is not known among Amazonian tribes, unless they are culturally related to Inca descendants in the borderland areas of the Amazon jungle, the *ceja de selva* (the eyebrow of the jungle).

The hierarchy of this dichotomy and rupture established between the past and present may only be subverted through a revolutionary proposition—namely, a radical reinterpretation of the meaning reflected in the imagery embedded in the representation of such a historical space. Along these lines, the analysis of particular spaces, including the one in question, must be examined within the context of space as such. Henri Lefebvre claims that the organization of space is a symptomatic dimension of societies, and it both reflects and influences societal relations. Consequently, justice and injustice become visible in space. This is also Edward Soja's central argument in *Seeking Spatial Justice*, in which he, too, considers the imprint of social justice in a specific space. Although Soja focuses more on planning and creating spaces, his concepts are applicable to the interpretation of existing sites.

Correspondingly, we are concerned with the way in which historical spaces may be interpreted as manifestations of the representation of aforementioned identities—in which case discourses are emitted from a *thirdspace* of enunciation (examined in detail below) to manifest agency. We are also concerned with discourses as embedded within the dominant hierarchy to reaffirm and reconstitute the status quo—in which case they can be considered representations of zones of *deadspace* where not only the physical but also the cultural dimensions of a site are either denied or radically reinterpreted. Machu Picchu exemplifies such space and, through our focal object of analysis, this mode of inquiry is by no means limited to this historical site alone.

THIRDSPACE AND *DEADSPACE*

The idea of *thirdspace* is understood in various ways by different theoreticians.[17] Homi Bhabha was the first to define the term as "a challenge to the limits of the self in the act of reaching out of what is liminal in the historic experience, and in the cultural representation, of other peoples, times, languages, texts."[18] He further notes that "third space" is a "locus of acts of translation,"[19] which, combined with the idea of a liminal and historical interpretation of culture, sheds light on the limitation of any particular cultural perspective. In the self-reflexivity of *thirdspace* discourses, power relations are open for suspension and readjustment. Edward Soja, who coined the term *thirdspace* (in one word, precisely to be distinguished from Bhabha's two-word concept), defined it as such: "Thirdspace is a purposefully tentative and flexible term that attempts to capture what is actually constantly shifting."[20] In our understanding, *thirdspace* is a discursive middle ground between two binary opposites that ultimately relocates the discourse itself from its vertical antagonism by introducing new elements that are not reflexive of either one of the antagonist constituents.

We define *thirdspace* as a space, physical or symbolic, in which dominant hierarchies are suspended in a move of critical openness toward dynamic and inclusive change manifest in hybridity and *métissage*. *Deadspace* refers to a space in which dominant modes of oppression are continued, regardless of how either element of the dichotomy (self/other) would be accepted or rejected. This centers the colonizing dichotomy enforced and re-created by the tourism industry. By representing the current inhabitants of the Machu Picchu area as exotic, emphasizing their alterity by recontextualizing them in the tourists' gaze as such, self-manifestation and agency are denied to the present-day inhabitants, part and parcel of the Andean cultural area.

Soja's *thirdspace* offers a "both/also" choice between apparent opposites instead of forcing an "either/or" selection. Such choices are further separated from either *firstspace*, which Soja defines as "perspectives focused on the *real* material world," or *secondspace*, understood as "*imagined* representations of spatiality."[21] The possibility of an essential fourth term that Soja does not address in his work must be mentioned primarily to expose spaces of repression applied to the colonizer/colonized dichotomy—in other words, a forced "either/or" choice. As noted above, we suggest a name for this fourth term, here defined as *deadspace*. *Deadspace* does not simply fall prey to the strict dichotomy of the *real* (*firstspace*) and the *imagined* (*secondspace*); rather, it is itself a space of *repression* coming from both the real and the imaginary. The distinction between *thirdspace* and *deadspace* is nevertheless not necessarily one of mutual exclusivity. Instead, the greater issue regarding these two concepts is not the question of either/and/or/both, but rather the possibility for *thirdspace* growing stagnant into *deadspace*—or, to put the matter conversely, the dream of a *deadspace* being (re)vitalized as *thirdspace*.

When contextualized within the discourses of power, the issue of the forced "either/or" choice is only one of multiple avenues in the configuration of *deadspace*. The paradoxical idealization or despising of a repressed minority, such as the glorification of the ancient Incas coupled with an attitude of discrimination toward the indigenous Quechua,[22] their descendants, presents the forced "either/or" choice between the idealization of the past Inca glory and the present repression. The discursive modality of repression, in terms of power structures, is characteristic of *deadspace*. British cultural critic Stuart Hall refers to the "rupture" in cultural identity by the "either/or" choice as embodied in the cultural "vectors" of continuity[23] (the survival of the Inca/Quechua people and their cultural practices) and vectors of discontinuity (the representation of the Inca past and the Quechua present as two different cultural entities).

As it had been asserted by a number of critics (cf. Homi Bhabha, Alberto Moreiras, Julia Lossau, among others), discourses based on such dichotomy will do no more than re-create a Eurocentric notion of center and periphery. In order to break the discursive cycle of binary opposition, we propose that a contact zone must introduce Bhabha's idea of the "third space" of enunciation as applied to Edward Soja's idea of *thirdspace*, in which "everything comes together . . . subjectivity and objectivity, the abstract and the concrete, the real and the imagined."[24] Moreover, we make use of *deadspace* to signify the rupture in the continuity of cultural vectors[25] from the representation of the fifteenth-century indigenous builders of Machu Picchu to the representation of the Quechua.[26]

Deadspace represents a concept in contrast to *thirdspace* that uses the appearance of cultural exchange to crush the possibility of revolutionary change through cultural agency. It is here that the possible source of pride, potential, and communication between groups is replaced with postcards, cost-benefit analysis, and cultural pastiche. Stuart Hall has established cultural identity as "not outside but *within* representation." With this in mind, following the potential signs, signifiers, references, and referents of Machu Picchu is to navigate a tangled web of different, often-hybrid cultural substrata with the potential for several divergent modes of representations. The ruins of buildings, terraces, and temples become spaces of both rupture and sedimentation. The indigenous identity in Peru embodied in Machu Picchu is constituted by zones wavering between *deadspace* and *thirdspace*.

MACHU PICCHU: MIRROR OR PHOTOGRAPH?

Machu Picchu does not currently function as a source of indigenous cultural agency, mainly due to the commodification of its history witnessed in the imagery transmitted by tourism. The tourism industry includes a variety of actors, including several in the Peruvian government itself—namely, officers of the Ministry of Foreign Commerce and Tourism, as well as the Ministry of Justice and Human Rights, among others. These entities permit and promote the penetration of foreign agencies to assign cultural identities to Peruvian indigenous sites and their inhabitants. However, the commodification process itself stems from more than just the act of making a space into a recognizable tourist destination. bell hooks refers to such cultural commodification as "eating the other," meaning that cultural expressions may be sold to and by the dominant culture. It is seen in everything from the magnets and tokens for tourist keepsakes to overpriced food venues dotting the entrance gate when one enters the site itself.

The space of a UNESCO world heritage site is presented as a ghost town, as something that has been and is no more. It may be argued that it is precisely the tourists who breathe new life into the ruins, as the site has been culturally configured for tourist consumption. The historical narrative is reduced to ten- to thirty-minute talking points and is articulated to appeal as much as possible to most people. Often devoid of historical and social significance about those living today in the surrounding areas and, thus, the owners of the cultural heritage of Machu Picchu and its significance, the new, commercialized meaning is attached to the site and converts it into a *deadspace*. Within the business of tourism, the natives' viewpoints are often positioned vis-à-vis a Eurocentric viewpoint to cater to tourists who would harbor and share such views. The power structures manifest in the discursive representation of the site also point toward *deadspace* within the parameters of the culture industry best defined by Adorno and Horkheimer as "the general designation [that] already contains, virtually, the process of identifying, cataloging, and classifying which imports culture into the realm of administration."[27] The administration of cultural sites today cannot be separated from the material and economic forces that control the production of culture, which is enacted within and propelled by the power structures of capital.

Another space to consider, in the case of Machu Picchu, is what lies next to, but outside of, the "boundaries"[28] of the site itself, the physical structure of the buildings and land leading up to the entrance to the site, particularly if one travels via bus instead of foot.[29] This space of gift shops, overpriced food, and groups of tour guides emitting their explanations in the flavor of the dominant discourse implicitly articulates that Machu Picchu is truly a ruin, a relic of things long past that has come to represent little more than a memorial. "Here are found," one is told, "the *remnants* of the great Incan civilization, which has fallen and *no longer exists*." Taken at one level, one may consider the fact that in the presentation of Machu Picchu as a historical site—in colonial terms with the last Inca of Vilcabamba,[30] Túpac Amaru I, executed by Viceroy Toledo in 1572—the Incan civilization, as such, no longer exists. However, the totalizing assertions about the Incas fail to take into account their descendants, who, since then and until now, inhabit that space.

Tourists themselves become the center and the protagonist of their "adventure," and Machu Picchu is demoted to be nothing more than colorful wallpaper. Jaume Martí-Olivella pointed out the "double bind" of tourism in which even a self-conscious and self-reflective tourist may be caught between being the *tourist subject* and the *subject of tourism*.[31] From the presence of the tourist gaze,[32] the distinction between *deadspace* and *thirdspace* enters into a new interrelation where a breakdown of the "either/or" logic may occur. *Either* subjugation *or* dialogue (vertical or horizontal): the fusion of these concepts tied to Soja's *secondspace* destroys the very effectiveness of *thirdspace* as a theoretical tool. How can we theorize over the difference between the following attitudes displayed by tourists: one who falls in love with (the romantic notion of) Machu Picchu; another, who is disgusted by the overly commercialized atmosphere of the site and disappointed by its apparent lack of authenticity; or yet another, who considers Peru, including Machu Picchu, a primitive, inferior space (compared to Europe or the United States), refusing to engage with either the glorious past or the postcolonial present.

From within the differences between these attitudes emerges the understanding of culture as a *production*. In a way, with Machu Picchu broken from its original context (as an Incan winter retreat, contextualized by the historical narrative of the Incas as a colonizing power, itself subsequently colonized by Spain) and metamorphosed into a tourist site, the notion of authenticity as related to tourism has cornered Machu Picchu into a zone of *deadspace*. The image of Machu Picchu is (re)constructed by discourses of tourism that thrive on emphasizing exotic alterity (both the historical and the present-day Other, for the exotic sells) without a subsequent reflection on the nature of the *tourist* as a possible source of alterity. However, if Machu Picchu were not defined as a ruin, or as a space marked as something *dead*, but instead as an entity representative of those who are still living, the situation could change. Thus conceived, it would be a continuum or, in Stuart Hall's words, "a place, a narrative of displacement, that gives rise so profoundly to a certain imaginary plenitude, recreating the endless desire to return to 'lost origins.'"[33] This narrative circle that encloses the present with the origin may be the device needed to circumvent the binary logic of the colonization and break from the image of *deadspace*.

The key to this break is to conceive of Machu Picchu though the image of a *mirror* instead of the image of a *photograph*. The site is thus recontextualized in its physical layout as well as in its historic significance, to the point where one understands Machu Picchu as the *reflection* of Andean identity not solely from the *past* but surrounding us in the *present* by tracing the continuity between ancient and modern times to dissolve the "either/or" dichotomy. This way Machu Picchu becomes a site for the representation of indigenous identity as constituted "not outside but within representation"[34] through non-Eurocentric discourses by which alternative Andean identities can be understood and represented. To further reference Hall's terminology, the broken cultural vector thus may find continuity by which Andean agency may be recovered as the first step toward cultural self-determination.

REVOLUTION AND REAPPROPRIATION

Our aim in this article was very similar to that of Renee Wirth and Robert Freestone's in their endeavor to provide a critical understanding of how "historical places are transformed into places of consumption by investigating the relationship and conflict between culture as a resource for social meaning and a touchstone for economic growth."[35] Cultural agency should be understood as *both* cultural practices at the site itself along with access to self-determination of cultural meaning tied to references of other historical sites in the Andes. Heritage sites could thus be the source of more authentic cultural agency, concerning both the management of the physical sites themselves and the dominance of the metaphorical discursive spaces representing the sites. However, through commodification (or sometimes even disneyfication[36]) heritage sites are more often than not tied to the tourism industry, and through hegemonic discourses tied to and reflective of the commodification process. These heritage sites are transformed to mere tourist sites (presented as "exotic" and divorced from authentic historical meaning) and the possibilities of cultural agency are either obliterated or prohibited. One way of resisting this vertical discursive direction is to develop a discourse through a "third space of enunciation" that liberates the subject positions from the binary and carries within resistance and horizontality at the same time. The encounter of the vertical with the horizontal discursive dynamism results in a revolutionary reinterpretation of the discursive representation of the space. The movement between *deadspace* and *thirdspace* therefore becomes intertwined with the management of the site.

In the specific case of Machu Picchu, the management question is rather complicated. The site is currently managed by "Cosituc," a regional entity that reports to the Ministry of Culture. According to a proposal presented to the Peruvian Parliament in 2012 (but not yet approved or denied as of 2015), the revenues for Machu Picchu (currently $385 million annually, according to the Global Heritage Fund organization, or about 70 percent of the tourism revenue of the country, according to the National Tourism Chamber's figures) should be transferred to the Ministry of Culture in the Peruvian capital, Lima, and managed there. It is evident from the centralized control of revenue that, although regional organizations are involved in the management of the site, the Peruvian government, via its Ministry of Culture, is the major authority over Machu Picchu. The rivalry and hostility toward locals is evident in the latest declaration of Fernando Astete, head of the Machu Picchu Archaeological Park: "There are local authorities and each of them does what he feels like. . . . The problem is one of governability."[37] In view of the above, it is evident that the challenge of the management question is twofold, both economic and ideological.

One central tenet to the ideological part is positioned on the ideology of Hispanism created by nineteenth-century historian José de la Riva Agüero (1753–1858), who (re)wrote the country's history, dividing it into two periods (pre-Hispanic, or "primitive," and post-Hispanic, from the colonization until the nineteenth century, the time of his writing), discarding the non-Hispanic contributions to the country's culture.[38] All this was stated in spite of the heavily indigenous genetic (and consequently cultural) composition of the country that was confirmed in a 2013 study by National Geographic.[39] According to the study, the DNA of 68 percent of the population of Lima (considered as the "whitest" area of Peru) contains indigenous blood. In the mountain area (Sierra), this number is 95 percent. In spite of this, Hispanism still constitutes the foundation of Peru's self-image as a homogeneous nation of European origin and culture.

One way to address the ideological problem may be what Steve Brown suggests regarding Australian heritage sites and the creation of spaces surrounding them (his term is *cultural landscapes*), where "complex and conflicting meanings can be revealed" and histories (i.e., interpretations of history) of recent times are privileged.[40] In the case of Machu Picchu, the creation of such spaces would empower the Quechua population (who do not currently benefit from the revenues of the site, except in nonsystemic, minimal ways, by selling their trinkets, food, etc.). The inheritors of the Inca tradition and history could thus be empowered with cultural agency by managing the representation of their own cultural history so that it would not be considered as "alternative knowledge" (alternative to the Eurocentric version, the main point of reference) but instead would form the core of what is transmitted to tourists about the site. This could take shape in the form of an added museum, or community center, or some such space managed by indigenous "organic intellectuals," to use the Gramscian term,[41] recovering the cultural vector of continuity[42] in the representation of their cultural identity.

The reinterpretation and reappropriation of the meanings associated with historical sites previously imbued by commercially motivated symbolism is the process through which the "decolonized mind"[43] reclaims historical agency and actively resists cultural domination in a postcolonial reality. Nevertheless, the reappropriation of meaning is not a quest for recapturing a sense of "authenticity" from external sources, but rather the ability to articulate cultural identity from an *internal* plurality of meanings that have the potential to either open or suppress new modes of interpretation. This plurality of meaning can only be played out at Machu Picchu if it becomes a *thirdspace* instead of a *deadspace*. Making the shift is a movement of active resistance that leads to change. We submit that such movements may entirely be considered a revolution.

NOTES

1. Uzi Baram and Yorke Rowan, "Archaeology after Nationalism: Globalization and the Consumption of the Past," in *Marketing Heritage: Archaeology and the Consumption of the Past*, eds. Uzi Baram and Yorke Rowan, 3–26 (Lanham, MD: Rowman & Littlefield, 2004), 5.

2. *Commodification* commonly refers to the transformation of goods and services or cultural manifestations into a commodity. In classical economy, a commodity is created to satisfy a specific need. According to Jernej Prodnik, commodity is central to capitalism: "Processes of transforming literally anything into a privatized form of (fictitious) commodity that is exchanged in the circulation process are of fundamental importance for the rise and reproduction of capitalism" ("A Note on the Ongoing Processes of Commodification: From the Audience Commodity to the Social Factory," *Triple-C: Cognition, Communication, Co-operation* 10, no. 2 [2012]: 274). The recontextualization of historical sites for tourist consumption is just an example of such "fictitious" commodity.

3. *Criollo* in the Latin American and specifically Peruvian context refers to a person born in the Americas but of European descent.

4. With the method "carbon 14," the date of the construction of the citadel of Machu Picchu was determined (*El País*, October 12, 1987).

5. Garcilaso de la Vega, El Inca (1539–1616)—the son of a captain of the Spanish conquest of Peru, Sebastián Garcilaso de la Vega, and of Palla Chimpu Occlu, a noblewoman of Inca origin (foreword of *Comentarios Reales de los Incas* [Lisbon, Portugal: Pedro Crasbeeck, 1609], facsimile). His chronicle, the *Comentarios reales de los Incas* (Royal Commentary of the Incas), is a vast encyclopedia of the geography, economy, history, and culture of the Inca Empire.

6. In a typical gesture of a universalist and colonialist perspective that favors hegemonic sources, foreign and *criollo* writings coincided in their supposition that Machu Picchu was "lost." However, indigenous sources were not considered and people were not consulted. For them Machu Picchu was never "lost."

7. In Peru, the geographical division between the *costa* (coast), the *sierra* (mountain), and the *selva* (jungle) corresponds to a racial, social, and cultural division of the country: "Historically, the geographic landscape has given rise to a Peru divided

between a semi-feudal, largely Native American highland interior and a more modernized, capitalistic, urbanized, and mestizo coastal regions" (Joseph S. Tulchin and Brian Fonseca, *Peruvian Strategic Culture* [Miami: Florida International University Press, 2010], 14).

8. Mariana Mould de Pease, "Machu Picchu: A Failed Historic Management," *Peru This Week*, July 26, 2011, www.peruthisweek.com/blogs-machu-picchu-failed-historic-management-50021.

9. According to Mould de Pease, Bingham took a photo of the boy and Sergeant Carrasco, who would have been with him at the time of his "discovery," but he never published this photograph.

10. The term was coined by Mary Louise Pratt in 1992 (*Imperial Eyes: Travel Writing and Transculturation*, 2nd ed. [London: Routledge, 2007 (1992)]), and it refers to spaces (in both the geographical and the social sense) where disparate cultures meet. These places exhibit cultural *métissage* and hybridity as a consequence of such cultural encounters.

11. Cheung argues that "most tourism studies simplify the contest over heritage as foreign tourists versus local peoples" and there is much greater cultural complexity in terms of national and foreign tourism ("The Meanings of a Heritage Trail in Hong Kong," *Annals of Tourism Research* 26, no. 3 [1999]: 572).

12. The Barcelona Field Studies Centre has done a pertinent study on the beneficial and detrimental effects of tourism specifically on the Machu Picchu site (http://geographyfieldwork.com/MachuTourismImpact.htm).

13. Dean MacCannell, *The Tourist: A New Theory of the Leisure Class* (New York: Schocken Books, 1976), 1.

14. Allard Schmidt, "Machu-Picchu-c03," Wikimedia Commons Public Domain, http://commons.wikimedia.org/wiki/Machu_Picchu#mediaviewer/File:Machu-picchu-c03.jpg.

15. Evie Liu, "Peru to Tourists: 'Stop Getting Naked at Machu Picchu!'" *CNN*, March 20, 2014, www.cnn.com/2014/03/20/travel/naked-tourists-machu-picchu-peru.

16. www.machupicchutour.com.

17. The quest for an idea that expresses this in-between space of enunciation that would be able to circumvent the stalemate of binary oppositions would resurface in Antonio Cornejo Polar's concept of heterogeneity. Heterogeneity is embodied in the resistance to the homogenizing forces of colonialism, and to the equally Eurocentric ideologies of the nation-state.

18. Homi K. Bhabha, "In the Cave of Making: Thoughts on Third Space," in *Communicating in the Third Space*, eds. Karin Ikas and Gerhard Wagner, ix–xiv (New York: Routledge, 2009), xiii.

19. Ibid., ix.

20. Ibid., 2.

21. Edward W. Soja, *Thirdspace: Journeys to Los Angeles and Other Real-and-Imagined Places* (Cambridge: Blackwell, 1996), 6.

22. The *Runakuna* (meaning "people" in their language, Runasimi, or better known as Quechua) are the Quechua-speaking indigenous inhabitants (also called

Quichua or Quichwa in Ecuador and Ingas in Colombia) who live in Peru, Ecuador, Bolivia, north of Argentina, north of Chile, and in southern Colombia. These are the areas where the Inca Empire (twelfth to sixteenth centuries) extended, and the Quechua people are the descendants of the Incas.

23. Hall discussed Caribbean identities as "framed by two axes or vectors, simultaneously operative: the vector of similarity and continuity; and the vector of difference and rupture" ("Cultural Identity and Diaspora," in *Colonial Discourse and Postcolonial Theory: A Reader*, eds. Patrick Williams and Laura Chrisman, 392–403 [New York: Columbia University Press, 1994], 26).

24. Soja, *Thirdspace*, 57.

25. Hall, "Cultural Identity and Diaspora."

26. It is important to note that any and all possible representations of Machu Picchu are necessarily loaded with diverse subjectivities. As a result, it would be a mistake for anyone to suggest that the application of *thirdspace* and the power of Machu Picchu rest solely or completely in reconfiguring dichotomies, or any other cultural vectors, into a new form. Instead, we suggest that the representation of such spaces should be a reminder that the powers of the areas are grounded in the mutually beneficial exchanges between individuals and groups.

27. Theodor W. Adorno and Max Horkheimer, "The Culture Industry: Enlightenment as Mass Deception," in *Dialectic of Enlightenment: Philosophical Fragments*, ed. Gunzelin Schmid Noerr, trans. Edmund Jephcott (Stanford: Stanford University Press, 2002), 104.

28. *Boundaries* by definition correspond to a binary conception of space. Therefore, our concept of *thirdspace* and/or *deadspace* is introduced, precisely to extract the conceptualization of the site from the realm of dichotomy.

29. Machu Picchu may be approached by train, by bus, or on foot; the latter choice involves an arduous trekking trip. For more on the topic, see Mark Adams, "Top Six Alternative Routes to Machu Picchu," *National Geographic*, http://travel.nationalgeographic.com/travel/peru/machu-picchu/alternate-trails.

30. At the time of the Spanish colonization, the Inca (emperor) was Atahualpa. Many consider him the last Inca. However, after his execution, ordered by Francisco Pizarro in 1533, there was active resistance to the colonization by four successive monarchs (Incas) between 1537 and 1572: Manco Inca Yupanqui, Sayri Túpac Inca, Titu Cussi Yupanqui, and Túpac Amaru I. Because Cuzco had been occupied by the colonizers, the resistance had to retreat to the mountains of Vilcabamba. This is why these four consecutive Incas are known as the "Incas of Vilcabamba" (cf. Juan Betanzos, *Suma y narración de los Incas* [Madrid: Imprenta de Manuel G. Hernández, 1880], Project Gutenberg, www.gutenberg.org/files/25705/25705-h/25705-h.htm; Garcilaso de la Vega, *Comentarios Reales de los Incas*).

31. Jaume Marti-Olivella, "The Hispanic Post-colonial Tourist," *Arizona Journal of Hispanic Cultural Studies* 1 (1997): 23–42, especially 27 and 30.

32. The term *gaze* is used as defined by Roland Barthes in *Camera Lucida*, where the author proposes a new "history of looking" focusing on the photograph that "mechanically repeats what could never be repeated existentially" since its essence

is "never transcended for the sake of something else" (*Camera Lucida: Reflections on Photography*, trans. Richard Howard [New York: Hill and Wang, 1982], 4). The photograph itself is not distinguished from its referent. Looking at a photograph, it is its representation we see, not the actual photo, which is, thus, rendered invisible.

33. Hall, "Cultural Identity and Diaspora," 402.

34. Ibid., 397.

35. Renee Wirth and Robert Freestone, "Tourism, Heritage and Authenticity: State-Assisted Cultural Commodification in Suburban Sydney, Australia," *Perspectivas urbanas = Urban Perspectives* 3 (2003): 1, www.etsav.upc.es/urbpersp/num03/index.htm.

36. *Disneyfication,* while closely akin to commodification, involves the process of making historical objects into thematic attractions. In other words, if commodification is what Marx described as the abstraction of exchange-value from use-value, then disneyfication is the abstraction of ahistorical-attraction from historical-time. Moreover, insofar as this temporal abstraction is necessarily anachronistic, at best, it sets the stage for making a contact zone into a *deadspace*. Disneyfication is also tied to the Baudrillardian term *hyper-reality*, which functions based on seduction and replacement: a convergence toward a "simulated" version of reality up to the point of manifesting an inability or unwillingness to distinguish the real from its simulacrum. Of course, the "real" is already a disputable term for it presupposes the possibility of an objective view of itself.

37. "Peru Celebrates Machu Picchu Anniversary," *Fox News Latino*, July 7, 2011, http://latino.foxnews.com/latino/entertainment/2011/07/07/peru-celebrates-machu-picchu-anniversary.

38. Betford Betalleluz Meneses, "La imagen de la historia nacional peruana," *Revista Diálogos* 7, no. 1 (2003): 219–34.

39. Quoted in *Chirapaq: Centro de Culturas Indígenas del Perú*, Chirapaq, www.chirapaq.org.pe.

40. Steve Brown, "Landscaping Heritage: Toward an Operational Cultural Landscape Approach for Protected Areas in New South Wales," *Australasian Historical Archeology* 25 (2007): 35.

41. Antonio Gramsci distinguished two types of intellectuals, "traditional" and "organic." The first type is not moved by interest but searches for truth and reason. The "organic" intellectuals act on behalf of the interest of a class (or group) and present counterhegemonic ideas (as opposed to "traditional intellectuals," who follow the discourses of the hegemonic order). See *Selections from the Prison Notebooks* (New York: International Publishers, 1971), 3–14.

42. Hall, "Cultural Identity and Diaspora," 226–27.

43. This is a reference to Ngugi wa Thiongo's book *Decolonising the Mind: The Politics of Language in African Literature* (London: Heineman, 1986), in which the author argues that cultural production (in his case, literature) cannot be "meaningfully" considered "outside the context of those social forces which have made it both an issue demanding our attention and a problem calling for a resolution" (4).

BIBLIOGRAPHY

Adams, Mark. "Top Six Alternative Routes to Machu Picchu." *National Geographic*. http://travel.nationalgeographic.com/travel/peru/machu-picchu/alternate-trails.

Adorno, Theodor W., and Max Horkheimer. "The Culture Industry: Enlightenment as Mass Deception." In *Dialectic of Enlightenment: Philosophical Fragments*, edited by Gunzelin Schmid Noerr, translated by Edmund Jephcott. Stanford: Stanford University Press, 2002.

Baram, Uzi, and Yorke Rowan. "Archaeology after Nationalism: Globalization and the Consumption of the Past." In *Marketing Heritage: Archaeology and the Consumption of the Past*, edited by Uzi Baram and Yorke Rowan, 3–26. Lanham, MD: Rowman & Littlefield, 2004.

Barcelona Field Studies Centre. "Some Potential Benefits and Costs to the Community from Tourism." May 2009. http://geographyfieldwork.com/MachuTourismImpact.htm.

Barthes, Roland. *Camera Lucida: Reflections on Photography*. Translated by Richard Howard. New York: Hill and Wang, 1982.

Baudrillard, Jean. "Simulacra and Simulations." In *Modern Literary Theory and Criticism: A Reader*, edited by David Lodge and Nigel Wood, 403–12. New York: Longman, 1988.

Betanzos, Juan de. *Suma y narración de los Incas*. Madrid: Imprenta de Manuel G. Hernández, 1880. Project Gutenberg. www.gutenberg.org/files/25705/25705-h/25705-h.htm.

Bhabha, Homi K. "In the Cave of Making: Thoughts on Third Space." In *Communicating in the Third Space*, edited by Karin Ikas and Gerhard Wagner, ix–xiv. New York: Routledge, 2009.

Bingham, Hiram. *Lost City of the Incas: The Story of Machu Picchu and Its Builders*. New Haven, CT: Phoenix Press, 2003.

Brown, Steve. "Landscaping Heritage: Toward an Operational Cultural Landscape Approach for Protected Areas in New South Wales." *Australasian Historical Archeology* 25 (2007): 33–42.

Cheung, Sidney. "The Meanings of a Heritage Trail in Hong Kong." *Annals of Tourism Research* 26, no. 3 (1999): 570–88.

Chirapaq: Centro de Culturas Indígenas del Perú. Chirapaq. www.chirapaq.org.pe.

Cornejo-Polar, Antonio, and Susan Casal-Sanchez. "Indigenist and Heterogeneous Literatures: Their Dual Sociocultural Status." *Latin American Perspectives* 16, no. 2 (1989): 12–28. www.jstor.org/stable/2633579.

Danto, Arthur C. *Beyond the Brillo Box: The Visual Arts in Post-historical Perspective*. Berkeley: University of California Press, 1992.

Garcilaso de la Vega, El Inca. *Comentarios Reales de los Incas*. Lisbon, Portugal: Pedro Crasbeeck, 1609. Facsimile.

Gramsci, Antonio. *Selections from the Prison Notebooks*. New York: International Publishers, 1971.

Hall, Stuart. "Cultural Identity and Diaspora." In *Colonial Discourse and Post-colonial Theory: A Reader*, edited by Patrick Williams and Laura Chrisman, 392–403. New York: Columbia University Press, 1994.

hooks, bell. "Eating the Other: Desire and Resistance." In *Black Looks: Race and Representation*, 21–41. Cambridge, MA: South End Press, 1992.

Lefebvre, Henri. *Espace et politique*. Paris: Anthropos. 1972.

Liu, Evie. "Peru to Tourists: 'Stop Getting Naked at Machu Picchu!'" *CNN*, March 20, 2014. www.cnn.com/2014/03/20/travel/naked-tourists-machu-picchu-peru.

Lossau, Julia. "Pitfalls of (Third) Space: Rethinking the Ambivalent Logic of Spatial Semantics." *Communicating in the Third Space*, edited by Karin Ikas and Gerhard Wagner, 62–78. New York: Routledge, 2009.

MacCannell, Dean. *The Tourist: A New Theory of the Leisure Class*. New York: Schocken Books, 1976.

Machu Picchu. Cosmic Travel Network, 2014. www.machupicchu.info.

Marti-Olivella, Jaume. "The Hispanic Post-colonial Tourist." *Arizona Journal of Hispanic Cultural Studies* 1 (1997): 23–42.

Meneses, Betford Betalleluz. "La imagen de la historia nacional peruana." *Revista Diálogos* 7, no. 1 (2003): 219–34.

Moreiras, Alberto. *Tercer espacio: Duelo y literatura en América Latina*. Santiago, Chile: Arcis Lom, 1999.

Mould de Pease, Mariana. "Machu Picchu: A Failed Historic Management." *Peru This Week*, July 26, 2011. www.peruthisweek.com/blogs-machu-picchu-failed-historic-management-50021.

Ngugi wa Thiong'o. *Decolonising the Mind: The Politics of Language in African Literature*. London: Heineman, 1986.

"Peru Celebrates Machu Picchu Anniversary." *Fox News Latino*, July 7, 2011. http://latino.foxnews.com/latino/entertainment/2011/07/07/peru-celebrates-machu-picchu-anniversary.

Pratt, Mary Louise. *Imperial Eyes: Travel Writing and Transculturation*, 2nd edition. London: Routledge, 2007 [1992].

Prodnik, Jernej Amon. "A Note on the Ongoing Processes of Commodification: From the Audience Commodity to the Social Factory." *Triple-C: Cognition, Communication, Co-operation* 10, no. 2 (2012): 274–301.

Roach, John. "Machu Picchu under Threat from Pressures of Tourism." *National Geographic News*, April 15, 2002. http://news.nationalgeographic.com/news/2002/04/0415_020415_machu.html.

Rutherford, Jonathan. "The Third Space: Interview with Homi K. Bhabha." In *Identity: Community, Culture, Difference*, edited by Jonathan Rutherford, 207–21. London: Lawrence & Wishart, 1990.

Schmidt, Allard. "Huayna Picchu." Wikimedia Commons Public Domain. http://commons.wikimedia.org/wiki/Machu_Picchu#mediaviewer/File:Huayna_Picchu.jpg.

———. "Machu-Picchu-c03." Wikimedia Commons Public Domain. http://commons.wikimedia.org/wiki/Machu_Picchu#mediaviewer/File:Machu-picchu-c03.jpg.

———. "Peru Machu Picchu Sunrise." Wikimedia Commons Public Domain. http://commons.wikimedia.org/wiki/File:Peru_Machu_Picchu_Sunrise_2.jpg.

Soja, Edward W. *Postmodern Geographies: The Reassertion of Space in Critical Social Theory*. London: Verso, 1989.

———. *Seeking Spatial Justice*. Minneapolis: University of Minnesota Press, 2010.

———. *Thirdspace: Journeys to Los Angeles and Other Real-and-Imagined Places*. Cambridge: Blackwell, 1996.

Tulchin, Joseph S., and Brian Fonseca. *Peruvian Strategic Culture*. Miami: Florida International University Press, 2010.

Wirth, Renee, and Robert Freestone. "Tourism, Heritage and Authenticity: State-Assisted Cultural Commodification in Suburban Sydney, Australia." *Perspectivas urbanas = Urban Perspectives* 3 (2003). www.etsav.upc.es/urbpersp/num03/index.htm.

World Tourism Organization. *UNWTO Annual Report 2013.* UNWTO, Madrid, 2013. Accessed July 17, 2014. http://dtxtq4w60xqpw.cloudfront.net/sites/all/files/pdf/unwto_annual_report_2013_0.pdf.

7

Hugo Chávez, Iconic Associationism, and the Bolívarian Revolution

Joshua Frye

This chapter analyzes late Venezuelan president Hugo Chávez's imagistic appropriation of Simón Bolívar, nineteenth-century anticolonial Venezuelan revolutionary, while rolling out his Bolívarian Revolution. Chávez appropriated Bolívar's image by strategically positioning himself in front of sculptures, paintings, and 3-D digital reproductions of Bolívar during political ceremonies and addresses over the past decade. Visual images, artifacts, and performances play an important role in public persuasion. Chávez employed visual rhetoric strategically during his fourteen-year presidency. Rhetoric, and particularly visual rhetoric, is instrumental in shaping national identity, collective memory, and stories of origin for a people. History has repeatedly demonstrated this. *Slate* magazine recently conducted a memory experiment by inserting fictitious places or figures into previously developed photographs of political figures and events. The results suggest that image manipulation can reshape public memory. Audiences exposed to these doctored photographs imagined these fictitious images had historical veracity to the point where they would articulate imagined memories of their own to coincide with the figures and places shown to them.[1]

Hugo Chávez is a powerful example of the use of visual rhetoric to help render Venezuela's story of origin. His appropriation of Bolívar's image to help him retell Venezuelans this story is complicated. Venezuelans may be particularly susceptible to Chávez's Bolívarian rendering of their history and national identity. John Lynch argues that the cult of Bolívar was able to reach the heights of religiosity that is has because Venezuela was "a country without a distinguished prehistory."[2] In fact, it is not that Venezuela did not have a distinguished prehistory prior to Bolívar, but rather that colonized peoples have difficulty preserving unbroken, continuous narratives. It is not an amorphous lack of a compelling story of origin but ruptured memory that has perhaps contributed to Chávez's success with re-creating the national identity via a dominant narrative construction casting Bolívar as the anachronistic protagonist. Chávez has delivered a performance par excellence in that many Venezuelans seem to resonate with the insinuation that Chávez was working with the spirit of Bolívar or that Bolívar was working *through* Chávez in twenty-first-century Venezuela.

The Venezuelan public has seen the compound image of [Bolívar + Chávez] during numerous public addresses and press conferences at Miraflores Palace and in the president's office. President Chávez strategically placed Bolívar's image—Venezuela's dominant cultural icon—in the background to help frame Venezuelans' public perceptions and attitudes toward their president, as well as his policies and programs. Chávez appropriated the image of Bolívar to build popular support and legitimize his ideological architecture of the Bolívarian Revolution. Visual rhetoric was a primary strategy for Chávez to build his credibility and legitimate the Bolívarian Revolution during his tenure as Venezuela's president. This chapter theorizes the tactic of *iconic associationism* as one of many tactics available to rhetors employing a strategy of visual rhetoric. I define *iconic associationism* as a political leader's deliberate appropriation of an icon to reconstitute a nation's story of origin, identity, *telos*, and collective agency.

The circulation of images associating Bolívar and Chávez has multiplied in recent years. The association of Bolívar and Chávez has surfaced in campaign materials, posters, banners, and museum art. This significant image has not reached the level of a popular culture meme, but the broader it diffuses, the more effectively it yields rhetorical power. One of these powers is the power of remembering, which shapes a story of origin for Venezuela. Venezuela's revolutionary war with Spain becomes the rhetorically constructed "story of origin" for contemporary Venezuelans. Discounting Venezuela's noncolonial prehistory and anchoring contemporary Venezuelan's identities at this one historical juncture shapes their collective vision for the future, or *telos*.[3] The strategic use of Simón Bolívar, cultural icon, enables Chávez's followers to "read the present through the past."[4] This is a rhetorical maneuver because there is no inherently necessary connection between a predetermined past and this present moment. It is rather a dialectic where rhetors select and connect points from the past with points in the present, accompanied by different renderings and leading to foster this rather than that national identity or political program. Chávez has appropriated the image of Bolívar to enable his social and political programs, which he has framed as antagonistic to the political and economic character of contemporaneous imperialistic power. The ideological divergences between Bolívar and Chávez become less noticeable with Chávez's use of visual rhetoric due to visual rhetoric's ability to reinforce perceptions with a nonrational form of appeal. In Stuart Hall's words, iconic visual signs, accompanied by discourse, are still codes and, because of the cultural resonance of a visual icon, have the "(ideological) effect of concealing the practices of coding which are present."[5]

Chávez has used the visual rhetorical tactic of iconic association to build widespread public support for his late twentieth- and early twenty-first-century socialistic experiment in the Western Hemisphere. Building on the work of semantics,[6] visual theories,[7] rhetorical theory,[8] and gestalt psychology,[9] this chapter introduces the theoretical construct of iconic associationism and explains how it has been used by a contemporary Latin American political actor to accomplish myriad rhetorical effects and accommodate certain political actions. First, the iconicity of Simón Bolívar for Venezuelans is established. Second, the chapter synthesizes, explains, and applies relevant theories to Chávez's iconic associationism. Third, the circulation of the Chávez-Bolívar association and the appropriation, iconic augmentation, and deification of Simón Bolívar's image in the context of the Bolívarian Revolution are analyzed. Finally, the chapter summarizes the argument for iconic associationism and draws conclusions regarding this expansion of the repertoire and practice of visual rhetoric for rhetors and audiences in the twenty-first century.

SIMÓN BOLÍVAR: VENEZUELAN ICON

Simón Bolívar lived from 1783 to 1830. He was born in Caracas, Venezuela, and he died near Santa María, Colombia. As a member of the Creole nobility in Venezuela during Spanish colonial rule, Bolívar spent many years of his young adulthood in Europe, where he was educated and married. Bolívar's upper-class Venezuelan birthright, alongside his aspirations for a prosperous South America, and political theorization of the cruel tyranny of Spain's colonial model of serfdom for American inhabitants contributed to his complex character. From the beginning of his military leadership and expeditions against Spanish occupation of territories in South America in 1813 to the beginning of the decline of his power in

1826, he labored to unite indigenous peoples of South America in resistance and revolution against Spanish colonial rule. However, the public memory of Bolívar in Venezuela as the definitive anticolonial mythic war hero is complicated by evidence that suggests Bolívar was sympathetic to paternalistic but humane forms of colonial power.[10] It was Spain's severe hierarchy that left little room for the meso-level aristocratic authority of colonial governors and viceroys that Bolívar disdained. By 1826, he had united New Granada and Venezuela into the Republic of Colombia, convened a congress to oversee both provinces, published laws for these new states, ousted the Spaniards from upper and lower Peru, signed many proclamations of constitutions, assumed centralized power, and labored to establish a pan-American federation.[11] As one of the most prominent agents of Venezuela's political independence from Spain, Bolívar took on the symbolic status of the definitive revolutionary war hero, much like George Washington did for the United States and Gandhi did for India. Bolívar's status for Venezuelans far surpasses his leadership in South America's revolution against Spain, however.

The fact that Simón Bolívar has achieved the status of a cultural icon is apparent in a variety of ways. South America, like most other regions of the world, has numerous iconic heroes. What sets Simón Bolívar apart is his profound reception in cultural, political, economic, and religious history and identity in Venezuela. Many scholars agree that Bolívar's significance to Venezuelan culture cannot be overstated.[12] For example, the national currency of Venezuela is the Venezuelan Bolívar. There is a Universidad Simón Bolívar. The tallest mountain peak in Venezuela is Mount Bolívar. Venezuela's largest state is Bolívar State, and its capital is Ciudad Bolívar. Many, if not most, Venezuelan cities have a park or a square named after Bolívar. According to Thor Halvorssen, a distant relative of Simón Bolívar, the cultural significance of Bolívar to many parts of Latin America would be roughly equivalent to combining the cultural significance of Washington, Jefferson, Madison, and Lincoln in the United States.[13] Not surprisingly, then, Bolívar is celebrated in numerous educational and cultural forms. In Venezuelan textbooks, for instance, he is called *El Libertador* ("the Liberator").[14] When Bolívar's body was exhumed from the Cathedral Santa María in Colombia and relocated to Caracas in 1841, the cult of Bolívar in Venezuela was born and the Sociedad Bolivariana was formed. Bolívar's power as a mythic hero is also evidenced by the use of his name as an adjectival modifier. Chávez has continued this usage by using "Bolívarian" to rename the country and to refer to the Venezuelan people, his revolution, his political party, policies, social reforms, universities, and institutions.[15] Perhaps having the corporeal remains of the Liberator in the political center of Venezuela provided a material cue to his importance. His remains were treated as religious relics and buried in the National Cathedral. Indeed, Bolívar's significance transcends his use as a mythic war hero and cultural icon for Venezuelan unity. His image is found pervasively across Venezuela, in paintings, murals, and statues. As a figure, "his image is suggested as a supreme type of being."[16]

The maneuver to cultivate and exploit loyalty, identity, and unity from association with a heroic figure is well documented.[17] As Brunk and Fallaw argue, "Political leaders often invoke heroes in an effort to bolster their legitimacy through association with admired predecessors."[18] Political leaders who invoke the name, image, or memory of a past hero draw upon this hero as an authorizing figure who resonates with public memory.[19] According to Edwards, the rhetoric of the authorizing figure is used to (1) define and unify a movement; (2) sanction interpretations and events; and (3) legitimize future goals.[20] Mixon argues that Chávez used Bolívar as an authorizing figure for his version of the Bolívarian Revolution.[21] The appropriation of Bolívar as an authorizing figure for Chávez's revolutionary ideology can be traced to the second printing of the Marxist philosopher J. R. Nuñez Tenorio's *Reencarnar el Espiritu de Bolívar* in Venezuela during Chávez's 1998 rise to power.[22] However, these scholarly treatments examine the discursive appropriation of Bolívar for Venezuela's Bolívarian Revolution, not the visual. The chapter now turns to theoretical treatments of iconicity, the iconic augmentation of Bolívar's image, and Chavez's appropriation of Bolívar's image.

ICONICITY: SIGNS, AUGMENTATION, AND APPROPRIATION

Iconicity is the re-writing of reality.[23]

In his theory of signs, Charles Peirce devises a triadic set of relations. The elements in the triad consist of an object, a sign, and an interpretant. Peirce explains that the object determines the sign through the sign-vehicle. The sign-vehicle is the part of the sign that allows the sign to stand for the object. Not just any part of a sign entails an ability to stand in for its object. In other words, the object places certain limitations on the sign-as-signifier. In figure 7.1, I have taken the liberty of diagraming Peirce's theory of signs, adding some additional symbolic and semantic components.

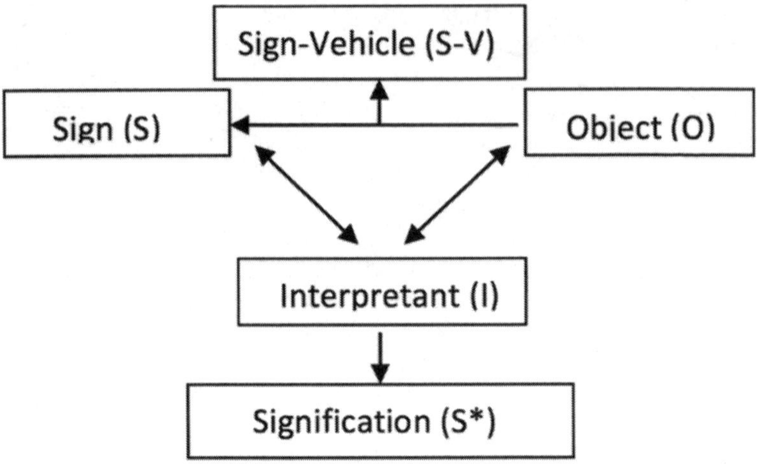

Figure 7.1. Sign diagram (original line drawing by Joshua Frye)

The diagram shows that an object (O) determines a sign (S) through the sign-vehicle (S-V). It further shows how an interpretant (I) both influences and is influenced by the sign-object relation. The interpretant's understanding of the sign-object relation is encoded by the interpretant as a signification (S*). This model helps illustrate a number of subtleties. First, by using bidirectionality between an interpretant, a sign, and an object, I show not only that the interpretant is influenced by the sign, as Peirce explains, but also that consequent to an interpretant's signification of a sign-object relationship, both the sign and the object are semantically altered. This clarification approaches Peirce's notion of infinite semiosis.[24] Additionally, the signification arrived at by a specific interpretant is only one among many understandings possible. Thus, a given signification is a special case of the sign-object relation.

In addition to conceptually mapping the basic components and relationships in a theory of signs, Peirce divides signs into three basic types: icons, indices, and symbols. Icons are signs that gain their significance through the resemblance they bear to the object they represent to the interpretant.[25] Peirce utilizes portraits as an example of an iconic sign and originally proposes that the interpretation of the iconic sign's signification derives from "community in some quality."[26] Thus, the recognition of the same or a similar community of quality in a sign and an object leads an interpretant to acknowledge that sign as a qualitative representation of that object. This type of sign relation is iconic. The second class of sign—indices—are signs that derive their significance through a correspondence of fact, typically a causal relationship. The classic example is "Where there is smoke there is fire." Symbols are Peirce's third class of sign. Symbols derive their significance through an imputed character, which is to say, a culturally or discursive community-specific meaning. The significance of colors, for example, is culturally specific. Peirce's early work on sign theory is useful in setting up a basic understanding of the components and relationships in sign theory. To complement Peirce's analysis of signs, Ricoeur's notions of iconic augmentation and appropriation are helpful in deepening the philosophical and psychological connections between iconic signs, interpretants, and potential significations.[27]

Peirce's theory of iconicity resists the Platonic treatment of art as imitation.[28] Peirce articulates the iconic sign-vehicle as a community of quality shared between the sign and the object. Ricoeur goes even further than Peirce in constructing a nonreductive theoretical understanding of icons. For Ricoeur, a painted portrait resists and ultimately transforms ordinary vision. Through painting's techniques of miniaturizing and contracting an object, as well as painting's ability to enhance contrast and luminosity in an iconic sign, the universe has added meanings and transformed significations.[29] These techniques, in the space of a framed two-dimensional image, generate optical effects of saturation and culmination. These optical effects, far from Plato's reductionism, not only resist a vacuous duplication of reality but also add meaning. This added meaning through artistic portraiture is what Ricoeur called *iconic augmentation*. Because artists are transcribing reality, they have the power to "write a new text of reality."[30] Ricoeur's notion of iconic augmentation deepens Peirce's theory of iconic signs and complicates the nature of the iconic sign-vehicle as well as the resultant range of potential significations. Next, Ricoeur's conceptualization of the appropriation of meaning will be explained in order to show that not only is the S-O relationship important in applying sign theory to particular cases, but the S-I-S* nexus is also grounded in temporal, spatial, and cultural contingencies.

The term *appropriation* has acquired negative connotations. It is commonly thought that to appropriate something is to take it unrightfully or unrighteously. In the post-Lockean ideological context of private property ownership,[31] appropriation is easily misunderstood as someone seizing or possessing something that does not rightfully belong to him or her. Yet appropriation is a perfectly natural—indeed, inevitable—occurrence. As Ricoeur explains, appropriation is the adoption of something from a distance. Ricoeur argues that any discursive product functioning as a new text of reality has semantic autonomy. In other words, any form of art or discourse will eventually become distanced from its original author and contain potentialities other than those inscribed by its author. The greater the distance (e.g., temporal, spatial, cultural) between a new text of reality (e.g., a portrait of Simón Bolívar) and its author, the greater the likelihood that its meaning will be appropriated. This is because, according to Ricoeur, appropriation is the counterpart to semantic autonomy achieved through distanciation. As such, distance is not a correspondence of fact but a dialectical trait in the struggle to reclaim—appropriate—for one's own the meaning of an "other" that has obtained autonomy in its own right. Appropriation, then, is a form of interpretation, ontologically inherent in the human experience, wherein the estranged meaning of a text (which is itself a unique but distant transcription of reality) is made proximate to a new interpretant.

Now that theoretical formulations of iconic signs, iconic augmentation, and appropriation have been explained, the argument for iconic associationism will be presented, building off of the theoretical concepts explained in this section. It will be argued that iconic associationism can function as a visual rhetorical tactic and that this is the case with Hugo Chávez's appropriation of Simón Bolívar's iconicity.

HUGO CHÁVEZ, ICONIC ASSOCIATIONISM, AND THE BOLÍVARIAN REVOLUTION

Chávez's appropriation of Bolívar's image has been instrumental in justifying and legitimizing Chávez's political program, aptly labeled the "Bolívarian Revolution." This section shows how Chávez used Bolívar's image to manipulate the Venezuelan public's perceptions through the juxtaposition of distance and proximity, sending the message of extending Bolívar's work into twenty-first-century South America, and using iconic associationism as a visual rhetorical tactic to retell Venezuela's story of origin, shape collective memory, and reconstitute national identity.

Recalling the sign diagram presented earlier (figure 7.1), figure 7.2 applies to Hugo Chávez's visual rhetorical appropriation of Simón Bolívar. The sign-object relation is complicated by the fact that the sign is not a single object. If the sign (S) were simply a portrait of Simón Bolívar, one would conclude fairly easily that the object (O) would be Simón Bolívar the man. The nature of the relationship between the sign and the object would be a community of quality and the sign would be classified as an icon. However, the fact that the portrait is placed in the background and in the foreground is Venezuela's head of state, the nature of the sign (S), as well as its signifying vehicle (S-V) and significance (S*), is problematized.

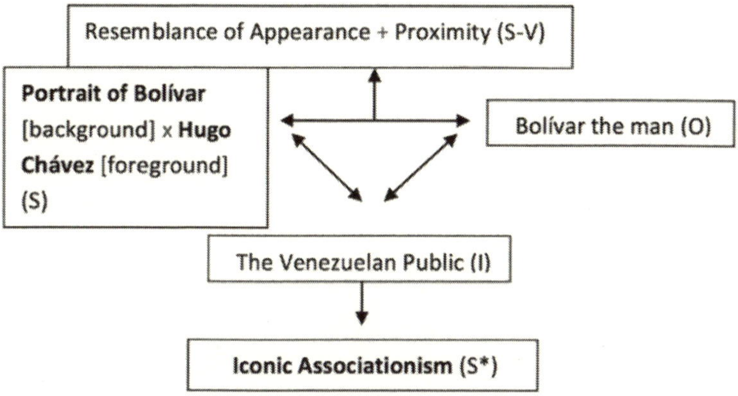

Figure 7.2. Sign diagram of Hugo Chávez's iconic associationism (original line drawing by Joshua Frye)

Chávez complicates the nature of the meaning generated by the sign-vehicle (S-V) for the interpretant (I), who is in this case the Venezuelan public. He effectively takes an iconic sign—Simón Bolívar's portrait/image—and transforms it into a symbol, thus generating an imputed character of meaning for the sign-vehicle. Instead of functioning only as an icon, Bolívar's image is appropriated by Chávez because when Chávez is added to the picture, the result is [Bolívar + Chávez]. This rhetorical move carries multiple complex potential significations and opens up a range of options for the persuader. The significance (S*) is ultimately a new rendering of political identity, history, and mission for Venezuelans and occurs through what is introduced here as *iconic associationism.* Figures 7.3–7.7 document the chronological development of this visual rhetoric, from 2003 to 2012, covering almost a decade of this increasingly built association. Different features of particular images will be referred to and analyzed throughout this section. Of particular interest is the development of iconic associationism, and the analysis will elaborate on the transformation of perception made possible with the help of these particular images.

Chávez has been able to strategically build the iconic association with Bolívar through a deft form of visual rhetoric. The physical proximity between Bolívar's image and Chávez in his rhetorical presidency[32] is one of the most important characteristics that enables the iconic associationism. In his theory of iconicity, Peirce mentions the sheer physical connection between a sign and an object, but gestalt psychology is more helpful in explaining the psychological manipulation of perception occurring with iconic associationism.

The gestalt principle of *emergent features* (or EFs) suggests that there are "features that are possessed by wholes—groups of parts—but not by any individual part nor by any single group of parts."[33] Thus, certain perceived features emerge from parts combined into a whole. In this sense, Chávez creates a compound sign, wherein Bolívar's portrait—an iconic augmentation—is placed in close proximity in the background with Chávez delivering mass-mediated political messages in the foreground. One of the physical characteristics of *Gestalten* perceived through emergent features is proximity. Proximity can lead to a *configural superiority effect*, or CSE. In a CSE, an observer perceives a whole before a part.[34] The relentless iconic associationism over the past several years can/will lead Venezuelan audiences to perceive the compound symbol of [Bolívar + Chávez] as a whole rather than as discrete parts. The emergent features of this compound sign would be difficult to ascertain, but it is certain that the Venezuelan public as the interpretants of these mass-mediated political images construct creative connections and shared features between Bolívar and Chávez. The evolution of this iconic associationism is instructive. The chapter will now analyze the specific features, contexts, and significations of [Bolívar + Chávez].

Since Bolívar is such a powerful cultural icon in Venezuela, it is not unusual that public displays of Bolívar's image by *Chavistas*, like the one during a 2003 commemoration of Venezuela's independence from Spain (see figure 7.3), became common after Chávez renamed the country and ratified this change by rewriting the constitution. Chávez was originally elected to the presidency in 1998, and in 1999 he spearheaded the rewriting of the constitution and the renaming of the country. The country formerly known as Venezuela was renamed the Bolívarian Republic of Venezuela to function as a naming device to legitimize Chávez's Bolívarian Revolution. Chávez is the quintessence of a contemporary iconoclast and revolutionary. Iconoclasts destroy sacred religious symbols, established conventions, and agreed-upon dogma. Evidence of Chávez's iconoclasm lies in his rewriting of Venezuela's constitution and renaming of the country in 1999 and again altering the country's constitution in 2009 to suspend presidential term limits. Thus it is ironic that Chávez, a contemporary iconoclast, built his power in part through the iconicity of Bolívar: an iconoclast benefiting from a long-standing Venezuelan icon. Chávez was a highly controversial political leader. Both his programs and his rhetoric polarized audiences, particularly within Venezuela.[35] It was a *Chavista* in military attire who held up a framed portrait of Bolívar during the 2003 commemoration of Venezuela's independence from Spain. In the context of this celebration of national independence, Bolívar's portrait

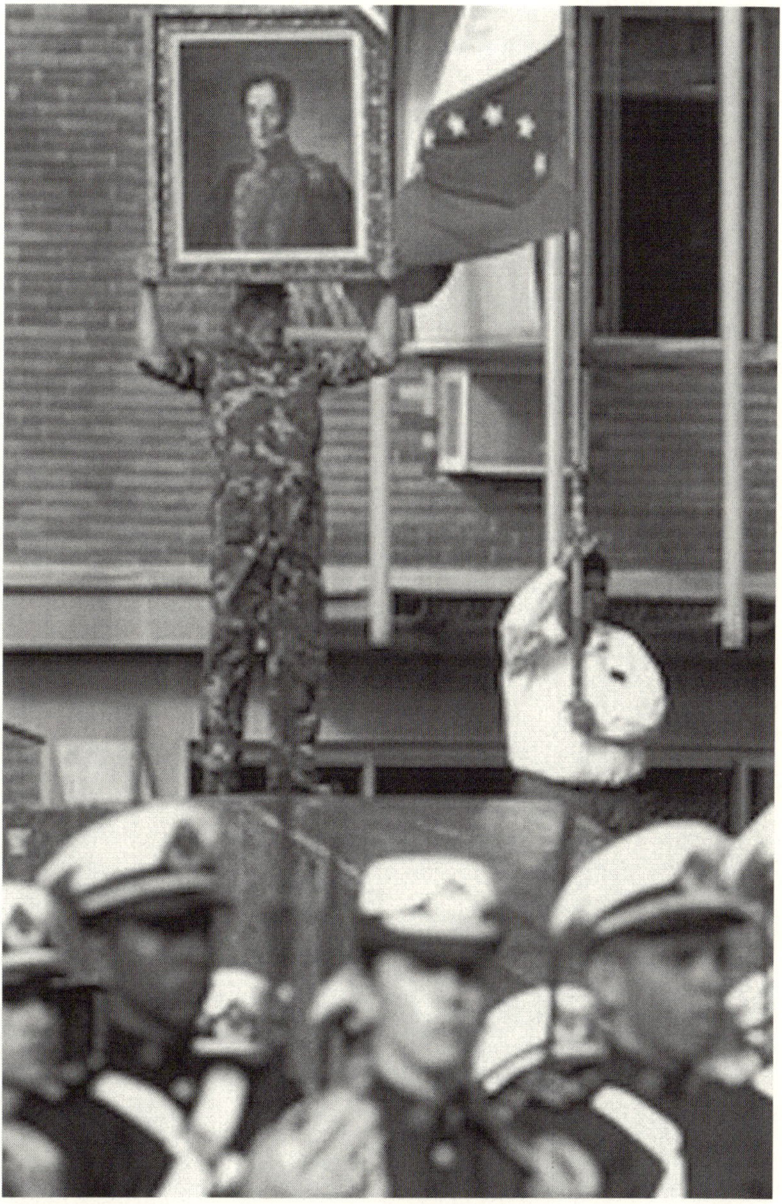

Figure 7.3. A *Chavista* standing on a platform and holding up a portrait of Simón Bolívar next to the Venezuelan flag during a 2003 commemorative celebration of Venezuela's independence from Spain. (Photo credit: European Pressphoto Agency/Miraflores.)

gains a heightened significance. It was a *Chavista* in the Bolívarian Republic of Venezuela that helped to forge an imagistic connection between Chávez, Bolívar, and national identity.

However, it was Chávez's rhetoric that interpellated Venezuelan audiences to reconstitute their identity and agency on the late twentieth- and early twenty-first-century's world stage. Interpellation occurs when an audience acknowledges being addressed. By renaming their country the "Bolívarian" Republic of Venezuela, Chávez created a new ideological subject to whom he could address his claims for the policies and programs of the "Bolívarian Revolution." In his first inaugural address as president, Chávez stated, "We have to revolutionize ourselves, even ourselves, it is time to hear Bolívar once again, and now is when the Venezuelans will hear me speak of Bolívar."[36] Such a move reveals the constitutive nature of rhetoric. It called into being a specific "character, nature, or essence"[37] for Venezuelans under Chávez's leadership. Chávez's proposed Bolívarian Revolution wasn't a revolutionary war against a colonial yoke; it was rather a revolution of identity. Maurice Charland argues that this kind of rhetoric is persuasive because "identity defines inherent motives and interests that a rhetoric can appeal to."[38] Under Chávez's leadership, Venezuelans have been goaded to imagine themselves in the present as embroiled in an ongoing revolution from the continuing imperial powers of the north. A decade and a half ago, Chávez was already doing rhetorical work to exploit Bolívar's cultural capital. Three years later, the visual rhetoric associating Chávez and Bolívar was stronger and more explicit (see figure 7.4).

Figure 7.4 illustrates one of the first explicit public images circulating among Venezuelans whose interpellated subjecthood as members of the Bolívarian Republic and agents of the Bolívarian Revolution becomes inscribed in public imagery. As Charland explains:

> Note, however, that interpellation does not occur through persuasion in the usual sense, for the very act of *addressing* is rhetorical. It is logically prior to the rhetorical *narratio*. In addition, this rhetoric is ongoing, not restricted to one hailing, but usually part of a rhetoric of socialization. Thus, one must already be an interpellated subject and exist as a discursive position in order to be part of the audience of a rhetorical situation in which persuasion could occur.[39]

Thus, the man in figure 7.4 holding the painting has identified with his reconstituted identity. He is a member of the Bolívarian Republic. This image portrays an explicit association between Bolívar and Chávez, as if they were partners or contemporaries. This painting suggests they are co-present in 2006 and coexist in the work of the Bolívarian Revolution. Chávez's renaming of the country created interpellated subjects whose identities

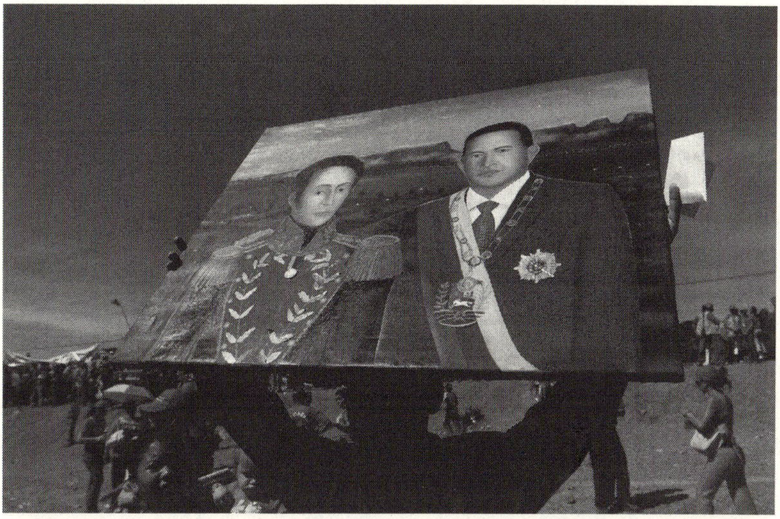

Figure 7.4. A *Chavista* on Margarita Island holding a portrait of President Hugo Chávez standing next to Simón Bolívar, 2006. (Photo credit: European Pressphoto Agency/Chico Sanchez.)

transformed them into reconstituted audiences ready to identify with and be motivated by the appeals of Chávez's ideological rhetoric of the Bolívarian Revolution. As the effects of a rhetoric of interpellation are ongoing, the imagery of contemporary Venezuelans' public art reveals a progressively strong bond between their national identity, their collective agency, and their perceptions of Chávez's ideological program. Additionally, this visual imagery works to reify and strengthen these bonds of identification, thus disseminating and amplifying Chávez's constitutive rhetoric. Chávez's constitutive rhetoric of renaming the country and interpellating Venezuelans into a reconstituted national identity was evident in much of his public address. As Rice affirms, "The ability to employ preexisting authority is a key to gaining and maintaining authority in the present."[40]

Also in 2006, before his appearance at the Kremlin for a Russia-Venezuela summit, Chávez made an appearance at Moscow's Foreign Literature Library, where he delivered remarks in front of Bolívar's statue during an unveiling ceremony (see figure 7.5). Moments such as these are rhetorical situations. Chávez has already reconstituted Venezuelans' identity and their sense of collective agency. This visual rhetoric now allows for a transformation of perception within his target audiences. The transformed perception aligns with Chávez's audiences as interpellated subjects whose identification with Bolívar now extends to Chávez and the ideological work

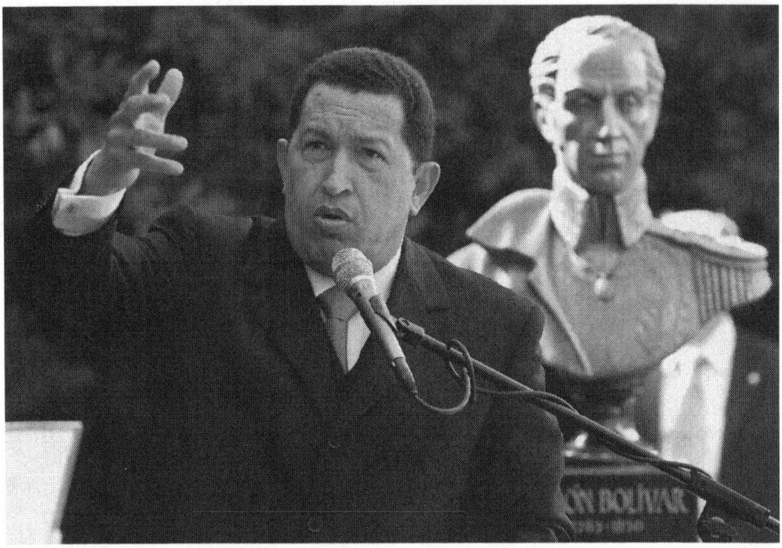

Figure 7.5. Venezuelan president Hugo Chávez delivering remarks in 2006 at Moscow's Foreign Literature Library during an unveiling ceremony of a statue of Simón Bolívar. (Photo credit: European Pressphoto Agency/Sergei Chirikov.)

of the Bolívarian Revolution. Such visual rhetoric presents ongoing socializing and legitimizing functions.

Another way that the visual rhetoric of iconic associationism affects audiences is to provide the visual semantic cue that Chávez is a political agent serving Venezuelans by resuscitating Bolívar's radical program of political independence and cultural unification for the twentieth and twenty-first centuries. According to Conway, "Bolívar represents the continuity and coherence of key terms and concepts, such as independence, liberty, and the nation."[41] Bolívar was the liberator of both Colombia and Venezuela. Bolívar's vision included not only political independence from Spain but also a greater unity among Americans, the project of Gran Colombia, where Venezuela, Colombia, New Grenada, and Ecuador were all unified in a larger republic.[42] Chávez has attempted to appropriate Bolívar's cultural capital through iconic associationism, and through his symbolic association with Bolívar he has taken actions that parallel Bolívar's vision of South American unification. For example, Chávez's foreign aid to the region has surpassed virtually every other nation over the last decade. According to Corrales and Penfold,[43] this is a pointed program of regional ally building.

Additionally, Chávez has become notorious for his anti-U.S. rhetoric. Chávez's anti-imperialism rhetorically shadows Bolívar—only the target of Bolívar's military campaign was Spain and the target of Chávez's rhetorical campaign was the United States. During his visit to Russia in 2006, Chávez met with Russian president Vladimir Putin. During their meeting, Chávez revealed his appropriation of Bolívar to build a foreign policy that privileges economic independence from the United States and social integration through an anti-imperialist struggle:

> We visited a major factory that produces oil refining equipment. Workers, managers and technicians in the factory all told us about reestablishing production after the awful situation at the beginning of the 1990s. . . .
>
> My present visit has a much deeper significance. I am fully determined to continue strengthening relations with Russia. And you well know that this stems from my soul, my heart and the vision of the world that I think we both share. . . .
>
> Just now in the [Foreign Literature] Library we recalled Simón Bolívar. We uncovered a bust in his honour. I remembered an oath that Bolivar made in 1805 when he said: "I will not fail, and neither my heart nor my hand will fail." In our struggle we also should not allow either our minds or our hands to get tired. Venezuela will be always with you in this.
>
> As you said, we are ready to expand and strengthen bilateral relations. And in this sense we can continue our efforts towards establishing a multipolar world. I am very grateful for your personal solidarity and Russia's solidarity.[44]

The anti-U.S. foreign-policy rhetoric here is subtle, but Chávez's allusion to former president George W. Bush as the devil in a speech to the United Nations—also in 2006—is not and illustrates the depths to which he was willing to take this demonization.[45] Even though Venezuela is a politically independent nation, Chávez has captured the hearts and minds of his followers by polarizing them against the United States and creating a strong identification by antithesis.[46] These elements of political rhetoric and foreign policy in Chávez's attempts to reincarnate Bolívar's vision of South American unification have been propelled by visual rhetoric's ability to shape Venezuelans' public memory and craft a story of origin.

If Chávez can retell Venezuelans and other potential allies the anti-imperialist revolutionary war against Spain is their story of origin, he can remold the *telos* for Venezuela and anti-imperialist audiences by crafting a strategic parallel-case narrative. Stephen Toulmin identifies a parallel case as a reasoning process that functions effectively as a policy argument warrant.[47] Chávez propels the work of the Bolívarian Revolution by extrapolating his story of origin to the present. This is a hybridization of deliberative policy-making rhetoric and imaginative storytelling. In order for the story to be believable, Chávez needed to create narrative rationality.[48] This narrative rationality would come from making the story cohere internally, or making the parts of the story appear consistent and "ring true." If Chávez was to stand in for Bolívar, almost as if he were an authorized intervener, the story would only be coherent if Venezuela had a Spain to struggle against. Recasting Spain as the United States supplied Chávez with this symbolic resource, and he matched his rhetoric to the task, positioning the United States in a parallel relation to Venezuela almost two hundred years after its first Bolívarian revolution. The visual rhetoric Chávez used flattened the complexities and potential historical and ideological divergences that could be used to detect a false analogy in the parallel-case narrative. Rather, Venezuelans and other potential anti-capitalist allies—such as Russia—were repeatedly socialized to identify with the visual rhetoric of [Bolívar + Chávez] and internalize this identity as sufficient to warrant belief in Venezuela's story of origin, *telos*, and all of the accompanying policies and programs of the Bolívarian Revolution.

By 2009, a portrait of Bolívar similar to the one publicly displayed by a *Chavista* in 2003 was hanging in the president's office in Miraflores Palace in Caracas (see figure 7.6). Figures 7.3 and 7.6 show that the artist of each portrait has taken the liberty of creating an aura of luminosity behind Simón Bolívar's head. A technique similar to Warner Sallman's[49] famous portrait of Christ, the icon gains a supernatural *ethos*. This feature alone is evidence in support of Ricoeur's notion of iconic augmentation being present in the appropriation of Bolívar's image. Given Bolívar's mythic heroism, these artistic portraits optically transcribe Bolívar's significance in a fashion that augments perceptions of his power even more than what can be found in educational or political discourse. If the artistic portrait is the quintessence of an inconic sign and enables the transformation of meaning through iconic augmentation, what kind of image could possibly add more meaning? The answer to this question is found in religious rhetoric, whose transposition to the political realm creates the ultimate argument for social disorder/broken covenant, sacrifice, redemption, and transcendence. As Burke explains in *The Rhetoric of Religion*, "The 'fall' and the 'redemption' are but parts of the same cycle, with each part implying the other."[50] In 1980, the cardinal archbishop of Caracas equated the exile of Bolívar's remains to Colombia as the reason for Venezuela's modern plight, as well as deifying Bolívar:

> The infamous proposal of exile against the Father of the Patria, accepted without protest by the Venezuelan nation, was a clear rejection of his character as the divine chosen one. And this is the reason why ever since 1830, when this iniquity was committed, our national history for the whole of the past century can be summarized as one of devastating civil wars and prolonged tyrannies.[51]

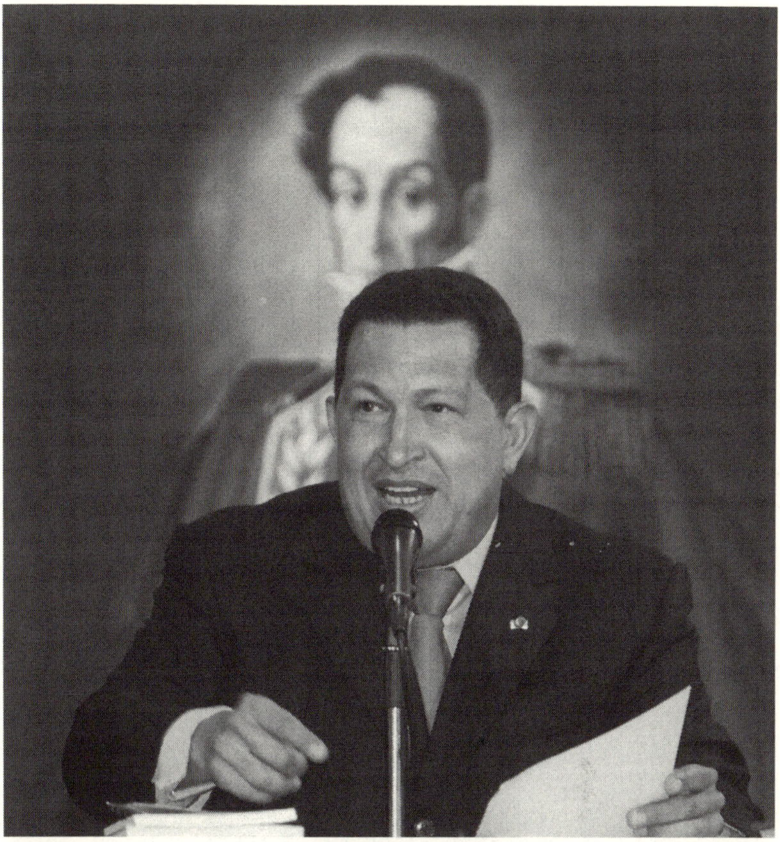

Figure 7.6. Venezuelan president Hugo Chávez speaking from the President's Office in 2009 in front of a portrait of Simón Bolívar. During this speech, he announced the upcoming release of the journal *Correo del Orinoco,* named for a newspaper founded by Simón Bolívar during Venezuela's independence war with Spain in the nineteenth century. (Photo credit: European Pressphoto Agency.)

Here Bolívar's exile is the broken covenant and the social disorder resulting from it will require some ritual to move Venezuelans toward redemption. In 2010, Chávez consummated the cardinal archbishop's rhetoric by decreeing that the skeletal remains of Simón Bolívar were to be exhumed. Chávez himself presided over the exhumation. During a passionate allegorical reenactment fusing Pablo Neruda poetry and biblical scripture, Chávez had televised the following sequence of images: (1) a painted portrait of Bolívar; (2) Bolívar's skeletal remains; and (3) images of Chávez, all set to the musical score of Venezuela's national anthem.[52] This conflation of nationalism and supernaturalism at once imbued Bolívar with enhanced cultural capital as well as reifying his "demigod" status.[53] Bolívar's demigod status combined with Chávez's advanced rhetorical manipulation of his image created a kind of superordinate meaning. This form of iconic associationism delivered extraordinary religiopolitical significations.

Figure 7.7 illustrates the most recent, most official, and eeriest iconic associationism between Chávez and Bolívar. In this figure we see a giant

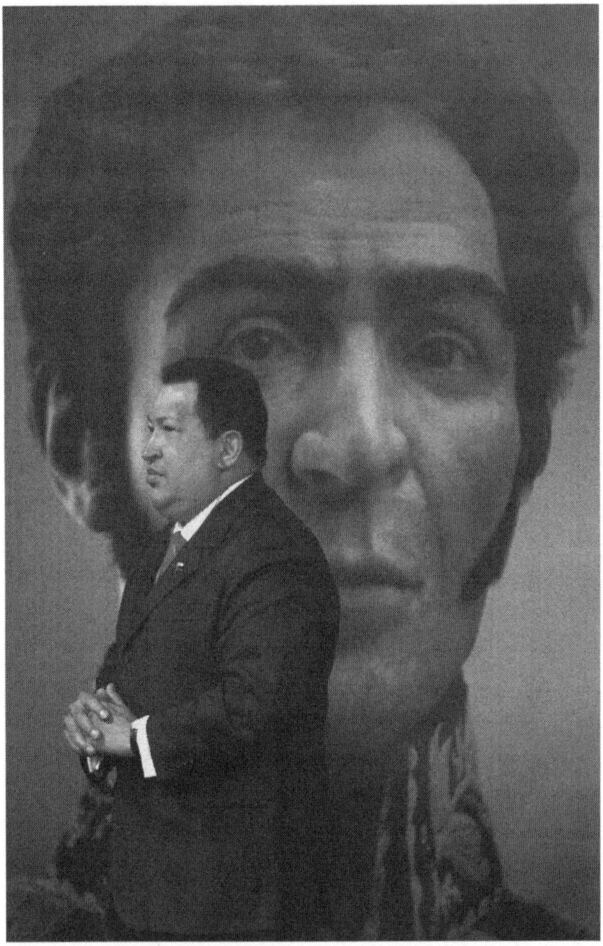

Figure 7.7. President Hugo Chávez posing in front of the newly unveiled scanned image of Simón Bolívar in Miraflores Palace, 2012. The image was generated from a three-dimensional reconstruction of Bolívar's skull structure. (Photo credit: European Pressphoto Agency/David Fernandez.)

three-dimensional reconstructed image of Bolívar, derived from his skull structure. This procedure was made possible from the public ritual exhumation of Bolívar's skeletal remains in 2010. The larger-than-life scanned image was framed and hung in Miraflores Palace. In figure 7.7, Chávez is poised in front of Bolívar's reconstructed image; he is in effect performing iconic associationism. The fact that this instance of imagistic appropriation portrays Bolívar as having a gigantic presence cues the growth of the significance of Bolívar in Venezuela in 2012 and perhaps the concomitant advancement of the Bolívarian Revolution.

The process of converting archaeological remains to a digitized image is itself a form of appropriation. An exact reproduction of Bolívar's physical appearance is impossible. His reappearance, in form, style, and place, is premised on co-optation. The 3-D image is based on numerous scans of Bolívar's skull and the latest forensic techniques of facial reconstruction. Nevertheless, this verisimilitude of Bolívar's appearance reduces the figurative distance between Bolívar and Chávez and fosters a new and different tenor of proximity and a heightened significance. The resultant compound symbolic sign, of Bolívar's facial reproduction framed in the background with Chávez in the foreground, is an extreme example of the dialectic of appropriation: distance and proximity. It is only because of the great literal distance originally between Chávez and Bolívar in terms of both time and space that this uncanny proximity of the two is an extreme example of appropriation; it is the juxtaposition of distance and proximity that insinuates near-total appropriation.

In the unveiling ceremony for this image, Chávez declared, "Now we know with precision and receive with infinite intensity the luminous presence of this gaze, this living face."[54] In many of his speeches, Chávez "extol[ed] the demi-god Liberator the way Priests summon Christ at mass."[55] When Chávez unearthed Bolívar's remains in 2010, he enacted a moment of inspiration, fusing high culture and the divine word. If Bolívar's portrait could be iconically agumented like Warner Sallman's famous depiction of Christ to confer supernaturalism through a halo of light behind his head, the next step in manufacturing divinity could come from skeletal scans and three-dimensional digital projections: you cannot get much closer to reincarnation than this. It is not Bolívar in the flesh, but it is a scientifically modeled, larger-than-life, three-dimensional digital projection of Bolívar's face based on scans of his skull.

Chávez has positioned himself between this image of Bolívar and his Venezuelan audience. In discussing the role relationship between an authorizing figure, a political leader, and an audience, Laura Mixon contends that "one could even view the speaker as a mediator between the audience and the authorizing figure, perhaps similar to the role of the Roman Catholic priest as an intercessor before God on behalf of his parishioners in the act of consecrating bread and wine in Mass."[56] Mixon is not discussing visual rhetorical strategy, however. In the ceremony of Mass, the priest-as-intercessor is strengthened by the presence of religious icons and symbols. Hugo Chávez's iconic associationism with Bolívar's "infinite intensity" and "luminous presence" indeed suggests an intercession.

Chávez is able to accomplish more than an intercession, however. With this extreme appropriation and advanced iconic associationism, Chávez plays with superordinate meaning. In practice, Chávez has attempted a profane version of reincarnation. And alongside Chávez's performance of Bolívar's infinite intensity, luminosity, and presence, the Venezuelan audience is once again interpellated. This time, however, they are meant to be more than empowered agents of the Bolívarian Republic and Revolution. Through Chávez's visual rhetoric of iconic associationism, *Chavistas* are reconstituted as heightened moral combatants with a virtuosity insinuating sainthood. The fact that the images in figures 7.6 and 7.7 are strategically placed in Miraflores Palace is further evidence in support of Chávez's appropriation and manipulation of Bolívar's image and mythos for his own ideological purposes.[57]

CONCLUSIONS

This chapter has introduced and coined the theoretical construct of *iconic associationism* as a visual rhetorical tactic. Building on work in semantics, visual theory, rhetoric, and psychology, iconic associationism is based on principles of cultural iconicity, iconic augmentation, configural superiority effects, strategic placement, and appropriation through the distance-proximity dialectic. Numerous potential rhetorical, political, and psychological consequences of Hugo Chavez's appropriation of Simón Bolívar's image were discovered through this analysis. These include reconstituting audience identity through interpellation, building collective agency, flattening ideological differences of an authorizing figure through use of visual iconography, extending the justification of a political ideology, selective storytelling of origins and destiny, and strategic parallel-case narrative.

Through his rhetorical presidency, Hugo Chávez has inserted himself into the unfinished legacy of Simón Bolívar. He has taken the religiosity of Bolívar to new political heights. His iconic associationism with Bolívar has been a powerful form of visual rhetoric to assist him on his mythic reconstruction of Venezuela's story of origin, national identity, collective agency, oppressors, and *telos*. Chávez has appropriated Bolívar's image through iconic associationism and in so doing he has justified his Bolívarian Revolution and retold Venezuela's story of origin and destiny. Since Chávez contributed to changing the Constitution of Venezuela in 1998 to accommodate the insertion of Bolívar's name into the very name of the country, he has worked rhetorically to build on this connection. The iconic associationism technique as used by Chávez has functioned to strengthen the connections between contemporary Venezuelans, the Bolívarian Republic, and the Bolívarian Revolution.

This chapter has several limitations. Notably, the construct of iconic associationism developed in this work has been built on the examination of one instance of its use. Other instances would no doubt modify the articulation of this form of visual rhetoric and contribute to the arguments developed here. Also, any cross-cultural or intercultural study of visual rhetoric with political and ideological facets will potentially pose issues of cultural insensitivity or ideological bias. The focus of this chapter has not been on the political ideology of the Bolívarian Revolution, Chávez's successes and failures, or specific programs and policies. Rather, this chapter has articulated a visual rhetorical tactic that was put to use during the rise of the late iconoclastic and populist president of Venezuela. Additionally, the focus on Chávez and his attempts to persuade Venezuelans poses the risk of excluding the agency, social organizing, and political advances made through this provocative form of participatory democracy. Lastly, oppositional voices and images were not taken into account. These may have shed light on the resistance to Chávez's appropriation and use of Bolívar's image.

In terms of future research, the construct of iconic associationism could be further developed by comparative analysis with studies in iconography and visual rhetoric. Also, further inquiry into the theoretical construct of iconic associationism as a form of visual rhetoric could apply this model to other historical and cultural cases in order to refine and elaborate the construct and explore their rhetorical, psychological, and political usages and consequences.

NOTES

1. Will Saletan, "The Memory Doctor," *Slate*, June 4, 2010, accessed March 5, 2013, www.slate.com/articles/health_and_science/the_memory_doctor/2010/06/the_memory_doctor.html.

2. John Lynch, *Simón Bolívar: A Life* (New Haven, CT, and London: Yale University Press, 2007), 301.

3. William F. Lewis, "Telling America's Story: Narrative Form and the Reagan Presidency," *Quarterly Journal of Speech* 73 (1987): 280–302.

4. Lester C. Olson, Cara A. Finnegan, and Diane S. Hope, *Visual Rhetoric* (Thousand Oaks, CA: Sage, 2008).

5. Stuart Hall, "Encoding/Decoding," in *Media and Cultural Studies: Key-Works*, eds. M. G. Durham and D. M. Kellner (Oxford: Blackwell, 2006), 167.

6. Charles S. Peirce, *Collected Papers of Charles Sanders Peirce*, vols. 1–6, eds. C. Hartshorne and P. Weiss (Cambridge, MA: Harvard University Press, 1931–1935); Paul Ricoeur, *Interpretation Theory: Discourse and the Surplus of Meaning* (Fort Worth: Texas Christian University Press, 1976).

7. Hall, "Encoding/Decoding"; Lewis, "Telling America's Story"; Olson, Finnegan, and Hope, *Visual Rhetoric*.

8. Kenneth Burke, *The Rhetoric of Religion: Studies in Logology* (Berkeley: University of California Press, 1961); Kenneth Burke, *A Rhetoric of Motives* (Berkeley: University of California Press, 1969); Maurice Charland, "Constitutive Rhetoric: The Case of the Peuple Quebecois," *Quarterly Journal of Speech* 73 (1987): 133–50; Jason A. Edwards, "Sanctioning Foreign Policy: The Rhetorical Use of President Harry Truman," *Presidential Studies Quarterly* 39 (2009): 454–72; Walter R. Fisher, *Human Communication as Narration: Toward a Philosophy of Reason, Value, and Action* (Columbia: University of South Carolina Press, 1987); Laura Mixon, *Use of the Authorizing Figure, Authoritarian Charisma, and National Myth in the Discourse of Hugo Chávez: Toward a Critical Model of Rhetorical Analysis for Political Discourse* (Ann Arbor, MI: ProQuest, 2009); Stephen Toulmin, *The Uses of Argument* (Cambridge: Cambridge University Press, 1958); Donald E. Rice, *The Rhetorical Uses of the Authorizing Figure: Fidel Castro and Jose Marti* (Westport, CT: Praeger, 1992).

9. Johan Wagemans et al., "A Century of Gestalt Psychology in Visual Perception: II. Conceptual and Theoretical Foundations," *Psychological Bulletin* 138 (2012): 1218–52.

10. Simón Bolívar, *La Carta de Jamaica*, 1815, accessed December 14, 2013, http://history202.wikispaces.com/file/view/Jamaica+Letter.pdf.

11. Karl Marx, "Bolívar y Ponte, Simón," in *The New American Cyclopaedia, Vol. III*, eds. G. Ripley and C. A. Dana (New York: D. Appleton, 1858).

12. Samuel Brunk and Ben Fallaw, "Heroes and Their Cults in Modern Latin America," in *Heroes & Hero Cults in Latin America*, eds. Samuel Brunk and Ben Fallaw, 1–20 (Austin: University of Texas Press, 2006); Christopher Conway, *The Cult of Bolívar in Latin American Literature* (Gainesville: University Press of Florida, 2003); Alejandro Cañizáles, *En Venezuela la batalla es simbólica: Uso de la historia en la confrontación política actual* (Caracas, Venezuela: Universidad Católica Andrés Bello, 2007); Lynch, *Simón Bolívar*; Mixon, *Use of the Authorizing Figure, Authoritarian Charisma, and National Myth in the Discourse of Hugo Chávez*.

13. T. Halvorssen, "Behind Exhumation of Simon Bolivar Is Hugo Chavez's Warped Obsession," *Washington Post*, July 25, 2010.

14. *Día de Simón Bolívar* (n.d.), retrieved January 8, 2016, http://classzone.com/books/en_espanol_shared/ML1/ML_1_Bolivar/ml_1_bolivar.html.

15. Mixon, *Use of the Authorizing Figure, Authoritarian Charisma, and National Myth in the Discourse of Hugo Chávez.*

16. Cañizáles, *En Venezuela la batalla es simbólica*, 175.

17. Benedict Anderson, *Imagined Communities: Reflections on the Origins and Spread of Nationalism* (London: Verso, 1991).

18. Brunk and Fallaw, "Heroes and Their Cults in Modern Latin America," 3.

19. Rice, *The Rhetorical Uses of the Authorizing Figure.*

20. Edwards, "Sanctioning Foreign Policy."

21. Mixon, *Use of the Authorizing Figure, Authoritarian Charisma, and National Myth in the Discourse of Hugo Chávez.*

22. Manuel Anselmi, *Chávez's Children: Ideology, Education, and Society in Latin America* (Lanham, MD: Lexington Books, 2013).

23. Ricoeur, *Interpretation Theory*, 42.

24. Albert Atkin, "Peirce's Theory of Signs," *The Stanford Encyclopedia of Philosophy* (Winter 2010), ed. Edward N. Zalta, accessed February 23, 2013, http://plato.stanford.edu/archives/win2010/entries/peirce-semiotics.

25. Ibid.

26. Peirce, *Collected Papers of Charles Sanders Peirce*, vol. 2, 56.

27. Ricoeur, *Interpretation Theory.*

28. Plato, *Republic*, trans. C. Emlyn-Jones and W. Preddy (Cambridge, MA: Harvard University Press, 2013), book 10.

29. Ricoeur, *Interpretation Theory.*

30. Ibid., 41.

31. John Locke's epistemology conveniently enabled and encouraged the political philosophy of private property. For a provocative and extensive treatment of this rhetorical phenomenon, see John D. Peters, *Speaking into the Air: A History of the Idea of Communication* (Chicago: University of Chicago Press, 1999).

32. Jeffrey K. Tulis, *The Rhetorical Presidency* (Princeton, NJ: Princeton University Press, 1988).

33. Wagemans et al., "A Century of Gestalt Psychology in Visual Perception," 1220.

34. Wagemans et al., "A Century of Gestalt Psychology in Visual Perception."

35. Pro-Chávez audiences, or *Chavistas*, as they are called, believe in Hugo Chávez's revolutionary rhetoric and reforms, or "missions," as they are called. Others, anti-Chávez audiences, believe him to be a demagogue and likely to follow in the footsteps of so many other Latin American dictators. There is scant objective literature on *Chavista* audience characteristics. Those accounts that do exist, whether academic, media, or oppositional, tend to oversimplify and caricaturize pro-Chávez audiences as young, poor, uneducated, and state controlled (Damarys Canache, *Venezuela: Public Opinion and Protest in a Fragile Democracy* [Miami, FL: North and South Center Press, 2002]; Philip Oxhorn, "Social Inequality, Civil Society, and the Limits of Citizenship in Latin America," in *What Justice?*

Whose Justice? Fighting for Fairness in Latin America, eds. S. Eckstein and T. P. Wickham-Crowley, 35–63 [Berkeley: University of California Press, 2003]; Mark Ungar, "Contested Battlefields: Policing in Caracas and La Paz," *NACLA Report on the Americas* 37 [2003]: 30–36). These analyses tend to be Chávez-centric. Ramirez has written a more-recent and objective account of *Chavista* organizations and individuals as "politically experienced and relatively autonomous components of a complex counter-hegemonic social movement that shares a political overview and is allied with the state" (138). According to a recent poll conducted by Columbia University's Earth Institute, Venezuela is the happiest country in South America (John Helliwell, Richard Layard, and Jeffrey Sachs, *World Happiness Report* [New York: The Earth Institute at Columbia University, 2012]). And according to the Gallup organization's world well-being polls, Venezuela is the fifth-happiest country in the world (Julie Ray, "High Wellbeing Eludes the Masses in Most Countries Worldwide," *Gallup*, 2011, accessed September 27, 2012, www.gallup.com/poll/147167/High-Wellbeing-Eludes-Masses-Countries-Worldwide.aspx#1). Others have called for more objective analyses of the high level of politically engaged individuals in Venezuela committed to democratic change and the rich level of civil society that they have created. More research needs to be conducted to explore the possible linkages between a sense of agency and happiness.

36. Hugo Chávez, "Discurso de la Toma de Posesion," 1999, accessed December 7, 2013, www.analitica.com/bitblioteca/hChávez/toma.asp.

37. Charland, "Constitutive Rhetoric," 137.

38. Ibid.

39. Ibid., 138.

40. Rice, *The Rhetorical Uses of the Authorizing Figure*, 131.

41. Conway, *The Cult of Bolívar in Latin American Literature*, 4.

42. Lynch, *Simón Bolívar.*

43. Javíer Corrales and Michael Penfold, *Dragon in the Tropics: Hugo Chávez and the Political Economy of Revolution in Venezuela* (Washington, DC: Brookings Institution Press, 2003).

44. Hugo Chávez, "Beginning of the Meeting with the President of Venezuela, Hugo Chávez," Ministry of Foreign Affairs of the Russian Federation, 2006, accessed December 7, 2013, www.mid.ru/brp_4.nsf/e78a48070f128a7b43256999005bcbb3/b54269f706d09c0cc32571b9003c4449?OpenDocument.

45. David Stout, "Chávez Calls Bush 'the Devil' in UN Speech," *New York Times*, September 20, 2006, accessed March 2, 2013, www.nytimes.com/2006/09/20/world/americas/20cnd-Chávez.html?_r=0.

46. In *A Rhetoric of Motives*, Burke (1969) argues that the strongest form of identification is identification by antithesis. Rather than locating commonalities shared between a rhetor and an audience, identifying a common enemy is a sure way to foster a strong bond and articulate an "us-them" polarization.

47. Toulmin, *The Uses of Argument.*

48. Fisher, *Human Communication as Narration.*

49. Warner Sallman's portrait of the head of Christ was very familiar in the United States during World War II. The image was reproduced by the YMCA and

the Salvation Army and distributed to soldiers, libraries, and schools. According to its publishers, the image has been reproduced more than five hundred million times. It hung in many schools across the United States until the Supreme Court ordered that these art pieces be taken down. You can see the image here: www.warnersall man.com/collection/images/head-of-christ.

50. Burke, *The Rhetoric of Religion*, 218.

51. Germán Carrera Damas, *Venezuela: Proyecto Nacional y podel social* (Barcelona, Spain, 1986).

52. Halvorssen, "Behind Exhumatin of Simon Bolivar."

53. Germán Carrera Damas, *El culto a Bolívar* (Caracas, Venezuela, 1969).

54. "Venezuela's Chávez Unveils 3D Image of Hero Bolívar," *Terra*, 2012, accessed February 12, 2013, http://news.terra.com/venezuelas-Chávez-unveils-3d-image-of-hero-Bolívar,53d2cf97d9ab8310VgnVCM3000009acceb0aRCRD.html.

55. Tim Padgett, "Why Venezuela's Chávez Dug Up Bolívar's Bones," *Time*, July 17, 2010, accessed March 5, 2013, www.time.com/time/world/article/0,8599,2004526,00.html.

56. Mixon, *Use of the Authorizing Figure, Authoritarian Charisma, and National Myth in the Discourse of Hugo Chávez*, 53.

57. J. L. Edwards and C. K. Winkler, "Representative Form and the Visual Ideograph: The Iwo Jima Image in Editorial Cartoons," *Quarterly Journal of Speech* 83 (1997): 289–310.

BIBLIOGRAPHY

Anderson, Benedict. *Imagined Communities: Reflections on the Origins and Spread of Nationalism.* London: Verso, 1991.

Anselmi, Manuel. *Chávez's Children: Ideology, Education, and Society in Latin America.* Lanham, MD: Lexington Books, 2013.

Aponte-Moreno, Marco, and Lance Lattig. "Chávez: Rhetoric Made in Havana." *World Policy Journal* 29 (2012): 33–42.

Atkin, Albert. "Peirce's Theory of Signs." In *The Stanford Encyclopedia of Philosophy* (Winter 2010), edited by Edward N. Zalta. Accessed February 23, 2013. http://plato.stanford.edu/archives/win2010/entries/peirce-semiotics.

Bolívar, Simón. *La Carta de Jamaica.* 1815. Accessed December 14, 2013. http://history202.wikispaces.com/file/view/Jamaica+Letter.pdf.

Brunk, Samuel, and Ben Fallaw. "Heroes and Their Cults in Modern Latin America." In *Heroes & Hero Cults in Latin America*, edited by Samuel Brunk and Ben Fallaw, 1–20. Austin: University of Texas Press, 2006.

Burke, Kenneth. *A Rhetoric of Motives.* Berkeley: University of California Press, 1969.

———. *The Rhetoric of Religion: Studies in Logology.* Berkeley: University of California Press, 1961.

Canache, Damarys. *Venezuela: Public Opinion and Protest in a Fragile Democracy.* Miami, FL: North and South Center Press, 2002.

Cañizáles, Alejandro. *En Venezuela la batalla es simbólica: Uso de la historia en la confrontación política actual*. Caracas, Venezuela: Universidad Católica Andrés Bello, 2007.

Carrera Damas, Germán. *El culto a Bolívar*. Caracas, Venezuela, 1969.

———. *Venezuela: Proyecto Nacional y podel social*. Barcelona, Spain, 1986.

Charland, Maurice. "Constitutive Rhetoric: The Case of the Peuple Quebecois." *Quarterly Journal of Speech* 73 (1987): 133–50.

Chávez, Hugo. "Beginning of the Meeting with the President of Venezuela, Hugo Chávez." Ministry of Foreign Affairs of the Russian Federation, 2006. Accessed December 7, 2013. www.mid.ru/brp_4.nsf/e78a48070f128a7b43256999005bcbb3/b54269f706d09c0cc32571b9003c4449?OpenDocument.

———. "Discurso de la Toma de Posesion." 1999. Accessed December 7, 2013. www.analitica.com/bitblioteca/hChávez/toma.asp.

Conway, Christopher. *The Cult of Bolívar in Latin American Literature*. Gainesville: University Press of Florida, 2003.

Corrales, Javíer, and Michael Penfold. *Dragon in the Tropics: Hugo Chávez and the Political Economy of Revolution in Venezuela*. Washington, DC: Brookings Institution Press, 2003.

Día de Simón Bolívar (n.d.). Retrieved January 8, 2016. http://classzone.com/books/en_espanol_shared/ML1/ML_1_Bolivar/ml_1_bolivar.html.

Edwards, Jason A. "Sanctioning Foreign Policy: The Rhetorical Use of President Harry Truman." *Presidential Studies Quarterly* 39 (2009): 454–72.

Edwards, J. L., and C. K. Winkler. "Representative Form and the Visual Ideograph: The Iwo Jima Image in Editorial Cartoons." *Quarterly Journal of Speech* 83 (1997): 289–310.

Fisher, Walter R. *Human Communication as Narration: Toward a Philosophy of Reason, Value, and Action*. Columbia: University of South Carolina Press, 1987.

Hall, Stuart. "Encoding/Decoding." In *Media and Cultural Studies: KeyWorks*, edited by M. G. Durham and D. M. Kellner, 163–73. Oxford: Blackwell, 2006.

Halvorssen, T. "Behind Exhumation of Simon Bolivar Is Hugo Chavez's Warped Obsession." *Washington Post*, July 25, 2010.

Helliwell, John, Richard Layard, and Jeffrey Sachs. *World Happiness Report*. New York: Earth Institute at Columbia University, 2012.

Koffka, Kurt. *Principles of Gestalt Psychology*. New York: Harcourt Brace Jovanovich, 1935.

Lewis, William F. "Telling America's Story: Narrative Form and the Reagan Presidency." *Quarterly Journal of Speech* 73 (1987): 280–302.

Lynch, John. *Simón Bolívar: A Life*. New Haven, CT, and London: Yale University Press, 2007.

Martinez, Carlos, Michael Fox, and JoJo Farrell. *Venezuela Speaks! Voices from the Grassroots*. Oakland, CA: PM Press, 2010.

Marx, Karl. "Bolívar y Ponte, Simón." In *The New American Cyclopaedia, Vol. III*, edited by G. Ripley and C. A. Dana. New York: D. Appleton, 1858.

McKim, Joel. "'Berlin's Memorial for the Murdered Jews of Europe' and the Problem of a Postmodern Monumental Rhetoric." In *The Rhetoric of Western*

Thought, 10th edition, edited by J. L. Golden, G. Berquist, W. Coleman, and J. M. Sproule, 401–10. Dubuque, IA: Kendall Hunt, 2011.

Mixon, Laura. *Use of the Authorizing Figure, Authoritarian Charisma, and National Myth in the Discourse of Hugo Chávez: Toward a Critical Model of Rhetorical Analysis for Political Discourse*. Ann Arbor, MI: ProQuest, 2009.

Olson, Lester C., Cara A. Finnegan, and Diane S. Hope. *Visual Rhetoric*. Thousand Oaks, CA: Sage, 2008.

Oxhorn, Philip. "Social Inequality, Civil Society, and the Limits of Citizenship in Latin America." In *What Justice? Whose Justice? Fighting for Fairness in Latin America*, edited by S. Eckstein and T. P. Wickham-Crowley, 35–63. Berkeley: University of California Press, 2003.

Padgett, Tim. "Why Venezuela's Chávez Dug Up Bolívar's Bones." *Time*, July 17, 2010. Accessed March 5, 2013. www.time.com/time/world/article/0,8599,2004526,00.html.

Peirce, Charles S. *Collected Papers of Charles Sanders Peirce*. Volumes 1–6, edited by C. Hartshorne and P. Weiss. Cambridge, MA: Harvard University Press, 1931–1935.

———. *Collected Papers of Charles Sanders Peirce*. Volumes 7–8, edited by A. W. Burks. Cambridge, MA: Harvard University Press, 1958.

———. *The Writings of Charles S. Peirce: A Chronological Edition*. Volumes 1–6 and 8, edited by Peirce Edition Project. Bloomington: Indiana University Press, 1982.

Peters, John D. *Speaking into the Air: A History of the Idea of Communication*. Chicago: University of Chicago Press, 1999.

Plato. *Republic*. Translated by C. Emlyn-Jones and W. Preddy. Cambridge, MA: Harvard University Press, 2013.

Ramirez, Cristobal V. "Who Are the Chavistas?" In *Venezuela: Hugo Chávez and the Decline of an "Exceptional Democracy,"* edited by S. Ellner and M. T. Salas, 121–39. Lanham, MD: Rowman & Littlefield, 2007.

Ray, Julie. "High Wellbeing Eludes the Masses in Most Countries Worldwide." *Gallup*, 2011. Accessed September 27, 2012. www.gallup.com/poll/147167/High-Wellbeing-Eludes-Masses-Countries-Worldwide.aspx#1.

Rice, Donald E. *The Rhetorical Uses of the Authorizing Figure: Fidel Castro and Jose Marti*. Westport, CT: Praeger, 1992.

Ricoeur, Paul. *Interpretation Theory: Discourse and the Surplus of Meaning*. Fort Worth: Texas Christian University Press, 1976.

Saletan, Will. "The Memory Doctor." *Slate*, June 4, 2010. Accessed March 5, 2013. www.slate.com/articles/health_and_science/the_memory_doctor/2010/06/the_memory_doctor.html.

Stout, David. "Chávez Calls Bush 'the Devil' in UN Speech." *New York Times*, September 20, 2006. Accessed March 2, 2013. www.nytimes.com/2006/09/20/world/americas/20cnd-Chávez.html?_r=0.

Sullivan, Mark P. *Venezuela: Political Conditions and U.S. Policy*. Washington, DC: Congressional Research Service, 2009.

Toulmin, Stephen. *The Uses of Argument*. Cambridge: Cambridge University Press, 1958.

Tulis, Jeffrey K. *The Rhetorical Presidency*. Princeton, NJ: Princeton University Press, 1988.

Ungar, Mark. "Contested Battlefields: Policing in Caracas and La Paz." *NACLA Report on the Americas* 37 (2003): 30–36.

"Venezuela's Chávez Unveils 3D Image of Hero Bolívar." *Terra*, 2012. Accessed February 12, 2013. http://news.terra.com/venezuelas-Chávez-unveils-3d-image-of-hero-Bolívar,53d2cf97d9ab8310VgnVCM3000009acceb0aRCRD.html.

Wagemans, Johan, Jacob Feldman, Sergei Gepshtein, Ruth Kimchi, James R. Pomerantz, Peter A. van der Helm, and Cees van Leeuwen. "A Century of Gestalt Psychology in Visual Perception: II. Conceptual and Theoretical Foundations." *Psychological Bulletin* 138 (2012): 1218–52.

8

❖ ❖

Crisis and Revolution

Activist Art in Neoliberal Buenos Aires

Leonora Souza Paula

As a response to worldwide crises and crashes brought about by the brutal march of neoliberal capitalism in the 1990s, numerous social movements around the globe have ever since been organizing various types of anti-capitalist protests and campaigns. Throughout the turn of the century, demonstrations such as the Seattle anti-globalization protests (1999), the first meeting of the World Social Forum (2001), and later the 15M Movement in Spain (2011), the Egyptian uprising (2011), the worldwide Occupy movement (2011), and the Chilean student protests (2013) have all denounced the sharp rise in economic and social inequality afflicting almost all parts of the world. Perhaps in no other place the anti-neoliberal sentiment that would take hold in twenty-first-century social movements was expressed so intensely as in Buenos Aires at the time of Argentina's worst financial crisis. The popular uprising of December 19 and 20, 2001, against government austerity measures recognized that the neoliberal economic program initiated decades earlier was responsible for the unforeseen levels of unemployment, poverty, and inequality that devastated the country. The magnitude of the economic collapse along with a crisis of political representation prompted a popular plea demanding, "¡Que se vayan todos!" ("Out with them all!").

In this chapter, I discuss how a 2001 art project by the Buenos Aires–based activist collective Grupo de Arte Callejero (Street Art Group), in tune with the general feeling of discontent, articulated the connection between Argentina's recent authoritarian past and the neoliberal economic model that led the country to its worst social, political, and economic crisis. Moreover, I demonstrate how Grupo de Arte Callejero's (GAC) action, more than simply attuned to the global anti-capitalist struggle, anticipated some of the self-organized participation models adopted by contemporary social movements such as Occupy Wall Street (2011) and the mass protests in Brazil (2013).

INVASIÓN

In the afternoon of December 19, 2001, just hours before the popular uprising that took over Buenos Aires in protest against the gravest economic crisis in Argentina's history, the downtown area was taken aback by an unexpected military occupation: ten thousand plastic toy soldiers in parachutes descended from the sky, disrupting trade and traffic in the financial center of the Argentine capital. While bystanders observed the scene, attempting to make sense of such a sudden interruption, others responded to the incursion by trying to grab the toys falling upon them. Drivers and commuters stopped for a moment to look at the sky; office workers halted their activities and went to the window to watch the rose-colored cascade unfolding in front of their eyes; when the last soldier reached the ground, the streets were temporarily paralyzed and the quotidian time suspended.

This scene describes the final phase of the remarkable urban intervention carried out by the Grupo de Arte Callejero, a collective of artists and activists active in Buenos Aires since the late 1990s. The first stage of the intervention, executed in the week prior to the parachute launching, involved the making and pasting of stickers displaying military imagery on consumer products and posters advertising mainstream media and

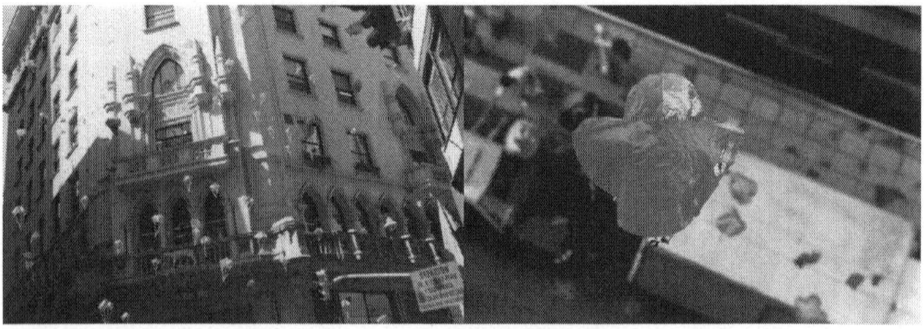

Figure 8.1. First phase of *Invasión*. (Photo by Grupo de Arte Callejero. 2009. *Pensamientos, Prácticas, Acciones*. [Buenos Aires]: Tinta Limón, 130–31.)

transnational businesses. On each decal, the image of a soldier, a tank, or a missile was juxtaposed to a blank target. The decals were then placed on a variety of products such as Marlboro cigarette packs and *El Clarín* newspaper announcements. During that entire week, the stickers were systematically pasted on commercial ads, street signs, as well as on banks and office windows in the area surrounding the location from which the parachutes were to be launched.[1]

A careful reading of the two stages of the art project reveals that by engaging in a symbolic occupation of downtown Buenos Aires, GAC's intervention, rightly named *Invasión* (Invasion), rendered visible the intersection between the country's past political history and the recent experiments of economic control in an era of implacable neoliberalism. In the following pages, I argue that *Invasión*'s synthesizing force lies in the precision with which it underlined the association between the repressive order of the military regime that ruled Argentina from 1976 to 1983 and its continuation by other means represented by the neoliberal reforms implemented in the 1990s. More than an instance of fortuitous timing, I contend, the art intervention was exceptional thanks to the explicit allusion to a military takeover conveyed by the deliberate use of war codes that critically engaged the recent Argentine past with its most dire present. In that, *Invasión* was precise in exposing the relationship between state violence and the neoliberal economic program initiated during the dictatorship years.

Initially an all-female visual arts student group formed in 1997, the still-active GAC was, by the time of the 2001 intervention, a mixed-gender collective that had among its members artists, activists, teachers, and self-employed graphic designers. In general, GAC's actions and interventions use performance, graphic, and textual strategies to draw attention to social and economic justice issues, broadly speaking. The group's previous projects include public actions against state-sponsored human rights violations, police brutality, and corporate-controlled media as well as public action in favor of rights to dignified housing and indigenous people's land rights. Although they describe themselves as a self-governed group, GAC does not work in isolation. The group has worked with artistic institutions such as museums and art institutes and has collaborated with other art and activist groups in Argentina, across Latin America, and in Europe in various projects.[2]

Understood here as an activist/artistic practice, urban intervention is commonly used for creating spaces that momentarily interrupt what is considered the normalcy of everyday life. In the urban setting, interventions are usually tied to anti-establishment activism and to the growing urban resistance to corporate takeover, enclosure, and segregation. With clear disruptive propositions about space, the main purpose of these interventions is to engage in creative and critical social production of space. Echoing Henri Lefebvre's space-centered understanding of social environments, urban interventions work with the idea that rather than a neutral medium or a container where humans and objects are located, space should be regarded as a process in constant production. In other words, as the result of social, political, and economic relations, space is being constantly produced by the activities of those inhabiting it. Thus, rather than a passive locus of social relations, space exists as a product of social interaction; it exists less as an abstraction and more as knowledge and action.[3]

On that account, activist/artistic interventions function as contesting practices that promote the production of disruptive spaces within the urban setting. More than the ordinary social protest, these actions use the language of signs and symbols found in the most diverse spheres of society to contest the norms established by the dominant order. A form of politically engaged art that is committed to challenging the limits between the cultural and the political, interventions are strategies used to re-signify the system through disturbances in its discourses. For its political implications, these kinds of work have been associated with *détournement* tactics—today known as culture jamming—first carried out by the French Situationists in the 1960s. *Détournement* has been defined as a strategy used to turn expressions of the system against itself, or, in Guy Debord's words, as a "language of contradiction . . . a critique of the totality and as historical critique."[4] Also known as "relational aesthetics," "social practice art," "social aesthetics," among others, urban interventions resemble what Nato Thompson calls "socially engaged art." Rather than an art movement, Thompson argues, "socially engaged art indicates a new social order—ways of life that emphasize participation, challenge power, and span disciplines ranging from urban planning and community work to theater and the visual arts."[5] A growing field of cultural production, these socially engaged interventions in the urban setting aim at advancing public awareness, engaging communities, and confronting specific social issues. In line with these ideas, the deliberate choice of using *intervention* to carry out my discussion is based on my understanding of the practice as a disruptive strategy used for creating spaces that question the construction of hegemonic versions of history and normalcy.

It was by taking up a normalcy-disruptive approach that GAC's symbolic invasion of downtown Buenos Aires challenged patterns of compliance put into effect by the media and consumer market, in the first stage of the intervention, and the state apparatus of repression as represented by the military takeover, in the second stage. Furthermore, while destabilizing the representation of Argentina as a successful neoliberal democracy,

Invasión exposed the intricate relationship between neoliberal reforms and authoritarian order. This is because the explicit allusion to a military takeover conveyed by GAC's deliberate use of war codes critically engaged Argentina's dire present with its traumatic past, promoting a radical form of historical critique.

RECLAIMING THE STREETS IN THE NEOLIBERAL CITY

The consequences of abusive economic practices reflected in the Buenos Aires of the late twentieth century serve as a critical example of the most aggressive neoliberal structural reforms in all of Latin America. In the late 1990s, in order to recover the economy's poor health due to years of hyperinflation, the Argentine state attempted to rescue the declining value of the peso by forcing the peso-dollar parity. As a result of the dollarization of the economy, an increasing number of Argentines were excluded from access to basic goods, services, and ultimately to their money when bank withdrawals were frozen in November 2001. Leading the way were neoliberal economic reforms that resulted in extensive privatization of national companies, the restructuring of the labor market, and the continuous cutbacks in state investments into social infrastructure while favoring private investments.[6] As a consequence, by the end of the twentieth century, an astonishing number of displaced populations and a mass of unemployed workers were added to the ranks of the new Argentine poor. The economic crises aggravated an already-growing crisis of state legitimacy in which the relatively new Argentine democratic state and its institutions failed to maintain the fundamental well-being of its citizens. The result was an unforeseen scale of mass protests in the capital in December 2001. The popular insurrection of December 19 and 20, 2001, also known as the *Argentinazo*, happened as masses of unemployed in the capital as well as other provinces joined forces with the declining urban middle classes and local activist groups to protest the long-standing abuse Argentines had been suffering. Even though martial law had been declared on December 19, the insurrection forced then president Fernando de la Rúa out of the presidential palace in a helicopter the next day.

In the evening of December 19, the population took the streets not only to protest against the alarming situation of mass dispossession afflicting a large part of the country but also to demand a substantial change in the failed political system that allowed for the country's economic depletion. Such a plea was eloquently expressed in the collective claim of the December popular revolt: "¡Que se vayan todos!" ("Out with them all!"). Driven by the rejection of a corrupt political system and characterized by a strong anti-neoliberal position, the popular uprising of December 2001 targeted the dominant economic model as much as the conjuncture that allowed the systematic abuse of the Argentine population to take place. Less than a statement announcing the "end of politics," as stated by Ernesto Laclau, the popular claim manifested an acute awareness of the need for a new way of doing politics. Laclau's claim that the "¡Que se vayan todos!" could lead to "the end of politics" is based on an interpretation that implicit in the popular demand is an invitation to authoritarianism: "Because saying '¡Que se vayan todos!' is equivalent to saying 'one of you stay'; someone must rule society. Against the myth of a society ruled in totality, '¡Que se vayan todos!' is the myth of a society unable to be ruled, which needs a master to re-establish order."[7] Laclau's main argument is that once ousted, power has to be restored or reorganized, and since the social movements offered no immediate alternative project at the time, the reorganization of Argentine society could once again fall in the hands of totalitarian forces. Yet what the popular slogan demonstrated (and GAC symbolically articulated) was the fact that Argentines were aware that a different form of authoritarianism had been already in place. Embedded in the demand for general resignation was a radical contestation of the alliance between the political class and economic forces that had depleted the country in the past decades and a plea for political reform.

Already in the 1990s, Buenos Aires was the scene of innumerous protests carried out by different groups reacting to the deterioration of working and living conditions. Workers blocked roads and overtook factories to protest the high levels of unemployment while garbage collectors trying to make a living out of scavenged material filled up the city's streets.[8] Other groups occupying the city were art and activist collectives that, together with other political actors, were contesting the decline of Argentine society. Among the groups formed in that period was H.I.J.O.S. (Hijos por la Identidad la Justicia contra el Olvido y el Silencio; Sons and Daughters for Identity and Justice against Oblivion and Silence), a collective formed by the children of the political dissidents disappeared during the military years.

GAC was first known for partnering with H.I.J.O.S. in preparing and executing the *escraches*—acts of denunciation or public shaming that intended to inform the public of the crimes of unpunished collaborators of the dictatorship. Escraches aim at raising public awareness about crimes committed during the dirty war and exposing the fact that the neoliberal economic policies in Latin America are a continuation of the status quo that allowed and supported the dictatorship in the 1970s. In a typical escrache, the group and its supporters take over the street where former agents of state terrorism live and expose their identities to the public via speeches, satirical theatrical performances, and musical acts. GAC's role in the public education campaign that usually precedes an escrache involves designing and posting informative street signage in the area where the act will occur.

This sign designed by GAC (figure 8.2) was used in an escrache done in 2003 that publicly condemned former military police commissioner Luis Juan Donocik, who had been accused of crimes against humanity during the dirty war but walked freely at the time of the protest. Later he was tried, found guilty, and jailed for life (2010).

In addition to being an act of public shaming, the collective effort that characterizes the escrache effectively adds a public dimension to the plea for truth and justice that comes with popular mobilizations demanding trial and punishment for the agents of the dictatorship. By shaming the unpunished agents of state violence in the public space of the streets, the demonstrators invite the present audience to join them in seeking accountability for the atrocities committed in the past. In denouncing the presence of a living past, embodied by the torturers living with impunity, the escrache creates a symbolic rupture with a history that conveniently situates state violence as a thing of the past, a past mistake that is better forgotten and left alone. Opposing that attitude, the escrache acts as a direct constituent of

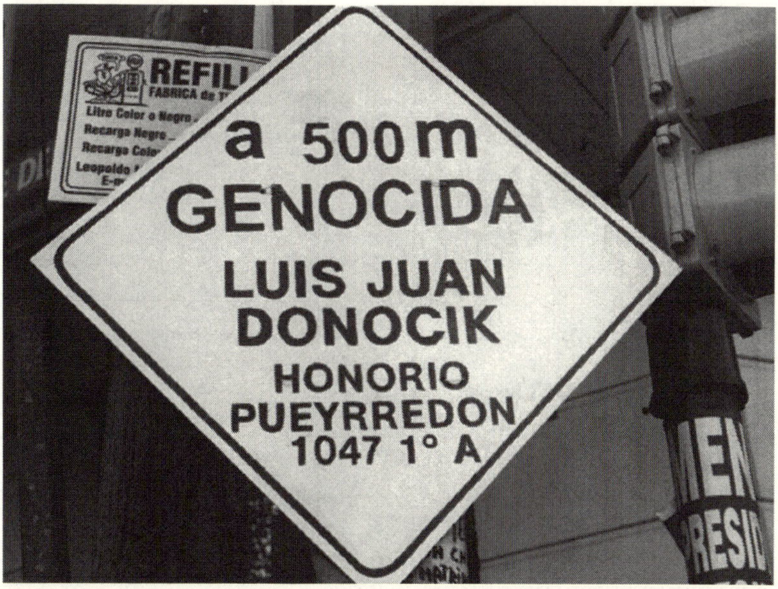

Figure 8.2. Street sign used in a 2003 escrache. (Photo by Grupo de Arte Callejero. 2009. *Pensamientos, Prácticas, Acciones*. [Buenos Aires]: Tinta Limón, p. 92.)

Argentina's process of construction of active memory. According to Hugo Vezzetti, "This form of intervention, which in some ways sanctions and inscribes meanings upon a living past, takes on an important role when it seeks to create a symbolic cut with the past."[9] In fact, the demonstrations carried out by H.I.J.O.S. and its supporters as well as the ongoing protests carried out by the Madres of Plaza de Mayo[10] enact a culture of production of active memory in the public sphere that has greatly contributed to human rights efforts and has successfully brought to justice those responsible for killing and disappearing thousands of Argentines. In other words, the political memory of a shared traumatic past is evoked and kept alive by these groups and shared with the entire society as responses to the culture of impunity normalized by the "forgive and forget" discourse of post-dictatorship Argentina, thus rendering it into an act of active remembering.[11] As it is widely known, in postmilitary Argentina amnesties were granted and torturers went free as they were judged to have been "just following orders" and were therefore pardoned.[12]

In Argentina, as in most of Latin America, the combined processes of military dictatorships, conservative governments, and the application of an initial version of neoliberal reforms acted together throughout the 1970s to facilitate the transfer from state-regulated economy to free-market capital. Neoliberal reforms developed by economists at the University of Chicago under the direction of Milton Friedman were adopted as the guiding principles for an economic experiment that could guarantee unprecedented levels of profitable capital accumulation. As a response to a thriving political scene in 1960s Latin America, where alternative models to capitalism were being shaped, an era of military coups ensued. Among the coups, the Chilean (1973) and the Argentine (1976) were at the same time the most violent and the most overtly supportive of the neoliberal state formation, both backed by the world's fiercest defender of capitalism, the United States.

In Chile, University of Chicago–trained economists sided with General Augusto Pinochet and began restructuring the economy by introducing the privatization of public assets, cuts to social spending, stimulating international loans, and facilitating foreign direct investment. Massive repression to any form of dissent via the torturing, killing, and exiling of civilians followed while the economic plan was put forward.[13] Similarly, in Argentina, the most brutal repression of mass disappearing and assassination was used to silence and control the population while a substantial part of public resources was handed to private capital. The main objectives of the social and economic reorganization carried out by the Argentine military in a program known as Proceso de Reorganización Nacional (National Reorganization Process) were "to eradicate subversion and to promote economic development based on the equilibrium and responsible participation of the various sectors of society."[14] During the years of the dirty war, the disappearance of more than thirty thousand people, most of them leftist activists critical of the Proceso, was integral to an overarching logic of reorganization of society led by economic reform in which terrorizing and harnessing the public were means to prepare the ground for the introduction of radical free-market reforms.[15] Not unlike warfare raids, "among some of the bombs dropped by the neoliberal war on underdeveloped countries were the forced privatization of national enterprises and services like education and healthcare; the imposition of austerity measures; and the adoption of so-called 'free trade agreements.'"[16] Unsurprisingly, the 1980s Latin American debt crisis that afflicted Argentina, Brazil, and Mexico more directly, a direct consequence of conservative governments' excessive high-rate borrowing from international creditors a decade earlier, can be traced back to the Chile economic restructuring model.

Similarly, the marriage between democratic principles and neoliberal practice adopted in postdictatorship Argentina, rather than an alliance that necessarily opposed authoritarianism, is evidence of the state's complicity with the economic model imposed by the military. Therefore, it only makes sense to talk about the return to democracy in post-1983 Argentina if we take into account that rather than a clear-cut process of transition from dictatorship to democracy, the return to civilian rule in Argentina was in fact a long-term process of substitution of a national state for a market-regulated state.

That tells us that the very idea of neoliberal democracy embodied then, as it does now, a fundamental contradiction—that is, if most of the economy is dominated by massive corporations with tremendous control over markets, media, and population, basically operating as totalitarian organizations, any attempt to bring about genuine participatory democracy is considered a threat and should be avoided at all costs. Even though a formal electoral democracy is maintained, meaningful participation in decision making is rendered a mere formality in a system that exists to assure the well-being of market rule. The various narratives of neoliberalism, however, do not acknowledge the real nature of the relationship between democracy and economic deregulation. They rather talk about individual freedom, consumerism, and limited-sized government and evoke a strong belief in the free market, placing an entire economic, political, and social order under the sign of freedom.[17] Disguised as a principle of freedom for all, such rhetoric serves to ensure that practices of economic deregulation, privatization, and the downsizing of the state as a guarantor of rights are declared legitimate strategies for the continuation of concentration of power in the hands of few. According to Pierre Bourdieu, one of the most powerful ideological strategies of neoliberalism consists of "severing the economy from social realities and thereby constructing, in reality, an economic system conforming to its description."[18] In that sense, this discursive operation of constructing a new reality adds its own symbolic force to already-existing relations of power and ensures its continuity.

ANOTHER DIRTY WAR

With a strikingly aware sense of the country's recent history, the warfare imagery used in *Invasión* exposed a contemporary version of a dirty war of sorts taking place in Argentine society at the turn of the century. Although the images of soldiers, tanks, and missiles had not been gone for too long from the collective consciousness of Argentines, in reclaiming and re-signifying these symbols, GAC revealed that the institutions of economic control and the military apparatus had been operating together in the creation and preservation of structures of domination. "The tank," they argue, "stands for the financial power of the multinationals while the missile represents mass media ideologies, and finally the soldier refers to the repressive forces needed to sustain the neoliberal order."[19] Therefore, more than a mere allusion to a familiar discourse with high impact potential, GAC's use of war codes critically evoked an ideological and economic battle taking place in Argentina at the time and denounced the fact that the oppressive system of the earlier decades had not left entirely.

At the time of the intervention, downtown Buenos Aires was altered by a temporary transformation of everyday economic transactions and consumption into a site for the articulation of a discourse contesting the coalition between capital and control. The disruption and reorganization of the corporate-occupied territory, for that matter, was fundamental to the execution of the intervention. Significantly, situated in this corporative territory are the local offices of companies such as Sulzner, BBVA, JP Morgan Chase, DuPont, Citibank, Heidrick & Struggles, HSBC, IBM, Microsoft, and Santander Bank. Therefore, the invasion of Buenos Aires's corporate center by symbols of domination stamped on ten thousand toy soldiers in parachutes exposed the overwhelming experience of economic domination to which Argentine society was subjected.

Moreover, the recuperation of warfare imagery demonstrated how the re-signification of such codes inserted in a different discursive space invited a break from the neoliberal democracy dominant discourse and encouraged a reflection about the concealed relationship between capital accumulation,

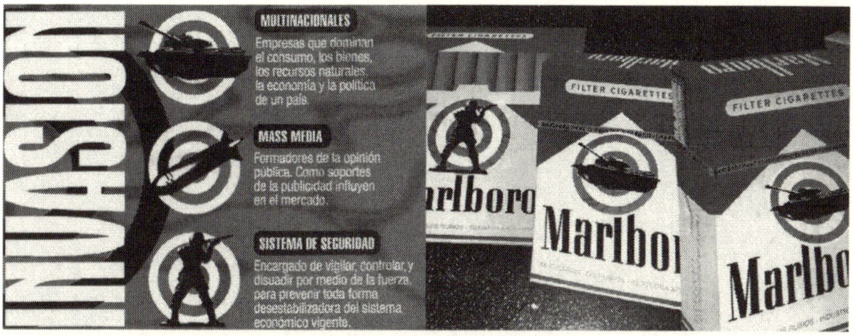

Figure 8.3. Stickers used in the second phase of *Invasión*. (Photo by Grupo de Arte Callejero. 2009. *Pensamientos, Prácticas, Acciones*. [Buenos Aires]: Tinta Limón, 126–27.)

political oppression, and inequality. More than a mere suggestion, the juxtaposition of war codes and consumer products made a clear reference to the extent to which the neoliberal order was responsible for driving millions of Argentines into poverty. As stated by the GAC, "The registering of military imagery that accompanies the definition of three agents [tank, missile, and soldier] or forces responsible for implementing and developing the neoliberal model, clearly show the terrible existence of a silent economic genocide."[20] With *Invasión*, the group employed a visual and discursive grammar typical of authoritarian regimes to denounce how an essentially antidemocratic model is embedded in the current democratic regime. In fact, the intervention successfully articulated the mutual functionality of market strategies and military tactics in the reenactment of a contemporary version of the dirty war.

On another dimension, the action carried out by GAC engaged with a notion of the cityscape as a space overexposed to mass media and consumer symbols typical of neoliberal capitalism. In their words, "Our working methodology revolves mostly around the subversion of the institutional messages in place (for instance, the highway sign, the advertisement, the aesthetics of TV shows, etc.), covering from graphic intervention to performative action, always taking into account that codes work differently in each place, for each community has their own cultural features."[21] Therefore, it was by shedding light on the neoliberal ideology embedded in the daily discourse of mass media and consumer market that *Invasión* sought to destabilize a celebratory discourse free market. Likewise, GAC's use of urban cultural imagery as seen in public ads, billboards, and corporate brands underlined the significance of processes of re-signification of the urban space, especially spaces of domination. That is, by publicly challenging the local agents of the repressive forces that had ushered and implemented the neoliberal reforms, *Invasión* offered alternative strategies for how the city could be seen and experienced, thus asserting the possibility to refunctionalize that existing space, ultimately reshaping its social relations vis-à-vis a logic of social justice. Fundamentally, *Invasión* generated a collective form of political action in which the city's occupation by the military was revisited, this time with an unconcealed critical function.

GAC's discursive framework, as did much of twenty-first-century grassroots critique of social injustice in Argentina, argues Brian Holmes, had its foundation in "a sharp awareness that the same classes that had profited from the dictatorship could always reassert their power, if their impunity was simply accepted and their crimes left unremembered."[22] In that sense, GAC's intervention functioned as an act of active remembering in which the present violence was seen as a reverberation of the atrocities of the past. Clearly influenced by the political art project known as *Siluetazo*,[23] one of the most important works of collective political art in the social history of Argentina, and a work of great influence to the art and activist groups of the late 1990s, *Invasión* engaged in the recuperation of history to make sense of the present. The *Siluetazo* was held in Buenos Aires on September 1983 with the support of the Madres de la Plaza de Mayo and other human rights organizations and was done by tracing the outline of a human body lying flat on large pieces of paper and hanging them on the city's walls in a symbolic occupation. The traces of the *desaparecidos* (missing political dissidents) that temporarily took over the streets exposed to public scrutiny horrific actions of torture and assassination that had occurred behind those same walls just a few years prior. With the *Siluetazo*, the city as a space of impunity was revisited as the public space where justice, institutional and social, was once again possible.

In a similar fashion, GAC's military occupation can be read as a warning sign alerting Argentine society against a coup d'etat of sorts disguised as economic development. Like the *Siluetazo*, *Invasión* used the occupation of the cityscape as a strategy to expose and challenge a culture of fear and intimidation. Effective in multiple dimensions, critically occupied spaces, argues Manuel Castells, "are not meaningless: they are usually charged with the symbolic power of invading sites of state, or financial institutions. Or else, by relating to history, they evoke memories of popular uprisings that had expressed the will of citizens when other avenues of representation were closed."[24] Thus, in reclaiming the symbolic power of collective dissent against the repressive regime and actively evoking the memory of the *Siluetazo*, GAC's occupation of the city by toy soldiers intervened in the contemporary discourse of democratic stability and neoliberal freedom. At the same time, the recent traumatic past was brought back to the city's streets as a means to recover a notion of the city as a public and collective space that had been undermined by capital and control and as a reminder that the implementation of the neoliberal program was made possible via an imposed regime of forgetting. It is thus against the violence of forgetting that remembering dirty war atrocities was deemed a necessary task; it not only made visible the brutal origins of the Argentine neoliberal order but also highlighted its disastrous repercussions years later.

GRUPO DE ARTE CALLEJERO: A NEW GENERATION OF POLITICAL ACTIVISM

The political, social, and economic turbulence that marked Argentina's passage to the twenty-first century had transformed the urban landscapes and opened up spaces for the articulation of several forms of oppositional interventions. In those years, Argentine cities, particularly Buenos Aires, became stages for the eruption of diverse forms of social mobilizations, such as road blocks known as *piquetes*[25] and factory takeovers by unemployed workers, that aimed at questioning the local experience of decline vis-à-vis the neoliberal process. The extreme experience of social deterioration combined with a strong sense of historical memory generated the ideal conditions for the mobilization of various social movements that ultimately offered an effective critical examination of the alliance between the political and economic control of the time.

It was precisely at a moment of intense criticism against the 1990s neoliberal shift implemented during the peak of neoliberal reforms in Argentina during the Carlos Menem administration years (1989–1999) that GAC appeared. In early 1997, the teachers' union CTERA (Confederación de Trabajadores de la Educación de la República Argentina) installed a large white tent in Plaza del Congreso and went on a hunger strike in protest against the increasingly precarious state of public education, the extremely low wages, and the appalling conditions of public schools in Argentina. They demonstrated against the terrible consequences of the education reform implemented by the 1993 Federal Educational Law (Ley Federal de Educación—LFE). The reform was designed to rescue an educational system deemed in crisis and involved transferring policy-making decisions from the nation to the provinces, curricular reform, and the extension of the years of compulsory education from seven to nine. A budget of approximately US$3 million provided by the World Bank and the Inter-American Development Bank was allocated for the implementation of the reform. According to Zappa-Hollman et al., these sponsors "played a significant role in outlining the direction of the LFE. Consequently, the reform was seen as representing the triumph of oppressive external globalizing forces whose aim was ultimately to control rather than provide autonomy to the nation's institutions."[26] The alliance between global financial institutions and local government served as proof of how the state was effectively under the direct control of financial capital.

GAC's founding members, then a group of four female students of visual arts in the Escuela Nacional de Bellas Artes Prilidiano Pueyrredón, seeing themselves affected by the changes in education, took to the streets in support of and in solidarity with the strikers and against the dire state of Argentina's public education. It is in that context that GAC's first intervention took place. Titled *Docentes Ayunando* (Starving Teachers), the action involved painting empty white smocks on the walls in different parts of Buenos Aires. The white smock[27] worn by students and teachers in public education was deliberately left empty as to mark the absent bodies of teachers and students, signaling their lack of participation in educational policy decision-making. Evoking the *Siluetazo*, the empty white smock traced by GAC was used to challenge the democratic practices of the Argentine state that, like in the dictatorship years, continued to subjugate supporters and active seekers of social justice.

While infused with a keen critical gender approach to the disastrous consequences of neoliberalism, a closer look into their practices reveals that the group's politics is greatly informed by rather than strictly defined by feminist politics. Having started as a group of four female artists and continued as a women majority group, GAC's first action clearly demonstrated how women's cultural imagery articulated responses to the system of oppression in place. After all, the painting of empty white smocks on the city's walls not only aimed at protesting the unjust, neoliberal nature of the educational reform but also exposed ways in which relations of patriarchal domination were concealed in the neoliberal order. Upholding the same critical attitude through the years, GAC has continuously collaborated with other groups in denouncing the gendered nature of neoliberal violence. Such is the case of the 2003 protest against the eviction of the employee-run Brukman textile factory, an action known as *Maquinazo* (Sewing Machine Action). In that action, the female workers that had been running the factory since its attempted closure in 2001 installed dozens of sewing machines on the street just steps away from the factory—at that time at risk of eviction and surrounded by a police fence—and donated all the garments they sewed to the victims of the Santa Fe Province floods. GAC participated in the protest by designing and displaying in the surrounding area a street-like sign with the image of arms-linked female figures followed by the caption "*obreras trabajando*" ("women at work").[28]

Much like the protests initiated by the Madres de la Plaza de Mayo in its defiant act of remembering and in its gendered occupation of space, GAC's interventions demonstrate how a patriarchal system oppresses not only women but also other marginalized social groups. Both GAC and Madres have established a practice that simultaneously exposes and opposes those dynamics of oppression. In the case of the Madres, the persistent appropriation of the Plaza de Mayo—a focal point in the political life of Buenos Aires and a space that under the military regime symbolized fear and control, as dictated by the patriarchal ideology—simultaneously challenged the regime of forgetting and called attention to the gendered logic of the regime. In a similar fashion, by temporarily occupying part of the city, GAC's works intervened in the experiences of everyday life with a clear attempt to render visible the close link between the equally oppressive neoliberal and military order. Another point of intersection between the two groups is the marking of the urban space with visual codes infused with an awareness of the critical potential of public space. Besides occupying the plaza with their bodies, the Madres also inscribed their emblematic kerchiefs in white paint on the pavement around the square's perimeter, which renders that space incomplete without their presence. Likewise, the space of the city is GAC's primary site of intervention as seen with the white smocks and the altered street signage.[29] To GAC, the appropriation of street signs and their re-signification into a form of political signage stresses the importance of the city as a legitimate space for demanding justice.

In effect, GAC's interventions, *Invasión* in particular, while maintaining a critical gender perspective, succeeded in mobilizing categories of masculinity to illustrate how, rather than a gender-neutral model, the logic of neoliberalism is grounded on a male, patriarchal order. It goes without saying that the consequences of the neoliberal reconfiguration of the labor market in the global south negatively affected working-class families and women in particular by significantly reducing, if not cutting, direct access to jobs, which in turn compromised access to basic needs such as food security, housing, and health care. A direct result of neoliberal globalization, argues Chandra Mohanty, "the material, cultural, and political effects of the process of domination and exploitation that sustains what is called the new world order are devastating for the majority of the people in the world—and most especially for impoverished women and Third World women."[30] Under a new and accelerated regime of work, where productivity is counted by the seconds, the further intensification of women's labor in low-income households is celebrated in a discourse that renders women more efficient workers. However, this discourse contributes to, rather than subverts, the already-gendered division of labor and responsibilities adopted by the neoliberal model.[31] Therefore, GAC's acuity in confronting the gendered violence of the "democratic" neoliberal state lies in the ingenious use of visual codes marked by masculinity to challenge the correlation between real material conditions and patriarchal discursive constructs.

But it is as a platform for plural identities that the group has defined itself. Aiming since its formation to become a space for the creation of fluid identities intentionally challenging hegemonic modes of identification, "GAC intended, from the very beginning, to be a place for the creation of a space outside the limits of identities imposed and proposed by the system to be recognized as of a given sector, movement or trend. We tried to remain in that state of motion; of individual and collective motion."[32] Therefore, it becomes clear that the group's approach seeks to destabilize self-contained identities and to disengage from predetermined or expected social roles. It was precisely this self-determining principle that gave room to the formation of an openly feminist branch. In 2003, some members of GAC founded Mujeres Públicas (Public Women), a separate group that engaged in protesting gender oppression using the streets as the main stage. Clearly informed by a critical gender perspective, the group's main goal was "to report, make visible and trigger off reflections around the variety of oppressions that women are subjected to, along with de-naturalizing sexist discourses and practices, from a feminist perspective."[33] While critiques of gender violence have been an integral part of GAC's strategies, the unequivocally feminist Mujeres Públicas suggests that the creation of a gender-specific platform allowing for the critical exploration of specific identity experiences was a necessary derivation from the original group. Evidently, by revealing the patriarchal nature of the neoliberal model represented in the use of the gender-coded masculine image of the toy soldier and warfare employed in *Invasión*, GAC succeeded in denouncing the exclusion of women as one of the groups that suffer more intensely the negative impacts of the neoliberal regime. Nevertheless, rather than be bound by clearly defined categories, GAC's identity as a group eludes easy classification. This is because the group is invested in creating social practices that put to work more broad forms of engagement that are not bound by specific modes of identity. That is to say, it is against various forms of imposed social roles that the group aims at creating alternative forms of political agency.

CONCLUSION

It was motivated by a desire to promote social change, weary of traditional forms of political affiliation, and aware of the exhaustion of the vertically structured organizations model, that GAC, as part of a new generation of activists, rejected old forms of political identification and promoted new forms of social protagonism. These new forms, as stated by Colectivo Situaciones, "were not strictly political in the sense that they did not focus on resisting a centralized state, which allowed them to aggregate more heterogeneous concerns."[34] Operating within a system of alliances, contemporary social movements have been offering ways to redefine political practices. Characterized as collaborative in nature, the new forms of collective organizing emerged from the need to reevaluate the old hierarchical political model in favor of the more context-sensitive experience of political transversality.[35] Transversal politics, states Doreen Massey, is "an attempt to find a way of doing things which is neither the imposition of a single universal claim which refuses to recognize that there really are 'differences', nor the retreat into those differences as tightly-bound, exclusivist and essentialist identities."[36] The multidimensional approach taken by this "new way of doing politics" sees in the heterogeneous claims made by different groups valuable sources of political imagination that inform the creation of new forms of participation. In that sense, the work done by GAC and its contemporaries takes on a dynamics of collaboration across social movements, connecting different forms of knowledge and practices that are mobilized as alternative modes of organizing oppositional stances against neoliberalism and its progenitors.

Beyond any doubt, GAC's awareness of Argentina's pervasive state of crisis was representative of the widespread collective sentiment of betrayal and disappointment that so visibly marked the last days of 2001. Amid a climate of profound social changes taking place at the time, a new political consciousness unfolded—one that, aware of the relationship between the worsening of working and living conditions under neoliberalism, saw the necessity to rethink forms of political participation. This new generation of political activists played an important role in reevaluating traditional leftist political practices and in finding different ways of bringing public debate up to date.[37] This is not to say that traditional forms of leftist organizing (such as political parties and labor unions) had disappeared completely. Rather, it means that the principles promoted by social movements had been reshaped by and infused with notions of horizontality, nonhierarchy, and self-governance.[38] As a result, the most diverse social movements have exploded all over the world in the first years of the twenty-first century.

Much like the protests in Argentina, the 15M movement in Madrid and the global Occupy movements ignited by the New York–based Occupy Wall Street have sought "some kind of response to a brutally neoliberalizing international capitalism that has been intensifying its assault on the qualities of daily life since the early 1990s," states David Harvey.[39]

It is no coincidence that the 1994 Zapatista uprising against NAFTA (North American Free Trade Agreement) regulations, one of the first self-identified anti-globalization social movements, emerged in Latin America; after all, that part of the world was the first target of neoliberal economic experiments. The concentration of global power in the hands of a few international financial institutions, private companies, and media corporations, alerted the Chiapas revolt, meant that the neoliberal power structure should be fought on a global scale. Since then, ideals of participatory democracy, nonhierarchical decision-making, organizing through popular assemblies, and occupying public space have been largely embraced by social movements worldwide as an alternative answer to the neoliberal democracy model. Amid contemporary global movements for social change, the critical perspective offered by groups like GAC delves deep into the core of what is at stake when celebratory narratives of freedom and liberty conceal a project of domination.

NOTES

1. In 1981, the Chilean art group CADA (Colectivo de Acciones de Arte) carried out an art action titled *¡Ay Sudamérica!* in which six small airplanes flown by retired military pilots dropped 400,000 flyers over the city of Santiago. The flyers launched from the planes encouraged passersby to question Chile's normal standards of living and declared that the only valid works of art were those that aimed to change Chile's social and political reality. Significantly, the action recalled the bombardment of the House of Government (La Moneda), which marked the fall of Salvador Allende's democratic government and the beginning of Augusto Pinochet's dictatorship in Chile in 1973. Separated by twenty years, the two actions, *¡Ay Sudamérica!* and *Invasión*, not only share remarkable similarities in format but also demonstrate the everlasting reach of military repression in Chilean and Argentine societies.

2. Among these partners and institutions we can cite the Buenos Aires Parque de la Memória, the Fiftieth Venice Biennale, the Instituto Hemisférico (Brazil), the Instituto de Perfomance y Política de las Américas (Mexico), and INJUVE (Spain).

3. Henri Lefebvre, *Espace et politique* (Paris: Anthropos, 1972).

4. Tom McDonough, ed., *Guy Debord and the Situationist International: Texts and Documents* (Cambridge, MA: MIT Press, 2002), 204.

5. Nato Thompson, *Living as Form: Socially Engaged Art from 1991–2011* (New York: Creative Time, 2012), 19.

6. Miguel Bonasso, *El Palacio y la Calle: Crónicas de Insurgentes y Conspiradores* (Buenos Aires: Planeta, 2002); Hugo Vezzetti, "Scenes from the Crisis," *Journal of Latin American Cultural Studies* 11, no. 2 (2002): 163–71; David Harvey, *A Brief History of Neoliberalism* (Oxford; New York: Oxford University Press, 2005).

7. "Porque decir '¡Que se vayan todos!' es decir que se quede uno, porque alguien tiene que reglamentar la sociedad. Contra el mito de la sociedad totalmente gobernada, el '¡Que se vayan todos!' es el mito de una sociedad ingobernable, que necesita de un amo que restablezca el orden." Ernesto Laclau, "Entrevista a Ernesto Laclau," *Cuadernos del Cendes* (Venezuela) 22, no. 58 (2005): 124. Unless otherwise indicated, translations are mine.

8. Maristella Svampa, *La Sociedad Excluyente: La Argentina Bajo el Signo del Neoliberalismo* (Buenos Aires: Taurus, 2005); Naomi Klein and Avi Lewis, *The Take: La Prise* (Montreal: Alliance Atlantis, 2004).

9. "Ese rasgo de intervención que, en cierta medida, sanciona y prescribe sentidos sobre un pasado que pervive en el presente, adquiere un carácter relevante cuando pretende instalar un corte simbólico con ese pasado." Hugo Vezzetti, "Activismos de la Memoria: El 'Escrache,'" *Punto de Vista: Revista de Cultura* 21, no. 62 (1998): 5.

10. Each Thursday afternoon, since 1977, mothers of disappeared political dissidents have met in Plaza de Mayo to repeat their plea. Week after week in the plaza, the Madres have accused the military of disappearing their children and demanded that they be returned alive (*aparición con vida*).

11. Diana Taylor argues that more than merely a youth-centered movement, the escrache entails the transmission of a traumatic memory from one generation to another (from mothers to children of the disappeared) while rendering past experiences something "felt affectively and viscerally in the present" (*The Archive and the Repertoire: Performing Cultural Memory in the Americas* [Durham, NC: Duke University Press, 2003]).

12. The 1986 Ley de Punto Final (Full Stop Law) stopped prosecution of human rights violations committed during the military years, and the 1987 Ley de Obediencia Debida (Due Obedience Law) granted immunity to all members of the military except those in positions of command. In 2005, both laws were overturned.

13. A direct result of neoliberal reforms implemented during General Augusto Pinochet's regime (1973–1990), Chile's universal public education system was largely privatized and deregulated. Since 2011, Chilean students have been protesting to reform the country's highly unequal education system into one that provides free, quality education to everyone. It is worth noting that the "NO +" (no more) slogan used by the student protesters first appeared in Santiago during the 1980s as part of an art action by the CADA group in which the "NO +" phrase was graffitied on the walls and left to be completed by the city's residents, which in most cases expressed their discontent with the military regime. Reclaimed by the students, the slogan has been used to encourage dissent and critical discourse.

14. Marguerite Feitlowitz, *A Lexicon of Terror: Argentina and the Legacies of Torture* (New York: Oxford University Press, 1998), 25.

15. Harvey, *A Brief History of Neoliberalism*; Klein and Lewis, *The Take*.

16. Berta Joubert-Ceci, "US Economic Wars and Latin America," in *Feminism and War: Confronting US Imperialism*, 238–42 (London: Zed, 2008), 240.

17. Pierre Bourdieu, "The Essence of Neoliberalism: What Is Neoliberalism? A Programme for Destroying Collective Structures Which May Impede the Pure Market Logic: Utopia of Endless Exploitation," *Le Monde Diplomatique*, 1998, accessed January 4, 2016, https://mondediplo.com/1998/12/08bourdieu; Harvey, *A Brief History of Neoliberalism*.

18. Bourdieu, "The Essence of Neoliberalism," 2.

19. José Miguel G. Cortés, "Buenos Aires/Grupo de Arte Callejero," in *Dissident Cartographies* (Barcelona: SEACEX, 2008), 123.

20. "La homologación de las imágenes militares que acompañan las definiciones de tres agentes [tanque, misil escrache soldado] o entes responsables de implementar y desarrollar en concreto el modelo neoliberal muestran de manera concreta el peso descarnado de un genocidio económico silencioso." Lorena Fabrizia Bossi and Grupo de Arte Callejero (Argentina), *GAC: Pensamientos, Prácticas, Acciones* (Buenos Aires: Tinta Limón, 2009), 123.

21. Cortés, "Buenos Aires/Grupo de Arte Callejero," 1.

22. Brian Holmes, "Remember the Present: Representations of Crisis in Argentina," in *Escape the Overcode: Activist Art in the Control Society*, 172–93 (Eindhoven, Netherlands: Van Abbemuseum, 2009), 6.

23. *Siluetazo* was, in turn, influenced by *Tucumán Arde* (Tucumán Is Burning), a political and artistic collective work, which is considered the most influential avant-garde experience in Argentine art and the origins of activist art in the country. The work involved multimedia exhibitions combining photography, documentary film, and public lectures; the event took place in Buenos Aires and Rosario in 1968. The collective project sought to expose and condemn the closure of the sugar mills and the consequent crisis in the Tucumán province, which drove the population into poverty and brought about the destruction of the local trade union movement.

24. Manuel Castells, *Networks of Outrage and Hope: Social Movements in the Internet Age* (Cambridge, UK; Malden, MA: Polity, 2012), 10.

25. Having emerged in the early 1990s as a response to the growing unemployment brought about by neoliberal reforms, the *piqueteros* movement's main strategy of protest was to block roads in order to obstruct the trade routes that fed the most important cities in the country; meanwhile, laid-off industrial workers refused to let their factories close down and took them over, managing the factories themselves.

26. Sandra Zappa-Hollman, Vaidehi Ramanathan, and Brian Morgan, "EFL in Argentina's Schools: Teachers' Perspectives on Policy Changes and Instruction," *TESOL Quarterly* 41, no. 3 (2007): 617.

27. The uniform code was implemented in the late nineteenth century by the Argentine state and carried a discursive element that articulated a direct association between uniforms and signs of democracy, hygiene, and morality. For its implied erasure of markers of difference, such homogenizing discourse promoted a form of abstract equality and concealed class differences (Beatriz Sarlo, "Cabezas Rapadas y Cintas Argentinas," *Prismas: Revista de Historia Intelectual* 1, no. 1 [1997]: 187–91).

28. The purpose of hanging the signs, states GAC, was to "reveal two elements: the significance of female labor and the space where the occupation took place, both united in the demand for dignified work." ("Visibilizar dos elementos: la fuerza de trabajo de las mujeres y el espacio del acampe, ambas reunidas en la exigencia de un trabajo digno.") Bossi and Grupo de Arte Callejero, *GAC*, 326.

29. GAC's street signs are also found in the Parque de la Memória (Memory Park), a memorial dedicated to the victims of state terrorism along the coast of Rio de la Plata in Buenos Aires. The group's contribution to the memorial is made up of signposts with information revealing the truth about repressive spaces in the city and it is titled "Carteles de la Memoria" ("Memory Signs"). The memorial, a collection of sculptures and installations, has since its creation in 1998 received severe criticisms for functioning as a site for the aesthetization of memory in a theater-like setting as if staging an experience of memory for the spectator (Silvia R. Tandeciarz, "Citizens of Memory: Refiguring the Past in Postdictatorship Argentina," *PMLA* 122, no. 1 [2007]: 151–69).

30. Chandra Talpade Mohanty, *Feminism Without Borders: Decolonizing Theory, Practicing Solidarity* (Durham, NC; London: Duke University Press, 2003), 146.

31. Kalpana Wilson, "'Race,' Gender and Neoliberalism: Changing Visual Representations in Development," *Third World Quarterly* 32, no. 2 (2011): 315–31.

32. "El GAC se planteó, desde sus inicios, ser un lugar de creación de un espacio más allá de las identidades impuestas y propuestas por el sistema para reconocerse como de tal o cual sector, movimiento o corriente. Intentamos permanecer en ese estado de movilidad, de los sujetos individuales y colectivos." Bossi and Grupo de Arte Callejero, *GAC*, 175.

33. Paper read at the European Social Forum, Malmö and Privilege Walk Symposium, organized by the YES! Association and Lilith Performance Studio, Malmö, Sweden, 2008. Accessed June 9, 2011. http://www.mujerespublicas.com.ar/.

34. Edgardo Fontana and Colectivo Situaciones (Buenos Aires, Argentina), *19 y 20, Apuntes Para el Nuevo Protagonismo Social* (Buenos Aires: Ediciones de Mano en Mano; Colectivo Situaciones, 2002), 12.

35. Doreen Massey, "Space for Co-existence?" in *Transversal Politics*, 1–4 (London: Soundings 12, 1999).

36. Ibid., 1.

37. Another form of visual activism, wall stenciling in Buenos Aires boomed as a postcrisis urban manifestation that began as a precrisis response to socioeconomic structural changes. The culture of stenciling Buenos Aires walls appeared at a time of political uncertainty in which the traditional channels of political participation and representation were being intensely questioned. Stencils were most commonly found in Buenos Aires's central areas, its more economically active space and the main target of urban renewal programs. The culture of stenciling speaks to the appropriation of the urban space as a central factor in the development of what has been called "the new Argentine social movement" of the early twenty-first century.

38. David Harvey, *Rebel Cities: From the Right to the City to the Urban Revolution* (New York: Verso, 2012).

39. Ibid., xii.

BIBLIOGRAPHY

Bonasso, Miguel. *El Palacio y la Calle: Crónicas de Insurgentes y Conspiradores*. Buenos Aires: Planeta, 2002.

Bossi, Lorena Fabrizia, and Grupo de Arte Callejero (Argentina). *GAC: Pensamientos, Prácticas, Acciones*. Buenos Aires: Tinta Limón, 2009.

Bourdieu, Pierre. "The Essence of Neoliberalism: What Is Neoliberalism? A Programme for Destroying Collective Structures Which May Impede the Pure Market Logic: Utopia of Endless Exploitation." *Le Monde Diplomatique*, 1998. Accessed January 4, 2016. https://mondediplo.com/1998/12/08bourdieu.

Carassai, Sebastián. "The Noisy Majority: An Analysis of the Argentine Crisis of December 2001 from the Theoretical Approach of Hardt and Negri, Laclau and Zižek." *Journal of Latin American Cultural Studies* 16, no. 1 (2007): 45–62.

Castells, Manuel. *Networks of Outrage and Hope: Social Movements in the Internet Age*. Cambridge, UK; Malden, MA: Polity, 2012.

Cortés, José Miguel G. "Buenos Aires/Grupo de Arte Callejero." In *Dissident Cartographies*. Barcelona: SEACEX, 2008.

Dussel, Ines. "When Appearances Are Not Deceptive: A Comparative History of School Uniforms in Argentina and the United States (Nineteenth–Twentieth Centuries)." *Paedagogica Historica: International Journal of the History of Education* 41, nos. 1–2 (2005): 179–95.

Feitlowitz, Marguerite. *A Lexicon of Terror: Argentina and the Legacies of Torture*. New York: Oxford University Press, 1998.

Fontana, Edgardo, and Colectivo Situaciones (Buenos Aires, Argentina). *19 y 20, Apuntes Para el Nuevo Protagonismo Social*. Buenos Aires: Ediciones de Mano en Mano; Colectivo Situaciones, 2002.

Harvey, David. *A Brief History of Neoliberalism*. Oxford; New York: Oxford University Press, 2005.

———. *Rebel Cities: From the Right to the City to the Urban Revolution*. New York: Verso, 2012.

Holmes, Brian. "Remember the Present: Representations of Crisis in Argentina." In *Escape the Overcode: Activist Art in the Control Society*, 172–93. Eindhoven, Netherlands: Van Abbemuseum, 2009.

International Center for the Arts of the Americas, Museum of Fine Arts, Houston. "ICAA Documents Project Working Papers: The Publication Series for Documents of 20th-Century Latin American and Latino Art." *ICAA Documents Project Working Papers: The Publication Series for Documents of 20th-Century Latin American and Latino Art 3*. 2013.

Joubert-Ceci, Berta. "US Economic Wars and Latin America." In *Feminism and War: Confronting US Imperialism*, 238–42. London: Zed, 2008.

Klein, Naomi, and Avi Lewis. *The Take: La Prise*. Montreal: Alliance Atlantis, 2004.

Laclau, Ernesto. "Entrevista a Ernesto Laclau." *Cuadernos del Cendes* (Venezuela) 22, no. 58 (2005): 117–25.

Lefebvre, Henri. *Espace et politique*. Paris: Anthropos, 1972.

Longoni, Ana. "Is Tucumán Still Burning?" *Sociedad* (Buenos Aires) 1 (2006).

Massey, Doreen. "Space for Co-existence?" In *Transversal Politics*, 1–4. London: Soundings 12, 1999.

McDonough, Tom, ed. *Guy Debord and the Situationist International: Texts and Documents*. Cambridge, MA: MIT Press, 2002.

Mesquita, André. *Insurgências Poéticas: Arte Ativista e Ação Colectiva*. São Paulo, Brazil: FAPESP; AnnaBlume, 2011.

Mohanty, Chandra Talpade. *Feminism Without Borders: Decolonizing Theory, Practicing Solidarity*. Durham, NC; London: Duke University Press, 2003.

Sarlo, Beatriz. "Cabezas Rapadas y Cintas Argentinas." *Prismas: Revista de Historia Intelectual* 1, no. 1 (1997): 187–91.

———. "Cultural Landscapes: Buenos Aires from Integration to Fracture." In *Other Cities, Other Worlds: Urban Imaginaries in a Globalizing Age*, 27–50. Durham, NC: Duke University Press, 2008.

Svampa, Maristella. *La Sociedad Excluyente: La Argentina Bajo el Signo del Neoliberalismo*. Buenos Aires: Taurus, 2005.

Tandeciarz, Silvia R. "Citizens of Memory: Refiguring the Past in Postdictatorship Argentina." *PMLA* 122, no. 1 (2007): 151–69.

Taylor, Diana. *The Archive and the Repertoire: Performing Cultural Memory in the Americas*. Durham, NC: Duke University Press, 2003.

Thompson, Nato. *Living as Form: Socially Engaged Art from 1991–2011*. New York: Creative Time, 2012.

Vezzetti, Hugo. "Activismos de la Memoria: El 'Escrache.'" *Punto de Vista: Revista de Cultura* 21, no. 62 (1998): 1–7.

———. "Scenes from the Crisis." *Journal of Latin American Cultural Studies* 11, no. 2 (2002): 163–71.

Wilson, Kalpana. "'Race,' Gender and Neoliberalism: Changing Visual Representations in Development." *Third World Quarterly* 32, no. 2 (2011): 315–31.

Zappa-Hollman, Sandra, Vaidehi Ramanathan, and Brian Morgan. "EFL in Argentina's Schools: Teachers' Perspectives on Policy Changes and Instruction." *TESOL Quarterly* 41, no. 3 (2007): 618–25.

9

Mexican Spring

#YoSoy132's Images of Resistance

Nasheli Jiménez del Val

On May 11, 2012, in the midst of a highly charged electoral campaign season, a group of students from the Universidad Iberoamericana (Uia) in Mexico protested against the presence of PRI-PVEM (Partido Revolucionario Institucional–Partido Verde Ecologista de México) presidential candidate Enrique Peña Nieto on campus to deliver a campaign speech. Through homemade posters, body paint, and unified shouts of "Atenco no se olvida" ("Atenco, never forgotten"), they denounced Peña Nieto's involvement in the Atenco police raid of 2006, his close ties to former Mexican president Carlos Salinas de Gortari (1988–1994), and his manufactured media image sustained by the two main television networks in Mexico, Televisa and TV Azteca. That evening on these same officialist networks, the student protest at the Uia was covered as the work of a few infiltrated troublemakers who were not students at the university. In response, 131 Uia students posted a video on YouTube where they provided their names and student numbers in order to rebuff the claim that the protest had been a manufactured boycott against Peña Nieto. The video went viral, support for the students grew nationwide, and their new followers started to call themselves the 132nd student, leading to the naming of the collective as #YoSoy132 (#IAm132).

The movement snowballed and quickly grew in size, incorporating students from other universities, members from civil society, intellectuals, and so forth. As this happened, #YoSoy132 drew on a two-pronged activist platform: (1) in favor of media democratization and political democratization nationwide and (2) a critique of the authoritarian Mexican political regime. Taking inspiration from the Chilean student movement, the Arab Spring, the Occupy movement, and the Spanish 15M movement,[1] yet firmly situated in the Mexican context of the democratic failings of the current and past regimes, #YoSoy132 made a very effective use of social networking in order to promote their agenda, rally for protests, and even organize an online presidential debate. As part of their communication strategy, they produced a wide array of visual media, from online videos and digital posters to onsite performances at demonstrations.

This chapter aims to explore the visual production of a student movement that is highly horizontal in organization, democratic in its decision-making processes, and nationally grounded, yet globally connected. Centrally, this text will analyze the movement's imagery of revolution in the twenty-first century as a reflection of its variegated composition, its national and international influences, and its political agenda for media democratization.

THE RETURN OF THE PRINOSAUR

2012 was the year of highly anticipated presidential elections in Mexico. After seventy-two years of PRI "partidocracia" (hegemonic one-party rule), the country had undergone twelve years of democratic transition through PAN (Partido Acción Nacional) rule. In the spring of 2012, it seemed that the PRI was back, profiling itself as the lead runner for the presidential elections through the figure of Enrique Peña Nieto, a young, photogenic politician who had been the governor of the state of Mexico from 2005 to 2011. He was the product of a PRI subset called Grupo Atlacolmulco, a long-standing group of politicians hailing from the state of Mexico that was the focus of allegations of corruption and authoritarianism.[2] In addition, Peña Nieto was frequently associated with the more retrograde branch of the party, frequently dubbed "the dinosaurs" or "PRInosaurs" for their backward approach to political rule, their lack of democratic practice, and their institutional weaknesses.[3]

For the presidential race of 2012, Peña Nieto had preempted his candidateship as early as 2005 by forging political ties with the main players on the Mexican political stage, including controversial former president Carlos Salinas de Gortari. Throughout 2005, both politicians were seen together publicly in several events, the most noteworthy of which was Salinas's presence at Peña Nieto's inaugural ceremony as the governor of the state of Mexico. The Salinas de Gortari connection was especially notorious because Salinas represented one of the darkest moments in recent Mexican political history, with a presidential term characterized by electoral fraud, political assassinations, and the Zapatista uprising of 1994.[4] In 2008, Salinas de Gortari gave his political blessing to Enrique Peña Nieto by stating in the *Financial Times* that Peña Nieto represented a new generation of PRI politicians that were heading the renewal of the party.[5]

Peña Nieto also invested heavily in his media image throughout his term as governor of the state of Mexico. He quickly became a media darling, not in the least because of his marriage to Mexican soap-opera star Angélica Rivera, but more so due to his alleged purchasing of favorable coverage in Mexico's biggest television network, Televisa. As reported by Jenaro Villamil and the *Guardian*, several documents leaked by a Televisa source outlined the fees "apparently charged for raising Enrique Peña Nieto's national profile when governor of the state of Mexico."[6] For the 2005–2006 budget, over two hundred news reports, interviews, and features are listed, at a total cost of $346,326,750 Mexican pesos (US$36 million at the time).[7] While not strictly illegal, the favorable coverage of Peña Nieto under the guise of "news" was deeply unethical and equally contentious.

Peña Nieto was also the center of controversy following the San Salvador Atenco police raid of 2006. On May 3, a group of flower vendors had set up their stalls at the Texcoco market without a permit, according to the city council. The municipal police were sent in and violently dispersed the vendors, resulting in a full-scale confrontation between the two groups. There were several arrests, the violence escalated, and state and federal police forces were called in. After two days of battle, it is alleged that the San Salvador Atenco raid resulted in the death of a minor, the brain death of a twenty-year-old male, the systematic rape and sexual abuse of forty-seven female activists, and two hundred arrests including torture and police brutality,[8] all under Peña Nieto's watch. In short, Enrique Peña Nieto embodied two of the elements that were foremost in critiques of Mexican politics at that moment: a national media monopoly that unfailingly sold itself out to the highest political bidder and the potential return of an authoritarian party that had historically quelled attempts at democratization processes in the country.

"BLACK FRIDAY"

It was within this context that the student protest at the Universidad Iberoamericana (Uia) took place on Friday, May 11, 2012. Other presidential candidates, such as Andrés Manuel López Obrador (Coalición

Movimiento Progresista) and Gabriel Quadri (Partido Nueva Alianza), had previously taken part in the university-organized forum "Buen ciudadano Ibero" ("Good Citizen Ibero"). On the eve of Peña Nieto's participation in the forum, there were already rumblings as to whether he would be well received. In that morning's edition, *El Universal* reported that students from Uia had been organizing several forms of protest through the Facebook event "Los candidatos a la Presidencia en la UIA" ("The Presidential Candidates at UIA").[9] Communicating through the social networking site, various "protest actions" had been agreed on, including the seeding of "uncomfortable questions" for Peña Nieto during the Q&A section of the forum, instructions for making masks of ex-president Carlos Salinas de Gortari to wear on the day, and other performance-like actions.

On the morning of May 11, Peña Nieto arrived at the Universidad Iberoamericana for the forum "Buen ciudadano Ibero." As he took to the stage, he was welcomed by a wave of supporters' cheers and detractors' boos, many shouting "¡Peña! ¡Peña!" while others cried "¡Fuera! ¡Fuera!" ("Out! Out!"). During his programmed speech, the audience remained in respectful silence while the PRI presidential candidate elaborated on his campaign platform; however, when the Q&A session began, several students expressed their criticism of the presidential candidate.[10] While many of the questions highlighted Peña Nieto's poor performance as governor of the state of Mexico and his highly manufactured media image, perhaps the most controversial moment was related to the Atenco police raid of 2006. As Peña Nieto was closing up the Q&A session, exclamations of "¡Atenco! ¡Atenco!" were heard, and the PRI-PVEM candidate returned to address these clamors. Regarding accusations of police brutality in Atenco,[11] Peña Nieto admitted that, as governor of the state of Mexico at the time, he had "made the decision to make use of the public forces to reestablish order and peace. . . . It was a determined action that I assumed personally in order to reestablish order and peace in the legitimate right that the Mexican state has to use public force."[12] The auditorium erupted in shouts following this admission, and as Enrique Peña Nieto walked out he was followed by a chorus of students chanting "murderer" and "We are all Atenco."

Outside the auditorium the mood was equally tense. A large group of students who had not managed to enter the forum were grouped around the exit, and they joined in the chants of "Atenco no se olvida" ("Atenco never forgotten") and "La Ibero no te quiere" ("Ibero doesn't want you here"). Many showed placards criticizing the candidate; others wore Salinas de Gortari masks with the inscriptions "Tu papá. Asesino" ("Your father. Murderer"). Some students had colored the university fountains with red dye, and another group held up a large sign reading "Todxs[13] somos ATENCO" ("We are all ATENCO"). Faced with the unsympathetic multitude, Peña Nieto was led through the university by a thirty-man-strong security team in search of an exit; a large number of protestors followed the candidate around campus continuing their chants. Making a brief pit-stop at the campus toilets in order to regroup with his security staff, Peña Nieto finally managed to board his vehicle and exit the university in the midst of shouting students.[14]

The intensity of the student reaction at the Uia took the presidential candidate and his campaign team by surprise. Until that day at the Ibero, his highly staged, highly mediatized campaign had run relatively according to script. Following Peña Nieto's "Black Friday," his media team hastily put together a promotional video attempting to gloss over the controversy.[15] However, the protest organizers at Uia had previously agreed on Facebook to bring along electronic devices such as photographic and video cameras in order to "document everything."[16] (This is visible in many of the student-recorded videos of the protest available on YouTube; numerous students can be seen holding up their mobile phones and iPads.[17]) By that evening, the student protest at Uia had been widely uploaded on YouTube and was receiving numerous hits, as well as being shown on some of the mainstream media outlets. The student-made videos provided a contrasting account of what, according to Peña Nieto's promo, had been a warm reception at the university.

Peña Nieto and his team were swift on damage control. Even prior to his participation in the forum, he had asserted that plans to protest his presence on campus were a "show set up in order to disqualify me."[18] That evening after the "Black Friday" at the Universidad Iberamericana, the conspiracy theory was quickly backed by PRI president Pedro Joaquín Coldwell, who addressed the events at Uia in an interview on Radio Ibero 90.9. Coldwell stressed that the protestors at the university were a handful of young people who were not representative of the academic community; in fact, he argued, it would be up to Uia authorities to investigate whether those who participated in the protest were Ibero students at all.[19] Similarly, Emilio Antonio Gamboa Patrón, another prominent PRI member, qualified the protest as a boycott, a trap, and a provocation, insisting that an investigation be conducted in order to determine where the attacks were coming from.[20] More direct accusations were forwarded by the Senate leader for the PVEM, Arturo Escobar, who affirmed that the protestors were hardly young students—according to him, most of them seemed to be around thirty to thirty-five years old—and no more than twenty people had participated in the protest. In short, he asserted that the group that had "insulted" Peña Nieto was orchestrated by the candidate's political rivals and that he was convinced that they were not students at the university: "The information that we have is that groups close to Andrés Manuel López Obrador were prompting and organizing these kind of events."[21] In addition to these claims by politicians, a number of dailies belonging to the consortium Organización Editorial Mexicana (OEM) covered the protest as an attempted boycott, with headlines ranging from "Peña Nieto Succeeds in the Ibero in Spite of Orchestrated Boycott Attempt" to "He Succeeds Boycott!"[22] Similarly, news programs on Televisa and TV Azteca highlighted the politicians' reactions to the protests while excluding the activists' point of view.[23]

The following Monday, 131 students from the Universidad Iberoamericana responded to the mainstream media's coverage of the protest through a video on YouTube.[24] Opening with a sound clip from Escobar's interview where he claimed that the protest had been orchestrated by groups from outside the academic institution, the students read the following message:

> The Students respond: Dear Joaquín Coldwell, Arturo Escobar, Emilio Gamboa, as well as mass media of doubtful impartiality. We are using our right of reply to deny [your version of the events of Friday, May 11, 2012]. We are students at the Ibero, not "acarreados" [paid political fodder] or "porros" [professional troublemakers]. And no one has trained us to do anything.[25]

The 131 students then went on to state their names and student ID numbers, as well as display their student ID cards.[26] The video went viral and, by that evening, the hashtag *#131alumnosdelaIbero* became a worldwide trending topic on Twitter.[27] Within the first week of the video being uploaded, students from other universities quickly showed solidarity with the Ibero activists, with hundreds of students from private and public higher education institutions joining in to organize the "Demonstration for Truth" in front of Televisa Studios on May 18. As students from other universities started to claim that they were the 132nd student, the hashtag *#YoSoy132* was coined and soon became the identifier for the movement.[28]

#IAM132

#YoSoy132 increasingly grew in presence, adherents, and organization. One of the early defining moments was the Estela de Luz demonstration on May 23, when the original protestors from the Uia joined with other university students and read the burgeoning movement's declaration and demands. In this statement, they asserted that the movement centered on the defense of freedom of expression and on the right of information in

Mexico. Stressing that they were concerned with the political role played by the national press and mass media, they declared that their movement sought the democratization of the media in order to guarantee transparent, plural, and impartial information for the advancement of critical consciousness and thought. Their demands, therefore, included real competition in the mass-media market, particularly with reference to the television duopoly held by Televisa and TV Azteca; Internet access as a constitutional right effective in the terms established by Article 1 of the Carta Magna; a widening of the debate between the activists and the mass media concerning the demands of the movement; and the guarantee of personal safety for all the members of #YoSoy132 and, particularly, those journalists who have been the victims of violence in Mexico. In closing, they invited other university students, Mexican youth, and citizens to join the movement and adopt its demands.[29]

As the movement rallied around this series of demands, it also began to produce a rich variety of visual media in order to circulate information and gain wider support. One of the earliest images was the "Soy 132" ("I Am 132," figure 9.1) digital poster that designer Emiliano Molina made for the Estela de Luz demonstration. As Molina explained in interview, he chose to make an attractive poster that would catch people's eye as well as capture the political mood at the time. The students in the image were represented with very determined countenances in order to convey the message that their movement was serious: "They mean this isn't a TV commercial, this is real," Molina stresses. For him, the poster was the product of the "very immediate" need to make an image that would "put some weight on the balance so that all the weight wouldn't be on the powerful's side (that power represented by the government and the media)."[30] He recounts that he had designed the image and posted it on Facebook on the dawn of May 21. By morning it had gone viral, receiving a thousand views and circulating widely on Twitter. For some, it became the "protest banner that brought together thousands of people."[31] The "Soy 132" poster, as well as the great variety of visual material produced by #YoSoy132 in the following months, effectively became the cultural artifacts that brought together and gave voice to the demands of the thousands that participated in the movement.

#YoSoy132's visual production is highly varied and prolific. Much of it has a base in Mexican postrevolutionary images, such as the prints produced by the Taller de Gráfica Popular (Popular Arts Workshop) artists' collective in the 1930s, and in the imagery of the 1968 Mexican student movement. Yet much of it equally draws inspiration from Russian constructivism, socialist realism, World War II propaganda, 1960s antiwar posters, stencil art, British punk, Japanese manga, contemporary pop

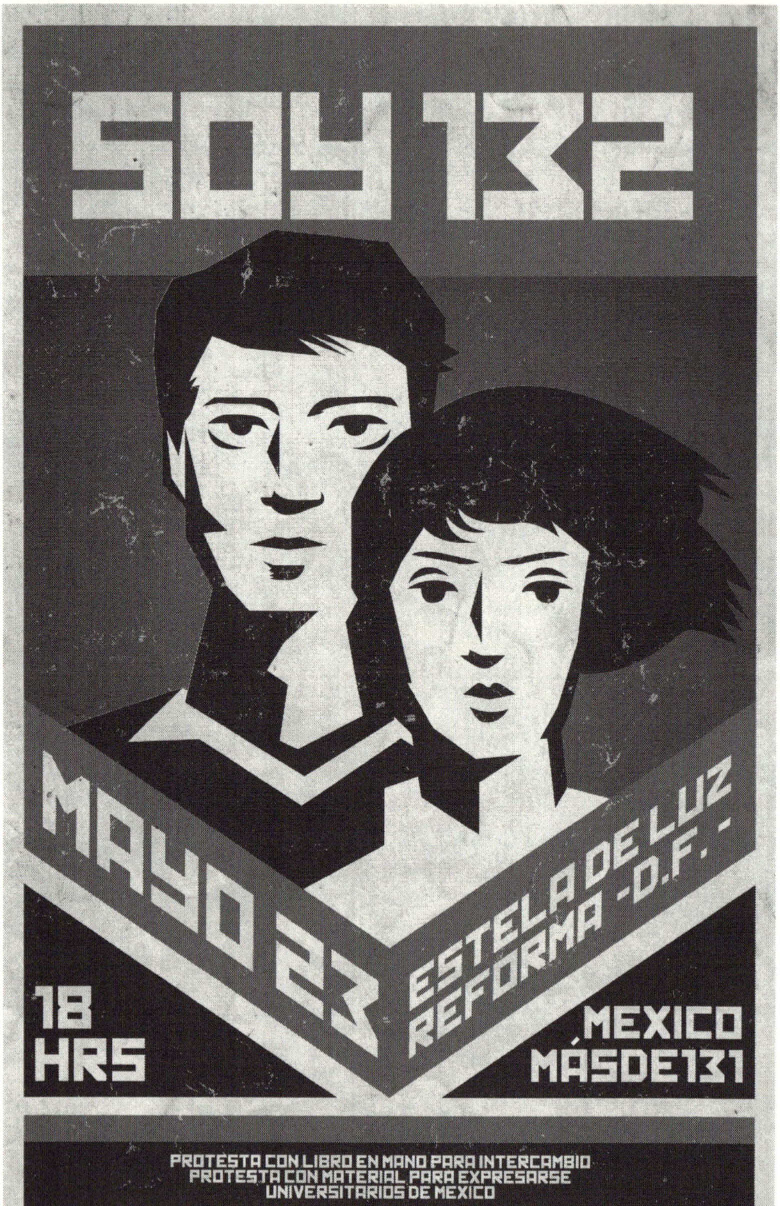

Figure 9.1. "YoSoy132," by Emiliano Molina, available on his website: http://emilianomolinadiseno.wordpress.com/2012/05/22/soy-132/. (Printed with the artist's permission.)

culture, and digital media.[32] It has circulated mostly in street demonstrations and through online networks such as the Facebook groups Cartel 132, Gráfica 132, and Resistencia Gráfica; the Twitter hashtags #yosoy132arte and #YoSoy132media; and blogs such as *FrenteGráfico*, *LaManufacturera*, and *RevolutionUAM*.[33]

While many of the digital posters seem to have been designed on an individual basis, artists' collectives have also emerged. The Frente Gráfico 132 "Arte, diseño y libertad" brings together designers and artists from two of most well-established art schools in the country, the Escuela Nacional de Artes Plásticas (ENAP) and the Escuela Nacional de Pintura, Escultura y Grabado "La Esmeralda." The collective Artistas Aliados also groups members from art schools and independent artists, stating the following in their manifesto:

> Our aim is to produce alternative information that is humanly objective, reliable and contributing to strengthen social consciousness. . . . We propose to combat the television duopoly through alternative media. . . . We rebel against media invisibility. We resist and struggle to make visible the invisible. Our weapons are art, culture, creativity, satire and irony.[34]

They appear to have been successful in this regard. Prominent Mexican painter and sculptor Vicente Rojo has praised the posters, commenting that they are excellent in terms of design and very useful to the movement given that they communicate its objectives clearly.[35] As part of a communication strategy that aimed to garner wide citizen support and break through the media blackout, the visual production of #YoSoy132 revived a strong Mexican tradition of art activism.

One of the most evident points of reference for #YoSoy132's imagery is the Mexican student movement of 1968. That year the country was hosting the Nineteenth Olympics, and the government was eager to showcase a modern, vibrant Mexico to the outside world. However, on the flipside of the Olympic *furore*, the PRI's heavy-handed authoritarianism was common policy. Following a student altercation between two rival university football clubs, the Mexican federal police force (called *granaderos* at that time) violently repressed the fight. As student persecution by federal police forces escalated over the following days, students from both universities began to organize and in the short space of two months became a nationwide movement against the PRI regime's authoritarian and antidemocratic practices. The student movement was brutally quelled on October 2, 1968, when hundreds of students demonstrating at Tlatelolco plaza were massacred by military and paramilitary forces, resulting in an estimated two hundred dead.[36]

Before that fateful October 2, the student movement had been highly active in the production of visual propaganda. Student artist collectives were formed, in many cases printing and distributing hundreds of linotype posters in a matter of weeks. The iconography of the 1968 student protest included what Álvaro Vázquez Mantecón describes as "quintessential left-wing representations": raised fists, fingers making the sign of "V" for Victory, portraits of Che Guevara, and so on.[37] Many of the 1968 posters also adopted the imagery of socialist realism from the Taller de Gráfica Popular artist collective, while others drew inspiration from the French students' movement posters.[38] Others still applied the Situationist technique of *détournement*—what would currently be termed *subvertisement*—to parody the design logos for the Mexico 1968 Olympics.

Many of the political and iconographical objectives of the 1968 Mexican student movement were similar to those of their contemporary counterparts. Politically, the 1968 movement sought to open up the field of democratic action through its capacity to strive toward freedom of expression and the rejection of all forms of sectarianism and dogmatic positioning.[39] The visual production of the movement was key to achieving these goals; for Arnulfo Aquino, one of the figureheads of the student movement, "the capacity for communication through images played a transcendental role that, it may be said, gave the movement a character all its own."[40] Iconographically, the aim was to generate images that would break through the media barrier and disseminate the ideas and objectives that fueled the protest. Students at the ENAP and La Esmeralda created images collectively as members of the movement's propaganda brigades and used all the techniques at their disposal—such as linoleum print, mimeographs, offset, and silkscreen—to create banners, picket signs, posters, leaflets, or stickers.[41]

#YoSoy132 recouped this legacy of art activism, emphasizing the influence of the Mexican 1968 movement through various symbolic acts and iconographic borrowings. #YoSoy132 online galleries host numerous digital posters that make reference to the 1968 and 1971 student movements. The Facebook group Cartel 132, for example, has uploaded a good number of original Mexico 1968 prints and has added contemporary posters referring to the governmental repression of the student movement. This is in line with #YoSoy132's emphasis on the importance of exercising historical memory; perhaps their slogan "#YoSoy68" (#IAm68) best expresses this commitment. Their questioning of the *PRI-ato*, their awareness of the Mexican history of democratic struggle, and their championing of freedom of expression are consistent with their statement that "#YoSoy132 is the proof that there is a collective historical consciousness."[42]

This is reflected in the historical and iconographical references to 1968 in their visual production. Several digital posters refer to the PRI's authoritarian regime by associating Enrique Peña Nieto with other controversial PRI politicians such as Gustavo Díaz Ordaz (the Mexican president at the time of the 1968 protests) and Carlos Salinas de Gortari (more on this below). In terms of iconography, several of the images remix the symbols and characteristic typography from the Mexico 1968 Olympics; others reproduce the linoleum print aesthetic typical of the 1968 movement, representing human figures silhouetted in black against a white background. A good example is "Simbología de servicios en 1968" ("Symbology of Services in 1968," figure 9.2), a student remix of the Olympic logos highlighting the repressive government behind the Olympics. In short, 1968 is a historical and iconographical point of reference that figures prominently in the visual production of #YoSoy132.

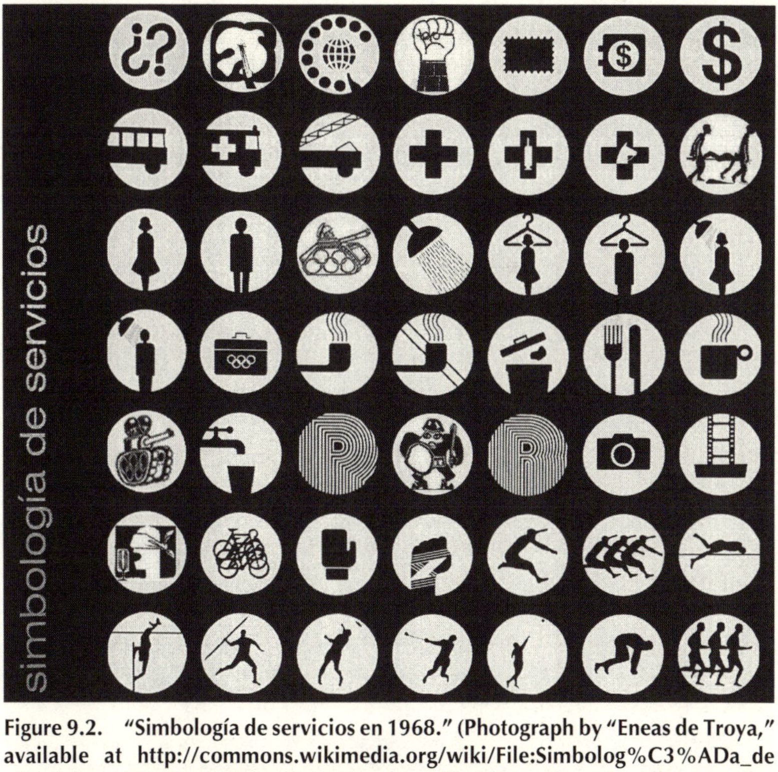

Figure 9.2. "Simbología de servicios en 1968." (Photograph by "Eneas de Troya," available at http://commons.wikimedia.org/wiki/File:Simbolog%C3%ADa_de_Servicios_1968_%283134634478%29.jpg; file licensed under the Creative Commons Attribution 2.0 Generic license [public domain].)

While making reference to its historical background, #YoSoy132 also clearly positioned itself in relation to the contemporary world context. As expressed in their *General Principles*, "the chaotic world situation that has resulted in different protest movements was also reflected in our country, presenting us as part of a context of international protest."[43] The mass protest movements that had taken place around the world in 2011, such as Occupy Wall Street (OWS), 15M, the Greek Indignant Citizens Movement, the Arab Spring, and the Chilean student movement, were a continuing point of reference for the Mexican activists. And in 2012, precisely when #YoSoy132 was starting to consolidate as a movement, the 2011 uprisings were commemorating their anniversaries. Only a few days after the "Black Friday" at the Uia, the *indignados* were celebrating their one-year anniversary by holding demonstrations in over three hundred cities around the world, including Mexico City; in Madrid, they were violently dispersed from Plaza del Sol by anti-riot police.[44] The Occupy movement in the United States was attempting to reoccupy Zuccotti Park on their six-month and one-year anniversaries, resulting in the arrest of numerous activists.[45] The global moment was one of resistance. As philosopher Enrique Dussel eloquently states, "Recently I was writing that the Arab, Israeli, Spanish, Greek, Chilean and North American youth was part of a 'political revolution that will span all the 21st century', and that you [#YoSoy132], and many other young people in other parts of the world have already started [it]."[46]

In the wake of the student uprising in Mexico, many journalists and political analysts drew comparisons between the world movements and the national situation, some openly dubbing #YoSoy132 as the Mexican Spring.[47] Effectively, there were many similarities between the Mexican youth and the global protests that had marked 2011. In several cases, the movements were initiated by young people, many with a university education. Importantly, the initiators were proficient in the use of social networking sites such as Facebook, Twitter, and YouTube as resources that allowed them to organize events, reach out to sympathizers, and share information.[48] They promptly took advantage of the technological platforms that allowed them to communicate their stance and break through media blackouts. Online networks also provided them with resources that helped them hone their activist tactics, such as organizational advice from other movements and tactical manuals used to communicate their demands through nonviolent means.[49]

However, some believe that the comparisons between #YoSoy132 and the indignados, Occupy Wall Street (OWS), and the Arab Spring are oftentimes amplified.[50] For political analyst Genaro Lozano, the demands of all these movements varied greatly according to each context, and even though some of them shared in the struggle for greater democratic freedom, the degree to which this was demanded differed from country to country.[51]

In spite of claims that #YoSoy 132 was not necessarily a Mexican Spring in the same sense as the Arab Spring, the indignados, or OWS, the Mexican activists clearly identified themselves with the resistance movements taking place around the world. This is frequently referenced in their visual production. One of the movement's most viewed and copied digital posters is "La Primavera Mexicana" ("Mexican Spring," figure 9.3) by

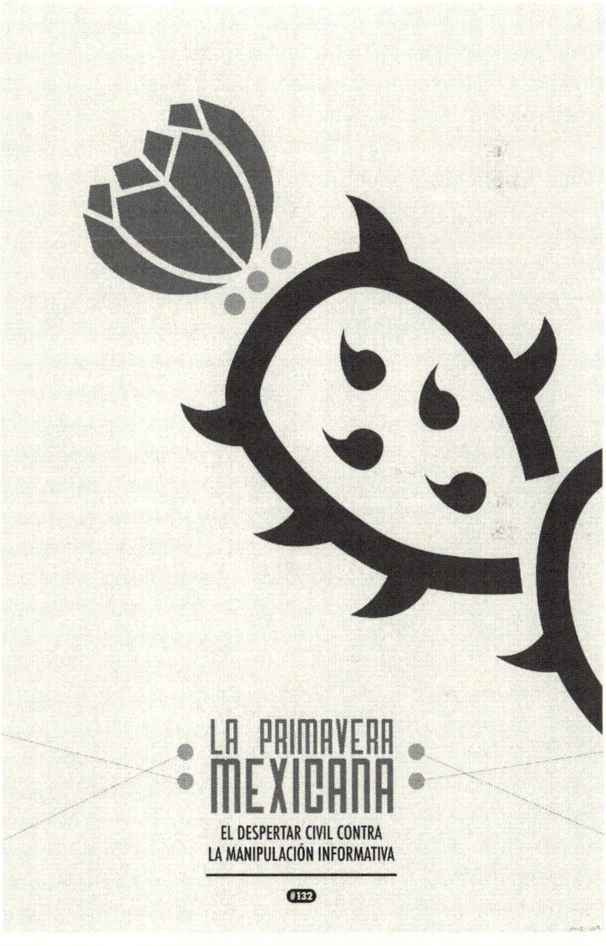

Figure 9.3. "La Primavera Mexicana," by Eduardo Salles, available for open download on the artist's blog: http://www .cinismoilustrado.com/2012/05/la-primavera-mexicana.html. (Courtesy of Eduardo Salles.)

publicist and illustrator Eduardo Salles. For "La Primavera Mexicana," he wanted "to make reference to the Arab Spring and represent the possibility of rebirth after adversity,"[52] a concept symbolized through the synthetic rendering of a flowering cactus. The Anonymous mask was also adopted as part of #YoSoy132 iconography, except that it became "Mexicanified" so that the Anonymous *charro* was a regular character at many of the rallies. Instructions for making a Zapatista Anonymous mask, complete with the Zapata moustache, were posted online to "use in the event of a revolution." OWS slogans were adopted by the Mexican students; during the first rally in front of Televisa Studios, many placards read "Occupy Televisa #YoSoy132." The activists' links with the Chilean student movement were also visually represented through the poster "Soy/Eres 132" ("I Am/You Are 132"), designed on the occasion of Chilean student leader Camila Vallejo's visit to Mexico in June 2012. As will be developed in more detail below, #YoSoy132 was especially active in cultivating networks between their movement and others worldwide, and much of their visual production reflects this.

In short, the visual corpus of #YoSoy132 is extremely varied and prolific; as many as hundreds of digital posters are available through Facebook groups such as Cartel 132 and Gráfica 132. With regard to content, the images touch on a number of different themes, many of them resulting from the communicational needs of the movement as they emerged. Taking #YoSoy132's demands as a starting point, this chapter will now go on to examine only three of the main themes that are deployed throughout the visual corpus: the rejection of an authoritarian political regime, resistance against the media duopoly, and the practice of a renewed, participatory democracy.

MÉXICO, SIN PRI

The original impetus for the movement was sparked by the events at the Uia and by the entrenched powers' reaction to the student criticisms of the PRI candidate. As historian Lorenzo Meyer has argued, Peña Nieto's party members reacted to the protests at the Uia in a very authoritarian manner, much within the PRI's logic of "no one is allowed to question me and if they *do* question me, it must be a conspiracy."[53] What is more, Meyer underscores that Peña Nieto's very admission of having ordered the Atenco repression, a la Díaz Ordaz (the Mexican president who ordered the Tlatelolco massacre), signals that for the PRI it is acceptable for one person to unilaterally call for the use of public force against a people in order to "maintain the peace."[54]

The original 131 student activists, and then their adherents, were frankly opposed to this authoritarian way of doing politics as usual in Mexico; as the Artistas Aliados "Manifesto" states, "We reject the authoritarian and antidemocratic verticality of the current political and economic system."[55] Numerous digital posters and online videos make reference to this, some addressing Peña Nieto's poor record as governor of the state of Mexico, others drawing links between the PRI candidate and other party members of sketchy morals. For example, the poster "Nunca más" ("Never More") draws on the Mexico 1968 aesthetic of linoleum print silhouettes in order to highlight Peña Nieto's track record as governor, with accusations of rising murder tolls, state debt, femicides, robberies, and electoral fraud. The manga-inspired cartoon "¡La Extinción Está Cerca!" ("Extinction Is Near!") by designer Ubaldo caricatures the main PRI politicians as a troop of dinosaurs running from an asteroid labeled "#YoSoy132." The digital posters "El PRInosaurio pertenece a los libros de historia" ("The PRInosaur Belongs in History Books") and "¿Volver?" ("Return?") further emphasize the backwardness of the PRI by relegating it to a past historical moment.

However, here it is important to clarify that for all the anti-PRI images and the "México. Sin PRI" ("Mexico. Without PRI") slogan at rallies, the student's rejection of the political party referred more to their discontent with a particular way of doing politics than to a specific partisan position. Very early on, #YoSoy132 made clear that they were a nonpartisan movement and did not support any political candidate in particular. Analyst Denise Dresser has highlighted this dimension: the students presented "a positioning far away from ideological imperatives and close to citizen concerns. . . . They have exposed the authoritarian features of the Mexican political system."[56] For writer Sabina Berman, it was the case that the Mexican youth found a way to enunciate the following statement: "The political system that all of you [politicians] belong to is nothing more than a bunch of amoral deal-making."[57] In short, they rebelled against a political regime that was authoritarian as a whole; in political theorist Benjamin Arditi's words, "To rebel is to say 'enough!' to business as usual and to disturb the given because you don't want things to go on as they are."[58]

Moreover, #YoSoy132 was firmly situated within the political juncture of the 2012 presidential elections. Statistically, the number of young citizens (eighteen to thirty-four years old) registered to vote in the elections made up a total of thirty-four million Mexicans (40 percent of the total voting population).[59] In this electoral context, the youth population held the real potential to sway the results one way or another. #YoSoy132 maintained their neutral stance and refused to endorse any particular candidate or political party, declaring themselves to be "a non-partisan movement—this [is] understood as the inexistence of any link between the movement and any political party."[60] Yet this positioning was fundamentally political. As Dussel states, "Choosing not to opt for a particular party does not mean refusing to be deeply political. And the [#YoSoy132] movement is political because it takes on the responsibility of cleaning up a corrupt *electoralera* [form of political] representation."[61] The students' main goal was never to support one politician over another in their ascent to the presidency, but rather to provide the adequate conditions for the citizenry to exercise a well-informed vote.

Much of the media produced by the movement directly addresses the students' dissatisfaction with the way campaign information was being handled by the private media duopoly Televisa and TV Azteca. As communicator and illustrator Diego Martínez stresses, the movement's visual production "emerges in response to the disinformation or the manipulation of information on the part of the television duopoly, and also as a rejection to the imposition [to the presidency] of a character such as Enrique Peña Nieto."[62] In this vein, many of the digital posters encourage voters to exercise their electoral rights with full information on the candidates and their platforms. The posters incorporate slogans such as "Voto informado jamás manipulado" ("A well-informed vote can never be manipulated"), "Voto libre. ¡Infórmate! Lee, difunde y participa" ("Free vote. Get information! Read, share, and participate"), and "Yo soy 132. Por un voto libre y responsable" ("I am 132. For a free and responsible vote").

TELEVISA SAVE THE QUEEN

In essence, then, the main target of the movement was the privatized mass media in Mexico and the power it held to define the country's political landscape. The immediate point of contention was the media's lack of fairness in the way it covered the electoral campaigns; in many cases, Televisa and TV Azteca gave disproportionate amounts of airtime to Enrique Peña Nieto and presented a soap-opera rosy version of his background as a politician and public figure. The movement addressed this point directly in its "General Principles" charter: "#YoSoy132 was born in the midst of an electoral race that was devoid of content, constantly bombarded by [publicity] spots without any true proposals, full of empty messages, promises without a voice . . . and characterized by the noticeable imposition of a political figure that was constructed by the media."[63]

Since 2005, Peña Nieto had been paying the two television networks large amounts of money, channeled from the state of Mexico's budget, in order to build up his public image on news and entertainment programs. Yet the networks never made explicit reference to the purchased airtime—the spots were effectively adverts—nor did they clarify that the spots were not part of the enterprises' journalistic reporting.[64] This was the source of a great deal of controversy as it highlighted the media's overt complicity with the country's political regime.

For Dussel, it was no coincidence that many of the original 131 were Uia communications students, and that

> they focused on the essence of the process of public opinion formation (a crucial moment of democracy), which is mass media communications. By questioning the media monopoly, the #YoSoy132 movement touches upon the essence of democracy that in our times is characterized by electronic technology. Their opposition to a candidate produced like merchandise by a television monopoly is not a partisan choice; it is an essentially political one.[65]

This is reflected in the bulk of #YoSoy132's visual production that makes reference to the media's bias in favor of Peña Nieto. The "[Televisa logo] Save the Queen" poster is a remix of the original *God Save the Queen* album cover by the Sex Pistols and the Andy Warhol silkscreen portrait of Marilyn Monroe. Peña Nieto has been dressed in the screen siren's drag, complete with canary-yellow curls and bright-blue eye shadow. His lips have been painted bright red, but two sinister drops of blood trail down from his mouth to his chin. The coquettish angle of the politician's pose further emphasizes the combination of a carefully constructed media image with a disturbing authoritarian undertone. The poster's slogan reads, "[Televisa logo] Save the Queen," in reference to the network's backing of the politician and the construction of his image as merchandise. In "La alfombra roja ya está preparada . . ." ("The Red Carpet Is Ready . . ."), by designers Perre Quince and Sacre, Peña Nieto is wearing the presidential sash and standing over a bloody red map of Mexico. His head has been replaced by a television screen but he is still recognizable as Peña Nieto, with his trademark cowlick hairstyle topping the screen. Under the image, the poster's slogan is accompanied by a logo of the PRI, remixed to include the Televisa logo, a bullet hole, and streaks of blood. The "¿Quién quiere ser president?" ("Who Wants to Be President?") poster further emphasizes the impact of mediatization on the presidential race of 2012. Parodying reality shows in Mexico, the poster plays with the idea of a televised open casting to become president, reproducing all the over-the-top brashness of reality shows such as *Big Brother* and *La Academia*.

Similarly, during the movement's early defining moments it was confronted with media bias firsthand. Following the students' demonstration at the Televisa Santa Fe studios to protest media partiality in favor of the PRI candidate, Televisa continued to marginalize their voices by covering the protest in a ten-minute report while Peña Nieto's speech on perfecting democracy in Mexico received eighteen minutes of coverage on that evening's news.[66] In reaction to this and other instances of media bias, the students proclaimed the following at the Estela de Luz rally on May 23:

> We, the united students of this country believe that a condition necessary to correct [Mexico's current] situation is the empowerment of the citizen through access to information. Information allows us to make better political, economic and social decisions. Information makes it possible for citizens to demand and offer well-argued critiques of their government, political agents, entrepreneurs, and society itself. This is why "Yo Soy 132" upholds the right to information and the right to freedom of expression as its main demands.[67]

As a result of this stance, a great number of digital posters make reference to the media's overpowering control of the political situation in Mexico. In "#Yo Soy 132," a poster that once again makes reference to the 1968 silhouette aesthetic, a group of figures are in the process of toppling media tyranny as represented by a dictator's statue capped with a television head. Other posters represent the breaking of media control through images of a masked Mexican wrestler air-kicking a TV set, a *2001 Space Odyssey*–esque chimp pounding at a TV screen with a bone, and a figure with a television head opening its cage door to release a white dove labeled "freedom."

Another of the criticisms that #YoSoy132 directed at the networks was the poor quality of their programming content. The "Apaga la tele" ("Turn Off the TV Set") poster by Rodo Fredo "Tnk" makes reference to quotes from Televisa founder Emilio Azcárraga Milmo, such as "Los mexicanos tienen la televisión que se merecen" ("Mexicans get the television they deserve")[68] and "No estoy para educar" ("I'm not here to educate anyone"). The poster "Que no te heduke[69] la Rosa de Guadalupe" ("Don't let the *Rosa de Guadalupe* [Show] 'Hedukate' You") further highlights this theme. Recalling artist Barbara Kruger's *Your Body Is a Battleground* through its formal treatment of the subject matter and the use of digital collage, the poster refers to one of Televisa's most popular daytime TV shows, *La Rosa de Guadalupe*. The melodrama deals with a series of problems faced by individuals (mostly women) and how they are miraculously resolved through their faith in the Virgin of Guadalupe. Highly moralizing in content and badly acted and produced, the show is perhaps the flagship of Televisa's relationship with an audience that the network perceives to be feverously religious and, in many cases, poorly educated. For #YoSoy132, this show was a clear-cut example of Televisa's use of "bread and circus" to keep the Mexican audiences from developing a critical stance toward political life. Faced with this, the movement invites Mexican citizens to "Turn off the TV, turn on your mind," a slogan from another one of their posters.

Perhaps the most impactful visual piece that #YoSoy132 produced to counteract Televisa's media hegemony was the video shown at the *Fiesta por la Luz de la Verdad*. Part of the occupation of Televisa Chapultepec Studios on the evening of June 13, it was projected on the network's wall in order to demand truth and impartiality from the media; subsequently, it was circulated on YouTube.[70] The video opens with violent footage of the 1968 Tlatelolco masssacre and the 1995 Aguas Blancas killings (when a group of organized peasant farmers were ambushed by police forces, resulting in at least seventeen dead). It is worthwhile to quote the whole video script in detail:

> **What is being manipulated behind these walls?**
>
> —1968. At least 300 students killed or disappeared. TELEVISA reported 20, including the military and civilians. [This phrase makes reference to the Tlatelolco massacre.]
>
> **Who is hiding the truth from us?**
>
> —1971. 120 dead. The news was not reported. [This refers to the "Halconazo" or Corpus Christi massacre of student demonstrators on June 10, 1971.]
>
> **Who silences our voices?**
>
> —1988. TELEVISA covered up the largest electoral fraud in the history of our country. [Carlos Salinas de Gortari was "elected" president in one of the most impugned elections in recent Mexican history.]
>
> "I am the PRI's best soldier." —Emilio Azcárraga Milmo. [Televisa networks owner and chairman of the board from 1972 to 1997.]
>
> "I make television for *jodidos* because Mexico is a country of *jodidos.*" —Emilio Azcárraga Milmo. [*Jodidos* is a colloquial Mexican term that simultaneously means "people who are poor" and "people who are being fucked over."]
>
> —1994. Faced with a presidential candidates' assassination [TELEVISA] repeated the lone assassin theory until it was legitimated. [This makes reference to the assassination of PRI presidential candidate Luis Donaldo Colosio during a campaign speech, see note 3 for details.]
>
> **TELEVISA has justified abuse,**
>
> —AGUAS BLANCAS. 17 peasants murdered.

rape,

—ACTEAL. 45 dead including children and pregnant women. [A paramilitary organization ambushed the village of Acteal, killing numerous men, women, and children, while the state police forces camping nearby did nothing to intervene.]

and the omission of our rights.

—ATENCO. 2 dead, 201 injured and 23 women sexually abused.

FOR DECADES IT HAS BEEN IN THE PRI'S INTEREST THAT YOU REMAIN APATHETIC. THE APATHETIC DON'T QUESTION, THE APATHETIC GIVE UP, THE APATHETIC DON'T VOTE.

WAKE UP! DEMAND THE TRUTH PEACEFULLY. TELEVISA DOES NOT DECIDE FOR YOU. YOU ARE BIGGER THAN THEM. AND MORE IMPORTANT.

TURN OFF THE TV AND TURN ON THE TRUTH.

IF WE DO NOT BLAZE TOGETHER, WHO WILL ILLUMINATE THIS DARKNESS?

#LUZ132

Through this video, the movement highlighted the historical complicity between Televisa and the PRI regime ("I am the PRI's best soldier") throughout some of the country's most algid moments of political violence. At the end of the video, #YoSoy132 calls for action on the part of the average Mexican citizen to inform his- or herself, to question the information they are given, and to demand the truth peacefully. In other words, the movement encouraged passive TV audiences to become citizen agents in the construction of a more democratic Mexico.

As the *Luz de la Verdad* video and other forms of visual media demonstrate, #YoSoy132 was very creative in its tactics for breaking through the media blackout. One of the main tools at hand was the access to digital communication technologies such as social networking sites and blogs. As claimed in a placard bearing the Facebook, Twitter, and YouTube logos and the slogan "¡Ahora nosotros damos las noticias!" ("Now we are reporting the news!"), the student movement had found a platform to make its voice heard.

In its "General Principles," #YoSoy132 was explicit as to the importance of social networking for the movement: "We prefer a world of social networks over muted silences; . . . we prefer the Internet and the possibilities [it offers]."[71] María Elena Meneses, a professor in new technologies at the Tecnológico de Monterrey, stresses that the social media were a catalyst in triggering the protests, an event without precedent in Mexico: "The students understood that social networks can be spaces for the articulation of citizenship, and a counterweight to traditional discourse and power, including that of the media."[72] In fact, #YoSoy132 was very skillful in their understanding that the public sphere is also negotiated in the digital world. Their use of social networks and other forms of digital media redefined and reinvigorated participatory democracy as the right of every citizen; tired of a limited "citizenship" that involved stuffing a vote in a ballot box every six years, the students made a push to redefine politics in their own terms by using a (digital) forum in which all voices would be heard. Through its active engagement in the public sphere (be it online or offline), the students aimed to redefine political participation, and citizenship itself, beyond the constraints of a political system that silenced dissenting voices through its political and economic control of the (more traditional) media. In the case of #YoSoy132, the public space was digital as well as on the streets.

There is an abundance of #YoSoy132 digital posters and other forms of media celebrating the importance of social networking as a means for circulating alternative information and enhancing political activism. One of the simplest, yet most eloquent, posters by fco-e shows three mouse pointer icons in the shape of hands on a white backdrop. The first pointer icon signals the number 1, the second the number 3, the third the number 2, adding up to the digits for 132. Through a very simple formal means, the poster comments on the imbrication between the movement and the digital platforms that allow it to organize, share information, and reach out to the public. Another image using simplicity to get its point across is the "#YoSoy132" poster. On a Twitter-blue background, the Twitter bird logo is flying over Enrique Peña Nieto's head, having previously defecated on his luxurious hairstyle. Other posters are slightly more elaborate but deal with the same theme. One poster by Moi12 carries the slogan "The medium has changed. The control is ours. #YoSoy132," accompanied by the illustration of a hand holding a remote control and pointing hashtag and @ symbols at a black hole. The "1968-1971-2012" poster highlights the historical importance of social networking by drawing a comparison between the violence in 1968 and 1971 (the peace dove pierced by a bayonet) and the access to freedom of expression provided by digital platforms (the #YoSoy132, Twitter, and Facebook logos held by the beak of the Twitter bird).

However, it is important not to overstate the impact that social networks had on the movement's political successes. While much of the organization of events and the sharing of ideas took place online, the students' presence on the streets was crucial. Here it is important to highlight that much of the students' organization took place face-to-face at local and inter-university assemblies that functioned on a horizontal and representative level. It was the conjunction of both forms of visibility that allowed the movement to gain adherents and achieve public support.

What is more, the students were intent on practicing different forms of political resistance in the public arena. For instance, some of their first demonstrations were conducted by marching on the sidewalks, rather than interrupting traffic by walking on heavily congested roads. Other rallies included graffiti cleanups on city walls as a demonstration of positive civic action. Many of the demonstrations included onsite cultural presentations that ranged from ballet performances to impromptu jazz concerts, emphasizing the importance of public access to culture in tandem with political resistance (figure 9.4).

The Paris branch of #YoSoy132 was especially poignant in highlighting the role of culture in the political context. The *Resisting the Present* exhibition of contemporary Mexican art was showing at the Musée d'Art Moderne when several members of #YoSoy132-Paris walked into the gallery space under the guise of regular visitors. At 3:00 p.m. on the dot, all of them took off their jackets and revealed the "#YoSoy132" signs they had pinned on the front of their shirts. On their backs, they had pinned messages such as "over 60,000 dead since 2006," "over half of the Mexican

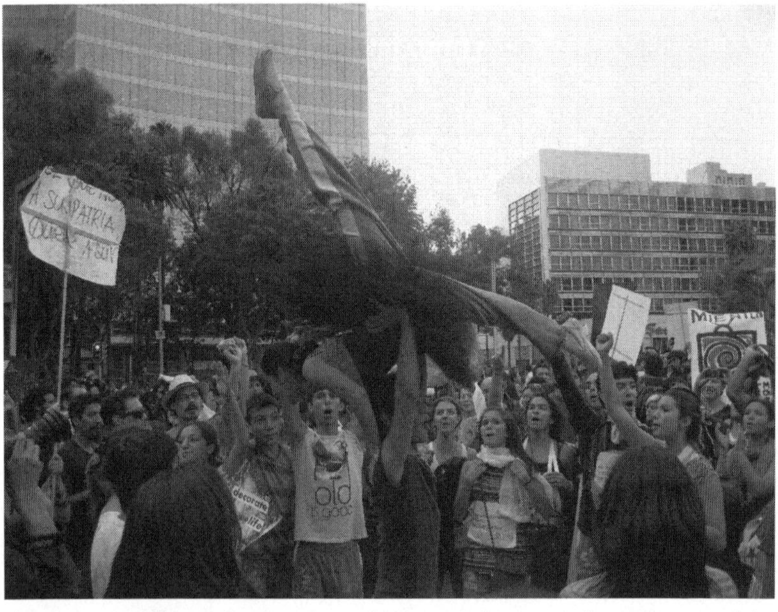

Figure 9.4. Ballet performance at a #YoSoy132 demonstration. (Photograph by Analí Sánchez Neri; printed with the photographer's permission.)

population in poverty," "2006–2012, 632 attacks on journalists," and so forth.[73] Gathering at Marcela Armas's artwork representing a map of Mexico made up of cogs dripping oil into the United States, the activists held a minute of silence with their backs toward the gallery visitors. Then they moved on to Arturo Hernández Alcázar's work with enormous black kites. Again, they stood before the piece for a minute of silence before going on to Bayrol Jiménez's mural representing a beheaded Felipe Calderón (the Mexican president at the time) hobnobbing with Peña Nieto and Genaro García Luna (former secretary of public security) vomiting dead bodies among scenes of violence.[74] #YoSoy132's first international flashmob found a way to use culture to bring international media attention to the political situation in Mexico.

The activists also proved themselves to be extremely media savvy in terms of infiltrating national media enclaves. On the occasion of the football soccer match between Mexico and Guyana at Televisa's Estadio Azteca stadium, a group of students pulled out an enormous banner in the shape of a football jersey with the lettering "México #132" on it. The match was being transmitted nationally and the student action received coverage on several media outlets, many remarking on the fact that the students had managed to question Televisa in its own "home."[75] As Dresser highlights, the movement was ultimately successful in breaking through the media blackout imposed by the television networks.[76]

DEMOCRACY 2.0

At its core, the student movement demanded, in Berman's words, "elections in which the citizens could vote knowing exactly who they were voting for. Isn't that what a true democracy is?"[77] In line with this stance, the students were especially scrupulous in practicing the participatory forms of democratic action that they demanded on a national scale. Student activists vindicated the movements' plurality and horizontality, stressing that "they practice an active, horizontal and inclusive form of political participation,"[78] and that

> #YoSoy 132 is a movement with its own organic organization . . . that is nurtured by the ties of solidarity between companions, of equality between citizens, of fraternity between brothers, of trust between colleagues, of love between comrades, and of respect between human beings . . . growing on the value of plurality itself.[79]

Perhaps the slogan that best expresses this concept of political togetherness is "Si no ardemos juntos, ¿quién iluminará esta oscuridad?" ("If we don't blaze together, who will illuminate this darkness?"), used in many of the movement's digital posters.

#YoSoy132's capacity for collective organization through online networking and onsite assemblies allowed them to complete several actions successfully. For instance, as part of their demand that the major networks transmit the first two presidential debates on prime-time slots, they requested that a third debate also be televised. When the idea of a third debate was rejected by the networks, #YoSoy132 decided to host their own citizens' debate and stream it online.[80] The organizational and logistical resources required were complex, from confirming the presidential candidates' attendance to determining the debate format to receiving and selecting the questions that would be posed.[81] The event was well publicized through social networks and received a high viewership, to the extent that while the debate was being streamed the server crashed.[82]

As election day drew near, #YoSoy132 launched the "Un voto una foto" ("One vote, one photo") campaign, a form of electoral invigilation that included the presence of #YoSoy132 volunteers at the electoral polls as citizen observers, the documentation of electoral counts at the voting stations, and the uploading of these counts on the http://fotoxcasilla.mx website in order to compare with the official results emitted by the Instituto Federal Electoral (Federal Electoral Institute, IFE).[83]

The movement's visual production reflects the importance accorded to the "Un voto, una foto" campaign. The "No solo se trata de votar" ("It's Not Just about Voting") poster reminds citizens that exercising the vote also implies observing any irregularities taking place at the voting station, reporting these to authorities if they should occur, and acting in case problems should arise. Other posters make stylistic reference to World War II propaganda and social realist aesthetics to underscore the importance of remaining vigilant on election day. The "Gane quien gane, vigilaremos por México" ("Whoever Wins, We Will Be Vigilant for Mexico") poster accompanies its text with the illustration of an eye that seems to have been directly borrowed from WWII posters, emphasizing the importance of maintaining vigilance under the wartime scenario. "Estamos observando" ("We're Watching," figure 9.5) draws on a remixed form of socialist realism combined with an Orwellian reference to a digital-age Big Brother. Several hands are holding their mobile phones up high, and each mobile phone bears the image of an eye on its screen; the text reads, "Operation July 1st. We are millions. We are watching. Effective suffrage, no imposition. Observe, photograph, record, report, defend. Take care of the vote." An exercise in inverse panopticism, the poster calls for the use of the technological means at the students' disposal to ensure a clean election.

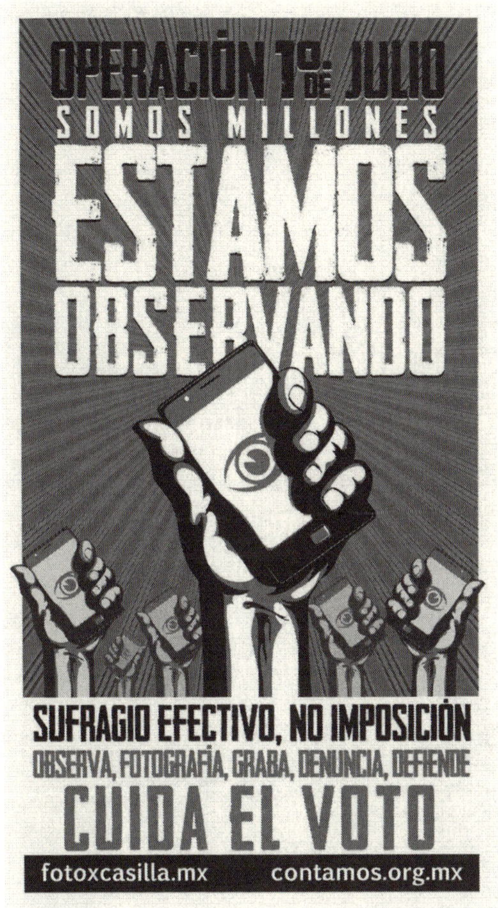

Figure 9.5. "Estamos observando" (anonymous), available at the Facebook group Gráfica 132. (Public domain.)

Through their actions and modes of collective organization, as well as their tangible results, #YoSoy132 enacted what Arditi terms "political performatives" following John Austin's theorization of performatives. Arditi has conceptualized *political* performances as utterances that are inseparable from the actions they announce: "They link stating and doing in the sense that what is sought for is already occurring within a context. Participants already begin to experience what they are fighting for *while* they fight for it."[84] In their horizontal organization and enactment of participatory forms of decision making, the students were setting a practical example of democracy for the politicians and the country at large.

This is also true regarding their stance on image property and copyright. In response to the mass media's commodification of political imagery, activist designers made their digital posters and videos widely available online. Much in the spirit of Mexico 1968, #YoSoy132 allowed their images to be widely circulated in order to break through the media siege and increase participation in the movement. The importance accorded to image sharing and circulation was paramount. None of the designers charged any money for the use of their designs online or otherwise; on the contrary, they facilitated the sharing of their work by uploading high-resolution versions of their posters. As Eduardo Salles, the designer of "La Primavera Mexicana," states, "The main goal is that people appropriate the images, take them, modify them, print them, reprint them, place them anywhere, because in the end it's all about the distribution of something that has to become everybody's."[85]

Artist collectives such as Artistas Aliados have also been clear on this point: "The re-use and handling of our individual or collective works is free, as long as the principles of this manifesto and the resolutions emanating from the Artistas Aliados assemblies are respected."[86] As Arditi argues with regards to the Egyptian context, "The circulation of images of that experience [of simply being there in Tahrir Square] precipitated an enhanced connectivity between bodies much further than what was happening in the Square."[87] In the same way, the production of freely circulating visual media allowed #YoSoy132 to share an experience of democracy with the rest of the country and with the rest of the world.

In fact, #YoSoy132 was quite well connected with similar movements around the globe. Ties were forged with activists from Egypt, Spain, and the United States;[88] tactical information and proclamations of solidarity were exchanged.[89] This was an exercise in "transnational, cross-border activism carried out by domestic actors": it is the capacity to forge networks beyond national borders, to build international assemblies, to carry messages of solidarity to similar movements.[90] Perhaps the best example of #YoSoy132's capacity to build international networks of resistance is the *2012* video produced by #YoSoy132gdl.[91] In it, representatives from OWS, 15M, the Arab Spring, and #YoSoy132 make a brief statement relating to their movement's main demands, and each representative closes with the phrase "We are not alone."

Effectively, these movements were not alone, as demonstrated at the *Cumbre mundial de indignados* (Indignados World Summit) that took place in Mexico City on December 7–10, 2012.[92] During the summit, representatives from the various movements discussed the current global situation, shared their experiences in activism, and exchanged tactical advice for using the Internet to its fullest potential for political resistance. This was, perhaps, the culmination of what Arditi calls "the exemplary role of insurgencies that capture the imagination of people in faraway lands. . . . Taking sides can mean solidarity but also replicating the insurgent spirit they have witnessed and wish to experience themselves."[93] If the Mexican youth had been inspired by the insurgent spirit of the Arab Spring, the indignados, and OWS, it could, in turn, capture the imagination of other peoples and other resistances around the world.

#1DMX

On December 1, 2012, #YoSoy132 had organized the #1Dmx demonstration against Enrique Peña Nieto's inaugural ceremony as president of Mexico. Elections had come and gone, with the PRI candidate as the winner amid claims of ballot stuffing and vote buying. In spite of many irregularities, Peña Nieto's triumph was ratified by the Federal Electoral Institute and the stage was set for the presidential inaugural ceremony. In response, the student movement and the Convención Nacional contra la Imposición (National Convention against Imposition, CNI) had rallied for a mass demonstration to surround the Palacio Legislativo de San Lázaro, where the inauguration would take place.

On the morning of December 1, however, San Lázaro had been preemptively surrounded by anti-riot fences and police squadrons. The peaceful demonstration still took to the streets, but at one point it was joined by masked individuals carrying Molotov cocktails, sticks, and stones who started to attack businesses along the demonstration route and the metallic fences surrounding San Lázaro. Police response was severe. They launched tear gas, pepper spray, and pressurized water. Some claim that rubber bullets were used.[94] After seven hours of clashes, the day's events resulted in 103 arrests and at least 23 people injured.[95] #YoSoy132 dissociated themselves from the masked individuals and claimed that they were not a part of their movement but rather infiltrated troublemakers there to provoke violence. Moreover, they declared that from the total of people arrested, at least half of them had not participated in the clashes and many had been lifted from streets where no riots had taken place; ten of them were passersby who had not participated in the demonstration at all.[96] In the following days and weeks, the movement focused on the release of their members, considered by them to be political prisoners.

The events of #1Dmx were a stiff blow to the movement, and one could argue that the government's repressive stance was a message meant to set the tone for the subsequent six years of PRI-ato. Since the inauguration of

Peña Nieto as president, the students have kept a lower profile and, generally speaking, #YoSoy132 has disbanded into smaller nodes of resistance focusing on more particular local issues.[97] It is still unclear what continuing role #YoSoy132 will play during Peña Nieto's term as president. For now, the movement has been central in changing the terms of the conversation under which politics is discussed in Mexico, even if only briefly. They demonstrated, through their inclusive, horizontal decision-making practices, that a different level of political practice is possible and desirable. We have yet to see whether they were ultimately successful in "changing the political climate" or making a difference "impregnating practices and institutions in ways of seeing and doing,"[98] but their tactics and practices remain a legacy in political activism, as a "political toolbox [available] for people everywhere."[99]

As discussed throughout this chapter, #YoSoy132's political imagery—as materialized in their visual production—is extremely varied and draws from many historical and global sources. For designer Emiliano Molina, there is no single image that can be said to represent the movement as a whole;[100] rather, #YoSoy132's diversity is expressed in the range of images that it produced throughout the few months that the Mexican Spring blossomed. Their digital posters and other forms of visual media are, in a way, heterotopic sites in the Foucauldian sense: heterotopias are the real places—the countersites—where utopias are effectively enacted and "simultaneously represented, contested and inverted."[101] In other words, they are places for experimentation; they are sites for symbolically pushing the boundaries of what is politically possible.

#YoSoy132's body of visual works is, in this sense, what Lieven De Cauter has termed an act of subversivity. While radical politics vindicate ideological dogma, subversivity is a "disruptive attitude that tries to create openings, possibilities in the 'closedness' of a system. . . . [It] consists in temporary disruptions of states of affairs."[102] The student movement effectively disrupted Mexican politics as usual, if only momentarily, and demonstrated that there were alternatives to Mexico's authoritarian and corrupt political system.

In their own words, "We are those [people] who have found new accesses to reality and new ways of acting. . . . [We are] motivated by the spontaneity of our actions and by the desire to achieve unexpected results for the future of our country."[103] Struggling for "a freer, more prosperous, more just Mexico,"[104] they belong "to a present that demands that we work hard in order to stop being *the country of missed opportunities*."[105] Using Slavoj Žižek's words, they are the agents of an *enacted utopia*: "In the short circuit between the present and the future we are—as if by Grace—for a brief period of time allowed to act as if the utopian future were . . . already at hand, just there to be grabbed."[106]

At its very core, #YoSoy132's political imagery is about invisibility and visibility. As they have stressed, "We rebel against media invisibility. We resist and struggle to make visible the invisible."[107] #YoSoy132 vindicates its "claim to political subjectivity and collectivity" in what Nicholas Mirzoeff has called "the right to look."[108] The student movement seeks to oppose the authority of visualization (media and political powers determining what futures are or are not possible) with the autonomy claimed by the right to look and be seen.[109] In sum, what #YoSoy132 demands

> is so simple that [the politicians and their media lackeys] don't understand it. . . . [The university students] are against lies. That simple. They are pro-truth. That fundamental. They believe that the distortion of truth is the origin of the moral disarray of the country. And they are right. . . . They are the pureness that can point its finger at the emperor and declare that he is naked.[110]

This is #YoSoy132's utopia. Quite simply, it is a utopia of truth.

NOTES

1. Throughout 2011, several organized citizens' groups emerged worldwide. Chronologically, the first movements to emerge were those grouped under the umbrella term "Arab Spring." This refers to the uprisings that took place in Tunisia (January 14), Egypt (January 25), Libya (February 15), and Syria (March 15), in many cases successfully overturning the governments they were protesting. On May 15, a group of citizens overtook the Plaza del Sol in Spain, spawning the 15M or *Indignados* (Indignants) movement against political corruption and the failing political and economic system of the Spanish state. The Chilean student movement organized in May 2011 as well, opposing tuition hikes, university privatizations, and the criminalization of social protest. The Occupy Wall Street movement emerged in the autumn of that year, occupying Zucotti Park in New York on September 17 to protest the economic divide between the richest 1 percent and the 99 percent of the rest of the American population.

2. One of its leaders, Arturo Montiel (former governor of the state of Mexico, 1999–2005), was processed for embezzlement, illicit enrichment, and influence peddling, only to be pardoned by Enrique Peña Nieto during his term as governor of the state of Mexico; he is also Peña Nieto's godfather and political mentor. Jenaro Villamil, "Peña Nieto y la sombra del tío Arturo," *Proceso*, September 10, 2012, accessed April 15, 2013, www.proceso.com.mx/?p=319413.

3. The most authoritarian and corrupt members of PRI have been colloquially referred to as "dinosaurs" or "PRInosaurs" in Mexican popular culture. This term is used in reference to their archaic—one could argue, primitive—approach to

exercising politics in Mexico, characterized by autocratic rule, electoral clientelism and fraud, nepotistic complicities, and backwater deal-making. Alma Soto Zárraga, "El origen del PRInosaurio," *Ciencias* 98 (April–June 2010): 52–53; and John M. Ackerman, "El retorno del dinosaurio," *Proceso*, July 2, 2012, accessed April 15, 2013, www.proceso.com.mx/?p=312937.

4. Carlos Salinas de Gortari reached the Mexican presidency under vociferous accusations of electoral fraud, perhaps best exemplified by the so-called caída del sistema, a technical "glitch" that interrupted the vote count on the eve of the 1988 presidential elections. When the counting system resumed a week later, Salinas de Gortari was declared the winner, with 50.4 percent of the votes ahead of his left-wing rival Cuauhtémoc Cárdenas Solórzano. His term was further marked by violence, culminating in the assassination of PRI presidential candidate Luis Donaldo Colosio while on his campaign trail to succeed Salinas and the assassination of José Francisco Ruiz Massieu, the secretary general of the PRI, both in 1994. "Episodios complicados de las elecciones de México," *CNN México*, June 30, 2012, accessed January 31, 2014, http://mexico.cnn.com/nacional/2012/06/30/de-la-caida-del-sistema-al-magnicidio-y-la-violencia.

5. Jenaro Villamil, "Los Ex Presidentes y Peña Nieto, Relaciones Peligrosas," *Jenaro Villamil: Medios, política y diversidad sexual* (blog), July 30, 2011, accessed January 31, 2014, http://jenarovillamil.wordpress.com/2011/07/30/los-ex-presidentes-y-pena-nieto-relaciones-peligrosas.

6. Jenaro Villamil, "Proyecto Jorge: El plan Televisa–Peña Nieto para alcanzar la Presidencia," *Proceso*, September 8, 2013, accessed April 15, 2013, www.proceso.com.mx/?p=319353; and Jo Tuckman, "Computer Files Link TV Dirty Tricks to Favourite for Mexico Presidency," *Guardian*, June 7, 2012, accessed April 15, 2013, www.guardian.co.uk/world/2012/jun/07/mexico-presidency-tv-dirty-tricks.

7. Tuckman, "Computer Files."

8. Comisión Civil Internacional de Observación por los Derechos Humanos, Cuarta visita, 29 de mayo a 4 de junio 2006, *Informe preliminar sobre los hechos de Atenco, México* (Mexico: Comisión Civil Internacional de Observación por los Derechos Humanos [CCIODH], 2006), 9, 27–31.

9. "Preparan alumnos de la Ibero 'bienvenida' a Peña," *El Universal*, May 11, 2012, accessed April 15, 2013, www.eluniversal.com.mx/primera/39432.html.

10. A full video of Peña Nieto's speech at the forum "Buen ciudadano Ibero," as well as student reactions, is available here: www.youtube.com/watch?v=AE2cTdgauho.

11. Comisión Civil Internacional, *Informe preliminar*, 9.

12. The original quote in Spanish is as follows: "Tomé la decisión de emplear el uso de la fuerza pública para reestablecer el orden y la paz . . . fue una acción determinada que asumo personalmente para reestablecer el orden y la paz en el legítimo derecho que tiene el Estado mexicano de hacer uso de la fuerza pública." EPN's speech at the Uia can be seen in full at www.youtube.com/watch?v=AE2cTdgauho.

13. The word *Todxs* in this slogan is intentionally spelled with an *x* in order to be gender-inclusive in the Spanish language.

14. "La Ibero grita 'asesino' y 'fuera' a EPN; lo meten al baño para cuidarlo; 9 etiquetas de Twitter lo vapulean," *Sinembargo*, May 11, 2012, accessed April 15, 2013, www.sinembargo.mx/11-05-2012/230979; Jesusa Cervantes, "Llega EPN 'engallado' a la Ibero, huye por corretiza y sale por puerta trasera," *Proceso*, May 11, 2012, accessed April 15, 2013, www.proceso.com.mx/?p=307196; Jesusa Cervantes, "Peña Nieto, amarga lección en la Ibero," *Proceso*, May 11, 2012, accessed April 15, 2013, www.proceso.com.mx/?p=307224; "Insultos, reclamos y porras en la visita de Peña Nieto a la *Ibero*," *La Jornada*, May 12, 2012, accessed April 15, 2013, www.jornada.unam.mx/2012/05/12/politica/005n1pol; and John M. Ackerman, "Opinión: 'Fuera Peña Nieto,'" *La Jornada*, May 12, 2012, accessed April 15, 2013, www.jornada.unam.mx/2012/05/14/opinion/021a1pol.

15. The PRI advert is available at www.youtube.com/watch?v=9iS3CYw_PyQ.

16. "Preparan alumnos de la Ibero 'bienvenida.'"

17. The videos with the highest number of views include www.youtube.com/watch?v=3OV0A8t1PfA, www.youtube.com/watch?v=MdE6aaI0SN4, and www.youtube.com/watch?v=4c7y4ucRnUM, among several others.

18. Juan Arvizu, "'Es un show montado con ánimo de descalificarme': EPN," *Red Política*, May 12, 2012, accessed April 15, 2013, www.redpolitica.mx/ruta-electoral/es-un-show-montado-con-animo-de-descalificarme-pena.

19. "Coldwell exige investigar a estudiantes que protestaron contra EPN; la Ibero dice que se expresaron libremente," *Sinembargo*, May 11, 2012, accessed April 15, 2013, www.sinembargo.mx/11-05-2012/231421.

20. Rocío Galván, "Ibero, boicot contra EPN: Emilio Antonio Gamboa," *El Sol de Tijuana*, May 13, 2012, accessed April 15, 2013, www.oem.com.mx/elsoldetijuana/notas/n2539677.htm.

21. María Luisa Vivas, "Estudiantes de la Ibero a EPN: 'Ni acarreados ni porros,'" *Proceso*, May 14, 2012, accessed April 15, 2013, www.proceso.com.mx/?p=307494; "AMLO responsable de críticas a Peña en la Ibero: PVEM," *El Economista*, May 11, 2012, accessed April 15, 2013, http://eleconomista.com.mx/sociedad/2012/05/11/amlo-responsable-criticas-pena-ibero-pvem.

22. "Éxito de Peña Nieto en la Ibero pese a intento orquestado de boicot," *El Sol de Morelia*, May 12, 2012, accessed April 15, 2013, www.oem.com.mx/elsoldemorelia/notas/n2538448.htm; "¡Supera Boicot!" *La Prensa*, May 12, 2012, accessed April 15, 2013, www.oem.com.mx/laprensa/notas/n2538553.htm; and "Intentan boicotear en la Ibero a Peña Nieto," *El Sol de México*, May 12, 2012, accessed April 15, 2013, www.oem.com.mx/oem/notas/n2538119.htm.

23. "Las noticias y las coberturas que 'molestaron' a los estudiantes," *Aristegui Noticias*, May 19, 2012, accessed April 15, 2013, http://aristeguinoticias.com/1905/uncategorized/los-videos-y-las-coberturas-que-despertaron-a-los-estudiantes.

24. The video has received over 1,200,000 views; it is available at www.youtube.com/watch?v=P7XbocXsFkI.

25. The original quote in Spanish is as follows: "Los Estudiantes respondemos: Estimados Joaquín Coldwell, Arturo Escobar, Emilio Gamboa, así como medios de comunicación de dudosa neutralidad. Usamos nuestro derecho de réplica para

desmentirlos. Somos estudiantes de la Ibero, no acarreados, no porros. Y nadie nos entrenó para nada."

26. Laura Poy Solano, "Alumnos de la Uia niegan *montaje* al expresar rechazo al candidato del PRI," *La Jornada*, May 13, 2012, accessed April 15, 2013, www.jornada.unam.mx/2012/05/13/politica/009n2pol; Emir Olivares Alonso, "No somos porros ni acarreados, responden alumnos de la *Ibero* que increparon a Peña," *La Jornada*, May 15, 2012, accessed April 15, 2013, www.jornada.unam.mx/2012/05/15/politica/011n1pol; and "131 alumnos de la Ibero responden al PRI y al PVEM, en VIDEO y con credenciales en mano: 'No somos acarreados ni porros,'" *Sinembargo*, May 14, 2012, accessed April 15, 2013, www.sinembargo.mx/14-05-2012/233335.

27. "La Piñata: Los golpes de 'color' de la política," *CNN México*, May 19, 2012, accessed April 15, 2013, http://mexico.cnn.com/nacional/2012/05/19/131-alumnos-de-la-ibero.

28. Roberto Ehrman, "Yo soy 132: Historia y perspectiva de un movimiento político," accessed April 15, 2013, http://elecciones2012mx.wordpress.com/2012/05/25/yo-soy-132-historia-y-perspectiva-de-un-movimiento-politico.

29. "Declaratoria y pliego petitorio," *Animal Político*, May 23, 2012, accessed April 15, 2013, www.animalpolitico.com/2012/05/declaratoria-y-pliego-petitorio-de-yo-soy-132/#ixzz2PoA50nm3.

30. Personal interview with Emiliano Molina.

31. Juan Carlos Mayorga, "Los carteles, una 'voz gráfica' del movimiento estudiantil #Yosoy132," *CNN México*, June 7, 2012, accessed April 15, 2013, http://mexico.cnn.com/nacional/2012/06/07/los-carteles-una-voz-grafica-del-movimiento-estudiantil-yosoy132.

32. Many of these forms of visual protest art are on an iconographical continuum, where many of the most recent visual statements borrow and rework the historical propaganda preceding it. In this sense, the visual production for #YoSoy132 is somewhat palimpsestic, insofar as it brings together many different influences and remixes them in order to bring their point across.

33. The full URLs for these blogs are: http://frentegrafico.wordpress.com, http://lamanufacturera.com/arte-yosoy132-yo-soy-132/, and http://revolutionuam.blogspot.com.es/2012/10/la-grafica-politica-yo-soy-1968.html.

34. The original text in Spanish is as follows: "Pretendemos producir información alternativa, humanamente objetiva, confiable, siempre con la voluntad de fortalecer una conciencia social. . . . Proponemos combatir el duopolio televisivo a través de medios alternativos. . . . Nos rebelamos contra la invisibilidad informativa. Resistimos y luchamos por hacer visible lo invisible. Nuestras armas son el arte, la cultura, la creatividad, la sátira y la ironía." Artistas Aliados, "Manifiesto," accessed March 15, 2013, www.artistasaliados.org/manifiesto.

35. Mayorga, "Los carteles."

36. Elena Poniatowska, *La noche de Tlatelolco: Testimonios de historia oral* (Mexico: Ediciones ERA, 1971).

37. Álvaro Vázquez Mantecón, "Visualizing 1968," in *Age of Discrepancies: Art and Visual Culture in Mexico, 1968–1997*, comp. Olivier Debroise (Mexico: Universidad Nacional Autónoma de México, 2006), 67.

38. Vázquez Mantecón, "Visualizing 1968," 67.

39. Grupo Mira, *La gráfica del '68: Homenaje al movimiento estudiantil*, 2nd ed. (Mexico: Ediciones Zurda, 1981), 14–15.

40. Grupo Mira, *La gráfica del '68*, 5.

41. Vázquez Mantecón, "Visualizing 1968," 39.

42. "Principios generales del movimiento," accessed April 15, 2013, www.yosoy132media.org/yosoy132oficial/principios-generales-del-movimiento.

43. Ibid.

44. "Se revitaliza el movimiento de 'indignados' en España," *La Jornada*, May 13, 2012, accessed April 15, 2013, www.jornada.unam.mx/2012/05/13/politica/002n1pol; and "Desalojan con violencia a indignados en Madrid," *La Jornada*, May 14, 2012, accessed April 15, 2013, www.jornada.unam.mx/2012/05/14/mundo/022n1mun.

45. "Occupy Wall Street: Dozens Arrested on One-Year Anniversary," *Guardian*, September 17, 2012, accessed April 15, 2013, www.guardian.co.uk/world/2012/sep/17/occupy-wall-street-arrests-anniversary.

46. Enrique Dussel, "Interpelaciones del movimiento #YoSoy132," *La Jornada*, June 9, 2012, accessed April 15, 2013, www.jornada.unam.mx/2012/06/09/opinion/021a2pol.

47. The full segment discussing #YoSoy132 on *Primer Plano* is available at http://vimeo.com/42877920.

48. Genaro Lozano, "OPINIÓN: ¿Qué puede aprender #YoSoy132 de otros movimientos en el mundo?" *CNN México*, May 24, 2012, accessed April 15, 2013, http://mexico.cnn.com/opinion/2012/05/24/opinion-que-puede-aprender-yosoy132-de-otros-movimientos-en-el-mundo.

49. For instance, #YoSoy132's Artistas Aliados website has a link to Gene Sharp's *How to Start a Revolution* documentary and the *From Dictatorship to Democracy* e-book, both tactical manuals for resistance referenced during the Arab Spring and OWS: http://edition.cnn.com/2012/06/23/world/gene-sharp-revolutionary, http://occupywallst.org/forum/how-to-start-a-revolution-gene-sharp, and www.youtube.com/watch?v=dHezFksIM68.

50. Lozano, "¿Qué puede aprender #YoSoy132."

51. Ibid.

52. Mayorga, "Los carteles."

53. "Caso Ibero: Analizan intelectuales excesivo cuidado de Peña Nieto," *Aristegui Noticias*, May 18, 2012, accessed April 15, 2013, http://aristeguinoticias.com/1805/post-elecciones/caso-ibero-analizan-intelectuales-excesivo-cuidado-de-pena-nieto.

54. "Caso Ibero."

55. Artistas Aliados, "Manifiesto."

56. Denise Dresser, "#YoSoy132: Los riesgos," *Proceso*, August 13, 2012, accessed April 15, 2012, www.proceso.com.mx/?p=316927.

57. Sabina Berman, "El estudiante 132," *Proceso*, May 28, 2012, accessed April 15, 2013, www.proceso.com.mx/?p=308961.

58. Benjamin Arditi, "Insurgencies Don't Have a Plan—They Are the Plan: Political Performatives and Vanishing Mediators in 2011," *JOMEC Journal* 1 (June 2012): 4.

59. María Elena Meneses, "OPINIÓN: Los jóvenes indignados mexicanos ya levantaron la voz," *CNN México*, May 22, 2012, accessed April 15, 2013, http://mexico.cnn.com/opinion/2012/05/22/opinion-los-jovenes-indignados-mexicanos-ya-levantaron-la-voz.

60. "Principios generales."

61. The original text in Spanish is as follows: "Pero no optar por algún partido no es dejar de ser profundamente político. Y el movimiento es político porque asume la responsabilidad de limpiar una representación electoralera corrompida." Dussel, "Interpelaciones del movimiento #YoSoy132."

62. Mayorga, "Los carteles."

63. "Principios generales."

64. Berman, "El estudiante 132."

65. Dussel, "Interpelaciones del movimiento #YoSoy132."

66. Berman, "El estudiante 132."

67. "Declaratoria y pliego petitorio."

68. Carlos Monsiváis, "Editorial: Esta noche nos honra con su ausencia," *El Universal*, January 24, 2010, accessed April 15, 2013, www.eluniversal.com.mx/editoriales/47153.html.

69. The misspelling here is intentional in order to emphasize the miseducation that Televisa's shows promote.

70. The video is available in its entirety on YouTube: www.youtube.com/watch?v=hYtmzuyGgqc.

71. "Principios generales."

72. Meneses, "Los jóvenes indignados."

73. Anne Marie Mergier, "Las aventuras de #YoSoy132 en París," *Proceso*, July 3, 2012, accessed April 15, 2013, www.proceso.com.mx/?p=313181.

74. Mergier, "Las aventuras de #YoSoy132."

75. Beatriz Pereyra, "Logra #YoSoy132 'meter gol' en el estadio Azteca," *Proceso*, June 9, 2012, accessed April 15, 2013, www.proceso.com.mx/?p=310244.

76. Dresser, "#Yosoy132."

77. Berman, "El estudiante 132."

78. Artistas Aliados, "Manifiesto."

79. "Principios generales."

80. The full video of the debate is available at www.youtube.com/watch?v=txWoCr1EXyE.

81. Enrique Peña Nieto declined to participate in the debate, arguing that it would lack conditions of impartiality and neutrality toward his person, www.eluniversal.com.mx/notas/854377.html.

82. The video's permalink on YouTube currently marks 1,425,908 views.

83. "Convoca YoSoy132 a la campaña foto por voto para evitar un fraude electoral," *La Jornada Michoacán*, June 30, 2012, accessed April 15, 2013, www.lajornadamichoacan.com.mx/2012/06/30/convoca-yosoy132-a-la-campana-foto-por-voto-para-evitar-un-fraude-electoral.

84. Arditi, "Insurgencies Don't Have a Plan," 4–5.

85. Mayorga, "Los carteles."

86. Artistas Aliados, "Manifiesto."

87. Arditi, "Insurgencies Don't Have a Plan," 12.

88. Some of these communications can be consulted here: http://temorisblog.wordpress.com/2012/06/06/yosoy132-explained-to-the-egyptian-revolutionaries-yosoy132-explicado-a-los-revolucionarios-egipcios, http://occupywallst.org/article/mexico-yosoy132, and www.youtube.com/watch?v=F_DgL81rBSQ.

89. Jesús Aldabi Olvera, "De la primavera árabe, mensajes para #YoSoy132," *Proceso*, June 12, 2012, accessed April 15, 2013, www.proceso.com.mx/?p=310630.

90. Arditi, "Insurgencies Don't Have a Plan," 9.

91. Available on YouTube at www.youtube.com/watch?v=6_A6LKR0h08.

92. Arditi, "Insurgencies Don't Have a Plan," 11.

93. Ibid.

94. "Siete horas de disturbios en el DF; daños severos a comercios y mobiliario urbano," *La Jornada*, December 2, 2012, accessed April 15, 2013, www.jornada.unam.mx/2012/12/02/politica/006n1pol.

95. "Estrategia maquiavélica, disturbios del 1 diciembre: #YoSoy132," *Aristegui Noticias*, December 4, 2012, accessed April 15, 2013, http://aristeguinoticias.com/0412/mexico/estrategia-maquiavelica-disturbios-del-1-de-diciembre-yosoy132.

96. "Más de la mitad de los detenidos son ajenos a los ataques, dice #YoSoy132," *La Jornada*, December 2, 2012, accessed April 15, 2013, www.jornada.unam.mx/2012/12/02/politica/007n2pol.

97. The Facebook group Acampada Revolucionaria chronicles this shift well.

98. Arditi, "Insurgencies Don't Have a Plan," 3.

99. Ibid., 15.

100. Personal interview with Emiliano Molina.

101. M. Foucault, *Of Other Spaces, Heterotopias* (1967), accessed February 15, 2013, www.foucault.info/documents/heteroTopia/foucault.heteroTopia.en.html.

102. Lieven De Cauter, "Notes on Subversion: Theses on Activism," in *Art and Activism in the Age of Globalization*, eds. Lieven De Cauter, Ruben De Roo, and Karel Vanhaesebrouck (Rotterdam, Netherlands: NAi Publishers, 2011), 9.

103. "Principios generales."

104. "Declaratoria y pliego petitorio."

105. Italics in the original text, "Principios generales."

106. Quoted in Arditi, "Insurgencies Don't Have a Plan," 5.

107. Artistas Aliados, "Manifiesto."

108. Nicholas Mirzoeff, *The Right to Look: A Counterhistory of Visuality* (Durham, NC; London: Duke University Press, 2011), 1.

109. Mirzoeff, *The Right to Look*, 28.

110. Berman, "El estudiante 132."

Bibliography

"131 alumnos de la Ibero responden al PRI y al PVEM, en VIDEO y con credenciales en mano: 'No somos acarreados ni porros.'" *Sinembargo*. Accessed May 14, 2012. www.sinembargo.mx/14-05-2012/233335.

Abraham, K. *Adwa: Decolonization, Pan-Africanism, and the Struggle of the Black Diaspora.* Addis Ababa: The Ethiopian International Institute for Peace and Development and the Horn of Africa Democracy and Development International Lobby, 2007.

Ackerman, John M. "El retorno del dinosaurio." *Proceso*, July 2, 2012. Accessed April 15, 2013. www.proceso.com.mx/?p=312937.

———. "Opinión: 'Fuera Peña Nieto.'" *La Jornada*, May 12, 2012. Accessed April 15, 2013. www.jornada.unam.mx/2012/05/14/opinion/021a1pol.

Adams, Mark. "Top Six Alternative Routes to Machu Picchu." *National Geographic*. Accessed September 1, 2015. http://travel.nationalgeographic.com/travel/peru/machu-picchu/alternate-trails.

Adorno, Theodor W., and Max Horkheimer. "The Culture Industry: Enlightenment as Mass Deception." In *Dialectic of Enlightenment: Philosophical Fragments*, edited by Gunzelin Schmid Noerr, translated by Edmund Jephcott, 1–34. Stanford: Stanford University Press, 2002.

Aldabi Olvera, Jesús. "De la primavera árabe, mensajes para #YoSoy132." *Proceso*, June 12, 2012. Accessed April 15, 2013. www.proceso.com.mx/?p=310630.

"AMLO responsable de críticas a Peña en la Ibero: PVEM." *El Economista*. Accessed May 11, 2012. http://eleconomista.com.mx/sociedad/2012/05/11/amlo-responsable-criticas-pena-ibero-pvem.

Amnesty International. *Amnesty International Report 2012: The State of the World's Human Rights*. New York: Amnesty International, 2012.

Anderson, Benedict. *Imagined Communities: Reflections on the Origins and Spread of Nationalism.* London: Verso, 1991.

Anselmi, Manuel. *Chávez's Children: Ideology, Education, and Society in Latin America.* Lanham, MD: Lexington Books, 2013.

Aponte-Moreno, Marco, and Lance Lattig. "Chávez: Rhetoric Made in Havana." *World Policy Journal* 29 (2012): 33–42.

Arditi, Benjamin. "Insurgencies Don't Have a Plan—They Are the Plan: Political Performatives and Vanishing Mediators in 2011." *JOMEC Journal* 1 (June 2012).

Armstrong, J. B. "'The People . . . Took Exception to Her Remarks': Meta Warrick Fuller, Angelina Weld Grimké, and the Lynching of Mary Turner." *Mississippi Quarterly* 61, nos. 1/2 (2008): 113–41.

Arrighi, Giovanni. *Adam Smith in Beijing: Lineages of the 21st Century*. London: Verso, 2009.

Artistas Aliados. "Manifiesto." Accessed March 15, 2013. www.artistasaliados.org/manifiesto.

Arvizu, Juan. "'Es un show montado con ánimo de descalificarme': EPN." *Red Política*, May 12, 2012. Accessed April 15, 2013. www.redpolitica.mx/ruta-electoral/es-un-show-montado-con-animo-de-descalificarme-pena.

Ater, R. "Making History: Meta Warrick Fuller's 'Ethiopia.'" *American Art* 17, no. 3 (2003): 12–31.

Atkin, Albert. "Peirce's Theory of Signs." In *The Stanford Encyclopedia of Philosophy* (Winter 2010), edited by Edward N. Zalta. Accessed February 23, 2013. http://plato.stanford.edu/archives/win2010/entries/peirce-semiotics.

Avila, Theresa. "Laborious Arts: El Taller de Gráfica Popular & the Meaning of Labor in *Las Estampas de la Revolución Mexicana*." *Hemisphere: Visual Cultures of the Americas* 1 (Spring 2008): 62–82.

———. "El Taller de Gráfica Popular and the Chronicles of Mexican History and Nationalism." *Third Text* 28, no. 3, Special Issue: Art and Revolution in Mexico (2014): 311–21.

———. "Zapata: Figure, Image, Symbol." Master's thesis, University of New Mexico, 2005.

Bakunin, Mikhail. *Statism and Anarchy*. Cambridge: Cambridge University Press, 1990.

Baram, Uzi, and Yorke Rowan. "Archaeology after Nationalism: Globalization and the Consumption of the Past." In *Marketing Heritage: Archaeology and the Consumption of the Past*, edited by Uzi Baram and Yorke Rowan, 3–26. Lanham, MD: Rowman & Littlefield, 2004.

Barcelona Field Studies Centre. "Some Potential Benefits and Costs to the Community from Tourism." Accessed May 1, 2009. http://geographyfieldwork.com/MachuTourismImpact.htm.

Barthes, Roland. *Camera Lucida: Reflections on Photography*. Translated by Richard Howard. New York: Hill and Wang, 1982.

Baudrillard, Jean. "Simulacra and Simulations." In *Modern Literary Theory and Criticism: A Reader*, edited by David Lodge and Nigel Wood, 403–12. New York: Longman, 1988.

Berman, Sabina. "El estudiante 132." *Proceso*, May 28, 2012. Accessed April 15, 2013. www.proceso.com.mx/?p=308961.

Betanzos, Juan de. *Suma y narración de los Incas*. Madrid: Imprenta de Manuel G. Hernández, 1880. Project Gutenberg. www.gutenberg.org/files/25705/25705-h/25705-h.htm.

Bhabha, Homi K. "In the Cave of Making: Thoughts on Third Space." In *Communicating in the Third Space*, edited by Karin Ikas and Gerhard Wagner, ix–xiv. New York: Routledge, 2009.

———. *The Location of Culture*. New York: Routledge, 2004.

Bingham, Hiram. *Lost City of the Incas: The Story of Machu Picchu and Its Builders*. New Haven, CT: Phoenix Press, 2003.

Blackburn, Robin. *The Overthrow of Colonial Slavery, 1776–1848*. London: Verso, 1988.

Bolívar, Simón. *La Carta de Jamaica*. 1815. Accessed December 14, 2013. http://history202.wikispaces.com/file/view/Jamaica+Letter.pdf.

Bonasso, Miguel. *El Palacio y la Calle: Crónicas de Insurgentes y Conspiradores*. Buenos Aires: Planeta, 2002.

Bossi, Lorena Fabrizia. Grupo de Arte Callejero (Argentina). *GAC: Pensamientos, prácticas, acciones*. Buenos Aires: Tinta Limón, 2009.

Bourdieu, Pierre. "The Essence of Neoliberalism: What Is Neoliberalism? A Programme for Destroying Collective Structures Which May Impede the Pure Market Logic: Utopia of Endless Exploitation." *Le Monde Diplomatique*, 1998. Accessed January 4, 2016. https://mondediplo.com/1998/12/08bourdieu.

Brigham, Robert K. *Guerrilla Diplomacy: The NLF's Foreign Relations and the Viet Nam War*. Ithaca, NY: Cornell University Press, 1998.

Brown, Steve. "Landscaping Heritage: Toward an Operational Cultural Landscape Approach for Protected Areas in New South Wales." *Australasian Historical Archeology* 25 (2007): 33–42.

Brundage, W. F. "Meta Warrick's 1907 'Negro Tableaux' and (Re)Presenting African American Historical Memory." *Journal of American History* 89, no. 4 (2003): 1368–1400.

Brunk, Samuel. *¡Emiliano Zapata! Revolution and Betrayal in Mexico*. Albuquerque: University of New Mexico Press, 2001.

Brunk, Samuel, and Fallaw Ben. "Heroes and Their Cults in Modern Latin America." In *Heroes & Hero Cults in Latin America*, edited by S. Brunk and B. Fallaw, 1–20. Austin: University of Texas Press, 2006.

Buck-Morss, Susan. *Hegel, Haiti, and Universal History*. Pittsburgh, PA: University of Pittsburgh Press, 2009.

Burke, Kenneth. *A Rhetoric of Motives*. Berkeley: University of California Press, 1969.

———. *The Rhetoric of Religion: Studies in Logology*. Berkeley: University of California Press, 1961.

Butzer, Karl W. "From Columbus to Acosta: Science, Geography, and the New World." *Annals of the Association of American Geographers* 82, no. 3 (September 1992): 543–65.

Cabrera Infante, Alberto, and Orlando Jiménez Leal. *P.M.* Havana, Cuba, 1961. DVD.

Calvente, Lisa B. Y., and Guadalupe García. "The City Speaks: Dis/articulating Revolutionary Cuba and Global Belonging." *Cultural Studies* 28, no. 3 (2014): 438–62.

Camín, Héctor Aguilar, and Lorenzo Meyer. *In the Shadow of the Mexican Revolution: Contemporary Mexican History, 1910–1989*. Austin: University of Texas Press, 1993.

Canache, Damarys. *Venezuela: Public Opinion and Protest in a Fragile Democracy.* Miami, FL: North and South Center Press, 2002.

Cañizáles, Alejandro. *En Venezuela la batalla es simbólica: Uso de la historia en la confrontación política actual.* Caracas, Venezuela: Universidad Católica Andrés Bello, 2007.

Carassai, Sebastián. "The Noisy Majority: An Analysis of the Argentine Crisis of December 2001 from the Theoretical Approach of Hardt & Negri, Laclau and Zižek." *Journal of Latin American Cultural Studies* 16, no. 1 (2007): 45–62.

Carrera Damas, Germán. *El culto a Bolívar.* Caracas, Venezuela: Editorial Alfa, 2003.

———. *Venezuela: Proyecto nacional y poder social.* Barcelona, Spain: Publicaciones Vicerrectorado Académico, 1986.

Carver, J., J. A. Ennels, and D. L. Haulman. *The Tuskegee Airmen: An Illustrated History, 1939–1949 with a Comprehensive Chronology of Missions and Events.* Montgomery, AL: NewSouth, 2011.

"Caso Ibero: Analizan intelectuales excesivo cuidado de Peña Nieto." *Aristegui Noticias*. Accessed May 18, 2012. http://aristeguinoticias.com/1805/post-elecciones/caso-ibero-analizan-intelectuales-excesivo-cuidado-de-pena-nieto.

Casteen, John Charles. *Born in Blood and Fire: A Concise History of Latin America*, 3rd edition. New York: W. W. Norton, 2011.

Castells, Manuel. *Networks of Outrage and Hope: Social Movements in the Internet Age*. Cambridge: Polity, 2012.

Castro, Fidel. *Palabras a los intelectuales*. Havana, Cuba: National Cultural Council, 1961.

———. Speech by Cuban prime minister Fidel Castro Ruz. Presented at the closing of the National Congress on Education and Culture, Havana, Cuba, May 3, 1971.

Cervantes, Jesusa. "Llega EPN 'engallado' a la Ibero, huye por corretiza y sale por puerta trasera." *Proceso*, May 11, 2012. Accessed April 15, 2013. www.proceso.com.mx/?p=307196.

———. "Peña Nieto, amarga lección en la Ibero." *Proceso*, May 11, 2012. Accessed April 15, 2013. www.proceso.com.mx/?p=307224.

Césaire, Aimé. *Discourse on Colonialism*. New York: Monthly Review Press, 2000.

———. "Letter to Maurice Thorez." *Social Text* 28, no. 2 (2010): 145–52.

Chamberlin, Paul Thomas. *The Global Offensive: The United States, the Palestine Liberation Organization, and the Making of the Post–Cold War Order*. Oxford: Oxford University Press, 2012.

Chanan, Michael. *Cuban Cinema*. Minneapolis: University of Minnesota Press, 2004.

Charland, Maurice. “Constitutive Rhetoric: The Case of the Peuple Quebecois.” *Quarterly Journal of Speech* 73 (1987): 133–50.

Chasteen, John Charles. *Born in Blood and Fire: A Concise History of Latin America*, 3rd edition. New York: W. W. Norton, 2011.

Chávez, Hugo. “Beginning of the Meeting with the President of Venezuela, Hugo Chávez.” Ministry of Foreign Affairs of the Russian Federation, 2006. Accessed December 7, 2013. www.mid.ru/brp_4.nsf/e78a48070f128a7b43256999005bcbb3/b54269f706d09c0cc32571b9003c4449?OpenDocument.

———. “Discurso de la toma de posesion.” 1999. Accessed December 7, 2013. www.analitica.com/bitblioteca/hChávez/toma.asp.

Cheek, W. F., and A. L. Cheek. *John Mercer Langston and the Fight for Black Freedom (1829–1865)*. Urbana: University of Illinois Press, 1996.

Cheung, Sidney. “The Meanings of a Heritage Trail in Hong Kong.” *Annals of Tourism Research* 26, no. 3 (1999): 570–88.

Chirapaq: Centro de Culturas Indígenas del Perú. Accessed September 1, 2015. www.chirapaq.org.pe.

Chong, Sylvia Shin Huey. *The Oriental Obscene: Violence and Racial Fantasies in the Vietnam Era*. Durham, NC: Duke University Press, 2012.

Clay, N. “Black Press Drive to Aid Ethiopia Gets in Gear.” *Chicago Metro News*, January 5, 1985, p. 3.

Cleaver, Eldridge, and Black Panther Party. *To My Black Brothers in Viet Nam*. 1970.

“Coldwell exige investigar a estudiantes que protestaron contra EPN; la Ibero dice que se expresaron libremente.” *Sinembargo*, May 11, 2012. Accessed April 15, 2013. www.sinembargo.mx/11-05-2012/231421.

Comisión Civil Internacional de Observación por los Derechos Humanos, Cuarta visita, 29 de mayo a 4 de junio 2006. *Informe preliminar sobre los hechos de Atenco, México*. Mexico: Comisión Civil Internacional de Observación por los Derechos Humanos (CCIODH), 2006.

Contee, C. “The Emergence of Du Bois as an African Nationalist.” *Journal of Negro History* 54, no. 1 (January 1969): 48–63.

“Convoca YoSoy132 a la campaña foto por voto para evitar un fraude electoral.” *La Jornada Michoacán*, June 30, 2012. Accessed April 15, 2012. www.lajornadamichoacan.com.mx/2012/06/30/convoca-yosoy132-a-la-campana-foto-por-voto-para-evitar-un-fraude-electoral.

Conway, Christopher. *The Cult of Bolívar in Latin American Literature*. Gainesville: University Press of Florida, 2003.

Copernicus, Nicolas. *On the Revolution of Heavenly Spheres*. Amherst, NY: Prometheus Books Great Minds Series, 1995.

Cornejo-Polar, Antonio, and Susan Casal-Sanchez. "Indigenist and Heterogeneous Literatures: Their Dual Sociocultural Status." *Latin American Perspectives* 16, no. 2 (1989): 12–28.

Corrales, Javíer, and Michael Penfold. *Dragon in the Tropics: Hugo Chávez and the Political Economy of Revolution in Venezuela.* Washington, DC: Brookings Institution Press, 2011.

Cortés, José Miguel G. "Buenos Aires/Grupo de Arte Callejero." In *Dissident Cartographies*. Barcelona, Spain: SEACEX, 2008.

Craven, David. *Art and Revolution in Latin America, 1910–1990*. New Haven, CT: Yale University Press, 2002.

———. *Diego Rivera as Epic Modernist*. New York: G. K. Hall, 1997.

Cushing, Lincoln. *Revolución: Cuban Poster Art*. New York: Chronicle Books, 2003.

Dagmawi Woubshet, D., S. Tillet, and E. Wolde Giorgis. "The Romance of Ethiopia." *Callaloo* 33, no. 1 (2010): 8–14.

Danto, Arthur C. *Beyond the Brillo Box: The Visual Arts in Post-historical Perspective*. Berkeley: University of California Press, 1992.

Davis, Clyde. "Black Consciousness and the Vietnam War." *Black Scholar* 5, no. 2 (October 1973): 2–8.

Davis, David Brion. *The Problem of Slavery in the Age of Revolution, 1770–1823.* Ithaca, NY: Cornell University Press, 1975.

Davis, H. L. "Feeding the World a Line? Celebrity Activism and Ethical Consumer Practices from Live Aid to Product Red." *Journal for Nordic Studies in English* 9, no. 3 (2010): 89–118.

De Cauter, Lieven. "Notes on Subversion: Theses on Activism." In *Art and Activism in the Age of Globalization*, edited by Lieven De Cauter, Ruben De Roo, and Karel Vanhaesebrouck. Rotterdam, Netherlands: NAi Publishers, 2011.

"Declaratoria y pliego petitorio." *Animal Político*, May 23, 2012. Accessed April 15, 2013. www.animalpolitico.com/2012/05/declaratoria-y-pliego-petitorio-de-yo-soy-132/#ixzz2PoA50nm3.

Della Porta, Donatella, and Mario Diani. "Collective Action and Identity." In *Social Movements: An Introduction*, 83–109. Oxford: Blackwell, 2006.

"Desalojan con violencia a indignados en Madrid." *La Jornada*, May 14, 2012. Accessed April 15, 2013. www.jornada.unam.mx/2012/05/14/mundo/022n1mun.

De Waal, Alex. *Evil Days: Thirty Years of War and Famine in Ethiopia.* New York: Human Rights Watch, 1991.

Día de Simón Bolívar (n.d.). Retrieved January 8, 2016. http://classzone.com/books/en_espanol_shared/ML1/ML_1_Bolivar/ml_1_bolivar.html.

El Diario del Hogar. In "Revolutionary Mexico in Newspapers, 1900–1929" (microfilm set), edited by Adán Benavides and Agnes L. McAlester. Nettie Lee Benson Latin American Collection, General Libraries, University of Texas at Austin, 2002.

Dohrn, Bernadine. "Communiqué #1 from the Weatherman Underground." *Berkeley Tribe*, May 21, 1970. www.freerepublic.com/focus/f-news/2098150/posts.

Dopico, Ana Maria. "Picturing Havana: History, Vision, and the Scramble for Cuba." *Nepantla: Views from the South* 3, no. 3 (2002): 451–93.

Douglass, F. *Frederick Douglass Papers* 7, no. 25 (1854): 3.

———. *North Star* 2, no. 12 (March 16, 1849): 1.

Dresser, Denise. "#YoSoy132: Los riesgos." *Proceso*, August 13, 2012. Accessed April 15, 2012. www.proceso.com.mx/?p=316927.

Du Bois, W. E. B. *The Star of Ethiopia.* Alexandria, VA: Alexander Street Press, 2001 [1913].

Dunbar, P. L. *The Complete Poems of Paul Laurence Dunbar.* New York: Dodd, Mead, 1926.

Dussel, Enrique. "Interpelaciones del movimiento #YoSoy132." *La Jornada*, June 9, 2012. Accessed April 15, 2012. www.jornada.unam.mx/2012/06/09/opinion/021a2pol.

Dussel, Ines. "When Appearances Are Not Deceptive: A Comparative History of School Uniforms in Argentina and the United States." *Paedagogica Historica: International Journal of the History of Education* 41, nos. 1–2 (2005): 179–95.

Edwards, Jason A. "Sanctioning Foreign Policy: The Rhetorical Use of President Harry Truman." *Presidential Studies Quarterly* 39 (2009): 454–72.

Edwards, J. L., and C. K. Winkler. "Representative Form and the Visual Ideograph: The Iwo Jima Image in Editorial Cartoons." *Quarterly Journal of Speech* 83 (1997): 289–310.

Ehrman, Roberto. *Yo soy 132: Historia y perspectiva de un movimiento político.* Accessed April 15, 2013. http://elecciones2012mx.wordpress.com/2012/05/25/yo-soy-132-historia-y-perspectiva-de-un-movimiento-politico.

Elkins, James. *Theorizing Visual Studies: Writing through the Disciplines*. London: Routledge, 2012.

———. *Visual Studies: A Skeptical Introduction*. London: Routledge, 2003.

"Episodios complicados de las elecciones de México." *CNN México*, June 30, 2012. Accessed January 31, 2014. http://mexico.cnn.com/nacional/2012/06/30/de-la-caida-del-sistema-al-magnicidio-y-la-violencia.

Escobar, Arturo. *Encountering Development: The Making and Unmaking of the Third World*, 2nd edition. Princeton, NJ: Princeton University Press, 2012.

"Estrategia maquiavélica, disturbios del 1 diciembre: #YoSoy132." *Aristegui Noticias*, December 4, 2012. Accessed April 15, 2013. http://aristeguinoticias.com/0412/mexico/estrategia-maquiavelica-disturbios-del-1-de-diciembre-yosoy132.

"Éxito de Peña Nieto en la Ibero pese a intento orquestado de boicot." *El Sol de Morelia*, May 12, 2012. Accessed April 15, 2013. www.oem.com.mx/elsoldemorelia/notas/n2538448.htm.

Fanon, Frantz. *Black Skin, White Masks*. New York: Grove Press, 1990.

———. *The Wretched of the Earth.* New York: Grove Press, 1963.

Feitlowitz, Marguerite. *A Lexicon of Terror: Argentina and the Legacies of Torture*. New York: Oxford University Press, 1998.

Fisher, Walter. R. *Human Communication as Narration: Toward a Philosophy of Reason, Value, and Action.* Columbia: University of South Carolina Press, 1987.

Folgarait, Leonard. *Mural Painting and Social Revolution in Mexico, 1920–1940*. Cambridge: Cambridge University Press, 1998.

Fontana, Edgardo. *Apuntes para el nuevo protagonismo social*. Buenos Aires: Ediciones de Mano en Mano; Colectivo Situaciones, 2002.

Foster, Hal. *Return of the Real: Critical Models in Art and Theory since 1960*. Cambridge, MA: MIT Press, 1996.

Foucault, Michel. "Of Other Spaces." *Diacritics* 16 (Spring 1986): 22–27.

———. *Security, Territory, Population: Lectures at the Collège de France, 1977–1978*. London: Picador, 2009.

———. *Society Must Be Defended*. London: Picador, 2003.

Freitag, Sandria B. "The Visual Turn: Approaching South Asia across the Disciplines." *South Asia: Journal of South Asian Studies* 37, no. 3 (2014): 398–409.

Frick, Richard. *The Tricontinental Solidarity Poster*, 1st edition. Bern, Switzerland: Comedia-Verlag, 2003.

Friend, Robert. "Review: *Anthologie de la littérature vietnamiene* by Nguyen Khac Vien, Nguyen Van Hoan, Huu Ngoc, Vu Dinh Lien, Tao Trang." *East and West* 24, nos. 3/4 (September 1, 1974).

Fuentes, Carlos. *Nuevo tiempo mexicano*. Madrid: Editorial Alfaguara, 1994.

Galván, Rocío. "Ibero, boicot contra EPN: Emilio Antonio Gamboa." *El Sol de Tijuana*, May 13, 2012. Accessed April 15, 2013. www.oem.com.mx/elsoldetijuana/notas/n2539677.htm.

García Espinosa, Julio. "For an Imperfect Cinema." *Jump Cut*. Accessed September 1, 2015. www.ejumpcut.org/archive/onlinessays/JC20folder/ImperfectCinema.html.

Garcilaso de la Vega, El Inca. *Comentarios Reales de los Incas*. Lisbon, Portugal: Pedro Crasbeeck, 1609. Facsimile.

Gebrekidan, Fikru Negash. *Bond Without Blood: A History of Ethiopian and New World Black Relations, 1896–1991*. Trenton, NJ: Africa World Press, 2005.

Getino, Octavio, and Fernando Solanas. "Towards a Third Cinema." *Tricontinental* 14 (October 1969): 107–32.

Giles, F. "Star of Ethiopia 1913." In *Black Theater USA Revised and Expanded Edition: Plays by African Americans*, volume 1, *The Early Period 1847–1938*, edited by James V. Hatch and Ted Shine. New York: Simon & Schuster, 1974.

Gilly, Adolfo. "Rural Economy and Society: 1920–1940." In *Encyclopedia of Mexico*, volume 2, edited by Michael S. Werner, 1309–13. Chicago: Fitzroy Dearborn, 1997.

Gleijeses, Piero. *Visions of Freedom: Havana, Washington, Pretoria, and the Struggle for Southern Africa, 1976–1991*. Chapel Hill: University of North Carolina Press, 2013.

Goldberg, David Theo. *Racist Culture: Philosophy and the Politics of Meaning*. Hoboken, NJ: Wiley-Blackwell, 1993.

———. *The Threat of Race: Reflections on Racial Neoliberalism*. Malden, MA: Blackwell, 2009.

Gombrich, Ernst H. *Meditations on a Hobby Horse and Other Essays on the Theory of Art*. London: Phaidon, 1963.

Gramsci, Antonio. *Selections from the Prison Notebooks*. New York: International Publishers, 1971.

Grossberg, Lawrence. *Cultural Studies in the Future Tense*. Durham, NC: Durham University Press, 2010.

———, ed. "On Postmodernism and Articulation: An Interview with Stuart Hall." In *Stuart Hall: Critical Dialogues in Cultural Studies*, edited by David Morley and Kuan-Hsing Chen, 131–50. New York: Routledge, 1996.

Grupo Mira. *La gráfica del '68. Homenaje al movimiento estudiantil*, 2nd edition. Mexico: Ediciones Zurda, 1981.

Guevara, Ernesto Che. *Guerrilla Warfare*. Minneapolis, MN: Ocean Press, 2006.

———. *Man and Socialism.* Atlanta, GA: Pathfinder Press, 1965.

Hall, Gwendolyn Midlo, ed. *A Black Communist in the Freedom Struggle: The Life of Harry Haywood.* Minneapolis: University of Minnesota Press, 2012.

Hall, Linda. *Álvaro Obregón: Power and Revolution in Mexico, 1911–1920.* College Station: Texas A&M University Press, 1981.

Hall, M. G., and H. Haywood. *A Black Communist in the Freedom Struggle: The Life of Harry Haywood.* Minneapolis: University of Minnesota Press, 2012.

Hall, Stuart. "Cultural Identity and Diaspora." In *Colonial Discourse and Postcolonial Theory: A Reader*, edited by Patrick Williams and Laura Chrisman, 392–403. New York: Columbia University Press, 1994.

———. "Encoding/Decoding." In *Media and Cultural Studies: KeyWorks*, edited by M. G. Durham and D. M. Kellner, 163–73. Oxford: Blackwell, 2006.

———. "Gramsci's Relevance for the Study of Race and Ethnicity." In *Stuart Hall: Critical Dialogues in Cultural Studies*, edited by David Morley and Kuan-Hsing Chen, 411–40. New York: Routledge, 1996.

———. "Ideology and Communication Theory." In *Rethinking Communication*, volume 1, edited by Brenda Dervin, Larry Grossberg, Barbara J. O'Keefe, and Ellen A. Wartella, 40–52. Newbury Park, CA: Sage, 1989.

———. "Notes on Deconstructing 'the Popular.'" In *People's History and Socialist Theory*, edited by Raphael Samuel, 227–40. Boston: Routledge & Kegan Paul, 1981.

———. "On Postmodernism and Articulation: An Interview with Stuart Hall." Edited by Lawrence Grossberg. In *Stuart Hall: Critical Dialogues in Cultural Studies*, edited by David Morley and Kuan-Hsing Chen, 131–50. New York: Routledge, 1996.

———. "What Is This 'Black' in Black Popular Culture?" In *Stuart Hall: Critical Dialogues in Cultural Studies*, edited by David Morley and Kuan-Hsing Chen, 465–75. New York: Routledge, 1996.

Hall, Stuart, and Jessica Evans, eds. *Visual Culture: The Reader*. Thousand Oaks, CA: Sage, 1999.

Halvorssen, T. "Behind Exhumation of Simon Bolivar Is Hugo Chavez's Warped Obsession." *Washington Post*, July 25, 2010.

Hanes, Travis, and Frank Samello. *The Opium Wars: The Addiction of One Empire and the Corruption of Another*. London: Sourcebooks, 2004.

Harris, Michael D. *Colored Pictures: Race and Visual Representation*. Chapel Hill: University of North Carolina Press, 2003.

Harvey, David. *A Brief History of Neoliberalism*. Oxford; New York: Oxford University Press, 2005.

———. *Rebel Cities: From the Right to the City to the Urban Revolution*. New York: Verso, 2012.

Hay, Samuel A. *African American Theatre: An Historical and Critical Analysis*. Cambridge: Cambridge University Press, 1994.

Helliwell, John, Richard Layard, and Jeffrey Sachs. *World Happiness Report*. New York: The Earth Institute at Columbia University, 2012.

Herzog, Tamar. *Defining Nations: Immigrants and Citizens in Early Modern Spain and Spanish America*. New Haven, CT: Yale University Press, 2011.

Hewett, R. "'Looking at One's Self through the Eyes of Others': Representations of the Progressive Era Middle Class in W. E. B. Du Bois's *The Star of Ethiopia*." *Theatre History Studies* 30 (2010): 187–201.

Hobsbawm, Eric, and Terence Ranger. *The Invention of Tradition*. Cambridge; New York: Cambridge University Press, 2010.

Holmes, Brian. "Remember the Present: Representations of Crisis in Argentina." In *Escape the Overcode: Activist Art in the Control Society*, 172–93. Eindhoven, Netherlands: Van Abbemuseum, 2009.

Hood, Adrienne D. "Material Culture: The Object." In *History Beyond a Text: A Student's Guide to Approaching Alternative Sources*, edited by Sarah Barber and Corinna M. Peniston-Bird, 176–98. New York: Routledge, 2008.

hooks, bell. "Eating the Other: Desire and Resistance." In *Black Looks: Race and Representation*, 21–41. Cambridge, MA: South End Press, 1992.

Howells, Richard, and Joaquim Negreiros, eds. *Visual Culture*, 2nd edition. Cambridge: Polity, 2012.

Hughes, Chris. *Chinese Nationalism in a Global Era*. London: Routledge, 2006.

Huu Ngoc. *Wandering through Vietnamese Culture*, 4th edition. Hanoi, Vietnam: Thế Giới, 2004.

"Insultos, reclamos y porras en la visita de Peña Nieto a la *Ibero*." *La Jornada*, May 12, 2012. Accessed April 15, 2013. www.jornada.unam.mx/2012/05/12/politica/005n1pol.

"Intentan boicotear en la Ibero a Peña Nieto." *El Sol de México*, May 12, 2012. Accessed April 15, 2013. www.oem.com.mx/oem/notas/n2538119.htm.

International Center for the Arts of the Americas, Museum of Fine Arts, Houston. *ICAA Documents Project Working Papers: The Publication Series for Documents of 20th-Century Latin American and Latino Art* 3 (2013).

International Labor Office. *Special Report of the Director-General on the Application of the Declaration concerning Action against Apartheid in South Africa and Namibia*. International Labor Conference, 77th session, 1990.

Iton, Richard. *In Search of the Black Fantastic: Politics and Popular Culture in the Post–Civil Rights Era*. London: Oxford University Press, 2010.

Jackson, Carlos Francisco. *Chicana and Chicano Art: ProtestArte*. Tucson: University of Arizona Press, 2009.

James, C. L. R. *The Black Jacobins: Toussaint L'Ouverture and the San Domingo Revolution*. New York: Vintage Books, 1989.

———. *A History of Pan-African Revolt.* Oakland, CA: PM Press, 2012.

Jameson, Frederic. "Third-World Literature in the Era of Multinational Capitalism." *Social Text* 15 (1986): 65–88.

Joubert-Ceci, Berta. "US Economic Wars and Latin America." In *Feminism and War: Confronting US Imperialism*, edited by Robin Lee Riley and Chandra Talpade Mohanty, 238–42. London: Zed, 2008.

Kaplan, Geoff, ed. *Power to the People: The Graphic Design of the Radical Press and the Rise of the Counter-Culture, 1964–1974*. Chicago: University of Chicago Press, 2012.

Kaplan, Robert D. *Surrender or Starve: Travels in Ethiopia, Sudan, Somalia, Eritrea*. New York: Vintage, 2008.

Kastfelt, Niels. "African Resistance to Colonialism in Adamawa." *Journal of Religion in Africa* 8, no. 1 (1976): 1–12.

Kelley, Robin D. G. *Race Rebels: Culture, Politics and the Black Working Class.* New York: The Free Press, 1994.

Klein, Naomi, and Avi Lewis. *The Take: La Prise*. Montreal: Alliance Atlantis, 2004.

Klemm, P., and M. Niederstadt. "Beyond Wide-Eyed Angels: Contemporary Expressive Culture in Ethiopia." *African Arts* 42, no. 1 (2009): 6–13.

Koffka, Kurt. *Principles of Gestalt psychology.* New York: Harcourt Brace Jovanovich, 1935.

Kopytoff, Igor. "The Cultural Biography of Things: Commoditization as Process." In *The Social Life of Things: Commodities in Cultural Perspective*, edited by Arjun Appadurai. Cambridge: Cambridge University Press, 1986.

Krasner, P. D. "The Pageant Is the Thing: Black Nationalism and *The Star of Ethiopia*." In *Performing America*, edited by J. Ellen Gainor and Jeffrey Mason, 106–22. Ann Arbor, MI: University of Michigan Press, 2000.

Kumaraswami, Par. "Cultural Policy and Cultural Politics in Revolutionary Cuba: Re-reading the Palabras a los intelectuales (Words to the Intellectuals)." *Bulletin of Latin American Research* 28, no. 4 (2009): 527–41.

Kunzle, David. "Public Graphics in Cuba: A Very Cuban Form of Internationalist Art." *Latin American Perspectives* 2, no. 4 (1975): 89–110.

Laclau, Ernesto. "Entrevista a Ernesto Laclau." *Cuadernos del Cendes* (Venezuela) 22, no. 58 (2005): 117–25.

Laclau, Ernesto, and Chantal Mouffe. *Hegemony and Socialist Strategy: Towards a Radical Democratic Politics*. London: Verso, 1985.

LaDuke, B. "Lois Mailou Jones: The Grand Dame of African-American Art." *Women's Art Journal* 8, no. 1 (1987).

"La Ibero grita 'asesino' y 'fuera' a EPN; lo meten al baño para cuidarlo; 9 etiquetas de Twitter lo vapulean." *Sinembargo*, May 11, 2012. Accessed April 15, 2013. www.sinembargo.mx/11-05-2012/230979.

"La Piñata: Los golpes de 'color' de la política." *CNN México*, May 19, 2012. Accessed April 15, 2013. http://mexico.cnn.com/nacional/2012/05/19/131-alumnos-de-la-ibero.

"Las noticias y las coberturas que 'molestaron' a los estudiantes." *Aristegui Noticias*, May 19, 2012. Accessed April 15, 2013. http://aristeguinoticias.com/1905/uncategorized/los-videos-y-las-coberturas-que-despertaron-a-los-estudiantes.

Lefebvre, Henri. *Espace et politique*. Paris: Anthropos, 1972.

Lenin, V. "Left-Wing Communism: An Infantile Disorder." In *Collected Works*, volume 31. Moscow: Progress Publishers, 1964.

Lewis, R. "Marcus Garvey and the Early Rastafarians: Continuity and Discontinuity." In *Chanting Down Babylon*, edited by Nathanial Samuel Murrell, William David Spencer, and Adrian Anthony McFarland, 145–58. Philadelphia: Temple University Press, 1998.

Lewis, William F. "Telling America's Story: Narrative Form and the Reagan Presidency." *Quarterly Journal of Speech* 73 (1987): 280–302.

Lichbach, Mark Irving. *The Rebel's Dilemma.* Ann Arbor: University of Michigan Press, 1998.

Liu, Evie. "Peru to Tourists: 'Stop Getting Naked at Machu Picchu!'" *CNN*, March 20, 2014. www.cnn.com/2014/03/20/travel/naked-tourists-machu-picchu-peru.

Longoni, Ana. "Is Tucumán Still Burning?" *Sociedad* (Buenos Aires) 1 (2006).

Lorde, Audre. "Age, Race, Class, and Sex: Women Redefining Difference." In *Sister Outsider: Essays and Speeches by Audre Lorde*, 114–23. Berkeley, CA: Crossing Press, 2007.

———. "The Master's Tools Will Never Dismantle the Master's House." In *Sister Outsider: Essays and Speeches by Audre Lorde*, 110–13. Berkeley, CA: Crossing Press, 2007.

Lorini, Alessandra. *Rituals of Race: American Public Culture and the Search for Racial Democracy.* Charlottesville: University of Virginia Press, 1999.

Lossau, Julia. "Pitfalls of (Third) Space: Rethinking the Ambivalent Logic of Spatial Semantics." In *Communicating in the Third Space*, edited by Karin Ikas and Gerhard Wagner, 62–78. New York: Routledge, 2009.

Lozano, Genaro. "OPINIÓN: ¿Qué puede aprender #YoSoy132 de otros movimientos en el mundo?" *CNN México*, May 24, 2012. Accessed April 15, 2013. http://mexico.cnn.com/opinion/2012/05/24/opinion-que-puede-aprender-yosoy132-de-otros-movimientos-en-el-mundo.

Lu, Xiufen. "Li Dazhao's Materialist Conception of History." *East-West Connections* 9, no. 1 (2009).

Lynch, John. *Simón Bolívar: A Life.* New Haven, CT: Yale University Press, 2007.

MacCannell, Dean. *The Tourist: A New Theory of the Leisure Class*. New York: Schocken Books, 1976.

Machu Picchu. Cosmic Travel Network, 2014. www.machupicchu.info.

Madero, Francisco I. "Plan de San Luis." In *Plan de San Luis: Documentos Facsimilares.* Mexico: PRI, Comisión Nacional Editorial, 1976 [1910].

Maldonado-Torres, Nelson. "On the Coloniality of Being: Contributions to the Development of a Concept." *Cultural Studies* 21, no. 2 (2007): 240–70.

Mao Tse-tung. "Statement Supporting the American Negroes in Their Just Struggle against Racial Discrimination by U.S. Imperialism of Aug 8, 1963." Reprinted in *Peking Review* 9, no. 33 (August 12, 1966): 12–13.

Martin, Susan. "Introduction: The Left Turn." Exhibition catalog. *Track 16 Exhibition: Decade of Protest: Political Posters from the United States, Viet Nam and Cuba, 1965–1975*, March 19, 1996. Accessed May 1, 2013. www2.iath.virginia.edu/sixties/HTML_docs/Exhibits/Track16.html#Viet.

Martin, Tony. *Race First: The Ideological and Organizational Struggles of Marcus Garvey and the Universal Negro Improvement Association.* Westport, CT: Greenwood Press, 1976.

Martínez, Carlos, Michael Fox, and JoJo Farrell. *Venezuela Speaks! Voices from the Grassroots.* Oakland, CA: PM Press, 2010.

Marti-Olivella, Jaume. "The Hispanic Post-colonial Tourist." *Arizona Journal of Hispanic Cultural Studies* 1 (1997): 23–42.

Marx, Karl. "Bolívar y Ponte, Simón." In *The New American Cyclopaedia*, volume 3, edited by G. Ripley and C. A. Dana. New York: D. Appleton, 1858.

Marx, Karl, and Frederich Engels. *The Communist Manifesto.* London: Penguin, 1967.

"Más de la mitad de los detenidos son ajenos a los ataques, dice #YoSoy132." *La Jornada*, December 2, 2012. Accessed April 15, 2012. www.jornada.unam.mx/2012/12/02/politica/007n2pol.

Massey, Doreen. "Space for Co-existence?" In *Transversal Politics*, 1–4. London: Soundings 12, 1999.

Mayorga, Juan Carlos. "Los carteles, una 'voz gráfica' del movimiento estudiantil #Yosoy132." *CNN México*, June 7, 2012. Accessed April 15, 2013. http://mexico.cnn.com/nacional/2012/06/07/los-carteles-una-voz-grafica-del-movimiento-estudiantil-yosoy132.

Mbembe, Achilles. "Necropolitics." *Public Culture* 15, no. 1 (Winter 2003): 11–40.

McAdam, Doug, Sidney Tarrow, and Charles Tilly. "Revolutionary Trajectories." In *Dynamics of Contention*, 193–226. New York: Cambridge University Press, 2001.

McDonough, Tom, ed. *Guy Debord and the Situationist International: Texts and Documents.* Cambridge, MA: MIT Press, 2002.

McKim, Joel. "'Berlin's Memorial for the Murdered Jews of Europe' and the Problem of a Postmodern Monumental Rhetoric." In *The Rhetoric of Western Thought*, 10th edition, edited by J. L. Golden, G. Berquist, W. Coleman, and J. M. Sproule, 401–10. Dubuque, IA: Kendall Hunt, 2011.

Meisner, Maurice. *Li Ta-chao and the Origins of Chinese Marxism.* Cambridge, MA: Harvard University Press, 1967.

Meneses, Betford Betalleluz. "La imagen de la historia nacional peruana." *Revista Diálogos* 7, no. 1 (2003): 219–34.

Meneses, María Elena. "OPINIÓN: Los jóvenes indignados mexicanos ya levantaron la voz." *CNN México*, May 22, 2012. Accessed April 15, 2013. http://mexico.cnn.com/opinion/2012/05/22/opinion-los-jovenes-indignados-mexicanos-ya-levantaron-la-voz.

Mergier, Anne Marie. "Las aventuras de #YoSoy132 en París." *Proceso*, July 3, 2012. Accessed April 15, 2012. www.proceso.com.mx/?p=313181.

Meriwether, J. H. *Proudly We Can Be Africans: Black Americans and Africa, 1935–1961.* Chapel Hill: University of North Carolina Press, 2002.

Mesquita, André. *Insurgências Poéticas: Arte Ativista e Ação Colectiva*. São Paulo, Brazil: FAPESP, 2011.

Metaferia, Getachew. "The Ethiopian Connection to the Pan-African Movement." *Journal of Third World Studies* 12, no. 2 (Fall 1995): 300–325.

Meyer, Hannes. *Taller de Gráfica Popular: Doce años de obra artística colectiva*. Mexico: La Estampa Mexicana, 1949.

Meyer, Hannes, and Johannes Itten. *"Mexikanische Druckgraphik": Die Werkstatt fur graphische Volkskunst in Mexico*. Zurich, Switzerland: Kunstgewerbemuseum, 1951.

Meyer, Michael C., William L. Sherman, and Susan M. Deeds. *The Course of Mexican History*. Oxford: Oxford University Press, 2011.

Mignolo, Walter. *The Darker Side of the Renaissance: Literacy, Territoriality, and Colonization*, 2nd edition. Ann Arbor: University of Michigan Press, 2003.

Mills, Charles. *The Racial Contract*. Ithaca, NY: Cornell University Press, 1999.

Minh, Ho Chi. *The Prison Diary of Ho Chi Minh*. New York: Bantam Books, 1971.

Mirzoeff, Nicholas. *An Introduction to Visual Culture*. London: Routledge, 1999.

———. *The Right to Look: A Counterhistory of Visuality*. Durham, NC; London: Duke University Press, 2011.

———. *The Visual Culture Reader*. London: Routledge, 1998.

Mitchell, W. J. T. "Showing Seeing: A Critique of Visual Culture." *Journal of Visual Culture* 1, no. 2 (2002): 165–81.

Mixon, Laura. *Use of the Authorizing Figure, Authoritarian Charisma, and National Myth in the Discourse of Hugo Chávez: Toward a Critical Model of Rhetorical Analysis for Political Discourse*. Ann Arbor, MI: ProQuest, 2009.

Mohanty, Chandra Talpade. *Feminism Without Borders: Decolonizing Theory, Practicing Solidarity*. Durham, NC: Duke University Press, 2003.

Monsiváis, Carlos. "Editorial: Esta noche nos honra con su ausencia" *El Universal*, January 24, 2010. Accessed April 15, 2013. www.eluniversal.com.mx/editoriales/47153.html.

Moreiras, Alberto. *Tercer espacio: Duelo y literatura en América Latina*. Santiago, Chile: Arcis Lom, 1999.

Moskvitch, K. "Ethiopia Clamps Down on Skype and Other Internet Use on Tor." *BBC News*, June 15, 2012. www.bbc.co.uk.

Mosquera, Gerardo, and Jean Fisher, eds. *Over Here: International Perspectives on Art and Culture*. Cambridge, MA: MIT Press, 2007.

Mouffe, Chantal. "Strategies of Radical Politics and Aesthetic Resistance." *Truth Is Concrete*, September 8, 2012. Accessed January 6, 2016. http://truthisconcrete.org/texts/?p=19.

Mould de Pease, Mariana. "Machu Picchu—a Failed Historic Management." *Peru This Week*, July 26, 2011. Accessed January 6, 2016. www.peruthisweek.com/blogs-machu-picchu-failed-historic-management-50021.

Ngugi wa Thiong'o. *Decolonising the Mind: The Politics of Language in African Literature*. London: Heineman, 1986.

Niblo, Stephen R. *Mexico in the 1940s: Modernity, Politics, and Corruption*. Wilmington, DE: Scholarly Resource, 1999.

Nkrumah, Kwame. *Neo-colonialism: The Last Stage of Imperialism*. New York: International Publishers, 1966.

Noble, Andrea. "Visual Culture and Latin American Studies." *CR: The New Centennial Review* 4, no. 2 (2004): 219–38.

"Occupy Wall Street: Dozens Arrested on One-Year Anniversary." *Guardian*, September 17, 2012. Accessed April 15, 2013. www.guardian.co.uk/world/2012/sep/17/occupy-wall-street-arrests-anniversary.

Okafor-Newsum, I. "A Passage to Afrotopia." *Research in African Literatures* 32, no. 4 (2001): 172–86.

Olivares Alonso, Emir. "No somos porros ni acarreados, responden alumnos de la *Ibero* que increparon a Peña." *La Jornada*, May 15, 2012. Accessed April 15, 2013. www.jornada.unam.mx/2012/05/15/politica/011n1pol.

Oliver, P. *Blues Fell This Morning: Meaning in Blues*. Cambridge: Cambridge University Press, 1960.

Olson, James S., ed. *The Vietnam War: Handbook of the Literature and Research*. Westport, CT; London: Greenwood Press, 1993.

Olson, Lester C., Cara A. Finnegan, and Diane S. Hope. *Visual Rhetoric*. Thousand Oaks, CA: Sage, 2008.

Olson, Mancur. "Logic of Collective Action." In *Social Movements: A Reader*, edited by Vincenzo Ruggiero and Nicola Montagna, 93–94. London: Routledge, 2008.

O'Malley, Ilene V. *The Myth of the Revolution: Hero Cults and the Institutionalization of the Mexican State, 1920–1940*. Greenwood, CT: Greenwood Press, 1986.

Ongiri, Amy Abugo. *Spectacular Blackness: The Cultural Politics of the Black Power Movement and the Search for a Black Aesthetic*. Charlottesville: University of Virginia Press, 2009.

Organization in Solidarity with the People of Africa, Asia, and Latin America (OSPAAAL). "Digital Archive." Accessed August 30, 2015. www.docspopuli.org/CubaWebCat/gallery-01.html.

———. *Il Manifesto Della OSPAAAL: Arte Della Solidarietà*. Paprio, Italy: Tricontiental, 1997.

———. "Ospaaal.com." Accessed May 6, 2013. www.ospaaal.com.

Oxhorn, Philip. "Social Inequality, Civil Society, and the Limits of Citizenship in Latin America." In *What Justice? Whose Justice? Fighting for Fairness in Latin America*, edited by Susan Eckstein and T. P. Wickham-Crowley, 35–63. Berkeley: University of California Press, 2003.

Padgett, Tim. "Why Venezuela's Chávez Dug Up Bolívar's Bones." *Time*, July 17, 2010. Accessed March 5, 2013. www.time.com/time/world/article/0,8599,2004526,00.html.

Pandey, Gyanendra. *Unarchived Histories: The "Mad" and the "Trifling" in the Colonial and Postcolonial World*. New York: Routledge, 2014.

Pegler-Gordon, Anna. "Seeing Images in History." In *Perspectives on History: The Newsmagazine of the American Historical Association* (February 2006).

Peirce, Charles S. *Collected Papers of Charles Sanders Peirce*. Volumes 1–6, edited by C. Hartshorne and P. Weiss. Cambridge, MA: Harvard University Press, 1931–1935.

———. *Collected Papers of Charles Sanders Peirce*. Volumes 7–8, edited by A. W. Burks. Cambridge, MA: Harvard University Press, 1958.

———. *The Writings of Charles S. Peirce: A Chronological Edition*. Volumes 1–6 and 8, edited by Peirce Edition Project. Bloomington: Indiana University Press, 1982.

Pereyra, Beatriz. "Logra #YoSoy132 'meter gol' en el estadio Azteca." *Proceso*, June 9, 2012. Accessed April 15, 2013. www.proceso.com.mx/?p=310244.

Pérez-Stable, Marifeli. *The Cuban Revolution: Origins, Course, and Legacy*, 3rd edition. Oxford: Oxford University Press, 2011.

"Peru Celebrates Machu Picchu Anniversary." *Fox News Latino*, July 7, 2011. Accessed January 6, 2016. http://latino.foxnews.com/latino/entertainment/2011/07/07/peru-celebrates-machu-picchu-anniversary.

Peters, John D. *Speaking into the Air: A History of the Idea of Communication*. Chicago: University of Chicago Press, 1999.

Pipes, Richard. *A Concise History of the Russian Revolution*. Vancouver, WA: Vintage, 1996.

Plato. *Republic*. Translated by C. Emlyn-Jones and W. Preddy. Cambridge, MA: Harvard University Press, 2013.

Plumber, B. G. *Rising Wind: Black Americans and U.S. Foreign Affairs, 1935–1960*. Chapel Hill: University of North Carolina Press, 1996.

Poikāne-Daumke, A. *African Diasporas: Afro-German Literature in the Context of the African American Experience*. Piscataway, NJ: Transaction, 2006.

Poniatowska, Elena. *La noche de Tlatelolco: Testimonios de historia oral*. Mexico: Ediciones ERA, 1971.

Poy Solano, Laura. "Alumnos de la Uia niegan *montaje* al expresar rechazo al candidato del PRI." *La Jornada*, May 13, 2012. Accessed April 15, 2013. www.jornada.unam.mx/2012/05/13/politica/009n2pol.

Pratt, Mary Louise. *Imperial Eyes: Travel Writing and Transculturation*, 2nd edition. London: Routledge, 2007.

"Preparan alumnos de la Ibero 'bienvenida' a Peña." *El Universal*, May 11, 2012. Accessed April 15, 2013. www.eluniversal.com.mx/primera/39432.html.

Prignitz-Poda, Helga. *El Taller de Gráfica Popular en México, 1937–1977*. Translated by Elizabeth Siefer. Mexico: Instituto Nacional de Bellas Artes, 1992.

"Principios generales del movimiento." Accessed April 15, 2013. www.yosoy132media.org/yosoy132oficial/principios-generales-del-movimiento.

Prodnik, Jernej Amon. "A Note on the Ongoing Processes of Commodification: From the Audience Commodity to the Social Factory." *Triple-C: Cognition, Communication, Co-operation* 10, no. 2 (2012): 274–301.

Putnam, A. "Ethiopia Is Now: J. A. Rogers and the Rhetoric of Black Anticolonialism during the Great Depression." *Rhetoric and Public Affairs* 10, no. 3 (2007): 419–44.

"Questionnaire." *October* 123 (Winter 2008): 9–10.

Quijano, Anibel. "Coloniality of Power and Eurocentrism in Latin America." *International Sociology* 15, no. 2 (2000): 215–32.

Ramirez, Cristobal V. "Who Are the Chavistas?" In *Venezuela: Hugo Chávez and the Decline of an "Exceptional Democracy,"* edited by S. Ellner and M. T. Salas, 121–39. Lanham, MD: Rowman & Littlefield, 2007.

Ray, Julie. "High Wellbeing Eludes the Masses in Most Countries Worldwide." *Gallup*, 2011. Accessed September 27, 2012. www.gallup.com/poll/147167/High-Wellbeing-Eludes-Masses-Countries-Worldwide.aspx#1.

Razetto, Francesco Augusto. *Vietnam, Plakty Propagandy [Vietnam, Propaganda Posters/Vietnam, Manifesti Di Propaganda]*. Exhibition catalog. Prague, Czech Republic: Nadacn Fond Eleutheria, 2010.

"Resolution Adopted by the General Assembly of the United Nations 3379 (XXX): Elimination of All Forms of Racial Discrimination." November 10, 1975. Accessed May 13, 2013. http://unispal.un.org/UNISPAL.NSF/0/761C1063530766A7052566A2005B74D1.

A Revolutionary Spirit: Vietnamese Propaganda Art from the Dogma Collection. Exhibition catalog. January 8–18, 2015. Hanoi: Vietnam Fine Arts Museum, 2015.

Riccio, Thomas. "Ethiopia and Its Double." *TheatreForum* 41 (2012): 46–55.

Rice, Donald E. *The Rhetorical Uses of the Authorizing Figure: Fidel Castro and José Martí*. Westport, CT: Praeger, 1992.

Ricoeur, Paul. *Interpretation Theory: Discourse and the Surplus of Meaning*. Fort Worth: Texas Christian University Press, 1976.

Rivera-Velázquez, Celiany. "The Importance of Being Rita Indiana-Hernández: Women-Centered Video, Sound, and Performance Interventions within Spanish Caribbean Culture Studies." In *Globalizing Cultural Studies: Ethnographic Interventions in Theory, Method, and Policy*, edited by Cameron McCarthy, Aisha S. Durham, Laura C. Engel, Alice A. Filmer, Michael D. Giardina, and Miguel A. Malagreca, 205–28. New York: Peter Lang, 2007.

Roach, John. "Machu Picchu under Threat from Pressures of Tourism." *National Geographic News*. Accessed April 15, 2002. http://news.nationalgeographic.com/news/2002/04/0415_020415_machu.html.

Robbins, Mary Susannah, ed. *Against the Vietnam War: Writings by Activists*. Syracuse, NY: Syracuse University Press, 1999.

Robinson, Cedric. *Black Marxism: The Making of the Black Radical Tradition*. Chapel Hill: University of North Carolina Press, 1983.

Rollins, L. "Ethiopia, African Americans, and African-Consciousness: The Effect of Ethiopia and African-Consciousness in Twentieth-Century America." *Journal of Religious Thought* 54/55, nos. 2/1 (2000): 1–25.

Ross, Stanley R. *Francisco I. Madero, Apostle of Mexican Democracy*. New York: Columbia University Press, 1955.

Rothwell, P. "Momple's Melancholia: Mourning for Mozambique." *Portuguese Studies Review* 10, no. 1 (2002): 185–93.

Rowell, C. "An Interview with Lois Mailous Jones." *Callaloo* 39 (1989): 357–78.

Rutherford, Jonathan. "The Third Space: Interview with Homi K. Bhabha." In *Identity: Community, Culture, Difference*, edited by Jonathan Rutherford, 207–21. London: Lawrence and Wishart, 1990.

Said, Edward. *Orientalism*. New York: Vintage Books, 1978.

Saletan, Will. "The Memory Doctor." *Slate*, June 4, 2010. Accessed March 5, 2013. www.slate.com/articles/health_and_science/the_memory_doctor/2010/06/the_memory_doctor.html.

Sarlo, Beatriz. "Cabezas Rapadas y Cintas Argentinas." *Prismas: Revista de Historia Intelectual* 1, no. 1 (1997): 187–91.

———. "Cultural Landscapes: Buenos Aires from Integration to Fracture." In *Other Cities, Other Worlds: Urban Imaginaries in a Globalizing Age*, 27–50. Durham, NC: Duke University Press, 2008.

Sartre, Jean-Paul. *Colonialism and Neocolonialism*. New York: Routledge, 2006.

———. "Preface." In Frantz Fanon, *The Wretched of the Earth*. New York: Grove Press, 1963.

Saunders, Tonya L. "The Cuban Remix: Rethinking Culture and Political Participation in Contemporary Cuba." PhD dissertation, University of Michigan, 2008.

Schaffner, Ingrid. *The Essential Andy Warhol*. New York: Wonderland Press, 1999.

Schell, Orville, and David Shambaugh. *The China Reader*. New York: Random House, 1999.

Schmidt, Allard. "Huayna Picchu." Wikimedia Commons Public Domain. http://commons.wikimedia.org/wiki/Machu_Picchu#mediaviewer/File:Huayna_Picchu.jpg.

———. "Machu-Picchu-c03." Wikimedia Commons Public Domain. http://commons.wikimedia.org/wiki/Machu_Picchu#mediaviewer/File:Machu-picchu-c03.jpg.

———. "Peru Machu Picchu Sunrise." Wikimedia Commons Public Domain. http://commons.wikimedia.org/wiki/File:Peru_Machu_Picchu_Sunrise_2.jpg.

Schumpeter, Joseph. *Capitalism, Socialism, and Democracy*, 3rd edition. New York: Harper Perennial Modern Classics, 2008.

Scott, William. "The Ethiopian Ethos in African American Thought." *International Journal of Ethiopian Studies* 1, no. 2 (Winter/Spring 2004): 40–57.

Seldon, Mark. *China in Revolution: The Yenan Way Revisited*. New York: M. E. Sharpe, 1995.

"Se revitaliza el movimiento de 'indignados' en España." *La Jornada*, May 13, 2012. Accessed April 15, 2013. www.jornada.unam.mx/2012/05/13/politica/002n1pol.

Sheth, Falguni A. *Toward a Political Philosophy of Race*. Albany, NY: SUNY Press, 2009.

"Siete horas de disturbios en el DF; daños severos a comercios y mobiliario urbano." *La Jornada*, December 2, 2012. Accessed April 15, 2013. www.jornada.unam.mx/2012/12/02/politica/006n1pol.

Soja, Edward W. *Postmodern Geographies: The Reassertion of Space in Critical Social Theory*. London: Verso, 1989.

———. *Seeking Spatial Justice*. Minneapolis: University of Minnesota Press, 2010.

———. *Thirdspace: Journeys to Los Angeles and Other Real-and-Imagined Places*. Cambridge: Blackwell, 1996.

Sotelo Inclan, Jesús. *Raíz y razón de Zapata*, 2nd edition. Mexico: Editorial CFE, 1970.

Soto Zárraga, Alma. "El origen del PRInosaurio." *Ciencias* 98 (April–June 2010).

Soyer, François. "Faith, Culture and Fear: Comparing Islamophobia in Early Modern Spain and Twenty-First-Century Europe." *Ethnic and Racial Studies* 36, no. 3 (2013): 399–416.

Sterkx, Henry Eugene, and Brooks Thompson. "Philemon Thomas and the West Florida Revolution." *Florida Historical Quarterly* 39, no. 2 (April 1961): 378–86.

Stout, David. "Chávez Calls Bush 'the Devil' in UN Speech." *New York Times*, September 20, 2006. Accessed March 2, 2013. www.nytimes.com/2006/09/20/world/americas/20cnd-Chávez.html?_r=0.

Sturken, Marita, and Lisa Cartwright. *Practices of Looking: An Introduction to Visual Culture*, 2nd edition. Oxford: Oxford University Press, 2009.

Sullivan, Mark P. *Venezuela: Political Conditions and U.S. Policy.* Washington, DC: Congressional Research Service, 2009.

"¡Supera Boicot!" *La Prensa*, May 12, 2012. Accessed April 15, 2013. www.oem.com.mx/laprensa/notas/n2538553.htm.

"Supplemental Foreign Assistance, Fiscal Year, 1966—Vietnam: Hearings before the Committee on Foreign Relations, United States Senate, Eighty-Ninth Congress, Second Session, on S. 2793, to Amend Further the Foreign Assistance Act of 1961, as Amended: January 28, February 4, 8, 10, 17 and 18, 1966." Washington, DC: U.S. Government Publishing Office, 1966.

Svampa, Maristella. *La Sociedad Excluyente: La Argentina bajo el signo del neoliberalismo*. Buenos Aires: Taurus, 2005.

Sweig, Julia. *Inside the Cuban Revolution: Fidel Castro and the Urban Underground.* Cambridge, MA: Harvard University Press, 2004.

Tandeciarz, Silvia R. "Citizens of Memory: Refiguring the Past in Postdictatorship Argentina." *PMLA* 122, no. 1 (2007): 151–69.

Tang, Xiaobing. "The Anxiety of Everyday Life in Post-revolutionary China." In *The Everyday Life Reader*, edited by Ben Highmore. London: Routledge, 2002.

Tarrow, Sidney. "Cycles of Contention." In *Power in Movement: Social Movements, Collective Action, and Politics*, 141–46. Cambridge: Cambridge University Press, 1994.

Taylor, Clyde. "Black Consciousness and the Vietnam War." *Black Scholar* 5, no. 2 (October 1973): 4.

———. *Vietnam and Black America: An Anthology of Protest and Resistance*. Garden City, NY: Anchor Press, 1973.

Taylor, Diana. 2003. *The Archive and the Repertoire: Performing Cultural Memory in the Americas*. Durham, NC: Duke University Press, 2003.

Thompson, Nato. *Living as Form: Socially Engaged Art from 1991–2011*. New York: Creative Time, 2012.

Tibebu, Teshale. "Ethiopia: The 'Anamoly' and 'Paradox' of Africa." *Journal of Black Studies* 26, no. 4 (1996).

———. "Modernity, Eurocentrism, and Radical Politics in Ethiopia, 1961–1991." *African Identities* 6, no. 4 (2008): 345–71.

Todorov, Vladislav. *Red Square, Black Square*. New York: SUNY Press, 1995.

Toulmin, Stephen. *The Uses of Argument.* Cambridge: Cambridge University Press, 1958.

Tricontenental. Accessed August 30, 2015. www.tricontinental.cu.

Tuckman, Jo. "Computer Files Link TV Dirty Tricks to Favourite for Mexico Presidency." *Guardian*, June 7, 2012. Accessed April 15, 2013. www.guardian.co.uk/world/2012/jun/07/mexico-presidency-tv-dirty-tricks.

Tulchin, Joseph S., and Brian Fonseca. *Peruvian Strategic Culture*. Miami: Florida International University Press, 2010.

Tulis, Jeffrey K. *The Rhetorical Presidency.* Princeton, NJ: Princeton University Press, 1988.

Ungar, Mark. "Contested Battlefields: Policing in Caracas and La Paz." *NACLA Report on the Americas* 37 (2003): 30–36.

Varshney, Ashutosh. "Nationalism, Ethnic Conflict, and Rationality." *Perspectives on Politics* 1, no. 1 (March 2003): 85–99.

Vaughan, Mary Kay. *Cultural Politics in Revolution.* Tucson: University of Arizona Press, 1997.

Vázquez Mantecón, Álvaro. "Visualizing 1968." In *Age of Discrepancies: Art and Visual Culture in Mexico, 1968–1997*, compiled by Olivier Debroise. Mexico: Universidad Nacional Autónoma de México, 2006.

"Venezuela's Chávez Unveils 3D Image of Hero Bolívar." *Terra*, 2012. Accessed February 12, 2013. http://news.terra.com/venezuelas-Chávez-unveils-3d-image-of-hero-Bolívar,53d2cf97d9ab8310VgnVCM3000009acceb0aRCRD.html.

Vezzetti, Hugo. "Activismos de la Memoria: El 'Escrache.'" *Punto de Vista: Revista de Cultura* 21, no. 62 (1998): 1–7.

———. "Scenes from the Crisis." *Journal of Latin American Cultural Studies* 11, no. 2 (2002): 163–71.

"Vietnam, Vietnam Culture: Leaf Hat." Accessed May 7, 2013. www.vietnampeace.com/vietnam/Leaf-hat.html.

Villamil, Jenaro. "Los Ex Presidentes y Peña Nieto, Relaciones Peligrosas." *Jenaro Villamil: Medios, política y diversidad sexual*, July 30, 2011. Accessed January 31, 2014. http://jenarovillamil.wordpress.com/2011/07/30/los-ex-presidentes-y-pena-nieto-relaciones-peligrosas.

———. "Peña Nieto y la sombra del tío Arturo." *Proceso*, September 10, 2012. Accessed April 15, 2013. www.proceso.com.mx/?p=319413.

———. "Proyecto Jorge: El plan Televisa-Peña Nieto para alcanzar la Presidencia." *Proceso*, September 8, 2013. Accessed April 15, 2013. www.proceso.com.mx/?p=319353.

Vivas, María Luisa. "Estudiantes de la Ibero a EPN: 'Ni acarreados ni porros.'" *Proceso*, May 14, 2012. Accessed April 15, 2013. www.proceso.com.mx/?p=307494.

Wagemans, Johan, Jacob Feldman, Segei Gepshtein, Ruth Kimchi, James R. Pomerantz, Peter A. van der Helm, and Cees van Leeuwen. "A Century of Gestalt Psychology in Visual Perception: II. Conceptual and Theoretical Foundations." *Psychological Bulletin* 138 (2012): 1218–52.

Walters, Ronald W. *Pan Africanism in the African Diaspora: An Analysis of Modern Afrocentric Political Movements.* Detroit, MI: Wayne State University Press, 1997.

Warren, Nagueyalti. "Pan-African Cultural Movements: From Baraka to Karenga." *Journal of Negro History* 75, nos. 1/2 (Winter/Spring 1990): 16–28.

Weisbord, R. G. "British West Indian Reaction to the Italian-Ethiopian War: An Episode in Pan-Africanism." *Caribbean Studies* 10, no. 1 (1970): 34–41.

Wilson, Kalpana. "'Race,' Gender and Neoliberalism: Changing Visual Representations in Development." *Third World Quarterly* 32, no. 2 (2011): 315–31.

Winter, Sylvia. "Unsettling the Coloniality of Being/Truth/Power/Freedom: Towards the Human, After Man, It Overrepresentation—an Argument." *CR: The New Centennial Review* 3, no. 3 (Fall 2003): 257–337.

Wirth, Renee, and Robert Freestone. "Tourism, Heritage and Authenticity: State-Assisted Cultural Commodification in Suburban Sydney, Australia." *Perspectivas urbanas* 3 (2003). www.etsav.upc.es/urbpersp/num03/index.htm.

Womack, John. *Zapata and the Mexican Revolution*. New York: Vintage Books, 1970.

Woods, Alan. *Bolshevism: The Road to Revolution*. London: WellRead Books, 1999.

World Tourism Organization. *UNWTO Annual Report 2013*. Madrid, Spain: UNWTO, 2013. Accessed July 7, 2014. http://dtxtq4w60xqpw.cloudfront.net/sites/all/files/pdf/unwto_annual_report_2013_0.pdf.

Wynter, Sylvia. "Unsettling the Coloniality of Being/Truth/Power/Freedom: Towards the Human, After Man, Its Overrepresentation—an Argument." *CR: The New Centennial Review* 3, no. 3 (Fall 2003): 257–337.

Young, Marilyn Blatt. *The Vietnam Wars: 1945–1990*. New York: HarperCollins, 1991.

Young, Marilyn Blatt, and Mark Bradley. *Making Sense of the Vietnam Wars: Local, National, and Transnational Perspectives*. Oxford: Oxford University Press, 2008.

Zappa-Hollman, Sandra, Vaidehi Ramanathan, and Brian Morgan. "EFL in Argentina's Schools: Teachers' Perspectives on Policy Changes and Instruction." *Tesol Quarterly TESOL Quarterly* 41, no. 3 (2007): 618–25.

Zeleke, E. C. "Addis Ababa as Modernist Ruin." *Callaloo* 33, no. 1 (2010): 117–35.

Zinoman, Peter. "Colonial Prisons and Anti-colonial Resistance in French Indochina: The Thai Nguyen Rebellion, 1917." *Modern Asian Studies* 34, no. 1 (2000): 57–98.

Further Reading

Alinsky, S. D. *Rules for Radicals*. New York: Vintage Books, 1971.

Arendt, Hannah. *On Revolution*. London: Penguin Classics, 2006.

Armitage, David, and Sanjay Subrahmanyam, eds. *The Age of Revolution in Global Context, c. 1760–1840*. New York: Palgrave MacMillan, 2010.

Cabral, Amilcar. *Return to the Source: Selected Speeches of Amilcar Cabral*. Edited by African Information Service. New York: Monthly Review Press, 1973.

Césaire, Aimé. *Discourse on Colonialism*. New York: Monthly Review Press, 2001.

Chamberlin, Paul Thomas. *The Global Offensive: The United States, the Palestine Liberation Organization, and the Making of the Post–Cold War Order*. Oxford Studies in International History. Oxford; New York: Oxford University Press, 2012.

Chong, Sylvia Shin Huey. *The Oriental Obscene: Violence and Racial Fantasies in the Vietnam Era*. Durham, NC: Duke University Press, 2012.

Craven, David. *Art and Revolution in Latin America, 1910–1990*. New Haven, CT: Yale University Press, 2002.

Cushing, Lincoln. *Revolución: Cuban Poster Art*. New York: Chronicle Books, 2003.

Davis, Angela Y. *The Angela Y. Davis Reader*. Edited by Joy James. Oxford: Blackwell, 1998.

DeFronzo, James. *Revolutions and Revolutionary Movements*, 5th edition. Westview, CT: Westview Press, 2014.

Dubois, Laurent. *Avengers of the New World: The Story of the Haitian Revolution*. Cambridge, MA: Belknap Press, 2005.

Dubois, Laurent, and John D. Garrigus. *Slave Revolution in the Caribbean, 1789–1804: A Brief History with Documents*. New York: Bedford/St. Martin's Press, 2006.

Fanon, Frantz. *Black Skin, White Masks*. New York: Grove Press, 1990.
———. *A Dying Colonialism*. New York: Grove Press, 1994.
———. *Toward the African Revolution*. New York: Grove Press, 1994.
———. *The Wretched of the Earth*. New York: Grove Press, 2005.
Ferrer, Ada. *Freedom's Mirror: Cuba and Haiti in the Age of Revolution*. Cambridge: Cambridge University Press, 2014.
Freire, P. *Pedagogy of the Oppressed*. New York: Continuum, 1970.
Fukuoka, M. *The One-Straw Revolution*. Emmaus: Rodale Press, 1978.
Goldstone, Jack A. *Revolutions: A Very Short Introduction*. Oxford: Oxford University Press, 2014.
Gramsci, Antonio. *Selections from the Prison Notebooks*. New York: International Publishers, 1971.
Guevara, Ernesto Che. *Guerrilla Warfare*. Minneapolis, MN: Ocean Press, 2006.
Haley, Alex, and Malcolm X. *The Autobiography of Malcolm X: As Told to Alex Haley*. New York: Ballantine Books, 1992.
Horne, Gerald. *The Counter-Revolution of 1776: Slave Resistance and the Origins of the United States of America*. New York: New York Press, 2014.
James, C. L. R. *The Black Jacobins: Toussaint L'Ouverture and the San Domingo Revolution*, 2nd edition. New York: Vintage Books, 1989.
———. *A History of Pan-African Revolt*. Oakland, CA: PM Press, 2012.
Mao Tse-tung. *On Guerrilla Warfare*. New York: Praeger, 1961.
Marable, Manning. *Race, Reform, and Rebellion: The Second Reconstruction and Beyond in Black America, 1945–2006*, 3rd edition. Jackson: University Press of Mississippi, 2007.
Meeks, Brian. *Caribbean Revolutions and Revolutionary Theory: An Assessment of Cuba, Nicaragua, and Grenada*. Kingston, Jamaica: University of the West Indies Press, 2005.
Meisner, Maurice. *Li Ta-chao and the Origins of Chinese Marxism*. Cambridge, MA: Harvard University Press, 1967.
Minh, Ho Chi. *On Revolution: Selected Writings, 1920–1966*. Kolkata, West Bengal: Signet, 1968.
Olson, Lester C., Cara A. Finnegan, and Diane S. Hope. *Visual Rhetoric*. Thousand Oaks, CA: Sage, 2008.
O'Malley, Ilene V. *The Myth of the Revolution: Hero Cults and the Institutionalization of the Mexican State, 1920–1940*. Westport, CT: Greenwood Press, 1986.
Ortega y Gasset, J. *The Revolt of the Masses*. New York and London: W. W. Norton, 1932.
Seldon, Mark. *China in Revolution: The Yenan Way Revisited*. New York: M. E. Sharpe, 1995.
Todorov, Vladislav. *Red Square, Black Square*. New York: SUNY Press, 1995.
Vaughan, Mary Kay. *Cultural Politics in Revolution*. Tucson: University of Arizona Press, 1997.
Woods, Alan. *Bolshevism: The Road to Revolution*. London: WellRead Books, 1999.
Wright, Thomas C. *Latin America in the Era of the Cuban Revolution*, revised edition. Santa Barbara, CA: Praeger Press, 2000.

Index

Page numbers in *italics* refer to images.

About the Contributors

Theresa Avila is a scholar and curator of Latin American and Latin@ art and culture in the School of Transborder Studies at Arizona State University. Her recent work includes the coedited special issue in *Third Text, Legacy of the Mexican Revolution* at the Maxwell Museum of Anthropology and *Imagined Regions: The ASU Simon Burrow Transborder Map Collection*.

Lisa B. Y. Calvente is assistant professor of intercultural communication at DePaul University. Her areas of research are the black Diaspora, performance studies, and cultural studies. Her interests lie in the critical interrogation of anti-black and -brown racism in the United States in order to generate possibilities of belonging and social justice. She has contributed to anthologies and journals in her field.

Joshua Frye is associate professor in the Department of Communication at Humboldt State University. His research includes strategic political and environmental communication, with interests in public policy, cultural change agency, social movement advocacy, and organizational forms and leadership. He actively contributes to sustainable and equitable practices and the cultivation of healthy democratic systems through volunteerism, consulting, and public education.

Guadalupe García is associate professor of history at Tulane University and specializes in Latin American colonial history, with an emphasis on Cuba and the Spanish Caribbean. Her research interests include colonial and port cities, urban governance, and contemporary urban studies. She is the author of *Beyond the Walled City: Colonial Exclusion in Havana.*

Brynn Hatton is a PhD candidate in the Department of Art History at Northwestern University. She specializes in art and visual culture of the twentieth century, with an emphasis on art and social movements, global aesthetic flows, and postcolonial and critical race theory. Her dissertation is titled "Via Vietnam: Racial Coalition and Social Collapse in Transnational Protest Art."

Alison Hulme is a teaching fellow at Royal Holloway. She is the author of *On the Commodity Trail* (2015) and is currently working on two more books: *21st Century Thrift* and *Imaginations of China.* She has also published two edited volumes on China and consumerism and has articles in various academic journals. She runs a blog at http://commoditytactics.wordpress.com.

Nasheli Jiménez del Val is a Beatriu de Pinós postdoctoral fellow in the Department of Art History at the University of Barcelona. Her research centers on the relationship between power and images, mostly in a Latin American context. Her research themes include othering and the body, coloniality and Latin American theory, visual culture, and activism and social movements in Mexico.

Silvia Nagy-Zekmi is professor of Hispanic and cultural studies and chair of the Department of Romance Languages and Literatures at Villanova University. Her publications include books and articles on cultural, postcolonial, and gender studies. For more information on her research and publications, see www.wix.com/snzekmi/cv.

Leonora Souza Paula is assistant professor of Brazilian literature at Rice University. She specializes in twentieth- and twenty-first-century Brazilian literature and culture. Her research and teaching interests include Brazilian and Latin American literature and culture, Afro-Brazilian culture, critical geographies, visual culture, and social movements. Her work has been published in Brazil and the United States.

Kevin J. Ryan Jr. is a PhD candidate in the Department of Philosophy at the University of Memphis. His primary research interests are in the philosophy of cognitive science, the philosophy of the mind, and aesthetics. Some of his current and previous work has focused on embodied music cognition, the social and political dimensions of popular music, social cognition, and direct perception.

Meron Wondwosen is an activist and serves as an attorney for Young Doctors DC, a mentoring pipeline to healthcare careers for young black boys in Washington, DC. She has practiced law in a range of areas, including corporate finance and securities, banking regulations, voting rights, and international human rights. Ms. Wondwosen has authored and coauthored several reports submitted to the United Nations.